JOINING
THE
Conversation

Dialogues by
Renaissance Women

JANET LEVARIE SMARR

THE UNIVERSITY OF MICHIGAN PRESS
ANN ARBOR

Copyright © by the University of Michigan 2005
All rights reserved
Published in the United States of America by
The University of Michigan Press
Manufactured in the United States of America
♾ Printed on acid-free paper

2008   2007   2006   2005   4   3   2   1

A CIP catalog record for this book is available from the British Library.

Library of Congress Cataloging-in-Publication Data

Smarr, Janet Levarie, 1949–
Joining the conversation : dialogues by Renaissance women / Janet
Levarie Smarr.
p. cm.
Includes bibliographical references and index.
ISBN 0-472-11435-2 (alk. paper)
1. Dialogue.   2. Dialogue in literature.   3. European literature—
Women authors—History and criticism.   4. European literature—
Renaissance, 1450-1600—History and criticism.   I. Title.
PN1551.S55 2004
842'.2099287—dc22   2004020268

*Every effort has been made to trace the ownership of all
copyrighted material in this book and to obtain permission for its use.*

Le taire me seroit louable
S'il ne m'estoit tant inhumain.

—*Marguerite de Navarre,*
Chansons Spirituelles

Acknowledgments

I owe thanks to many friends and colleagues for their help on this project: to Anne Larsen, Diana Robin, and Veena Kumar Carlson for generously sending me photocopies of Renaissance texts still unedited or not readily available to me; to Virginia Cox and Francine Daenens for sending me articles of theirs not yet in print; to Yelena Matusevich, whose dissertation work induced me to read Gerson; to Evelyne Berriot-Salvadore and Margaret King for helpful replies to my queries; and to all who responded to pieces of this work delivered at conferences, offering me their suggestions and ideas. I am very grateful to the support of the University of Illinois–Centre National de la Recherche Scientifique (CNRS) exchange agreement, which enabled me to pursue important research at the Bibliothèque Nationale and the Arsenal, and thankful to the kind assistance of scholars there, including especially Carla Bozzolo, Darwin Smith, and M. Maillard. Last but not least, I owe fond thanks to my father, who read through the entire manuscript at an early stage, and to the later anonymous readers, all of whom improved the work with their suggestions.

Pieces of this work have appeared in somewhat different form as articles. Discussion of Moderata Fonte in relation not to Marguerite but to Edmund Tilney appears in "The Uses of Conversation: Moderata Fonte and Edmund Tilney," *Comparative Literature Studies* 32 (1) (1995). The section on Tullia d'Aragona, the least revised, was published as "A Dialogue of Dialogues: Tullia d'Aragona and Sperone Speroni," *Modern Language Notes* 113 (1) (1998). A partial version of chapter 5 is forthcoming as "A Female Tradition? Women's Dialogue Writing in Sixteenth-Century France," in *Strong Voices, Weak History*, edited by Pamela Benson and Victoria Kirkham (University of Michigan Press).

Contents

1 Introduction

Dialogue is a field without edges. Mikhail Bakhtin (1986, 68–69, 72) proposed that all utterances are speech-acts within a larger conversation. Following his lead, other theorists have affirmed: "Every human word implies the existence of the other"; "Utterance is on the borderline between at least two consciousnesses where all dialogic discourse takes place" (Wesling and Slawek 1995, 25, 6). Moreover, the self is already "in reality plural, social in its very constitution. Its activities follow out dialogues that have begun well before one acts oneself to speak."[1] This study focuses on writings that take this act of dialogue into the very heart of the work.

The "dialogue" was one of the most popular genres during the Renaissance. It would be difficult indeed to count how many dialogues were published in the sixteenth century alone, either in Latin or in vernacular languages. As a genre based on the classics, it had its erudite aspect; yet as a form of casual conversation among acquaintances on a wide variety of topics, it had also a broader appeal than merely to the learned. Some women during the Renaissance wanted to insert their voices into the larger cultural conversation. Of the many hundreds of dialogues from this period, however, very few even included women speakers. Nonetheless, this was a genre that in many ways invited female participation, and a number of Renaissance women wrote their own examples. This study aims to explore the dialogues of Italian and French Renaissance women in the contexts, both literary and social, that might have helped to bring these works into being.

The genre includes a wide variety of types of writing. What we think of as Renaissance dialogues tend to have several speakers, in contrast to the two speakers of the medieval *débat*. Paul Zumthor has suggested the word *pluri-logue* to distinguish the multivoiced type.[2] Although *dia* does not really mean "two," as is commonly assumed, there does seem to be some usefulness in distinguishing between dialogues of two and more than two voices. Colette Winn (1993, 83) helpfully refers to diphonic and polyphonic dialogues, a pair of terms that I gratefully use. As we shall see, these two types had rather different models and could have different uses as well. Diphonic dialogues were just as popular during the Renaissance but have received much less general attention, whether they were written by women or by men. This type of dialogue traces its genealogy back only indirectly to the major classical models, deriving more directly from a long medieval history. It is also a type of dialogue that was possibly more welcoming to women and readily taken up by them. Dialogues by women tended more often to be diphonic than polyphonic, as a conversation between two female friends or relatives frequently seemed more plausible than either a gathering of women or a mixed gathering that would allow major participation by female voices. Women may be, by social requirement, modest and reticent in front of a group of men; but alone with a trusted friend, they are freer to speak honestly.

For Renaissance dialogues the basic classical models, used and mentioned repeatedly, were Plato, Cicero, and Lucian, but especially Cicero.[3] Eva Kushner (1977, 28) comments with specific reference to this trio: "The importance of the classical model is so great that it would not be impossible to attempt a classification of all Renaissance French dialogues in terms of the classical writers whom they imitate." Nonetheless, other writers, both ancient and eventually more modern, were also widely influential. It is worth noting how some of the more specific types of dialogue were either encouraging or discouraging to the inclusion of women as speakers and ultimately as writers.

Cicero's dialogues were to some extent an extension of Plato's.[4] Both made use of real historical persons as their speakers and set their conversations in real places. Cicero's men at leisure in a villa tend more toward lengthy, learned monologues with occasional interjections, while Plato's speakers, often meeting by chance on the street while on their way to other business, frequently exchange briefer statements in a more back-and-forth mode. But where Cicero's speakers—including Cicero himself—are friends and equals, Plato generally presents a teacher-student pattern, with Socrates as the driver of the discussion and the author absent from the cast of speakers. Plato's proposal in the *Republic* of a nearly equal education for men and women would certainly have endeared him to women writers, most of whom felt the need to defend and advocate women's education. Moreover, although his speakers are all male, the presence in the *Symposium* of a reported conversation between Socrates and Diotima became a frequent reference point in discussions of women's participation in Renaissance dialogue. Plato also offers moments of wit and irony that place him somewhere between the continual satire of Lucian and the sober tones of Cicero.

Cicero's conversations take place among educated and urbane friends in a pleasant private place, such as a villa or garden, and make use of historically real persons as speakers, thus as for Plato implying—whether or not it is true—that the text is a recording of conversations that actually took place. Cicero's dialogues not only record the content of these conversations but celebrate the friendship and leisure that make such discourse possible.[5] His inclusion of topics such as friendship and old age appealed to later writers who wanted to offer conversations based on lived experience rather than on a more abstract philosophical argument. These topics of lived experience are precisely the kind that one would talk about with good friends. Thus a domestic ambience and affectionate intimacy among participants work together with reflections rooted in daily life. Renaissance humanists saw their own intellectual friendships as a renewal of such classical conversations. Rejecting the cold logic of scholastic argumentation, they sought to bring moral and philosophical reflection back into connection with daily experience and to emphasize its sociality. Besides appealing to humanists, this Ciceronian framework opened possibilities of participation by women, even though Cicero himself does not seem to have imagined such participation.

Another classical model less often mentioned but with an abundant Renaissance progeny was Xenophon's *Oeconomicus,* in which Socrates, under the general topic of how to manage one's estate, discusses both proper self-management and the proper management of a young wife so as to produce ideal husband-wife relations. Combined or not with Plutarch's *Precepts of Marriage* (*Coniugalia praecepta*), it found an afterlife in Leon Battista Alberti's *Libri della famiglia* (1435–44); Erasmus's "Coniugium" and his other colloquies on marriage and family; Aonio Paleario's explicitly named *Dell'economia o vero del governo della casa* (1555), which was influenced by Erasmus as well as by Xenophon; and, directly or indirectly, the dialogues of Catherine des Roches and Moderata Fonte on the social roles of women and their relationships with fathers and husbands. This type of dialogue was first of all a means of practical instruction by men for each other; but given the role of wife as manager of the household, it became thinkable for women to participate in or even take over this topic of discussion. In a sense Xenophon prepares for this inclusion by asserting that men and women are naturally fitted for different types of work, the male outside the home and the female within, and that each would look foolish in the other's domain.[6] Along these lines, Paleario's work is a conversation among four women whose husbands are simultaneously discussing the government of the state.[7] So too Girolamo Razzi Silvano's *Della economica christiana, e civile . . .* (Florence, 1568) includes noblewomen and -men discussing how the family and state should be governed.

Plutarch's precepts are addressed jointly to a husband and wife. Even Alberti, although writing both through and for men, used the vernacular for this one work in order to give it a wider and more popular usefulness. Alberti's inclusion of a discussion about the value of friendship shows a merger of Cicero and Xenophon under this rubric of practical utility for daily life. Indeed, as David Marsh (1980, 78–79) has pointed out, Cicero's transmission of Greek philosophy in his own native Latin became a model for the vernacular imitation of classical models, such as Alberti's. The sense that this genre could be intended for common and practical use by a popular audience countered its more learned and philosophical aspects.

As men generally married much younger wives with the aim of training them, the topic of household management could readily be extended to include the education of women. While on the one hand a source of traditional precepts concerning wives—that they should remain at home and silent and should mirror their husbands's moods—Plutarch also advises men that reasoning with a wife is more effective than violence; that the husband should set an example for his wife and not expect from her restraints that he is unable to impose on himself; and finally that women are improved by the study of geometry, astronomy, philosophy, and history, which makes them less inclined to take an interest in frivolous pastimes and superstitions. His brief treatise ends with a list of women rendered famous by their wisdom and intelligence, more valuable than physical beauty: Theano the philosopher, Cleobuline the creator and solver of enigmas, Gorgo, Timocleia, Claudia, Cornelia, and others worthy of fame. The list ends with Sappho's just sense of her own superiority over a rich woman who would be soon forgotten. This appeal to women to study and to think about their own glory and fame runs counter to the suggestion that women should be unseen and unheard. The notion that women are improved by education, and certainly better than those women ruled by ignorance and passion, was more widely cited than this appeal to intellectual fame, but women readers, such as Catherine des Roches, were clearly attracted by the more radical possibilities.

A classical model popular with humanist men but much less useful to women was the banquet. Plato's *Symposium* on love; Xenophon's *Symposium* on the same topic; Plutarch's *Table-Talk* (*Quaestionum convivialium libri ix*) and *Banquet of the Seven Sages* (*Septem sapientium convivium*); Macrobius's

Saturnalia and Aulus Gellius's *Attic Nights* (*Noctes atticae*), with their conversations on scientific, philosophical, political, historical, grammatical, and literary topics; and Lucian's *Carousal,* with its satirical portraits of various schools of philosophy, may have been eagerly imitated by Francesco Filelfo, Alberti, Erasmus, Giordano Bruno, and others but were simply not a plausible form for women. For men such a scene might render more casual and amicable their philosophical conversations. For women to present themselves as a group eating and drinking together would only have undermined their efforts to represent themselves as intellectuals and would on the contrary have reinforced longstanding negative stereotypes associating women with the appetites of the flesh: gluttony; drunkenness; and their close companion, lust. Only Moderata Fonte comes close to this model, and her women do their talking not at the table but in a very formal garden after lunch. The formality of the garden is part of the indication of nature well under control.

Two more texts from the early sixteenth century joined the classical panoply as fundamental models for subsequent imitation. One was Baldassare Castiglione's *Il cortegiano.* Set in 1507, it was finally published for the first time in 1528, after twenty years of revision during which it had circulated as a manuscript. The work became widely acclaimed as a patternbook for both language and behavior, being reprinted more than twenty times in Italy during the sixteenth century with at least half a dozen more editions or translations in France.[8] The other model of widespread popularity was the *Colloquies* of Erasmus, first published in 1518 as a school text with helpful conversational formulas (*Familiarum colloquiorum formulae*) and then expanded with an increasing number of more elaborate dramatic dialogues on a wide variety of topics. It had appeared in eighty-seven editions or reprints by the time of Erasmus's death in 1536 and inspired translations, imitations, or borrowings by writers in nearly every country of Europe, both Catholic and Protestant.

Both Erasmus and Castiglione present their dialogues in relation to the concept of play. For Castiglione, the conversation is explicitly a game invented to pass the evenings at court in mixed company. For Erasmus, dialogues are part of a pedagogical theory that emphasizes learning through play, so that the student encounters learning as something enjoyable. Erasmus in "De utilitate colloquiorum" (3.742.16–17, 26–27) replies to critics who blame him for playing childishly in a way unbefitting an older man ("indecorum homini seni sic pueriliter ludere"): "Et haud scio an quicquam discitur felicius, quam quod ludendo discitur" [I'm not sure that anything is learned better than what is learned as a game].[9] Erasmus explicitly states his intention for his book: to improve both the Latin and the character of his young male pupils.[10] His conversations take place on the streets and in mid-dle-class homes rather than at court among the nobility, as in Castiglione's book, and aim at presenting scenes of daily life. This type of setting and char-acters was readily associated with dramatic comedy. The context and tone contrast with the melancholy of Castiglione's eulogy for an elite cultural gathering scattered and destroyed by time. Yet even within the nostalgic frame, Castiglione shows us the banter and merriment of a series of evening entertainments.

Both of these writers, working during the same years, went beyond their classical models—whether Cicero's dialogue on the perfect orator or Lucian's satiric discussions—in an important way: by including women in their conversations. The relaxed atmosphere of playfulness supported this inclusion, which the two settings, court gatherings and city life, made plau-sible. Yet both texts also remain somewhat ambivalent about the roles of women.[11]

Castiglione made widely available the discussion from Plato's *Republic* advocating that women receive an education similar to that of men and even be considered fit for public office. Despite the presentation—by Socrates and Castiglione both—of these notions as radical and the expectation that they will be laughed at by some auditors, their serious statement for consideration could only be helpful and encouraging to women. Yet Joan Kelly in her famous essay "Did Women Have a Renaissance?" observes accurately that the women in Castiglione's Urbino are not really part of the conversation, even when it is about women. They are there to set up a game in which men discourse; occasionally women may disrupt those speeches, but without offering their own. So too as the court lady is portrayed within the discourses even of her champions, whatever education or eloquence she may possess, she is viewed as an adornment or entertainment in the service of a totally male-centered culture.[12]

Considerable scholarly debate has ensued on the nature of women's roles in the book. Valeria Finucci (1989, 93), while conceding that the text seems to offer a progressive account of women, at first observes: "Purtroppo quello che è detto e quello che il testo mostra coincidono ben poco" [Unfortunately what is said and what the text shows coincide very little] and proceeds to demonstrate strategies by which the text works to exclude real women from serious consideration as it constructs a figure of the male imaginary.[13] How-ever, her expanded 1992 study sees at work in Castiglione's text not only this "official discourse," which constructs a disempowered "Woman," but also an occasionally intruding "unofficial discourse," which "presents a more threat-ening (because more real) woman" (21). Saccaro Battisti notes a continual contradiction in the position of the named court ladies, who, while seemingly freed from some of the restrictions of other women, function nonethe-less within the traditional assumptions of a patriarchal society, entertaining to men but chaste, modest, and dependent. Unlike the completely silent women at the gathering, they are named and speak; yet they remain mar-ginal to the real discourse. Even during the apparently radical proposals con-cerning women, it is clear that no one present expects real change in the society (1980, esp. 222, 224, 229, 231). Marina Zancan further affirms this sense that the society of courtiers is not really going to change women's sta-tus despite their apparently open-minded discussion. Nonetheless, she notes that the court lady's new "profession"—to participate in that conversation that is the primary activity of court life—requires considerable knowledge (1983a, 46, 28–29). Thus, Zancan notes, contradictory implications run through the *Cortegiano*.

The fact that women are there at all, listening and occasionally com-menting, is significant. As Virginia Cox (2000, 386–87) has observed, no previous text would have fully "prepared Castiglione's readers for the novelty of the appearance of women in a dialogue whose style and structure proclaim its affiliation to the hitherto exclusively masculine Ciceronian tradition. The importance of this fact for our reading of the *Cortegiano* can hardly be overemphasized. Where modern readers are struck by the silence of Casti-glione's women speakers, his contemporaries would have been more likely to be struck by the fact that there were women present at all," especially at a conversation involving politics.

Similar internal ambivalences characterize one of the classical models for dialogues in mixed company. Plutarch's *Banquet of the Seven Sages* indicates the presence of two women: Melissa, apparently a servant; and Cleobuline or Eumetis, daughter of the ruler Cleobulus, who is praised for her intelligence, political sense, and humanizing influence on her father. She is described with admiration as currently studying medicine. Despite her attendance at a discussion on both political and domestic government, however, she is not permitted to speak. When one of the men attacks her famous riddles as fit only for idle women, "Eumetis, who as one could easily see would have liked to reply, restrained herself with timidity, and her cheeks flushed." Aesop leaps to her defense with a counterattack on the foolishness of her belittler (10.214). He cites a riddle that she had proposed just before dinner; later her father recounts a fable that she had told at home (14.220–21). Thus her words are praised and cited but can be uttered in the text only through the mouths of men. After the meal and before the serious drinking begins, the women leave. Castiglione's court women are in a very similar position to Plutarch's, present and praised but basically silent, leaving even their own defense to men.

Erasmus's female participants are bolder—or perhaps just more middle-class—than Castiglione's courtly ladies, speaking sensibly and at length in a number of colloquies, where they are given equal time when talking with men.[14] The learned lady in her famous colloquy with a stupid abbot advocates learning and reading not only for the court lady but also for the middle-class, defending the usefulness of studies in fostering the "wisdom" needed by a wife and mother "administrare rem domesticam, erudire liberos" (3.405.73–74) [to manage the household and rear the children (221)]. Even with this domestic goal, and her repeated claim that her husband is pleased by her learning, this woman is an exception and probably not so much a model for women generally as a means of shaming the illiterate and worldly clergy and certainly of inculcating proper goals and values into the minds of young male students who might aspire to an ecclesiastical career;[15] after all, Erasmus's originally intended audience consisted of such boys. The other women who enter the varied scenes of Erasmus's work are chiefly involved in conversations about marriage: whether to marry or enter the convent, how to treat one's husband so as to foster a happy home life, whether to nurse one's own child or employ a wet nurse. If they speak with assurance, they may be expected to have some knowledge in these matters pertaining to their specifically female lives and duties.

The women who revive the Roman emperor's institution of a women's senate that might regulate women's affairs, in "Senatulus" or "The Council of Women," begin with high-sounding claims:

> frequentes hodie convenistis et alacres, unde spem optimam concipio futurum, ut Deus propitius cuique ea suggerat in animum, quae ad communem omnium et dignitatem et utilitatem pertinent. Scitis, opinor, omnes, quantum hinc commodis nostris decesserit, quod quum viri quotidianis conventibus suum agant negocium, nos colo telaeque assidentes causam nostram deserimus. Itaque res huc devenit, ut nec inter nos sit ulla reipublicae disciplina, et viri nos pene pro delectamentis habeant, vixque hominis vocabulo dignentur. (3.629.2–10)

> [Your full and prompt attendance at this meeting . . . gives me every hope that a gracious God may direct the mind of each one of you to what concerns the general welfare and the dignity of us all. You are all aware, I believe, of how much our interests have declined; aware that though men transact their business at daily assemblies, we have neglected our cause by sitting at distaff and loom. Hence matters have come to such a pass that we are entirely ignorant of political science; men treat us virtually as amusements and scarcely thinks us deserving of the name of human. (441–47)]

Cornelia, the main speaker in this piece, attacks male parliaments as "worse than womanish" [plusquam muliebra] for their wrangling, fickleness, and ill-judged counsel, all springing from male pride. Yet, citing Paul's restrictions against women's public speech, she defends women's right to speak only among women, not in the "meetings of men" [coetu virorum]. Moreover, her own council immediately sets about demonstrating that female vanity is no different: after discussing at length whom to exclude from their meeting, the women's first and only item of business is to regulate fashion so that differences in social standing not be obscured by the presumptuous garb of socially inferior women. Thus whatever seriousness they may seem to have had initially evaporates in what Craig R. Thompson calls "a gentleman's joke." (Erasmus 1965, 441)

Nonetheless, women readers may have taken something different from these pages, if they saw them. As Elizabeth McCutcheon (1992, 86) comments about Erasmus in general, "Whether or not he intended to do so, then, Erasmus established a variety of subject positions from which women (as well as himself) might speak . . . subverting the notion of [women's] silence to critique his own society." She is thinking of the voices of Folly and Peace as well as those of more realistic women in the *Colloquies*; that Erasmus himself chose to speak repeatedly through various female voices is one of those facts that can be used to argue opposite views: that the real author is always male while the female is merely a personification, and thus the strategy is not encouraging to women; or that the use of female voices critical of contemporary society is a model that women can appropriate. This is not a dispute to be answered one way or the other.

If Erasmus indeed did not have a female audience in mind, Castiglione certainly did, for he sent his draft of the *Cortegiano* to Vittoria Colonna for comment as one of its first readers.[16] His work is among those recommended for female readers: by Lodovico Dolce, for example, in his Italian version of Juan Luis Vives's enormously popular treatise on women's education *Dialogo della institution delle donne* (1547), and by Paleario as well.[17] Dolce updates Vives's recommendations by adding the *Cortegiano* to the list of permissible readings for a young woman; Vives (secs. 28–35; [1547] 1996, 39–53) had mentioned only sober ancients and church fathers, nothing contemporary. Finucci (1989, 90) cites Francesco Asolano's prefatory remarks to a 1533 edition of the *Cortegiano*: he dedicates it to the ladies, urging them to carry the book about with them tucked in their bosoms ("il possiate a vostro aggio portare in seno") as a work that truly belongs to them. There seems to be an odd convergence here of an erotic fantasy about female readers with attestations of convenient format and the usefulness of taking the work to heart.

It is easy from a modern point of view to see the limitations of these men's accomplishments for feminism, but we should also remain sensitive to the real openings that they created for the inclusion of women in what we can call the cultural conversation, whether written or oral. Castiglione's well-known influence on the fashion of neoplatonic love did make it easier for women to join in the social practice of lyric poetry, writing to express their admiration and praise for virtuous and learned men and receiving similar poems without dishonor. Although many women wrote lyric verses, several found in the dialogue form with its multiple speakers a way to insert their own voices, even their own multiple voices. Castiglione also provided a model for other male-authored dialogues that could vary the degree of women's participation.

As Virginia Cox has indicated, the hundreds of Renaissance conversations, like their classical models, rarely include women. When they do, the women's roles are usually limited either to asking questions or to talking about love, the one field in which women were presumed to have any competence.[18] As Cox points out (1992, 45), "Female interlocutors, guaranteed by their sex the right to be decorously ignorant, were much exploited in the vernacular dialogue as stand-ins for an unschooled audience." On the whole, this was a realistic or plausible position. We shall see in later chapters, however, that some women, writing their own dialogues, challenged and expanded these female speakers' roles.

Even some men participated in this challenge. Pietro Bembo's widely influential *Asolani*, as Valerio Vianello (1993, 29–30) has pointed out, is more liberal in its theory than in its practice.[19] Although, as usual, the three women present do not participate in delivering the long speeches of the discussion but only interrupt with occasional questions or objections, Bembo defends their presence as if they had a right to fuller participation. Indeed, the issue of female participation becomes a recurring topic throughout the work and is therefore worth observing in some detail.

Like the *Cortegiano*, which Bembo must have read somewhere between the first and second versions of his early sixteenth-century work, the *Asolani* discussion is set in a court run by a woman, in this case Caterina Cornaro, referred to as the Queen of Cyprus, a title not only historical but also poetically befitting the patron of a discussion on love. Bembo claims at the start to be reporting this conversation for the benefit of men and women alike. This mixed audience is represented within the work, for three married women are present at the rival discourses of their three male kinsmen and friends. Along with the garden setting and particular choices of phrase, the mixed company evokes the *Decameron* as the work's forebear, in relation to which, however, we see at once that the women's role has been reduced, for despite their equal numbers with the men, they do not have an equal turn to speak.

Although initially they seem to be invited to participate on equal footing, we quickly see that this invitation is not sincerely meant. Referring to the songs praising and complaining of love sung earlier by some ladies before the queen, Gismondo, one of the three men, proclaims that he will speak in praise of love and challenges any of his five companions to begin by speaking in opposition to him: "se alcuna di voi è, belle donne, o di noi, che so che ce ne sono, che creda insieme con la fanciulla primiera che Amore cosa buona non sia, dica sopra ciò quello che ne gli pare, che io gli risponderò" (1.6.323–24) [if there are any of you, lovely ladies, or of us, for I know that there are some, who believe along with the first girl that Love is not a good thing, speak about this as you see fit, and I will respond to it]. At first the ladies take this invitation seriously and hesitate but then realize that the challenge is really meant for Perottino, who has already been presented as a suffering lover. When Perottino acknowledges that the challenge is meant for him, the two men "arm" themselves for battle. Gismondo has set up the conversation as a disputation and thus as an armed battle in which women cannot be expected to participate. They can only laugh at these "due pronti cavalieri a battaglia" (326) [two knights ready for battle].

The image of dialogue as a battle fought with rhetorical weapons is part of a broader strategy to exclude women. Thus, for example, in the *Cortegiano*, Emilia Pia, giving il Magnifico the duty of defending women, speaks of debate as a battle, appropriate therefore only to men: "metteremo in campo un cavalier più fresco, che combatterà con voi" (2.97) [we will put into the field a fresher knight who will do combat with you]. Leonardo Bruni's fifteenth-century *De studiis et litteris liber*, dedicated to a woman, reluctantly discourages females from learning rhetoric, despite his own passionate interest in the subject, because rhetorical debates "Son cose da uomini; come le guerre e le battaglie, così anche le contese e le competizioni del foro" (Lenzi 1982, 79) [are things for men; as are wars and battles, so too the contests and competitions of the forum].

The *Asolani*'s second invitation to women's participation seems more sincere but is also later undermined. When Berenice, the oldest of the women, hesitates to interrupt Perottino's discourse with an objection, not wishing to be considered "senza rispetto e presontuosa" [disrespectful and presumptuous] for intervening in a male dispute ("il trametterci nelle *vostre* dispute"), she is cordially encouraged to speak up. We are all here to talk, says Gismondo generously; these are not "*nostre* dispute" (1.10.330; my emphasis) [*our* disputes] any more than "vostri ragionamenti" [your discussions]. After the oldest woman has broken the ice, the other women also speak up. However, Gismondo's invitation turns out to extend only to their interruptions of his rival's speech; when it is his turn to speak, he silences the women with rude remarks. First he tells Lisa that she is obstinate, the common defect of pretty women and fine horses. Lisa tries to deflect the insult by claiming that she is not pretty but concludes, "tu hai trovato la via di farmi oggi star cheta" (2.18.418–19) [you have found the way to make me keep quiet today]. Berenice, taking Lisa's hand in a "sisterly" manner, reproves Gismondo for "biting" and causing Lisa to feel excluded: "così bene dianzi ci sapesti mordere, che Lisa oggimai più teco avere a fare non vuole" [you knew so well how to bite us before that now Lisa does not want to have anything more to do with you]. Excusing herself as "poco maestra battagliera" [minimally a master of war], she reminds us of the way Gismondo has staged the discussion as a male battle in which women have no place. His second insult is to the youngest of the women, whom he embarrasses by staring at her shirtfront while describing the pleasure of the lover in imagining his lady's hidden beauties. Again Berenice, whom the ladies consider "lor capo" (2.6.323) [their chief], comes to the younger woman's defense with a reproach to Gismondo. "Madonna, tacete" (2.22.427) [Madam, be quiet], is his blunt reply, and he suggests that she is simply jealous. Finally Berenice objects, with the support of the other women, to Gismondo's statement that lovers take pleasure in seeing their ladies cry. His insult to her is the rudest of all: the hermit's son in the half tale at the start of the *Decameron*'s fourth day, had he seen Berenice, "non arebbe al suo padre chiesto altro papera da rimanere seco e da imbeccare che voi" [would not have asked his father for any other goose than you to keep with him and stuff things into its beak]. Gismondo repeats the association of women with animals, in this case a more stupid animal, and refers through the *Decameron*'s metaphor to the sexual act, thus reducing Berenice to an animal-like object of male sexual aggression. As Berenice sits in shocked silence, Lisa throws the horse image back at Gismondo, declaring that he has broken the bridle of his tongue: "egli ha oggi rotto lo scilinguagniolo." Berenice says that Gismondo has known how to silence them all. Gismondo, "che in quest'arte rade volte si lasciava vincere" [who in this art rarely let himself be conquered], shows no apparent shame, feeling rather "più libero . . . dalle donne ispeditosi" (2.24–25.429–31) [freer . . . having gotten the women out of his way]. These three insults and silencings in quick succession draw attention to themselves, surely not only from a female reader. Berenice at the end of the day reminds us of them, saying that she is glad Lavinello, the third speaker, will now have a turn because his words are more temperate; otherwise she would probably not come back (2.34.453).

The criticism of Gismondo, who ends the second day protesting his innocence ("E che ho io detto, Madonna . . . ?" [What did I say, Madam . . . ?]), comes not only from the women, and not only from Lavinello, who repeatedly reproves Gismondo as a brutish kind of lover, but also from Bembo himself, who introduces the third day with an explicit defense of the inclusion of women.

Quantunque io stimo che saranno molti, che mi biasimeranno in ciò, che io alla parte di queste investigazioni le donne chiami, alle quali più s'acconvenga negli uffici delle donne dimorarsi, che andare di queste cose cercando. De' quali tuttavia non mi cale. Perciò che se essi non niegano che alle donne l'animo altresì come agli uomini sia dato, non so io perché più ad esse che a noi si disdica il cercare che cosa egli sia, che si debba per lui fuggire che seguitare; e sono queste tra le meno aperte quistioni, e quelle per aventura, d'intorno alle quali, sì come perni, tutte le scienze si volgono, segni e berzagli d'ogni nostra opera e pensamento. Che se esse tuttavolta a quegli uffici, che diranno que' tali esser di donna, le loro convenevoli dimore non togliendo, negli studi delle lettere e in queste cognizioni de' loro ozii ogni altra parte consumeranno, quello che alquanti uomini di ciò ragionino non è da curare, perciò che il mondo in loro loda ne ragionerà quando che sia. (3.1.458–59)

[*Although I think that many men will blame me for calling in to participate in these investigations ladies, who would more suitably remain with their female duties than go inquiring about such matters, nonetheless about such men I do not care. For if they do not deny that women have been given a mind just as men have, I don't know why it should be more forbidden to them (women) than to us to inquire about what it is that we should flee or pursue; and these are among the least obvious issues, and ones, as it happens, around which, as around a hinge, all the sciences turn, the goals and targets of all our work and thought. So if ladies, not failing to perform their appropriate duties that are called those of women, sometimes spend the rest of their leisure in the study of letters, what some men may say about this is of no concern, for the world will speak in their praise at all times.*]

The phrase about seeking what to flee and what to pursue, with its echo of the preface to the *Decameron*, extends Boccaccio's inclusion of women from tale-telling to a more philosophical discussion, since both have the same morally educative intent. The passage defends not only the fitness of women's participation in the search for moral truth but also Bembo's own investment in a vernacular text about love, which is raised from a trivial entertainment to the status of a philosophical quest for a centrally important and difficult truth. Thus Bembo implicitly identifies himself with the women as someone who, though apparently trivial in his pursuits, is nonetheless to be taken seriously.

Yet on the third day, as Lavinello narrates his encounter and dialogue with the hermit, no one interrupts. The dialogue turns into a monologue that reports in turn the dialogue of Lavinello and his hermit. The removal of dialogue to a framed scene makes intervention impossible for men and women alike. Oddly, Bembo has intervened on behalf of women's participation just at the point where women have been silenced for good within the reported discourses of men. They speak only to each other, reporting to the queen the arguments presented in her garden. If the discussion were indeed a Socratic search for truth, Bembo assures us that women would be rightly part of it; but as it is instead a male performance and display of male rivalry, a battle of armed knights or verbal tournament, women have only the role of audience. The confusion, apparently on Bembo's part, about which kind of dialogue we have here, heuristic or disputational, causes the issue of the women's role to remain conflicted in its presentation. Yet this conflict also makes the issue become a major focus of anxiety throughout the work, both for its speakers and for its author.

Agnolo Firenzuola's *Ragionamenti* (Conversations) (1525) and his subsequent "Epistola in lode delle donne" (Letter in Praise of Women) (1525) go much further than Bembo. Firenzuola was a Florentine writer known best for his dialogues, tales, and an Italian version of Apuleius's *Golden Ass*. The letter on women responds to a Sienese gentleman who has criticized Firenzuola's *Ragionamenti* for implausibly introducing women who speak about philosophy: "io facevo troppo altamente parlare a quelle persone alle quali più si converrebbe cercare quante matasse faccian mestieri a riempire una tela che entrare per le scuole dei filosofanti" (1957, 185) [I made speak too loftily those female persons who would be better suited to seeking how many skeins they need to finish weaving a cloth than to entering among the schools of philosophers]. Arguing that women have the same mental capacities as men if they are not clouded over by "i tristi vapori che si levano d'in su i vili loro exercizi, ne' quali e i padri e le madri da picciole le hanno nutricate" (186) [the dismal vapors that rise from their lowly practices, in which both mothers and fathers have brought them up since early childhood], Firenzuola not only names examples to prove his point (Catherine of Siena; Isotta Novarola [sic]; Cassandra Fedele; Alessandra Scala, who wrote "arguti epigrammi" [clever epigrams] and "buone lettere di filosofia" [good letters of philosophy]; Vittoria Colonna; the Gambara sisters; and others)[20] but also maintains that the very women in his *Ragionamenti* were known by him to discuss philosophical topics in just the manner that they do in his book: "la quale, mentre vivea, ne poteva dottamente parlare; e ne parlò più volte" (192–93) [who, while she lived, could speak learnedly about it, and did so speak many times]. He points out to his Sienese critic the contemporary example of Onorata Pecci (193) as one of "vostre sanese" [your Sienese] who "così accortamente ragiona delle più ascoste cose di filosofia, che i più gentili spiriti di quelle contrade" [speaks as knowledgeably of the most recondite matters of philosophy as the finest intellects of that region]. The main speaker of the *Ragionamenti*, Gostanza Amaretta, addresses the other two women and three men alike as having not only intelligent minds but also considerable philosophical reading: "aver rivoltato ognuno di voi il più dei libri che ne insegnano le occulte cose" (72) [each of you has paged through many of the books that teach hidden matters]. She speaks to them at length initially about mathematics before the topic shifts to love. Firenzuola's dedication of the *Ragionamenti* to the learned Caterina Cibo reinforces his assertion that there are indeed women who can discourse eloquently on philosophical matters and that it is therefore not implausible to represent them this way in books. The issue has become not merely one of permissibility but one of plausibility, not of what women might ideally do but of what they do in fact within the writer's and reader's experience.

Firenzuola's prologue to the *Ragionamenti* offers the book as an answer to the question of whether reading books in solitude or engaging in conversation with educated people is the more useful. He claims that the conversations he is recording demonstrate the greater value of conversation, which he calls "le vive lettere" [living letters]—although paradoxically he is turning those conversations into a book to be read in solitude. Part of Gostanza's argument within the work for pursuing a Platonic love relationship is that conversations with a worthy man are an important part of a woman's education: "De' quali ragionamenti noi altre donne, ordinariamente parlando, che ne' vili nostri esercizi da piccoline avezze, non potiamo coi piedi scalzi camminar per li fruttiferi campi della filosofia come gli uomini, tanta commodità ne caviamo, che oltre allo imparar di ben vivere, sappiamo molte cose dei secreti della natura, che in altra guisa non avremmo possuto mai sapere" (80) [From such conversations we other ladies, ordinarily speaking, who, having been accustomed since we were small to our lowly practices, cannot walk barefoot like men through the fruitful fields of philosophy, draw so much benefit that besides learning how to live well, we come to know many things about the secrets of nature, which we would have had no other way of learning]. Friendly dialogue with an educated man—or with a learned woman— becomes the university that is open to women, the means by which they can access the kinds of learning from which they are otherwise excluded. It is, in a sense, an alternate educational institution. It makes possible in turn the occurrence of further conversations in which women can participate in a truly educated manner.

Although Firenzuola's conversations follow the models of Boccaccio and Castiglione,[21] and thus come under the rubric of "polyphonic," the conversation that Gostanza advocates within his text is a dialogue of two people joined by particular affection. Leone Ebreo's *Dialoghi d'amore* (1535), another sixteenth-century dialogue with enormous influence, is a dialogue of this type. On one hand, it presents Sofia in the traditional role of questioner. On the other hand, it shows her to be a thoroughly intellectual person, in some ways more rational than her ardent lover. As her name openly indicates, she represents in part the abstract wisdom that her lover seeks to obtain; to this extent she is an almost allegorical figure. Yet she never completely dematerializes into allegory and remains sexually attractive even as she argues and questions about philosophical matters. Her role is drawn from that of Socrates' Diotima and suggests the model of a neoplatonic relationship between the sexes based on intellectual conversation—exactly the kind of relationship Gostanza encourages. Thus even though Sofia is generally the listener, she evokes another female who held the teaching role. Jean-Claude Carron (1991, 94–95) has suggested that the publication in France of two translations of Leone Ebreo's work in the same year (1551) was a major factor in launching the popularity of dialogue writing in France. It certainly provided a model for the dialogues of Pontus de Tyard, one of its translators and a member of the des Roches's circle. It was also highly praised by Tullia d'Aragona, who, as we shall see, clearly preferred its use of the female to Sperone Speroni's.

A further encouragement potentially came from the proliferation of dialogues written for women and including female speakers, even if in a limited role. These included dialogues of spiritual counsel, such as the widely admired dialogues by Catherine of Siena as well as those by men for women. They also included dialogues concerning women's education. Lodovico Dolce, one of the advocates of developing a serious and gracious Italian prose, turned Vives's *De institutione feminae Christianae* (1547) not only into Italian but also into a dialogue initiated by a female. Eager for conversation, Dorothea accosts Flaminio, asks what he is reading, and urges him—since the book is in Latin—to tell her the gist of what it says. Here is an example of a conversation, provoked by a woman, that can supply women with the learning from which they are otherwise excluded. Flaminio laments that Dorothea cannot read Latin, advocates literacy in Latin as well as in the vernacular for women, and offers a long list not only of classical examples but also of recent or contemporary Italian women who combine learning and virtue. Catherine of Siena is one of them. So are the ubiquitous Cassandra Fedele, Vittoria Colonna, Veronica Gambara, and other women described as "private," as distinct from public examples such as queens. The readings that he recommends for such private women include a number of other writers of dialogic texts: Plato (presumably in translation), Cicero, Castiglione, Bembo, and Speroni. Vives is the source for the classical list and for the mention of Catherine of Siena (secs. 23–26; 1996, 31–39); but Vives's reading list does not include the recent Italian examples, which Dolce adds; notably, many of these more modern Italian works are dialogues. Their presence calls attention to the dialogic nature of some of the classical texts as well, making this a dominant genre in the reading list for women.

Sperone Speroni (1500–1588), the latest of the writers mentioned by Dolce, while including women in at least two dialogues, makes much more conservative use of them than either Castiglione or Dolce. His dialogue "Della dignità delle donne," written in the early 1530s, presents the defense of women's equality and liberty as a joke while using a praised and exemplary woman, historically real, to argue that women are naturally subservient to men and therefore enjoy their traditional role. Again, then, we are getting mixed messages. Dolce seems to encourage women—both within and by means of his dialogue—to develop their mental abilities, to read other dialogues that include a female presence, and to engage similarly in conversation with men about ideas, without, however, disrupting the basic patriarchal order of society.

One can apply to Dolce's work the same deconstructive reading that Janis Butler Holm has applied insightfully to Vives's treatise, and even more so: while addressing and instructing an apparently private, domestic female, he nonetheless cites with praise long lists of famous women who were active in the public sphere and who bested men with their intellectual or literary exploits. All the while, the woman in the dialogue is taught to be submissive to men. Holm (1991, 280) suggests that women in the sixteenth century might have read these lists without a sense of this contradiction: "Interpreting the passages as evidence that publicly active women may hold their exceptional places only by being so extraordinary that they are more extraordinary than extraordinary men, a 'middle-class' reader might have been led to view public life for women as a very remote possibility, but to see the possibilities for essential womanly virtue as fortunately closer to home." Nonetheless, Dolce recommends other texts that offer both more adventurous and more conservative messages about women's possible roles. The very mix of messages, for any woman who read everything on his reading list, would certainly have provoked further thought about the limits and possibilities of her life.

The models for diphonic dialogue, a form very attractive to women, tend to include more medieval examples along with the ancient and the new. Within the historical heritage of diphonic dialogue there is actually a continuum of more and less secular themes and a concomitant fluid variety of more and less human types of speaker. One can map out several types of two-speaker dialogue by considering who it is that speaks. The lines between human and nonhuman speaker, however, are often hard to maintain.

At one extreme is the dialogue of the soul with God. Augustine's *Confessions* delivers mostly the words of the human speaker; Catherine of Siena gives most of the speaking time to God, while her soul interjects brief questions and astonished exclamations of thanks and praise for God's love. The fact that pieces of her dialogues became labeled "tractato de la Providenza" or "tractato dell'obedienza" indicates the monologic nature of these expositions. As God explains to Catherine, this dialogue is a kind of speech by God with himself: "sonno un altro me, perché hanno perduta e annegata la propria volonta, e vestitisi, unitisi e conformatisi con la mia" (1912, 4) [They are another me, because they have lost and annihilated their own will, and dressed themselves in, united themselves with, and conformed themselves to my will]. Since "l'anima allora è in Dio, e Dio ne l'anima" (4–5) [the soul then is in God and God in the soul], the two speak from within each other rather than as clearly separate entities.

Similarly, Augustine's opening lines intermingle God's words and Augustine's own, appropriately for someone who ultimately expresses the belief that all communication takes place through God and is possible only in that way. Augustine cannot speak to us, nor can we understand his words, except through our common participation in God or God's presence and action in us. Thus, for example, *Confessions* 13.31: "Sicut enim recte dictum est: non enim vos estis, qui loquimini, eis, qui in dei spiritu loquerentur, sic recte dicitur: 'non vos estis, qui scitis' eis, qui in dei spiritu sciunt. Nihilo minus igitur recte dicitur: 'non vos estis, qui videtis' eis, qui in spiritu dei vident" [For as it is rightly said, unto those that were to speak by the Spirit, "It is not you that speak," so is it as rightly said to them that know through the Spirit of God, "It is not you that know." And no less then is it rightly said to those that see through the Spirit of God, "It is not you that see"] (trans. Watts, 2.461).

Although both Augustine and Catherine were widely read and powerfully influential, this is not a type of dialogue lightly undertaken outside a serious mystical vocation. I will mention here briefly one modest example: Marguerite de Navarre's "Dialogue de Dieu et de l'homme," which plays with a theme recurring in Marguerite's works: how man who is Nothing (Rien) can be raised by a God who is All (Tout) from a condition of Nothingness to a divine condition of unity with All.[22] Marguerite has summed up neatly the absolute imbalance between speakers, an imbalance that can be rectified only by their ultimate identity within the divine.

A second type of dialogue, a step down from these heights, involves a human and an abstraction. Although there are medieval scientific versions, such as Brunetto Latini's *Tesoretto*, involving the author in a conversation with Nature, women tend not to be engaged in scientific dialogues of that sort, except as the female personification of Nature herself. Women are similarly present chiefly through allegory in the predominant themes of this type of dialogue: moral or spiritual guidance and consolation. The most famous and influential model here is Boethius's *De consolatione philosophiae*, where the female teacher is Philosophy herself, not a role to which real women would aspire. Although Philosophy discusses divine providence and the perspective from beyond time, she is something less than God and closer to human. Indeed, she may be read in part as Boethius's own intellect in conversation with his more emotional self. Augustine's *Soliloquia* was perhaps a starting point for this type and certainly a model for Boethius. As in the dialogue with God, the distinction between the two speakers is not entirely clear. As Augustine puts it in the opening of his *Soliloquia* (1.1):

Volventi mihi multa ac varia mecum diu ac per multos dies sedulo quaerenti memetipsum ac bonum meum, quidve mali evitandum esset, ait mihi subito sive ego ipse sive alius quis, extrinsecus sive intrinsecus, nescio; nam hoc ipsum est quod magnopere scire molior. . . . (23)

[When I had been pondering many different things to myself for a long time, and had for many days been seeking my own self and what my own good was, and what evil was to be avoided, there suddenly spoke to me—what was it? I myself or someone else, inside me or outside me? (this is the very thing I would love to know but don't). . . .]

Reason, the sudden speaker here, is either Augustine's own reasoning faculty or else a more universal faculty that can speak to and for his readers as well as himself. Part of Augustine's anxiety involves the question of whether his love of wisdom is a love of God or a self-love of his own intelligence. In short, the topic like the form finds the distinction between internal and external difficult to draw.[23] So too Boethius's Philosophy is in part the external philosophical tradition but in part his own rational mind speaking to him in the solitude of his prison cell.

Augustine's and Boethius's search for wisdom brings Platonic models into a more Christian context, including prayer. Even though Boethius's prayers are not specifically Christian, they were certainly readily acceptable for a Christian readership and use. Rational argumentation predominates, but Augustine's implicit identification of Wisdom with God sets the object of the quest beyond its means. A certain progress is made toward a better understanding, but Augustine himself remains unsatisfied, though still hopeful for further enlightenment in the future. Boethius's Philosophy too may ultimately be giving her pupil an incomplete account, which must be complemented by faith.[24]

This type of dialogue had a long life, from the even earlier Ambrose's *Dialogus animae conquerentis et rationis consolantis* through, more famously, Petrarch's *De remediis utriusque fortunae*.[25] Petrarch's work dehumanizes both speakers, creating a pair of antithetical abstractions: Dolor or Metus, who laments about various losses—or Gaudium or Spes, who exults in good fortunes—and Ratio, whose arguments are, as Diekstra (Petrarch 1968, 49–51) observes for the Stoic tradition in general, a mix of cliché and sophistic exercise that is sometimes "hard-hearted and hardly in good taste." We can see in Petrarch's text the braiding of several strands: (1) the consolatory dialogue with reason or philosophy; (2) the stoic letter or essay, especially Seneca's *De remediis fortuitorum* (35–36, 40–41); and (3) the medieval debate between abstractions. Seneca's piece, as Diekstra points out (40–41), appeared in medieval versions as a dialogue between Sensus and Ratio and also as a dialogue between Seneca and Gallio, to whom Seneca was writing, or Seneca and Nero, in the traditions of teacher-student dialogue and education of the prince. In short, we have here an intermediate type that can be pushed antithetically either toward a pair of abstractions or toward a fully human interaction. Similarly, Cicero could remark in his *De finibus* (2.14.44): "relinquitur non mihi cum Torquato sed virtuti cum voluptate certatio" [there remains a duel in which the combatants are not myself and Torquatus, but Virtue and Pleasure]. Although Cicero maintains a human debate, the clear positions of each side allow it to be equated with a debate between the abstractions themselves.

When Philosophy presents herself to Boethius as a medical nurse and a compassionate mother, might women readers not have seen here the traces of real women's roles in consoling and advising men? Catherine d'Amboise certainly did identify with the female nature of this role, as we shall see (chap. 2). Leone Ebreo, while naming his female speaker "Sophia," nonetheless makes her a real human being rather than an abstract figure of Wisdom. His dialogue was praised by Tullia d'Aragona within her own, and his humanization of the wise female speaker was clearly encouraging to her as a woman writer. Furthermore, the figure of Reason or Philosophy might easily be confused with that of Diotima, with whom Tullia in part identifies herself (see chap. 3). In sum, the same kind of slippage that enabled Reason to become Seneca similarly enabled women as writers to embody a previously abstract or fictional female figure of wisdom. The shift between human and abstract figures can even occur within one writer. Catherine des Roches's dialogue of Beauty and Love is immediately followed by one between a beautiful girl—readily identifiable with Catherine herself—and her would-be lover.

Rudolf Hirzel (1894, 2: 364–65) observes that the dialogues of late antiquity tended to belong to either of two basic models: the teacher-student relation or the relationship of opposing views. We can see that the first is the more human and even the more individual; the second tends toward the typical figure and the abstract. Thus the teachings of wisdom concerning fortune and misfortune can be individualized as a particular sage and student or treated as opposing abstractions. Topical pairs (body and soul, virtue and fortune, winter and summer) could always be staged as a debate between the things or concepts themselves.[26] Cultural differences among women seem to have inclined them toward more abstract or more humanly embodied versions. Catherine d'Amboise's allegorical imitation of Boethius involves, as in the *De consolatione philosophiae*, the appearance of Reason to Catherine herself. Helisenne de Crenne, writing a debate between Reason and Sensuality, suddenly has her first-person narrator jump into the fray herself, directly interacting with Reason. Both she and Catherine des Roches wrote a series of dialogues that shift openly, in a rather unusual manner, between the abstract and the human.

The next step along the continuum, and the chief object of my focus in this study, is the conversation between two human beings. It may be a hierarchical relationship between teacher and student or a more equally conceived friendship. The two speakers will obviously have to disagree about something, but they can either remain fixed representatives of opposing views or else succeed in persuading each other toward an agreement. Where one side is clearly trying to teach or move the other, as is generally the case, narratives of more or less successful persuasion are possible. Ideally the speakers could also engage in a Socratic conversation in which they jointly pursue some truth originally known to neither, but this does not seem to happen, at least neither for the women writers of whose work I am aware nor for the dialogues written by men for and including women. Both male and female writers have a well-defined agenda and are using the dialogue to present it persuasively both to their conversational partner and to the reader.

Petrarch, the ubiquitous model for much sixteenth-century writing, provides examples that demonstrate the convergence of several traditions. His *Secretum* clearly follows Augustine's *Soliloquia*, replacing Reason with Augustine himself in a dialogue that, like Augustine's, is both internal and external and that ends without an entirely successful persuasion.[27] This dialogue is a response to another dialogue and as such uses Augustine to represent an external author with whose thought Petrarch is grappling. But Augustine is also a ghost rather than a living person and as such represents one of Petrarch's own inner voices expressing its doubts about his secular ambitions and desires. The same inner debate over how to live reappears in the first of Petrarch's eclogues. The eclogue offers a discussion between representatives of a more spiritual and a more secular life. On one hand, it draws on the historical realities of his own and his monastic brother's choices and the sort of conversation they might well have had, though not in those words, while on the other hand it reaches out to the bucolic tradition to distance this intimate rivalry and anxiety through the voices of classical pastoral figures. Clearly the Renaissance interest in bucolics is closely connected to the period's interest in dialogue forms for the expression and mutual testing of differing viewpoints. Boccaccio's eclogue "Olympia," unusual for putting a female in the position of teaching an older male, braids together the pastoral form with topics both of religious education and of consolation for the death of a beloved family member. Marguerite de Navarre's late plays pick up this connection of the personal and the pastoral with regard to both of those themes. Finally, Petrarch's invectives present one side of an explicit dispute, mingling rational argument with mocking satire in a way that Helisenne de Crenne found useful to her purposes.

Erasmus was a very influential model for the diphonic dialogue, both secular and spiritual. Many of his *Colloquies* have two speakers, and although several involve dinner parties with more, Franz Berlaire (1978, 95) has observed that Erasmus tends even there to engage only two speakers at a time or else to let each man take his turn in a circle, rather than coordinating a larger conversation. The topics tend to cluster around a few moral and religious themes prominently treated in Erasmus's other writings as well: marriage and celibacy, true piety and superstition, philology and textual interpretation—whether of scriptural passages or of the classical authors. Mingling Lucianic satire and playfulness with a Ciceronian realism of characters and domestic settings, and mixing allegorical names for typical figures with the use of named personal acquaintances as speakers, Erasmus offered a variety both of topics and of strategies for his readers and imitators. He repeatedly defended the dialogue as a lively and engaging method of teaching, but he obviously found it also a handy instrument for social satire.

What emerges predominantly from his volume of conversations, which increased in number over the years, is an attempt to find and articulate the morally good and humanly pleasant life among all the ridiculous or tragic follies of human society. That search for how to live the good life in its serious sense is a primary focus of the whole core of tradition in the dialogue genre: for Plato certainly, for Cicero as well, for Lucian by the negative approach of making fun of foolishness, for Augustine and Petrarch in a more Christian context. As Paul Pellison remarks in his mid-seventeenth-century discussion of the dialogue, "Car qu'y a-t-il de plus beau que de persuader aux hommes par de nouveaux moyens, ces maximes generales d'ou naist leur felicité . . . ?" (cited in Le Guern 1982, 146–47). The discussion of what might make for human felicity is not only good but also "beau"; it offers a convergence of intellectual, moral, and aesthetic pleasures. It combines the casual form of friendly conversation with one of the deepest issues of philosophy: how to live.

For women too, the best way to live, whether as a Christian or as a learned woman or both, is a recurring theme in the dialogues that we shall look at. These conversations are often moments of reflection on the women's major concerns both for themselves and for others. Religious issues are related to a personal quest for the right way of life; more secular issues are likely to involve the social debate about women's roles and possibilities. We shall see examples of both kinds in the chapters that follow.

Contradictions within social ideologies open up the possibilities for women to make use of conventional ideas for unconventional feminist purposes, as Ann Rosalind Jones (1990, 1–4) has rightly observed. Indeed, culture is even more complex; it offers not just contradictions but a whole gamut of attitudes, articulations, and ambivalences. One can see this gamut, for example, in Renaissance writings about women's education, which proffer a wide range of options along with internally ambiguous advice.[28] Some women writers could find within their culture an already articulated position that might suit their purposes. Others felt the need to introduce more radical options, possibly even while maintaining an ambivalent adherence to more conventional views.

I have been asked whether the women I am studying were truly "women writers" or rather writers who happened to be women. Often that question is difficult to answer. Yet it was impossible for these women to avoid the awareness that they were writing as women and that their gender made their position as writers always debatable. Dialogue offered an opportunity for such debates to find open expression.

Dialogue extends its connections in many directions. Michel Le Guern (1981, 142) has attempted to distinguish between dialogue and theater, while recognizing the basic overlap in a theater of ideas.[29] He defines the distinction thus: the truth value of statements by characters in a play is valid only within the play, whereas the truth value of statements by characters in a dialogue is valid in the real world, even though the speakers are just as fictional in both genres. The Renaissance dialogue writer Speroni, however, in his "Apologia dei dialoghi," returns repeatedly to the topic of close connections rather than distinctions between dialogue and "comedia," linking the two genres through the concept of imitation: both include a variety of characters, morally better or worse, intellectually more or less intelligent, and display the manners of speech and thought appropriate to these different persons; both leave out the direct expression of the writer's own views, presenting imitations of views and emotions rather than any kind of sincere expression. Sigonius too describes dialogue as presenting its material "quasi agatur in scena, non narratur" [as if it were acted on stage, not narrated].[30] Tasso qualified this notion by observing that the scene of dialogue can be readily imagined and does not need the stage for its realization. Questions about the high or low status of the dialogue genre were involved, for an association with theater implied a mass audience inappropriate to the contents of a learned conversation.[31] Marguerite de Navarre wrote both narrative and verse dialogues and also theater pieces; the topics and treatments of multivoiced conflict and persuasion overlap across her works in these genres. But of course the audience for her drama was a court audience and not a public theater. We shall see that the links of dialogue with theater are particularly strong among French women writers, to the point of apparently constituting a specifically French female tradition of dialogue writing.

Correspondence was another area that, as we shall see, had multiple relationships to women's dialogue writing. Vives and others explicitly suggested the use of model letters as an aid to the art of conversation as well as a pattern for letter writing (Massebieau 1878, 49). Humanist women, whether trying out their hand at the humanist letter or writing to a friend or advisor, could easily slide into epistolary dialogue.

Social conversations and oral games were yet another form that shaped the written genre. All of these together provided a field within which the idea of women's writing of dialogues became imaginable. Some of these connections will be further discussed in the chapters ahead.

The lyric too could be a dialogic form. Just as the women of Ovid's *Heroides* exchange verse epistles with their lovers, just as medieval *tenzoni* include *trobairitz* as well as troubadours in poetic exchanges, so too the sixteenth century cultivated the social exchange of verses: sonnets of mutual praise, sonnets of giving and thanking, sonnets of invitation and response, sonnets and *capitoli* of dispute. The social uses of the lyric made it very different from our later romantic conceptions of poetry. Tullia d'Aragona, defending her special honor above other courtesans because of her poetic skills, published a volume that displays the circle of powerful and intellectual men with whom she exchanged verse.[32] Veronica Franco, similarly a courtesan, used her series of capitoli to defend herself against a versified attack.[33] Some women wrote both sides of the exchange. Like Christine de Pizan, with her hundred poems forming a sort of epistolary narrative between a lady and her lover, Catherine des Roches nearly two hundred years later wrote a series of sonnets both to herself from a male admirer and to him in reply. This lyric exchange follows a set of prose dialogues ending with a dialogue of these same lovers. Her connection of the two forms clearly suggests that this culture of social poetry was one of the relevant contexts for women's dialogic writing in prose.

Any study requires some principle of subdivision; yet the categories one invents are always blurring into one another. Typologies of the dialogue tend to follow one of three factors: (1) ancient models: classifying according to Platonic, Ciceronian, and Lucianic models, each with its distinguishing features;[34] (2) themes or functions: distinguishing among consolatory dialogues, dialogues of religious instruction, love dialogues, scholastic dialogues, dialogues intended as a social game, and so on;[35] (3) formal aspects: distinguishing, for example, between "monologic" and truly "dialogic" or, along similar lines, between "open" and "closed" forms.[36]

A more structuralist approach to typology comes in Paul Zumthor's discussion of the genre: "D'un point de vue descriptif, deux principes de classification se conjuguent pour ordonner un corpus numériquement considérable: selon la nature des actants ou celle de fonctions narratives, implicites ou explicites" (1978, 181–85) [From a descriptive point of view, two principles of classification converge to organize a numerically large corpus: according to the nature of the actants or the nature of narrative functions, implicit or explicit]. He distinguishes "interlocuteurs," which can be allegorical, human, named personally or mythologically or by social role, and so on, and "actants," which can be, for example, questioner and answerer, or contrasting debaters, adding the further category of "narrative," which either juxtaposes their arguments or works toward a conclusion. Kushner (1983, 134) also makes use of this structuralist term of analysis "actants," observing that the number of speakers can be multiplied for each point of view. Michel Le Guern (1981, 143–44) suggests a typology according to the different possible relations between speakers: (1) "dialogue didactique"—one speaker represents the author, the other the reader; (2) "dialogue polémique"—one is the author, the other his or her adversary, while the reader becomes a witness of their debate; (3) "dialogue dialectique"—no one speaker represents the author, and truth is no longer the possession of one privileged speaker; the competing views can reach a synthesis or be left unresolved. Eva Kushner, in the same volume (1982, 149–50), notes that these relationships can be reduced to two: "adjuvant ou opposant."[37]

In another kind of formal typology, Reino Virtanen (1977, 3) cites Joseph de Maistre's distinction among real artless conversations, conversations recorded and shaped, and completely invented conversations. Virtanen, thinking about dialogues throughout history and not specifically Renaissance types, observes (46, 128) that the modern love for disputation is served by talk shows but that these clearly fall into the category of artless and unshaped language rather than a genre of literature. Giovanna Wyss Morigi ([1947], 12) sees the chief difference between dialogue and conversation in the focus on a set topic rather than the random associative sharing of ideas and impressions; thus, for her, talk shows would be true dialogues, even without further formal polishing. The writer is replaced by the host, who tries to shape the discourse in real time. Since many Renaissance dialogues, while artfully polished, tried to convey the impression of artless conversation, this set of distinctions seems less useful in our context.

Often these various typologies are used in combination, as indeed there is considerable overlap among them; for example, the Ciceronian model conveys not only certain formal features but also a certain range of thematic subject matter. Formal aspects also coincide with considerations of function. Some uses, such as the scholastic or catechetical, anticipate performance; Erasmus intended his colloquies, at least originally, to be recited aloud by schoolboys learning Latin, and they were so used in many schools. Other functions, such as the game or spiritual counsel, more often present the dialogue as the recording of a previous oral event. So too particular themes may lend themselves more to an open or closed form; matters of religious orthodoxy, for example, may be more difficult to leave in doubt than arguments about the use of the vernacular. Francesco Tateo (1967, 223), while comparing specific dialogues and noting particular features (such as the inclusion or omission of a narrative framework), shrugs off the possibility of theorizing the genre by defining any generic homogeneities either formal or substantial. So too Valerio Vianello (1993, 10–11) laments the difficulty of defining a genre that operates in "interference" with other forms such as satire, eclogue, letter, and comedy.[38]

In mapping out the strands of dialogue leading up to and including women's entry into this varied genre in France and Italy chiefly during the sixteenth century, I will need an eclectic approach. There are particular traditions involving both strong models and defined themes or functions. While the distinction between polyphonic dialogue and diphonic dialogue might seem trivial, for example, it carries with it in fact a number of differences, if not by any obvious intrinsic necessity, then simply by usage. For example, Le Guern notes (1981, 145) that most "open" dialogues are polyphonic rather than diphonic, although polyphonic dialogues need not be open and diphonic dialogues need not come to an agreed conclusion. On the other hand, more directly didactic dialogues tend to take the diphonic teacher-student form.

The material at hand can be ordered in a number of ways. Dolce lists literate women by region, both inside and beyond Italy. Cox similarly treats separately writings from Tuscany and Venice, from Italy and France, noting the regional distinctions. One could draw the dividing line between dialogues involving only women and those involving both sexes, for the social behavior of women is frequently different in those two cases. One could arrange this material chronologically, looking for developments. One could, as in Ann Rosalind Jones's book on women's lyric (1990), divide the material according to its more radical or conservative nature. The justification for any typology lies in its usefulness in helping us to see relationships and differences rather than in an accurate representation of any inherent system. Each has its particular insights to offer, and yet one cannot do all of them at once.

I have chosen to divide my material along formal lines, but in a manner that also involves different models, contents, and purposes. First I have distinguished between diphonic and polyphonic dialogues. Not only the possible range of views but also the positioning of authority works differently in a group of many voices; the models for a group interaction, Boccaccio and Castiglione, surely have something to do with the ambivalences concerning authority that permeate later polyphonic dialogues. Within the diphonic category, I have followed four overlapping lines of exploration: those dialogues that follow the model of spiritual counsel, those that make use instead of more secular social conversation, those that lean toward a connection with the epistolary genre, and those that lean toward a connection with drama. This last category happens to coincide with a cultural one as it is characteristic of French rather than Italian writers. Even these four categories, however, are not neatly distinguishable, and dialogue associated with drama readily adds in more than two voices.

I wish first of all to present women's dialogic writings, which are often not well-known, and to demonstrate that this was a genre that attracted women's wide and varied participation. That variety itself indicates the experimental nature of much of their writing and thus the liveliness of the genre as its possibilities in various directions were explored. I wish also to consider women's texts together with texts by men to or including women, texts that suggest the kinds of discourse available in the culture that might have encouraged women seeking to include their own voices in these con-

versations. Encouraging discourses include social conversation and epistolary correspondence as well as books of dialogue, and I will try to demonstrate some of the connections among them. Although focusing on human
dialogues, I have had to consider dialogues that cross the boundaries
between the human conversations that we think of as Renaissance dialogue
and the medieval débat between things or abstractions, which remained
(especially in France) an influential presence even in those later centuries.
Finally, having laid out the array of dialogues of various types by French and
Italian women, I will try in the end to survey the whole for any generalizations that we can draw about what encouraged these women to write dialogues, what seemed to them attractive about the genre, and what use they
made of it.

Studies on the dialogue as a genre, remarkably rare until recently, have suddenly proliferated. Rudolf Hirzel's two-volume history of the genre, published in 1895, reigned for a long time as master of the field and is still the
most ambitious contribution. Devoting the entire first volume and most of
the second to the ancients, especially the Greeks, he traces the genre more
briefly through its medieval Christian variants to its retransformation in the
Renaissance, focusing chiefly on Italian and German examples of that
period, and on into the eighteenth century. Since Hirzel, scholarly efforts
have tended to focus more modestly on one century or one type. David
Marsh (1980) focuses on the humanist dialogues of the fifteenth century as a
revival and transformation of classical models. Marcel Derwa and L. Massebieau investigate the school-text dialogue and its importance in Renaissance
pedagogy. Virginia Cox (1992, 10) has raised the question of "why it was
only in Italy that a strong tradition of documentary dialogue [i.e., using historically real speakers] developed, while elsewhere the vast majority of dialogues took a straightforward fictional form." Even within Italy, the culture
of her focus, she notices that the Venetians tended toward Lucianic models,
in contrast to a Tuscan Ciceronianism. Another strong theme of her study is
the extent to which dialogues were truly dialogic or merely disguised monologues, not only internally but also in relation to their readers: whether we
are "referees, actively engaged" or "relegated to the role of admiring specta-
tors" (2). More recently she has turned her attention to Italian dialogues
involving women speakers, work that obviously comes the closest to my own
and that I am thankful to her for allowing me to read in manuscript.

The social interests of her study are shared by Valerio Vianello, who
demonstrates the shifting context of Italian dialogue from courtly conversation to the urban circulation of printed texts and the function of the genre

in helping a new class of intellectual men define a role for themselves in society and find a way to insert their influence. Their problems and goals—"ansioso di reclamare nella penna un mezzo idoneo per intervenire nella realtà" (1993, 23) [anxious to reclaim via the pen a suitable means for intervening in reality] and their selection of dialogue as the means to a "cosciente progetto di atteggiarsi a maestro della nuova letteratura" (114) [conscious project of assuming a posture of master of the new literature]—were much the same as those of educated women, who found themselves in a similarly ill-defined situation within society. Italian social issues and their relations to different ways of writing are also important to the work of Raffaele Girardi.

Both geography and subgenre define the study of Mustapha Kemal Bénouis, which presents a number of different types of philosophical dialogue in France. Jon Snyder has turned his attention to dialogues about dialogues, looking at late Italian Renaissance dialogues that explicitly discuss the art of the genre even as they exemplify it. His discussion of how useful the dialogue seemed in the later sixteenth century to shield its writer from attack by allowing him to disavow the ideas expressed by his characters and to counter dangerous ideas with more conservative ones—and yet how thin a protection it actually offered—is readily applicable to some of the women's dialogues as well.

Carla Forni seeks to infer and map out the "rules of the game" for Italian Renaissance dialogues and their relationships to other genres, while recognizing the immense variety of dialogues and the fluidity of all boundary definitions. Eva Kushner has attempted in numerous essays to find a more modern way of theorizing the genre, especially in its French Renaissance form. All of these efforts add to our awareness of subgenres; of specific elements or features that vary from one case to another; of social uses for the genre, social contexts in which it arose, and social contexts that it realistically or wishfully represented.

These scholars have suggested a number of approaches applicable to women's dialogues. One is to inquire into the contexts, both literary and social or oral, that encouraged women to engage in this genre at all and that provided models for their efforts. What models did women find that enabled them to write as women, and how were these models used? Which types of written dialogue were more or less useful to women? How might these relate to social forms of dialogue? This means situating the texts in women's historical and literary relations with men or other women that might have produced thoughtful conversation; considering dialogues written for women and including women speakers; and looking at the ways that dialogues by, for, and with men nonetheless could be seen by women writers as available models for their own adoption.

The friendly visitor to Erasmus's Puerpera (New Mother), pointing out the importance of the mother-child relation for the child's education, says, "Praecipuus autem discendi gradus est mutuus inter docentem ac discentem amor" (1.3.468.545) [Now one of the main steps in the learning process is mutual affection between teacher and pupil (283)].[39] As someone who wrote a large percentage of his work either for or about education, Erasmus meant this seriously. We need to look at the personal relationships that inform women's dialogues, both internal and external to their writing. What kinds of difference do these relationships make? How different or similar are the relationships within dialogues between men and women or among women without men present? Is there a privileged voice of authority or not, and if so, how is that authority established? Is this an external authority, to be perhaps contested, or an authority granted by the text itself, and on what grounds? When women take for themselves the role of teacher, what sort of pupils do they envision? Does the inclusion of multiple female voices indicate multiple or ambivalent female views? How open-ended or conclusive are these conversations? How do these dialogues figure in a broader dialogue of dialogues; that is, how do they respond to previous examples of the genre or fit themselves into the preexisting cultural conversation?

Not only are the dialogues the results of real relationships, and the representation of relationships real or fictional, but they are also the producer of a new relationship, that between writer and reader. As Le Guern remarks (1981, 143), the dialogue is really a communication between writer and reader disguised as a communication between intermediary figures to which both writer and reader are presented as auditors. What array of responses does the writer seem to anticipate, and how does the text deal with them? Is the reader presumed to be male or female, or both? Would it make a difference? Last but not least, to what extent do these dialogues show women to be reading and imitating other women? Were women writing chiefly for the powerful men from whom they might hope to win approbation, or was there an awareness of, or a desire for, female models, a female readership, and a female friendship across the page?

These questions will guide my discussion of each writer's work. All of them can be summed up by the more general but harder to answer questions that we can ask of any text: Why and how did women do this? What did they think they were accomplishing? What do they want from us?

2 Dialogue & Spiritual Counsel

Since the time of Augustine and Gregory, dialogue has been seen as a useful form for the expression of Christian thought.[1] Women who wrote spiritual dialogues were doing so as part of a very long and venerable tradition. They could even point to the fact that Augustine sometimes included comments by his mother in dialogues on spiritual matters, such as *De beata vita*. Consolations had also been frequently written for women since the time of early Christianity, sometimes in dialogue form.[2] Gregory of Nyssa's fourth-century dialogue with his sister Macrina, *Dialogue on the Soul and the Resurrection*, even gives Macrina the authoritative speaking role. He expresses a typical Greek's doubts about Christian doctrines, while Macrina explains the new theology concerning the afterlife and interprets the Bible to him. The mystical dialogues of the fourteenth-century Catherine of Siena with God were still widely admired during the sixteenth century. Indeed, the century of printing opened with a volume of Saint Catherine's letters published by the Aldine press in 1500 (Prosperi 1994, 228). Her *Dialogo della divina provvidenza* had been among the earliest works in print, appearing already three times before 1500;[3] and her cult was promoted by the Dominicans throughout the sixteenth century. Another saintly Catherine, of Genoa, was widely known through several published volumes, including spiritual dialogues between the body and soul, or the soul and God, printed posthumously during the middle of the sixteenth century. Like the Italian Catherines, the French Margaret Porete wrote a dialogic work of mystical ardor emphasizing the overwhelming love between the soul and God. Despite her condemnation and execution for heresy in 1310, her writing remained known and admired into the sixteenth century. The many fifteenth-century manuscripts of her work include translations into Latin, Italian, and Middle English, attesting to a wide interest in it (Bryant 1984, 209). Her speakers are allegorical figures of Love, Reason, the Soul, and so on.

The sixteenth century is also full of spiritual dialogues that use two or more human speakers, usually written by men in ecclesiastical or monastic positions for the instruction and benefit of laymen and -women. We shall see some examples of these later. Sometimes a man of the church who was assigned to investigate the orthodoxy and claims to sanctity concerning a female visionary began as her inquisitor only to end as her disciple and devoted scribe, biographer, and public advocate. Thus, the hierarchy of authority could become confused or reversed between a holy woman and her spiritual advisor or assistant (Zarri 1994, 180). In the instructions to lay-women, however, the hierarchy remains clear-cut. Yet the women whom this chapter is considering—Marguerite de Navarre, Olympia Morata, and Chiara Matraini—were precisely laywomen, neither clergy nor mystical saints; what gave them the idea that they could write as well as read spiritual dialogues? Had not Paul written in 1 Timothy 2:11–12: "Let a woman learn in quietness with all subjection. But I permit not a woman to teach nor to have dominion over a man, but to be in quietness"? What might have encouraged them to write and teach, even sometimes to teach a male?

If we ask what forms of dialogue—in the broadest sense, that is, in life as well as in literature—included women and encouraged them to participate, we can point first of all to two religious situations within women's lives: catechism and confession. Both involve the woman's relation to a male of much greater authority, but whereas catechism asks the woman to reproduce memorized answers, confession calls for a deep self-searching and articulation of inner thoughts and feelings, of desires and fears, as well as of things actually done. This critical self-probing and resultant speech was a powerful type of dialogue for women, especially when carried out with a trusted and respected spiritual advisor. Michel Foucault (1988, 39–49) has observed how the habit of confession played an important role in the forming and cultivation of a sense of inner self.

Women also talked among themselves about religious topics. Investigations into heresy document some of their religious conversations (Rambaldi 1992, 37–38). During the course of the sixteenth century, Protestant anti-monastic sentiments and the widespread awareness of monastic corruption created an encouraging climate for the exploration of other options for a devotional life. Small groups for religious reading and discussion formed, often around charismatic leaders, male or female, reformist or staunchly Catholic, seeking authority not from the church but from the spiritual "mother" or "father" of the group (Zarri 1994, 197–98). Spiritual groups at the margins of institutionalized religion became centers for shared devotional reading (Zarri 1987, 140).[4] Indeed women also read the Bible together and undoubtedly discussed what it meant. Olympia Morata's letters repeatedly urge this kind of communal reading by a small group of women, especially her letters to her sister Vittoria and to the lady Orsini, in whose household her sister worked: "Vi priego, leggete questa lettera alla Vittoria, e esortatatela con esempio e con parole a onorare e confessare Dio. Leggete insieme con lei la Scrittura; pregate la mia cara signora Lavinia, che spesso vi legga qualcosa nella Scrittura, e voi sentirete efficacia della parola di Dio" (Caretti 1940, 1.111) [I beg you, read this letter to Vittoria and exhort her by example and word to honor and confess God. Read together with her the Scriptures; ask my dear lady Lavinia that she frequently read to you something in Scripture, and you will hear the efficacy of the word of God].[5]

Male devotional writers might also encourage such conversations. Battista da Crema declares that to learn the way to God requires not only a teacher and reading but also "compagnia spirituale."[6] Jean Gerson similarly assumes that his sisters, for whom he wrote various works of spiritual advice, were talking to each other and to other friends or relatives as well.

Similar discussions within a mixed group, and with a woman in charge of the scriptural readings, take place both within and beyond the edges of the text of Marguerite de Navarre's *Heptameron*,[7] where Oisille is not only the oldest member of the group but a kind of spiritual mother and leader. Paula Sommers (1983, 54–55) discusses the nature of Oisille's authority, noting as "significant that her Scriptural commentary is situated outside the chapel in an informal setting." Widows were encouraged in Vives's widely read books of advice not only to live chastely and piously but also to instruct those around them by both speech and example.

All of these types of spiritual conversation offered themselves as models for women in a much more immediate and lively—and much more encouraging—manner than the texts of Plato or Cicero, even when learned women were familiar with those too.[8] Nor were the topics totally unrelated to those of classical dialogue: how to live a good life was the basic theme for all of them.

Real conversations of these kinds found a written counterpart in books of spiritual advice written as dialogue. Research by Gabriella Zarri (1987, 132, 140, 141), looking at the proemial letters of printed devotional books and booklets in the late fifteenth and early sixteenth centuries, has indicated that these writings were expected to have a predominantly female readership. By the 1520s female convents were even becoming centers of book production. Zarri has shown further that works by Catherine of Siena and

Catherine of Bologna were among the few earlier devotional writings that remained in print; Catherine of Siena's work was, of course, dialogical, as its printed title made explicit.[9] Catherine of Bologna's advice was not in dialogue form but was addressed primarily to the female readership of other nuns. Women belonging to devotional groups or simply serious about their religious work might not write treatises, but they might write letters of instruction and exhortation to each other and to their relatives (Zarri 1987, 142–44).[10] Thus women felt specifically addressed by religious writing and also were aware of women who had participated in producing it, not only in moments of prophetic rapture but also in sober moments when kinsmen or community members had asked for their advice.

More intimate than a larger group, the duo offers a more intense occasion for focus on matters of inner disquiet and the search for salvation, in contrast to the more relaxed and urbane discussions of a larger number of speakers. Obviously this religious focus is one of the aspects that might well have attracted women writers, since pious texts were often allowed to women readers when more secular texts were not, and since a number of these texts were even specifically addressed to women and included them already as participants in discussion. Piety seemed an appropriate topic for women seeking to safeguard their honor while engaging in their own writing and even in making their writing public. Moreover, women were not only looking for approved topics. Given the religious turmoil and debate of the mid–sixteenth century, women writers show every indication of having been very seriously concerned with making the right spiritual choices. On the other hand, this religious focus might just as well have discouraged women from participating as writers, since to do so implied a certain authority to discourse on topics of religion, despite Paul's famous dictum that women should be silent in the church.

Several men, writing spiritual dialogues with and for intellectual women, may have provided the encouragement needed for women themselves to launch into this type of writing. Examples come from both Catholic and reform-minded writers. We can ask how these dialogues with women represent and situate their female speakers and how easily they might have been adapted by a woman writer.

Gerson, the most important and admired French theologian of the early fifteenth century and chancellor of the University of Paris, addressed a number of works to his sisters, including a *Dialogue spirituel*.[11] Referring to other texts that he has written for their spiritual education—he lists letters, treatises, and sermons and later has the sisters mention specifically his "livret de mendicité espirituelle, lequel fittes jadis pour nous" (1966, 167)—his sisters come to him with a request for four days of his time (though they acknowledge that he is a busy man) to pursue further discussion and to clarify some issues on which they or others with whom they have been speaking have some doubts. They ask him furthermore to write down the discussion both to aid their own memory and review and also to make it useful to others. Whether or not this request from his sisters is a fiction, it is plausibly presented and also maintained. The sisters do raise doubts and questions in the course of their conversation, doubts and questions that Gerson encourages by calling them thoughtful and intelligent. For example, when the sisters list four objections, beginning with their surprised, "Frere, que dittes vous?" [Brother, what are you saying?], his answer begins, "Mes suers, fortes sont, je le confesse, ces quatre objections . . ." (165) [My sisters, I admit that these four objections are strong ones . . .].[12] If he was inventing these questions and putting them into his sisters' collective mouth, nonetheless, the sisters in reading this would have seen that he expected them to have such questions or doubts as befit readers who truly desire to understand: "Vostre desir d'aprendre se monstre assez" (187) [Your desire to learn is very evident]. Moreover, it is clear that he imagines his sisters in turn instructing others, for they occasionally raise a question that they say is not their own but one they have heard and not known how to answer; they want to prepare themselves to give a reply the next time. For example, they ask, "Mais vecy que nous leur oyons dire: que vauroit ce que je feroie de bien quant il ne proffiteroit riens a ma salvacion? Si vouldrions scavoir de vous que nous responderons" (167) [But this is what we hear them say: what use would it be to do good works if they were no help at all toward my salvation? So we would like to know from you what we should reply]. This conversation, then, imagines itself as inserted among other conversations, previous and to come, involving Gerson's sisters.[13]

True, the sisters are treated as a unit rather than as five distinct persons, but Gerson describes both the mutual affections within this family and his own sense of duty to share with them the fruits of their parents' investment in his education: "Et a la verité aussi puisque nos bons parens, pere et mere ont exposé jadis leurs biens et heritages communs pour moy, vostre premier frere, aprendre la sainte escripture, raison veult que ou proffit vous y participiés" (158) [And in truth since our good parents, father and mother, spent their wealth and the common inheritance for me, your firstborn brother, so that I might learn holy Scripture, reason demands that you participate in the profit]. They in turn will pass on what they have learned from him in their instructive conversations with other acquaintances; thus they will get their turn at teaching.[14]

Indeed, in the *Montaigne de contemplation* he confesses to being himself no expert in the heights of mystical unity with God, but "j'en parlerai comme un aveugle de couleurs en recitant ce que li saint en dient en leurs escrips" (29) [I will speak of it as a blind man does of colors, by reciting what holy men have said in their writings]. He is passing on what he has learned from his teachers, in a chain of learning and teaching that neither begins with himself nor ends with the sisters.

If he is their superior because of his position as older brother and because of his education and position in the church, he is also explicit in his feelings of affection and respect and in his sense of duty to share with them whatever of his learning may be useful to their lives. The importance of affection in this teaching relationship is especially stressed: "je congnois asses l'amour que vous avez a moy; or est vray que medecine ou dottrine de tant plus prouffite qu'elle vient de celluy qui est aymé" (1966, 7.159) [I know very well the love that you have for me; now it is true that medicine or teaching is much more effective when it comes from someone who is loved]. This remains an important feature of these dialogues, both to and by women, distinguishing them sharply from the cold nature of a conversation with Reason or Philosophy.

Yet just as Boethius was both himself and a sort of Everyman, so too Gerson's *Dialogue spirituel* and the *Montaigne de contemplation*, another work for his sisters to which the dialogue refers (183), at the same time identify this intimate female audience with a wider audience of readers.[15] At the beginning of the *Montaigne*, defending his use of French and his aim at an audience of "simples gens" for the lofty topic of an ascent toward God through the contemplative life, he comments on how many such treatises exist in Latin and how little there is to guide uneducated people who seek to live in a way pleasing to God, "des simples gens, et par especial de mes seurs germaines, ausquelles je veuil escripre de ceste vie et de cest etat" (16–17) [simple folk, and especially my sisters, for whom I wish to write about this life and this condition]. He remarks on his seasoned experience of their ability to understand; indeed, his writings to them include references to Aristotle, Vergil, Seneca, and Terence as well as to a number of church fathers, implying that his sisters at least have heard these names and have an interest in learning their ideas.[16] He distinguishes furthermore between the helpful wisdom of the humble and the harmful knowledge of the educated but arrogant, citing Christ's own appeal to be humble "en guise d'ung petit enfant ou d'une simple femmelette" (17) [in the guise of a small child or simple little woman]. This reevaluation of the contrast between learned men and simple little women or children will reappear in the writings of Marguerite de Navarre, who would have been able to find Gerson's "Livre de contemplation" in the royal library, along with other of his writings, including another, internal dialogue between a contemplative man and his own soul.[17] In reviewing a list of others who have written about the contemplative ascent, Gerson (46–47) mentions Augustine's account of his experience with his mother (1961, 9) and Jerome's advice to the virgin Eustocium; that is, he makes the reader aware of a whole tradition of writing on this topic that includes women as appropriate participants.[18] His dialogue exists formally between the oral conversation between Augustine and his mother and the written exchange of letters between Jerome and Eustochium: as the written record of an oral exchange meant to be read beyond its first oral situation.

Gerson's use of dialogue is clearly connected with his desire to reach out to a less educated audience.[19] His *Canticordum du pélerin* (1966, 112–39; 1706, 3: 868–88) explains at the beginning:

> Mais affin que nostre doctrine soit plus plaisant et plus comprenable par les simples cuers espirituelz, in simplicitate cordis, quia cum simpli-cibus sermocinatio eius [Ps. 143:9], nous introduirons nostre matiere en guise de dyalogue ou personnaige ou quel parleront deux cuers: l'un se dit cuer mondain, l'autre se nomme cuer seulet.

> *[But in order that our teaching be more pleasant and more understandable to simple spiritual hearts, in the simplicity of the heart, because his speech is with the simple (Ps. 143:9), we will introduce our material in the guise of a dialogue or scene where two hearts speak: one is called Worldly Heart, the other is named Lone Heart.]*

These hearts are more than abstractions, for "cuer mondain" has various types of business that interrupt his seven days of conversation with the con-templative "cuer seulet": attending to the harvest, his household, the mar-ket. The dialogue of these two characters, one of whom slowly succeeds in enlightening the other, is indeed more lively as a conversation than it would have been as an expository treatise, while the "days" with their breaks sug-gest chunks of material to be digested by the reader before continuing. Cuer Mondain can express all the astonishment and doubt that a normal person might well feel before someone who has withdrawn from the world for con-templation, and his gradual growth of understanding can become a model for the reader.[20] In short, the writer-reader relationship can be included within the text itself, transforming the written text into a conversation with us. If this dialogue is not specifically addressed to his sisters, it is addressed to the same "simples" and vernacular readers with which they are elsewhere identified.

This broad audience was precisely what made Gerson's work of interest to Italian spiritual writers seeking to extend to a general public some basic

instruction in Christian doctrine. He was praised for having written sim-
plified and brief accounts that were useful to the reader, either for guidance
in mystical contemplation or for consolation or for teaching a general religious self-discipline. During the sixteenth century his writings—including
some not yet translated—were recommended by Serafino da Fermo, Pietro
da Lucca, Girolamo Regino, and Giovanni Cassiano (Zarri 1987, 144–46).

Two more reform-minded examples of dialogues with and for women
come from the pens of a pair of close friends, both of whom were well connected with learned women among the Italian nobility: Juan de Valdés and
Bernardino Ochino.

Valdés, at the age of eighteen, at the end of his very first year in the university, had published a *Dialogo de doctrina* (published in 1529 but probably
composed in 1524–27), a catechetical work intended for basic religious
instruction of the general public, a need apparently felt widely across Europe
a century after Gerson's remarking on it.[21] This early *Dialogo,* much like
some of Gerson's writings in French, runs through the Creed and the Ten
Commandments, the summary of Christian doctrine in chapters 5–7 of
Matthew's Gospel, the seven sins and seven virtues and the seven gifts of the
Holy Spirit, and so on.[22] Thanks to the recently elected Inquisitor of
Navarre's enthusiasm for this text, it was distributed in the Navarre region
and read by female as well as male readers.[23] Later, as imperial secretary and
chamberlain to the pope, Valdés moved in the very centers of power, both
secular and holy, and his own life, like Gerson's, was a constant endeavor to
combine political duties with piety, the demands of both this world and the
next.

In 1535 he met Giulia Gonzaga, the niece of a cardinal; and his second
dialogue, the *Alfabeto cristiano,* was written for her in 1536.[24] Documents of
the later investigations against Valdés and some of his associates, including
letters in code exchanged by Giulia Gonzaga and Pietro Carnesecchi, indicate that Valdés was leading group discussions of religion that included Giulia and that the group felt themselves to be a small community within the
kingdom of God (Nieto 1970, 148–49).[25]

Enthusiastic throngs in Naples, including male and female members of
the nobility, were attending the sermons that Bernardino Ochino was
preaching for the season of Lent. Even Charles V came to hear him with
pleasure. Giulia Gonzaga, at the age of twenty-four already a widow of eight
years, had come to Naples to be part of the festivities for Charles and was in
the audience for Ochino's preaching. Valdés, who had himself only recently
come to Naples, was working closely with Ochino at the time and presents
his dialogue as the record of a real conversation with Giulia following one of

Ochino's sermons. Valdés was by then in his forties and famous in his own right. Giulia's situation, poised between the interests of a powerful family and her personal spiritual state, was readily understandable to Valdés, with the tensions in his own life between political and spiritual needs. Their friendship was ongoing, and Valdés dedicated other works to her as well: for example, commentaries on Paul's epistles to the Romans and Corinthians. Clearly she was a woman whose seriousness and intelligence he admired. In 1536, not more than a few months after she had received his dialogue for her, Giulia moved into a Franciscan convent where she lived until her death at the age of thirty. Obviously, she was already in a state of mind conducive to spiritual conversations.

Valdés begins his text, like Gerson, by claiming that he is writing it at Giulia's request, setting down the conversation they had engaged in so deeply that only nightfall brought it to an end. We have every reason to believe that the originary conversation was not his invention but actually took place. Addressing her, he states that if he has left out or added anything, she should respond to him with the corrections. Other readers—and he does expect them—are only reading over her shoulder, as it were; he says explicitly that he is not concerned with their possible criticisms because he has written only for her and in a manner that he hopes will satisfy her wish.

Sforzata dal comandamento di V.S. Illustrissima, fuor d'ogni mia opinione ho scritto in dialogo tutto quello ragionamento cristiano nel quale l'altro dì, tornando dalla predica, tanto ci inebbriammo che fu necessario che la notte il conchiudesse. E se ben mi ricordo, non manca cosa veruna di quante là si ragionò. . . . Leggalo V.S. quando avrà tempo; e se alcuna cosa mancherà, e se altra ne troverà soverchia, e se nuovamente le si offerirà che replicare intorno a ciò ch'è stato detto, avertamene, peroché, aggiungendo l'uno e togliendo l'altro, alla fine il dialogo resterà assai conforme alla sua volontà. (1938, 4)

[Compelled by the command of your illustrious ladyship, outside from any judgment of my own, I have written in dialogue all that Christian conversation in which we were so caught up the other day, returning from the sermon, that only nightfall could put an end to it. And if I remember correctly, not a thing is missing of all that we spoke then. . . . May your ladyship read it when you will have time; and if anything is missing, and if anything is found in excess, and if you happen to think of something new to reply to what was said, let me know, for with my adding the one and removing the other, in the end the dialogue will conform entirely to your will.]

He writes, in sum, not as her master but as her servant and makes these dialogue hers rather than his. The title "alphabet" denotes, as the writer explains, that his text is only an elementary introduction to Christianity, for the perfection of which one must turn to more divine texts. The title reflects his own humility about his text, presented as a kind of preface to the Scriptures, although it may also imply the notion that Giulia is like a child ready only for an elementary religious education.[26] Certainly she had not, like Valdés, been studying theology at the university. On the other hand, Valdés urges her to go ahead and read the Scriptures for herself, in vernacular translation.[27] The text is thus an introduction to the spiritual path for intelligent but Latinless lay readers in general.

It is Giulia who begins the conversation, seeking someone she can trust through friendship in order to communicate freely her feelings. These opening pages resemble a confession, but her early sentences say that she is trying to express things that she would be reluctant to say even to a confessor. Raffaele Girardi (1989, 194) observes that it is a confession outside the usual institutional space. The relation of friendship allows even more than the situation of the confessional. It shares with it the privacy, intimacy, and spiritual seriousness; but it goes beyond a merely formal relationship into a real friendship. Here perhaps the Ciceronian dialogue of friends and the experience of confessional dialogue merge. Yet Cicero's dialogues were never so intense as this. Giulia, politely but firmly, requests Valdés's full attention; if he has other business or his thoughts are elsewhere, he should say so and postpone this conversation. He positions himself as completely at her service.

The long opening confession into which she launches is remarkable for the view it offers into her anguished inner conflicts and into her need and ability to conceal all this from everyone else around her, to live for years an outer life carefully separated from her tumultuous feelings and thoughts. Later she refers to the troubles "li quali mi tengono tanto alienata da me" (81) [that keep me so alienated from myself]. The divided self seeks colloquy with a "third" person, as it were, someone outside who can help to heal or adjudicate this division. In other words, the woman seeks external dialogue because she is already engaged in an internal dialogue. This is not the assured representation of a position, but the anguished search for a hidden truth.

> . . . voglio che sappiate ch'io per l'ordinario vivo tanto scontenta di me medesima, e similmente di tutte le cose del mondo, e tanto svogliata, che, se vedeste il cuor mio, son certa che n'areste compassione, perciocché in lui non trovereste se non confusione, perplessità e inquietudine.

. . . non sento mai tanta bonaccia nell'animo mio che, volendo far
conto con lui, possa finire d'intendere, che è ciò che io vorrei, che cosa
gli soddisfarebbe o con quale si contenterebbe:

. . . Di questa maniera che io vi dico, sono già molti anni ch'io vivo,
nelli quali, come sapete, mi sono intervenute tante cose che basterebbono per alterare uno spirito acchetato, tanto più per inquietare e confondere uno animo svogliato e confuso come è il mio. (7–8)

[. . . I want you to know that I ordinarily live so unhappy with myself
and with everything else in the world, and so listless, that if you saw my
heart, I am sure you would have compassion, for you would find in it nothing but confusion, perplexity, and unquiet.

. . . I never feel such tranquility in my mind that, wishing to make
accounts with it, I can manage to understand what it is that I want, what
would give it satisfaction, or with what it would be content.

. . . In this manner that I tell you I have lived for many years now, during which, as you know, so many things have happened to me that would be
enough to alter even a calm spirit, all the more sufficient to give anxiety and
confusion to a mind as listless and confused as mine.]

The sermon by Ochino, which she hoped might help bring peace to her
spirit, has only aggravated its wounds.[28]

Questa è una grandissima e crudelissima contradizione, che sento
dentro di me tanto noiosa e fastidiosa che per mia salute molte volte mi
vengono le lagrime agli occhi, per non sapere che far di me, né a cui
m'appoggiare. Questa contradizione hanno generato nell'animo mio i
sermoni del predicatore, mediante li quali mi veggio fortemente combattuta, da una parte dal timore dello'nferno e dallo amore del paradiso, e dall'altra dal timore delle lingue delle genti e dallo amore dell'onor del mondo. . . . Che se voi sentiste quel che io sento, vi
meravigliereste come io lo possa passare e dissimulare. (8–9)

[This is a very great and cruel contradiction that I feel within me, so irksome and tedious that for my own sake I often have tears come to my eyes
because of not knowing what to do with myself, nor on whom to lean. This
contradiction the sermons of the preacher have generated in my mind, by
which I see myself torn by violent combat, on the one hand the fear of hell
and love of paradise, and on the other the fear of people's tongues and the
love for worldly honor. . . . For if you perceived what I feel, you would marvel at how I can feign and dissimulate.]

Honor was not a light matter for a woman of Giulia's status and family. It involved not merely personal reputation but a sense of obligation to the whole family. The willingness to set aside considerations of honor might thus be construed as a selfish act of disregard for the family's needs. Yet the expectations of society have come to seem to Giulia in contradiction with the teachings of its faith. Moreover, women were regularly instructed to dissemble their feelings and behave dutifully as expected; therefore the length of this opening speech suggests truly the pouring out of a heart's flood that has been dammed up for too long. It is this inner restlessness and yearning for resolution that Valdés has been summoned to address. Giulia suggests that a man would not be able to hide his own feelings so well and so long and that men perhaps cannot even imagine how much is going on behind the façade of their women's outer comportment.

And yet he must have suspected, or even known, that other people, women and men as well, shared these feelings, for even though Giulia might indeed have requested a written record of their conversation for her own review, Valdés, for all the opening allusions to the special liberty of a private conversation between friends, clearly expects other readers—possibly even expects Giulia to want to circulate this text among other people whom it might similarly help. Valdés's assertions to be writing only at her request and for her own satisfaction may, then, be his way of excusing himself for putting into a text such personal confessions. Indeed, for all the personal nature of the opening complaint, the "tante cose," which might well have been immediately called to mind for people acquainted with Giulia, are left unspecified, thus making the sense of restlessness and inner conflict more generally applicable. Someone like Vittoria Colonna, for example, who was certainly aware of Valdés and acquainted with the Gonzagas, might have found herself in some empathy with this female speaker, for her poetry sometimes expresses a similar restlessness. Apparently Giulia or her family did control the circulation of this text, for only the Italian translation that she had made for her survives and was later printed after her death; the original Spanish by Valdés disappeared and was therefore presumably not circulated separately by him.

Valdés responds not with a lecture but with an invitation to Giulia to respond to each thing that he says (10). She takes him up on the offer, asking questions, protesting that certain things do not make sense to her, observing contradictions between his words and Ochino's, and even teasing Valdés gently at one point: when he has commented on a kind of preaching that he avoids because he considers it a waste of time, she ribs him for his lack of willing exercise in patience (106). The type of teacher-student dialogue in which this dialogue participates is qualified, in sum, by the combination of Giulia's social superiority and Valdés's obvious respect for her intelligence. This pairing of mutual superiorities helps to create a feeling of equality between friends, even in what is clearly a situation of requested advising.

Valdés seeks from the start to make Giulia feel empowered to change her own life (12):

> il rimedio sta in mano vostra. . . . il disonor vostro e'l vostro onore depende da voi sola. . . . E in questo modo, non ponendo l'onore vostro in mano né in cortesia delle persone del mondo, non avrete occasione né di sperare da loro l'onore, né di temere da loro il disonore, e con questo conversarete e tratterete con loro con molta libertà e molto dominio interiore.

> [. . . *the remedy lies in your hands . . . your dishonor and your honor depend on you alone. . . . And in this world, not placing your honor in the hand or at the discretion of anyone in the world, you will not have occasion either to hope for honor from them or to fear dishonor from them, and with this you will converse and deal with them with much liberty and much internal mastery.*]

He appeals to her as a noble soul ("animo alto, generoso e valeroso") for whom it should be easier than for others ("animo basso, plebeo e servile") to rise above the lowly nature of worldly goods and to free the will from slavery to such desires (95).

At the same time, he recognizes the true difficulty of her public situation. She asks him to set her on the road to God: "Ma si intende che tegnate sempre rispetto a portarmi tanto segretamente che nulla persona mi senta, perché, se io lo posso iscusare [=evitare], non voglio dare di che parlare alle genti" (56) [But let it be understood that you always keep an eye on bringing me there so secretly that no one notices, for if I can avoid it, I do not want to give people cause to talk about me]. Valdés himself knew only too well the need for this kind of secrecy, especially given the suspect nature of some of his preachings. He promises, therefore, to show her "uno camino secreto per lo quale andiate a Dio senza essere veduta dal mondo" (97) [a secret path by which you may go to God without being seen by the world]. He also warns her strenuously, however, about the dangers of seeking God without being willing to give up the world (29–30) or renounce self-love (23–24, 119).

As in Gerson's writings to his sisters, the emphasis is not on reason but on love. Indeed, reason is equated by Valdés with the darkness rather than the light (19), and its efforts aggravate the conflict between human and divine

impulses in Giulia. On the other hand, these feelings of conflict are in themselves a good sign, indicative of the workings of God within the soul: "La
lezione già v'ho detto che per ora vorrei che fusse di cose semplicissime, che
v'infiammassero la volontà e non v'occupassero lo'ntelletto" (106) [As I
have already told you, I want to keep the lesson for now to very simple things
that may inflame your will and not trouble your intellect]. The phrase "per
ora" makes it clear, however, that he thinks her intellect is up to more
difficult things. In fact, shortly after, he recommends that she read *De imitatione Christi* (107), not Kempis's text but another that was circulating in an
Italian translation from a Latin original attributed to Gerson, sometimes
under the title *De meditatione cordis*.[29] Both Gerson and Valdés are attempting to offer not theological arguments but practical advice for living a devout
Christian life.

The dialogue ends with an invitation for it to continue. Try out tonight
already some of the steps I have outlined, urges Valdés, and tell me in the
morning what you think (126). It is thus a text that both responds to a previous conversation and elicits a further oral response, specifically from Giulia. It is not a text that asks women to be quiet and listen, but a text that
invites them to participate in describing their inner experiences and considering how to live the perfect Christian life. It invites real questioning, testing and assessing the words of the teacher. Valdés may be acting as the secretary commanded to put this conversation into writing, but it is a dialogue
of which Giulia is as much the author and originator as Valdés.

Bernardino Ochino's dialogues with Caterina Cibo or Cybo, Duchess of
Camerino, were probably composed—at least some of them—at about the
same time as or shortly after Valdés's, that is, around 1536. Ochino was a
widely popular preacher and advocate for religious reform. Valdés and
Ochino may even have shared their ideas with regard to writing these dialogues. Granddaughter of Lorenzo de' Medici and niece of Pope Leo X, Caterina had learned Latin, Greek, and Hebrew, in contrast to Giulia Gonzaga
and Gerson's sisters, who were apparently limited to vernacular literacy. Like
Giulia, she was widowed early, by the age of twenty-six. Caterina was a supporter and defender of the radical Franciscans or Capuchins, of which
Ochino became the vicar general. The two had known each other since
Ochino's preaching in Rome in 1534–35. It was in her house that Ochino
changed clothing when he fled from Italy after a summons from the Inquisition, and she remained in touch with him after his departure. As with Juan
de Valdés and Giulia Gonzaga, we are dealing with a real friendship. Besides
the close bond between Valdés and Ochino, there were other shared
acquaintances between Caterina Cibo and Giulia Gonzaga from the reform-
minded groups within Italy.[30]

Another famous female connection between these two preachers was Vittoria Colonna, who, in her letters, thanked Giulia Gonzaga for sending her a copy of Valdés's commentary on Paul (1892, 240) and exchanged correspondence with Ochino about the story of Jesus and the woman taken in adultery (241–46). Later Ochino wrote to her explaining his decision to leave Italy rather than face martyrdom (247–49). Even in England, he sought out powerful female connections. Anne Cook, the mother of Sir Francis Bacon, translated his sermons into English in 1548; and Queen Elizabeth, who had spoken with him in person, translated one of his sermons into Latin (Tedeschi 1987, 92–93). One can certainly apply here the insight of Katherine Gill (1994, esp. 84) concerning the way the presence of a female audience in the writer's mind must have affected both his thought and his expression.

Ochino continued throughout his life to turn to dialogue as a form amenable to spiritual counsel and instruction. A volume of thirty dialogues, including a number of arguments with a Jew, and others between Ochino and figures such as "Spiritus" (who speaks in the words of Scripture) or "Meschinus" (Wretched), was published in 1563. Ochino's earlier *Dialogi sette* contains seven closely interelated pieces, of which four explicitly include Caterina. Several of Ochino's dialogues were circulating in manuscript by 1539, and the one that is now last of the seven had already appeared in print in Geneva during that year. Curiously enough, it was initially a dialogue between a "predicatore" (preacher) and a "gentilhuomo" (gentleman). Yet as Ochino began to write a few dialogues between himself and Caterina, he changed the speaker of this one as well and redirected it to her.[31] The importance of the speaker's gender was obviously small in this case. But that in itself is worth noting: here is a man who does not see a need to speak differently to men and to women, but who has the same message and the same language for both. Perhaps this is especially true when the woman's education makes her the equal of any man. Yet it is also true because of the spiritual nature of the message, for women's and men's souls are equally to be saved or damned.

A set of the last four dialogues was published in Venice in 1540, and then all seven were printed in that same year, with two further editions in 1542.[32] In this case, unlike that of Giulia Gonzaga, the recipient was still alive and well when the book appeared in print. Within the same year Ochino left Italy for Geneva. To be publicly conversing with Ochino then was a dangerous matter. Ochino is clearly the author of both voices, nor does he claim, like Valdés, to be transcribing a real conversation; indeed, we know that at least one of the dialogues preexisted its use of Caterina as a speaker. Nonetheless, Ugo Rozzo observes: "certo egli deve aver attribuito alla sua

nobile interlocutrice opinioni e 'interessi' che ella doveva sicuramente con-
dividere: del resto l'Inquisizione non mancherà di considerarla una vera e
propria eretica" (Ochino 1985, 24) [certainly he must have attributed to his
noble interlocutrice opinions and concerns that she must surely have shared:
furthermore, the Inquisition did not hesitate to consider her a true and
proper heretic].[33]

The topics of the first two dialogues, between "Duchessa" and "P. F.
Bernardino," are very close to those of Valdés's dialogue with Gonzaga: how
to turn oneself from a love of self and the world to the love of God, and how
to find peace within oneself. Like Gerson's and Valdés's dialogues, Ochino's
first one opens with the female speaker asking for counsel, although she does
not make an admission of inner disquiet, much less provide the very personal
inner description that Giulia gives. Like Valdés, Ochino emphasizes the act
of will by which one can freely choose to love what one knows is the ultimate good. Both men emphasize this notion of "libertà." To the duchess's
protest that loving is not in our power, he replies that although sensual love
may not be, spiritual love is "tutto volontario" [completely voluntary]. When
the duchess asks him how to accomplish this, he turns the questions back to
her, asking for her ideas and then confirming her right answers and correcting her errors.

One of her mistakes is placing too much importance on knowledge. We
recall that it was to this duchess that Firenzuola dedicated his defense of
women's learning.[34] Like Gerson and Valdés, Ochino rejects this intellectual approach, by which only the learned would be able to love God: "io
tengo che una semplice vecchiarella può tanto amare Dio, quanto il primo
dotto del mondo" (1985, 50) [I hold that a simple old woman can love God
as much as the most learned man in the world]. The image of the *vechiarella*
is significant and occurs as well in Gerson. Not only does Gerson contrast
the arrogance of the learned with the simplicity and humility of a "femmelette," as we have seen, but he also declares, in the dialogue with his sisters, that his *Mendicité spirituelle* was inspired by what he had heard about the
behavior of a devout and simple old woman (1966, 172). He emphasizes the
difference between cold-hearted *scientia* and a *sapientia* full of affection and
desire.[35] The attempt to take religion away from the scholastic disputes of an
educated elite and to popularize it, or make it widely accessible, involved a
more affective approach. It is not surprising, therefore, to see the close links
between Ochino's Franciscan order and the desire for a reform of the whole
church. The knowledge that is needed, says Ochino, is "notitia pratica"
[practical knowledge] rather than "vane, inutile e curiose dottrine" (51)
[empty, useless, and curious learning]. Here the image of a woman as uneducated but possessing a certain practical wisdom becomes valorized in opposi-

tion to the pride and vain disputation of the university-educated male. Surely this revalorization, along with the whole turn toward a more simple, democratic, and affective faith, encouraged the inclusion of women in discussions of religion.

Caterina's relation to this image is odd, however, for she was immensely well educated; she can refer to having read classical philosophers as well as citing Scripture. She seeks philosophical support for her own comments, introducing one, for example, by saying, "Si legge pure di molti philosophi" (48) [Yet one reads in many philosophers]. It is she who argues for the need to know and understand before one can love, while Ochino persuades her otherwise. He urges her to read not "poeti, historiographi, philosophi et fatti del mondo" [poets, historiographers, philosophers, and doings of the world] but rather Scripture and the lives of saints inflamed with love for God (53). Humanism, of which Caterina bore the fruit, is as much under attack here as scholasticism. Caterina is not, like Gerson's sisters, an example of the simple, uneducated folk. Rather she is closer to being identified with the proudly learned clergy. As for them so for her, her own learning is a potential danger to her.

Yet Ochino is not so distant from the philosophers himself. His method throughout the dialogue is one of Socratic questioning, the questioning of a teacher who is trying to draw out the truth from his student's own mouth. This method goes hand in hand with an obvious neoplatonism pervading the dialogues. To arrive at the love of God, he suggests, think of the beauty of flowers and fruits, of jewels and gold, and then raise your thoughts to the sun and stars, and then to the beauty of virtuous souls, and from there to the angels and the mother of God, then to the human Christ with a face full of love, and then think that all of this is nothing compared to divine beauty: "Bisogna farsi delle creature scala" (51–52) [One must make of created things a ladder].[36] He refers to the good that is in creatures as "ombratica, non vera, ma dalla divina pendente e participata" (43) [shadowy, not real, but dependent from and participating in the divine]. He uses Augustine's Platonic image of gathering into God the spirit that has been scattered into the world's multiplicity (54). And he openly mentions Plato and Socrates several times, always positively (64, 68, 106). Thus he has turned toward a Christian use of Socratic questioning as an approach to metaphysical truth.

The duchess's final phrases in the first dialogue offer an amusing resistance to the lesson: "Vorrei sommamente amarlo [Dio], se ben non l'amo quanto io dovrei" (58) [I would very much like to love God, even if I do not love him as I ought]. Ochino replies comfortingly, "Assai l'ama colui che in verità vuole amarlo" (58) [He who truly wants to love God loves him enough]. To which she responds, "Non basta che io vorrei volerlo amare?" (58) [Is it not enough that I want to want to love him?]. This kind of resistance or reluctance is a common feature of the spiritual dialogue, which one can see in Petrarch's *Secretum* and in the eclogue with his brother, as well as in later Renaissance dialogues. We will see it again further on.

The first dialogue ends, like Valdés's, with an exhortation to the lady to try out what has been said: "Vogli vostra signoria essercitarsi in tali essercitii" (58) [May your ladyship please to try out such exercises]. These texts are intended to be used beyond their mere reading as a guide for religious practice. Presumably, although Ochino does not end like Valdés with a request for her comments after trying out such practices, the exercise will lead to further discussion. Both 1540 editions (the four and the seven dialogues) were small and slim, easy to carry around. This is a text that seeks not only to persuade the text's historical reader through the woman in the dialogue but also to shape the actions of her daily life.

The second dialogue is unusual in containing a brief dramatic introduction: Ochino sees the duchess, whose name is now spelled out unequivocably as la Duchessa di Camerino, and comments that she seems afflicted and weary and in search of something. Like Giulia, the duchess is searching for peace. All my life, she says, "sono stata in continuo moto per haver quiete" (61) [I have been in continual motion seeking for peace]. But unlike Giulia's dialogue, this one has from the start clearly allegorical overtones. Ochino's opening question is, "Che la va cercando *in questo mondo?*" (61, my emphasis) [What are you looking for *in this world?*]. And when he asks where she has been searching for peace, she replies with a list of worldly goods.[37] Thus, where she is most precisely named, she is least personally present.

Thanks to a similar abstractness, the third dialogue, although it is between a teacher and student, could just as well be between the same speakers as before; we do not notice any change of character. Even the initial "D" for "Discepolo" could be "D" for "Duchessa." This dialogue turns into an allegory about self-government and opens up a dialogue within a dialogue between Intellect and Will. Given the genders of these words in Italian, Intelletto is the male servant and counselor to Volontà the queen. Therefore, even though this may not have been written originally with the duchess in mind, their relationship reemerges in the inner dialogue as well as in the frame.

The same mutual superiority that we noted between Giulia Gonzaga and Juan de Valdés is set forth between Volontà and Intelletto: he is the God-given advisor in accord with whose judgment she ought to rule; but he is also her subject and servant, obliged to consider whatever she bids him consider (68–69). As in the first dialogue, here too the desire of Intellect is to move

Will toward the love of God. But Intellect is unable to determine the right way to live; it is Will who declares that the love of God is the correct and only path: "e questa è grata a la divina volontà, la quale è imperatrice, regina, e madre di tutte le volontà create" (72–73) [and this is pleasing to the divine will, which is empress, queen, and mother of all created wills]. We have a female image of the divine will as an empress, queen, and mother. But this image is followed almost immediately by human Will's conclusion that she has decided to submit herself in rightful obedience to Intellect: "non voglio più andare innanzi a l'intelletto, ma seguirlo et haverlo per guida" (73) [I wish no longer to go ahead of Intellect but to follow him and have him as a guide]. The balance between intellect and will is represented as a balance between male and female powers. As between the duchess and her clergy-man, the woman has real power but has chosen to seek the guidance of her counselor. And just as Caterina's words are written by Ochino, so the words of Volontà within the inner dialogue are spoken by the male teacher as part of his lesson to his pupil. Ochino remains more solidly in control of his text—and of its circulation—than Valdés.

The fourth dialogue, between an unnamed "Huomo" and "Donna," still makes use of the same relationship, for the man calls the woman "vostra eccellenza" [Your Excellency]. Both the third and fourth dialogues are chiefly monologues set off by a few questions from the lady. The fifth and sixth dialogues do not apparently involve the duchess at all, being conversations between the soul and either Christ or an angel.[38] The soul, however, sounds considerably like Giulia in its wish to find a way to God that will not disrupt its worldly honor or cause people to talk: "S'io adesso mi parto, ogn'uno dirà la sua. Et io non vorrei dar che dire al mondo" [If I leave now, everyone will have something to say about it. And I do not wish to give the world cause to chatter]. The female gender of "anima" makes this concern for reputation seem particularly female, although it need not be. Christ replies, much like Valdés to Giulia, "Io t'intendo: tu vorresti tenir il pie' in due staffe, mi vorresti servire senza essere nemica a questo mondo, cosa che non è possibile" (92) [I understand you: you want to keep your foot in two stirrups, and to serve me without becoming an enemy to this world, a thing that is impossible].[39]

If the specific identification of Caterina has dropped out from the fifth and sixth dialogues, she reappears to frame the volume at its end as at its beginning. The speakers of the seventh and last dialogue, although initially listed simply as "Huomo" and "Donna," are clearly identified further on when the woman, making her formal testament, refers to herself as "io, C.D. di C." (111). The text of the testament includes a credo and a spiritualized version of the Franciscan vows (poverty, i.e., living without love for created things;

obedience, i.e., obeying divine inspiration; and chastity, i.e., thinking purely of God without any love for the things of this world). Allegory again overlaps with a more literal reading, as the woman promises "tirare al suo [God's] servitio, quanto mi sarà possibile, tutte le damigelle della casa mia, cioè tutte le potentie dell'anima" (117) [to draw to God's service, insofar as I can, all the young ladies of my household, that is, all the powers of the soul]. Several of the dialogues converge on this identification of the lady of the house with the soul.

The double identity makes the text address both women and men or implies perhaps that men who need to be guided, who are "weak" or concerned about their worldly honor, are somehow feminized. The appeal is ultimately to the indistinguishability of the human genders, as all who wish to be saved must recognize their complete nothingness and dependence on God (112): "la mia instabilità, la mia infirmità, debilità et nichilità" [my instability, my infirmity, weakness, and nothingness] is that of all "creatures." The ideal is to become completely "annichilata et in Dio tutta transformarmi" [annihilated and transformed into God] so that God can do through us what we cannot possibly do for ourselves. The woman speaker is half real and half allegorical, as the specified duchess and as the image of weak and dependent humanity. While the dialogues lean in places toward a more particular identity, mostly they lean toward universality, and it is not obvious why the duchess's identity should appear at all.

The final testament is peculiarly double voiced, for it is the "testament" that Caterina should speak but that is dictated to her by Ochino: "Vostra signoria . . . dira con tutto il cuore queste over simile parole" (110) [Your ladyship . . . will say with all your heart these or similar words]. Yet the final sentence ends: "et in fede di ciò, io, D.d.C., ho scritto la presente di mia propria mano. 1539" (118) [and in pledge of this, I, D. of C., have written the present declaration with my own hand. 1539]. This is pure fiction; it does, however, shift the final teachings of this text for its readers to a woman's hand. It might have been meant, like Boccaccio's famous women, to shame men into living up to standards that a woman could accomplish; but it would certainly have encouraged a female reader to feel that she was being earnestly addressed on a par with any man in being urged to read and discuss matters of faith and even to write and sign a testament of her belief. Given Ochino's control of the text all along, it is startling to find the final "signature" of the duchess at the very end of the book. As the duchess comments near the start of this final dialogue, "Sai bene ch'io ho posto l'anima mia nelle tue mani" (109) [You know well that I have placed my soul in your hands]. If at first she was a reluctant student, the final dialogue has become a unison in which his words and hers, his thoughts and hers, are indistinguishable.

Even among the few instructive dialogues that we have looked at in which women appear, we can see a range of differences in their positions. On one hand, the historical reality of these women can coincide smoothly with their rather abstract treatment as a collective: the undistinguished "sisters" of Gerson or the "Donna" of Ochino. Even though these women are specifically identified, that identity has very little effect on their role in the dialogue, which becomes generalizable to "simple" uneducated persons or educated but worldly persons in need of religious instruction. On the other hand, a figure like Giulia can take a much more personal and active role in the dialogue, making her particular history relevant to her quest and even getting in an occasional critical or instructive comment to the male. It is worth noting that this difference corresponds to a difference in who controls the circulation of the text: in Giulia's case, herself (or her family) rather than Valdés. Yet it is also worth noting that regardless of how the women are positioned in terms of historical specificity and active participation, all three writers treat these women with affectionate respect and a concern for their spiritual development and understanding, not simply for their rote learning of doctrine. This was the attitude most likely to encourage women's entry into dialogue on their own.

An example of the close connection between correspondence with a spiritual advisor and dialogue by a woman comes with one of the earliest writings of Marguerite de Navarre, sister of the French king Francis I and, at that time, Duchess of Alençon: the dialogic poem on the death of her niece, the king's daughter, written probably in 1524 and published later (1533) as *Dialogue en forme de vision nocturne*.[40] Christine Martineau and Christian Grouselle (1970, 573) have observed that an important source for the contents of this dialogue is Marguerite's own correspondence with Briçonnet, bishop of Meaux, a correspondence that had been going on for four years. Marguerite drew especially from two of his letters written in 1524 concerning the closely occurring deaths of Queen Claude, wife of Marguerite's brother, and their daughter Charlotte, particularly from the latter. The poem takes up, along with particular phrases and images, "the principal themes and developments of the prelate's letter": death as a liberation from prison, the lost potential of a future marriage on earth replaced by a divine marriage to God, the offense to Charlotte of grieving at her current felicity, the blessing of a short life that frees one from later temptations to sin, and other such ideas. While these may be more or less traditional images, Marguerite clearly indicates in subsequent correspondence that she was reading and rereading Briçonnet's letters of comfort, calling them "mon repos et nourriture."[41] Thus his letters are an immediate source for Marguerite's own reflections.

Indeed, they remained an inspiring influence on her writing throughout her life (Heller 1971, esp. 279).

Some of the topics most immediately recognizable from Briçonnet's letter on Charlotte were already written by him in a manner suggestive of dialogue (Briçonnet and d'Angoulême 1979, 264):

> Vous direz, "L'on eust faict ung beau mariage!" L'ombratil n'est à conferer au veritable. "Elle eust esté cause d'une bonne paix!" La sienne va devant la nostre. . . . Vous direz, "Le sang ne peult mentir, qui stimule le coeur." Qui l'a terrestre, plaingt ce qu'il ayme, terre estre en terre; qui l'a celeste, se consolle au bien de son sang digniffié de si excellent mariage. . . .

> [You will say, "She could have made such a fine marriage!" The shadowy is not to be preferred to the real. "She would have been the means of a good peace treaty!" Her peace comes before ours. . . . You will say, "Blood cannot lie, which stirs the heart." He who has earthly blood, laments what he loves, earth returned to earth; he who has celestial blood is consoled by the benefit to his blood dignified by so excellent a marriage. . . .]

It seemed natural to shift this dialogue, envisioned by Briçonnet as his own dialogue with Marguerite, into the dialogue of Marguerite's poem. Most of the borrowings from the letter about Charlotte, observe Martineau and Grouselle, occur in the first 350 lines of Marguerite's dialogic poem, where the focus is on grief and consolation; the latter part of the poem, with its shift to discussion of specific questions of doctrine, tends to draw instead from Briçonnet's previous letters but also goes off on its own trajectory.

For her dialogue Marguerite has changed the figure of spiritual counselor from the real male ecclesiastic comforter to her young niece, who speaks with the authority of a soul in paradise. Most of the bishop's remarks find their way into the mouth of Charlotte. The unusual result is a discussion about theology between two females, with the young girl as teacher of the older woman.[42] However, Charlotte is no longer of interest as an individual. Once Marguerite is assured of her niece's happiness in heaven, she turns her attention completely away from the girl to the theological issues of their discussion (Sommers 1995, 171).

Marguerite's epistolary relationship with Briçonnet, like the dialogic relationships of Valdés and Gonzaga, or Ochino and the Duchess of Camerino, balances the teacher-student hierarchy with an opposite social hierarchy. Marguerite at the start of this correspondence both asks for and commands counseling from her servant-advisor: "[je] vous emploie en mes affaires et vous demande le secours spirituel" (Briçonnet and d'Angoulême 1975, 25). Not only does she begin the correspondence, but she takes the initiative again when their exchange has temporarily lapsed, referring to her need for his letters and, when he is too busy, at least for his prayers: "necessité me faict vous demander adresse en ce desvoiement" (1979, 94). Briçonnet responds to her initial request by saying that he is ready to obey her wishes, although true aid can only come from God. Briçonnet is indeed, as he frequently signs, Marguerite's "très-humble et très-obeissant serviteur" [very humble and obedient servant]. Yet as her spiritual counselor, he dominates the correspondence with long, elaborately styled letters in reply to her short requests; her one sentence on feeling like a lost sheep, for example, is turned into an eight-page explication of four types of lost sheep (1975, 37, 41–48). When Marguerite signs herself "vostre fille" [your daughter], Briçonnet both scolds her gently—she is God's daughter, not his—and also responds in kind, calling himself her "fils" [son] and invoking her aid and "charité maternelle" [maternal charity] (1975, 31–32, 48). This mother-son image becomes a recurrent signature between them. Marguerite refers to herself variously as his old, poor, weak, fruitless, and ignorant mother, in need of the aid of her strong and laboring son (e.g., 1979, 49, 51, 60, 67, etc.). He in turn repeats his expressions of gratitude for her maternal charity and asks for her prayers just as she has asked for his, calling himself repeatedly "vostre inutile filz, G., indigne ministre" [your useless son, G., unworthy servant] (e.g., 1979, 106). Marguerite is the mother who is both needy and able to demand her son's attention; he is a loving son who is happy to oblige.

The two speakers mutually profess their unworthiness, yet Marguerite proposes an exchange of aid: at the royal court and at the court of heaven (1975, 33), an exchange dear to the bishop in need of her support for his programs of reform. Christine Martineau and Michel Veissière (1979, 8) point out that the years 1523 and 1524 saw a shifting set of relationships among the king, the papacy, and the bishop of Meaux. They describe 1523 as a low point in relations between the French court and the pope and a high point in the king's support of evangelical reformers, such that the pope was quoted as saying that Francis I was favoring the Lutheran heretics and trying to reorganize ecclesiastical affairs within France. By the following year, threatened by advances of the imperial army and by the defection of Bourbon to the emperor's side, Francis sought reconciliation with the papacy and began to make a show of cracking down on heretics in France. Briçonnet, opting carefully for moderate reform, distanced himself from the more radical members of his circle and forbade the circulation of Luther's writings. There is, then, an open acknowledgment of mutual need between Marguerite and Briçon-net. The authority of the duchess and the authority of the ecclesiast form counterweights that keep the relationship in a sort of balance.

Marguerite apparently needed Briçonnet not only as an advisor but also as an audience for her own self-expression, something for which she felt the need to apologize and explain:

> Helas, que veulx je dire ou yrai ge, contre le dict de sainct Pol, parler en l'eglise et devant vous? Ouy, car ma presumption n'a pas sy folle arrogance que de penser enseigner aultruy, mais le desir d'apprendre me faict demander, et le plaisir d'estre reprise et endoctrinée par la grace que Dieu vous donne me oste la craincte de faillir pour ne laisser sans exercice vostre filiale suportacion. (1979, 43)

> [Alas, what am I trying to say, or where am I going, speaking—against the statement of Saint Paul—in church and before you? Yes, for my presumption has not so much foolish arrogance to think that it can teach someone else, but the desire to learn makes me ask, and the pleasure of being corrected and taught by the grace that God gives you takes from me the fear of being at fault lest I leave unexercised your filial support.]

Especially the death of Charlotte seems to have triggered Marguerite's need to find some outlet or expression for her turbulent thoughts and feelings. She describes herself to Briçonnet as "celle qui n'eust esté à son aise sans vous avoir escript ce qu'elle en pense" (1979, 272) [she who would not have felt at ease without having written to you what she thinks]. In another letter, one of the last that we have, she mentions with pleasure the leisure that illness has given her to write and promises to show him soon something that she has been writing: it is the dialogue with Charlotte.

The end of this letter, unclear as its syntax is, deserves quoting at some length for the insights it offers into her project's connection with their correspondence.

> Vostre lectre m'a causé desir de vous prier de me vouloir ayder en lieu de la [Charlotte] resveiller de chanter si doulces louenges à Celluy qui l'a prevenue en grace que son doux repos ne soit empesché.
> Et si Dieu veult que quelque chose commencée soit finée, bien que mal et mauvais langaige, vous auriez le pouvoir de correction, où vous voirrez le debat que me faictes avant l'avoir veu estre, non si bien mais suivant vostre propos, comme si en pareil temps l'Esperit avoit aux deux parlé, vous priant en la charité qui vous est distribuée me faire ce

bien que de ne vous ennuyer de secourir la fille d'Adam absalonique et
telle que Dieu la congnoist qui, par l'abisme de sa sapience, voit ce que
mon abisme [d']ignorance ne congnoist, que toutesfois pour plus
esmouvoir à pitié, vostre esmue charité, voyant sa necessité, ne laissera
pour son inutillité se nommer vostre, bien que rien trop, mere, Marguerite (292).

> [*Your letter has caused me to desire to ask you to be willing to help me,
> not to reawaken Charlotte, but to sing such sweet praises of Him whose
> grace came before her, that her sweet sleep may not be disturbed.*
>
> *And if God wishes that something begun be finished, even though badly
> done and in poor language, you will have the power of correction where you
> will see the discussion that you sent me, before I had seen it, following your
> discourse though not so well, as if simultaneously the Spirit had spoken to
> two, begging you by the charity that has been given to you to do me the good
> of not refusing to help the absalonic daughter of Adam who is as God knows
> her, He who in the abyss of his wisdom sees what my abyss of ignorance does
> not recognize, anyway the better to move your already moved charity to pity,
> seeing the need of her who does not, despite her uselessness, cease to name
> herself your—although none too much—mother, Marguerite.*]

The tortured syntax, quite unusual for Marguerite's writing, conveys her
conflicted messages. She has been inspired by Briçonnet's letter of consolation no longer to wish Charlotte alive but rather to praise the Lord, who has
taken her in her innocence to be his love in heaven. The dialogue poem is
then, in part, meant to be a song of praise to God for his prevenient grace
and, in part, to be sent to Briçonnet in thanks for his comforting. Yet the
poem is not only the result of Briçonnet's discourse, which it follows
unevenly; it is also something that she was thinking of herself before seeing
his letter; indeed, she feels as if she has been inspired directly by the Holy
Spirit ("as if simultaneously the Spirit had spoken to two"). There is a vague
elation expressed here, although immediately hedged by expressions of her
own weaknesses as a writer. Moreover, the two texts, being partly independent of each other, do not entirely agree. "Le debat que me faictes" might
refer not only to the discussion within Briçonnet's letter but also to a discussion of differences between the two of them. Marguerite recognizes that her
deviance may be a result of her own ignorance and sinfulness (the reference
to Absalom draws from Briçonnet's letter contrasting the joy at an innocent
child's death with the grief at the death of a rebellious child like Absalom
who has been cut off from God). But it is also possible that God supports her
writing and will wish to see her work complete—as she did indeed complete

it. Because she anticipates some unhappiness when Briçonnet sees what she has written, Marguerite seeks in advance his correction, his charity, his pity; despite the elation with which she began to mention her poem, she is clearly apprehensive of Briçonnet's response. She presents herself as Adam and Absalom, offspring who are rebellious against their loving fathers. This suggests that she is concerned not only about her language skills but also about the contents of her dialogue, which may be in rebellion against her spiritual father Briçonnet.

Perhaps it was part of the strategy of winning his charitable reading that induced her to place near the front of the poem some of the strongest echoes of his recent letter, only then to launch into the poem's long and recurring theme that God alone is the source of aid to whom we should turn without seeking the mediation of saints or the Virgin Mary. Briçonnet had just the year before begun to defend his program of moderate reform by separating it clearly from the taint of more radical reformers. Besides banning the circulation of Luther's writings, he had condemned as heretical the teaching that purgatory does not exist and that prayers to the saints or the Virgin on behalf of the dead are therefore of no value (1979, 9). In 1526 Briçonnet preached at court "in a conservative manner and from then on appears to have washed his hands of the evangelicals" (Heller 1971, 282). Gérard Roussel, however, who had been a member of the evangelical group at Meaux, became Marguerite's confessor from 1528 until the end of her life. Marguerite took clear sides in the split of the Meaux circle.[43]

While Marguerite does not address the issue of purgatory or prayers for the dead, Charlotte argues repeatedly and at length that prayers should be addressed only to God, that prayers to the saints are not helpful because the saints will only want what he wants and have only the power that he gives them. Furthermore, God is angered if we do not sufficiently trust in his love to turn directly to him (Marguerite de Navarre 1926, vv. 343–465, 727–35, 805–43). In the midst of her grief and her sincere gratitude to Briçonnet for his consolations, Marguerite has used the opportunity of a sickbed leisure to articulate her beliefs in divergence from those of her bishop and to anticipate sending him this declaration.

It is perhaps no wonder, then, that Briçonnet does not appear as a speaker in this dialogue but has been replaced by the spirit of young Charlotte. The mutually superior, mutually dependent nature of their relationship, which we have seen before in the friendships between men of religion and women of nobility, is partially preserved in the *Vision nocturne* despite the change of speaker; for Charlotte, who was socially the child and dependent, has become, through death, the vehicle of divine truth. Briçonnet too had been described by both himself and Marguerite as a conduit for the action of God.

She is "endoctrinée par la grace que Dieu vous donne" (1979, 43) [taught by the grace that God gives you]; she has read "voz parolles (non vostres, mais lumiere de lumiere)" (1979, 108) [your words, not yours but the light of light]; she is grateful "au Tout-Bon par la grace qu'il luy plaist me donner de voz lettres" [to the All-Good for the grace that he has pleased to give me of your letters], for "Celluy qui les a faict escrire" (1979, 291) [He who has caused them to be written] has made them effective. Briçonnet himself is ever ready to assert that true understanding and faith can come only from God, not from his human efforts, which he repeatedly calls "inutille" [useless]. If the true teacher is always God, then it does not much matter who the human speaker may be.

Yet the use of Charlotte is not simply a matter of putting consolations into the mouth of the dead person herself. The literary mutation of Briçonnet into Charlotte goes along with the similar casting of speakers in Marguerite's early comedies, *Le malade* and *L'inquisiteur*, in which the evangelical voice is that of a young female servant—socially the lowest of the play's characters for all three reasons (age, gender, and class)—or a group of children, set in opposition, in both plays, to the arrogance of doctors or theologians with university degrees.[44] Despite her own learning, Marguerite, like Gerson, explicitly devalues learning on behalf of a more widely accessible piety. Thus Charlotte, asked about the debates on free will, tells her aunt to leave such debates "Aux grands docteurs qui l'ayantz ne l'ont pas; / Tant ont leurs cueurs d'inventions pressez, / Que Verité n'y poeut trouver sa place, . . . Laissez parler ceulx qui si cuydent saiges" (Marguerite de Navarre 1926, vv. 961–65, 971) [to the great doctors who, having it, have it not; Their hearts are pressed so full of cleverness that Truth can find no place there . . . Let those speak who think themselves wise]. Charlotte, the servant, the child, are the figures of humility opposed to intellectual pride; they are the babes through whose mouths truth issues. Even though in life Marguerite had turned to a bishop for spiritual aid, her writings seek to reinforce her emphasis on human inability and dependence on grace by denying even to the authoritative speaker of this dialogue any human authority of his or her own. In that way, of course, she shows herself a good pupil of the bishop's, for from the start he had emphasized that not he but God alone can offer any real aid. To express this lesson most fully, however, Marguerite needs to show a speaker who clearly speaks not from any personal learning or ecclesiastical rank, but purely as the recipient of grace. Out of the mouths of babes.

If some of the contents of the dialogue come from her spiritual correspondence with Briçonnet, other aspects of it, including ideas about its form, have completely different sources. Marguerite, like Caterina Cibo, was very well educated and widely read. Indeed, her sense of dialogue generally is

much broader in its varieties than almost any other writer's, for nearly everything she wrote involves dialogue in one way or another. The instructional
dialogue is certainly a model here, overlapping with the model of Marguerite's correspondence with Briçonnet. Whichever examples Marguerite
might have read—whether or not she knew, for example, the writings of
Gerson for his sisters—it is a form that welcomes the female participant in a
pupil role, such as Marguerite gives herself.[45] The oddity within this context
is that the teacher is also now female. But in a different context, which Marguerite consciously grafted here, that feature becomes less odd.

For the conversation with a dead girl now in paradise has specific sources.
One of these was undoubtedly Dante's *Commedia,* from which Marguerite's
Vision nocturne borrows a number of phrases—for example, Charlotte's
description of herself as sitting in heaven "dessus le dextre banc" (v. 93) or
her description of hell as "lieu où est ung immortel gémir" (v. 177)—as well
as the immediately obvious terza rima form.[46] We may notice further that
from Francesca's speech, Marguerite took the idea of beginning a series of
terzine with the word "Amour" (vv. 274–88); however, the erotic love of
Inferno 5 has become divine love, and the final terzina opens with the declaration that love is God. The passionate Francesca is thus "corrected." Moreover, even the erotic relation of Dante to the dead Beatrice is mocked by
Marguerite in a separate rondeau:

> A quarante ans vouloir encores faindre
> D'avoir le mal que l'âge doit refraindre
> Puis par despit courre à devocion
> Prenant tan pour ferme ficsion,
> C'este une fin plus qu'a ensuivre à craindre. . . .

(Pellegrini 1920, 8)

> [*At forty to be wishing still to feign*
> *to have that ill which age ought to restrain*
> *and then chagrined to run toward devotion,*
> *even if we take it as a fiction,*
> *this is an end to fear more than to follow. . . .]*

Thus Dante's eroticism comes in for a reprimand as well as Francesca's. However Charlotte might be idealized by her situation in paradise, she is not the
object of erotic fantasies but the darling of her aunt.

Another poem known to Marguerite and taking many of its features from
Dante—the terza rima form and the conversation with a dead beloved
lady—is Petrarch's *Trionfo della morte,* from which Marguerite also borrowed

phrases. Her question fairly early in the dialogue (vv. 205–37) concerning whether death is painful, and the reply, both echo the similar question and answer in Petrarch's poem—not only the standard image that death is a liberation from prison but especially the phrase "Le départir n'est riens qu'ung bref souspir" (v. 216): "che altro ch'un sospir breve è la morte?" (v. 51).[47] So too Laura's comment, "Et ora il morir mio, che sì t'annoia, / ti farebbe allegrar, se tu sentissi / la millesima parte di mia gioia" (vv. 37–39), returns in Charlotte's phrases: "Si poyvez de ma joye et soulas / Sentir la cent et millièsme partie, / En louenge tourneriez vostre hélas" (vv. 232–34). Places where Marguerite has closely translated one or two terzine indicate that she may even have had Petrarch's text at hand while she was writing.[48] But most of the rest of Petrarch's interview with Laura turns on the issue of whether she loved him and why she behaved toward him in life as she did. This amorous relationship, which is the prime focus for Petrarch, is, of course, utterly absent from Marguerite's poem.

One other aspect of the *Trionfi* more broadly does show up in the series of conquests outlined by Charlotte (vv. 265–76): reason must dominate the senses, but faith must overcome and mortify the pride of reason, and ultimately divine love overwhelms and humbles even faith. The elements in this sequence are not those of the Petrarchan triumphs, but the general idea and direction of this rising series of victories are similar. Petrarch's triumphs are those of Love, Chastity, Death, Fame, Time, and Eternity. Love ranks much higher in Marguerite's series, being a different kind of love. Where Petrarch sees one abstraction as more powerful than another in its universal manifestations, Marguerite shows the progress of a particular soul toward God.

I cannot help wondering whether Marguerite was not acquainted as well with Boccaccio's fourteenth eclogue, "Olympia," from his *Buccolicum carmen*, which is in many ways even closer to Marguerite's poem. Although not in vernacular terza rima but in Latin hexameters, it presents the nighttime appearance of a young girl, dead in childhood, who comes to comfort her grieving parent with a lesson in Christian faith and a description of paradise. Boccaccio's poem provides a familial instead of an amatory relationship like that of Dante and Beatrice or Petrarch and Laura. His daughter, like Charlotte, has died in childhood, not as a young lady. Charlotte was not quite eight when she died: "Avez esté d'ung petit corps delivre, / Lequel huyt ans acomplyz n'a sceu vivre" (vv. 4–5); Boccaccio's daughter was five and a half. The shift from a personal consolation into a more universal lesson on how to be a good Christian defines the basic structure of both works. Thus the "student" in this dialogue is partly to be identified historically with the specifically grieving author and partly to be read more broadly as any human being in the figurative dark, in need of comfort and instruction. Moreover, the young preacher repeatedly corrects the errors of her older relative, who remains even at the end only partially enlightened and still plunged in grief, calling out against the departure of the beloved spirit and returning to his or her tears. In both poems, the child must teach or recall to her older relative the most basic tenets of faith: the immortality of the soul, for example, and the possibility and means of salvation. Other moments or stylistic features are also shared. The two girls list and recommend the standard acts of mercy near the end of both poems, when the older parent has asked how to get to heaven, although Charlotte, unlike Olympia, follows this recommendation with a lengthy warning that works by themselves are of no avail (for Boccaccio, vv. 275–79; for Marguerite, vv. 1057–65). Both girls also launch into a lyrical list of images, one for the Virgin Mary—a traditional liturgical and lyrical effusion (Boccaccio, vv. 250–61)—and the other for Love itself, identified with God (Marguerite, vv. 274–88). Marguerite thus might be both imitating and correcting Boccaccio's poem with her own revised understanding of Christianity. Although Boccaccio's Bucolics are not included in the catalogs of works present in the royal library at the time,[49] almost all his other Latin writings were there, along with a number of his vernacular works, and some of them did have a profound impact on Marguerite's writing. Might the royal family's obvious interest in Boccaccio, or in Italian humanism more generally, have induced someone to mention or show this eclogue to the princess? We cannot know. But if Marguerite had the "Triumph of Death" at hand along with Briçonnet's letters, she was apparently seeking out texts that might address her situation of grief.

Whether we look to Dante, Petrarch, or Boccaccio, or to all three, Marguerite was definitely aware of and influenced by the writings of these famous Italians. The *Commedia*, *Trionfi*, and *Buccolicum carmen* all offer different models of dialogue with a female who is dead and can therefore speak with the authority of the blessed in heaven. Marguerite's innovation was to combine these poetic models with the form of spiritual counsel embodied in her correspondence with Briçonnet as in other dialogic works of religious instruction where the teacher is male.

One further example of which Marguerite was likely to have been aware offers a feminized version of such dialogues. This is the dialogue *La complaincte de la dame pasmée contre Fortune*, by Catherine d'Amboise, written either shortly before or shortly after Marguerite's *Vision nocturne*. Myra Dickman Orth (1997, 21), dating the piece to 1524 or 1525, considers it likely to have been written on an occasion similar to Marguerite's, that is, the death of a nephew. Drawing from the *Consolation* of Boethius, Catherine d'Amboise presents in the first person her complaint against Fortune and then her dialogue with Reason, who leads her from an encounter with Sadness to the home of Patience in the Park of Divine Love. She begins, like Marguerite, alone in her chamber in bed. All the figures encountered are female, as are most of the examples of suicide with which Sadness frightens the narrator. The narrator also meets a second noble lady whom she knows and loves, who is similarly distressed and similarly willing to accompany her and Reason to find Patience. The Boethian model thus becomes a conversation among females, some comforting and instructing others. The female figure of Reason becomes in part the voice of the female author, who, as in the case of Marguerite, is both the one in need of comfort and (as writer) the comforter. Orth points out (20) that Catherine had had herself portrayed as Reason in conversation with Boethius in an illustration to her earlier *Livre des prudens et imprudens* (1509). Both works were manuscripts produced for members of the family and probably not widely circulated; the family, however, included Anne de Graville, a member of the court of Queen Claude and certainly acquainted with Marguerite. The nephew whose death may have inspired the *Complaincte* was Anne's son. In sum, although we do not know which of the two consolatory dialogues came first, either Marguerite or Catherine may have become aware not only of male-authored dialogues with dead or personified females but also of a female-authored dialogue occasioned by a situation very similar to her own and involving all female speakers. While Catherine's work is executed in prose and in a more narrative and allegorical mode, both women almost simultaneously turned the symbolic female figure of traditional models into part of a philosophical and theological conversation among women.

Like the Italian models, Marguerite's correspondence with Briçonnet and her conversation with her dead niece are examples of writing as a response to absence. In this sense they fill in for rather than record real conversation. Marguerite had opened the correspondence with Briçonnet by writing in her first two letters to him that her husband had left with her brother for war; furthermore, her dear aunt was away for a wedding. Faced with extra duties that were causing her some anxiety, Marguerite complained of feeling alone and in need of counsel. She asked Briçonnet to be present for her at least through writing since he could not be there in person.[50] Left alone, Marguerite sought conversation through writing.

If Marguerite turned to writing correspondence when she had no one near to speak with in confidence, she wrote her dialogue when even written correspondence must fail: the *Vision nocturne* is a conversation produced by Marguerite because real conversation with her beloved niece has been rendered impossible by death. Marguerite is thus compelled to write both sides.[51] The dialogue is partly a request for a response from the dead—a desire to bridge that unbridgeable gulf that has suddenly opened—and partly a request for guidance in thinking about how to live with the fact of death. The role she gives herself within the text is that of a recipient to whom the girl's spirit suddenly comes; this is the position of the reader suddenly addressed by the text and its message.

Dialogues always present two relationships that must be measured against each other: the relationship of speakers within the text and the relationship of writer to reader beyond the text. This dialogue, and Marguerite's position within it, takes on different aspects depending on whom one conceives it to have been written for: whom is Marguerite seeking to address, and why? Jourda has suggested that she wrote the dialogue for her brother, not simply as a poem of consolation for his daughter's death but additionally as a means of persuading him to adopt a more evangelical religious position and thus to support a peaceful reform of the church.[52] In that case Charlotte would speak for Marguerite, while Marguerite, with her doubts, would represent her brother. In later publishing the poem, Marguerite, in this view, would be extending her preaching to other readers as well. If that was her intent, which it may have been in part—at least by the time she published the poem if not when she wrote it—then she certainly hides her own authority to preach. Using Charlotte as a speaker for her own ideas could be seen as either (or both) a precaution, allowing Marguerite to deny that she herself is advocating these things, or (and) a means of appeal to her brother Francis, suggesting that his own dear child, or heaven itself, wishes for his good and slyly positioning Marguerite as someone who needs the lesson herself rather than as someone who is telling her brother what to think.

It has also been suggested that she wrote the poem in part to demonstrate to Briçonnet that she had assimilated his lessons (Martineau and Grouselle 1970, 570). That case, in contrast, would call attention to the fact that Charlotte's words have, after all, been written by Marguerite even though her positioning herself as the pupil would reflect the initial relationship with her mentor. The transposition of his words into the mouth of a girl would signify their transposition into Marguerite's own mind and heart, her ability to reproduce them with understanding against her own moments of doubt and grief. There would at the same time be an implied compliment to Briçonnet by identifying his ideas with those of a soul securely among the blessed.

Yet to the extent that Marguerite anticipated that Briçonnet would disagree with parts of her poem, she may have had further reason to dissociate the speaker from him and from herself as well. Undoubtedly she recognized the dangers he was trying to avoid by maintaining an image as a moderate and did not wish to cause him trouble by ascribing to him ideas—such as the worthlessness of prayer to the saints—that he had openly condemned.[53] If, as her letter suggests, she intended him to be one of the poem's first readers, she may have seen it as an extension of their correspondence, in which she set forth her thinking for him, waiting to see not only whether he might correct her but whether he might be persuaded by her.

To the extent that she wrote the poem primarily for herself, to work through her grief and, under the impulse of that occasion, to review and express her religious beliefs, she compelled herself to articulate her own knowledge against the force of her questions and emotions, speaking for both points of view, "avouant la coexistence en elle du déchirement et de l'acceptation" (Martineau and Grouselle 1970, 573) [admitting the coexistence in herself of anguish and acceptance]. This self-consolation, however, cannot be effective because we cannot heal ourselves without divine grace. Charlotte argues that Marguerite (and we) cannot even choose how to respond to the poem's message, that is, cannot choose to be consoled, but must receive our consolation from God:

Ne vueillez point à vostre gré choisir
Penitence ou consolation:
Mais prenez tout de luy, sans desplaisir.

(vv. 1051–53)

[Do not try at your own will to choose
regret or consolation:
But take all from him, without displeasure.]

We can see this double attitude in the discrepancy between the beginning and the end of the text: while the neatly closed forms of the three rondeaux at the beginning express Marguerite's ultimate contentment with the will of God, the final speeches show her still lost in grief and wishing impossibly to retain her niece. As if in an extension of the rondeau form with its recurring phrase, the speaker Marguerite describes herself at both beginning and end of the whole narrative (vv. 58, 1293) as "pis que morte." This phrase too can be found in the correspondence with Briçonnet (1979, 228), where Marguerite refers to "l'esprit, qui sans vivification est pis que mort" [the spirit that without vivification is worse than dead]. By concluding the introductory set of rondeaux—itself a completed minidialogue—with the more consoled position ("Contente suis" is the rondeau's refrain), Marguerite as writer of the whole poem sets the recalcitrance of the speaker Marguerite after and against an initial statement of her acceptance. That is, she presents herself as responding to Charlotte with both possible conditions, reconciled and unreconciled, in tension with herself.

Marguerite's letter to Briçonnet announcing her work on the poem also refers to her mixed feelings and to her acceptance of the mix itself as having divine precedence. She even uses the same word, "contentement," as in the rondeaux (1979, 291): "je congnois que en la douleur est le contentement. Que vous diray je sinon que seroys trop ingratte si je ne vous declaroy les graces de l'infinie bonté, qui m'a faict, pare exemple, croire que en ung mesme instant passion et triumphe se trouvent en luy, honte et honneur, tristesse et joye, et toutes contrarietéz . . ." [I recognize that in grief is contentment. What shall I say to you except that I would be too ungrateful if I did not declare to you the graces of the infinite goodness that the belief has done me, for example, that in one same instant passion and triumph are found in him, shame and honor, sorrow and joy, and all contraries . . .]. The *Vision nocturne* is in this way a dialogue that expresses her own inner conflicts and awaits the grace that can resolve them.

As such it is one of a pair of examples by Marguerite, the other being the dialogic poem in terza rima on the death of her brother, *La navire, ou Consolation du roi François Ier à sa soeur Marguerite*, written nearly two dozen years later (1547). The two have naturally been compared because of their similar function and form, and the second dialogue's editor, Robert Marichal, has even suggested that Marguerite was clearly rereading or thinking about her earlier dialogue when she wrote the second, as the rare reuse of terza rima along with the funereal theme would certainly indicate.[54] Many of the images, standard for a consolation, also recur: death as a wedding with the divine spouse or as a liberation from prison, grief as an offense to the dead who is happier in heaven than in life, and so on. The differences are interesting not only as a source of information on the development of Marguerite's religious ideas over the course of many years, a topic that has been studied at length, but also as a comment on dialogue itself. For if the first dialogue, commonly described as "catechetical," offers straight answers on a number of current issues regarding faith, works, free will, and death, and opens with an indication of the potential success of its consolation, the second is much more complex, less inclined to preaching ("less explicitly doctrinal" [Cottrell 1986, 204]), and ultimately suggestive of the uselessness and ephemerality of human dialogue.

La navire is a more public work than the *Vision nocturne*. Robert Marichal (Marguerite de Navarre 1956) has argued that its formal features, such as the series of mourners summoned with references to their ranks (vv. 985–1314) and the inclusion of François's dying words to his son, which Marguerite knew only secondhand, indicate a wide intended audience rather than a merely private expression of grief. Certainly it includes both a public mourning and an exhortation to the people of France, as well as to the royal family, to cease mourning at last and to rejoice in François's salvation. Unlike the *Vision nocturne*, however, *La navire* was never published in Marguerite's lifetime and would have circulated only as a manuscript presumably in court and family circles.[55]

The poem is also more personally anguished than the dialogue with her niece, as befits the long and intensely close relationship between this brother and sister and the drastic change to Marguerite's life caused by his death. Without even the brief narrative opening of the *Vision nocturne*, where Marguerite seems to see her niece approach, *La navire* opens with the dramatic words of François speaking suddenly out of nowhere (Martineau-Génieys 1977, 558). Marguerite, instead of asking how to get to heaven, gives herself long speeches of remembrance, misery, and regret.

The first lament of Marguerite within the dialogue is precisely for the loss of "saige entretien" with her brother, a loss that the dialogue itself seeks to replace.

> Las! Maintefoys il m'en est souvenu,
> Luy respondis, mais j'ay perdu ce bien
> Que plus tu n'es de moy entretenu.
> Je l'ay perdu le plus saige entretien
> Qui oncques fut! Et le plus profitables!
> Plaisant sur tous: cela je ne soubstien!
>
>   (vv. 115–20)

> [Alas! I have recalled it many times,
> I answered him, but I have lost that good
> In that you no more speak with me.
> I have lost the wisest conversation
> That ever was! And the most profitable!
> Pleasant above all: that I cannot bear!]

Like good literature, the conversation of her brother was both pleasant and profitable.

The words "entretien" and "entretenu" evoke associations of mutual intimacy. But the voice that now addresses her with astonishing suddenness is "une venant des cieulx" [coming from the heavens], contrasted with her own "esploree voix" (vv. 62–63) [tearful voice]. The closeness of brother and sister has been replaced by a verticality with all the distance of heaven to earth. Their human love is the very object of François's attack, to be replaced by a "Parfaict amour" identified with God (v. 82) and with a total obliteration of the human self (vv. 88–93). He claims to have preached this even when alive, but what Marguerite within the poem remembers from his preaching is less the still valid content (though she acknowledges having heard it) than the sweetness of an intimate human conversation that has ceased.

There is no place for conversation in the ultimate oneness of the annihilated soul with God. Some scholars have suggested that the final goal of the dialogue is "silence," a silence that can never be attained by further persuasive speech.[56] Thus human conversation appears to be helpless: "Neither speaker moves from his original position. . . . Francis and Marguerite cannot speak to each other, for he moves outside time, she, within" (Cottrell 1986, 207–8). Jourda (1930, 583–84) expresses the impasse as a contrast between the "pleintes de la Reine" [laments of the Queen] and the "raisonnements dogmatiques du Roi" [dogmatic reasonings of the King], which cannot persuade the heart. As the dead François complains to his sister, "Tu le sces bien, mais tres mal tu l'entendz" (v. 204) [You know it well, but you understand it very poorly]. Impatient with each other's point of view, the siblings continually interrupt each other (e.g., vv. 244–45, 579, 619–20, 808, 1237).

Yet we are also made aware that Marguerite the writer shifts between the two positions, at times making fun of her own namesake within the poem. Her long childish argument that her grief is clearly God's will, which it would be worldly pride to resist, might elicit a rueful smile (vv. 625–30, 655–705, 940–57). So too her brother's protest that for all her exclamations of love, she is refusing to listen to him or obey him, preferring instead to weep "comme pressee esponge" (vv. 1317, 1319) [like a squeezed sponge]: "Ne mectz donc pas mes parolles au vent" (v. 1376) [Don't, then, cast my words to the wind]. Thus the gulf between speakers within the poem is played against our sense that the real Marguerite understands both sides and feels their mutual irritation. Yet while the *Vision nocturne* showed a Marguerite who seemed to be making steady progress in her lesson only to relapse into grief at the end, *La navire* shows a Marguerite who is recalcitrant all the way through but then, at the very end, a recipient of consoling grace.

With the emergence of the blinding sun following François's last departing words, Divine Light, Truth, and Love become the focus of the joyous final ten stanzas. Surely the number ten has a numerological significance for a work that from the start recalls Dante's *Commedia*: the sudden speech (in terza rima) of a voice that then indicates its past identity and enters into dialogue with a first-person narrator who has been nearly drowning in a dark sea.[57] Indeed, these ten ending tercets, which come closer to Dantean writing than anything else by Marguerite, contain a summary that is the most openly recognizable reflection of Dante's whole journey:

Par ceste mort tu m'as humiliee
Jusqu'en enfer: j'ay senty les lyens,
Et puis m'en as par grace deliee.

(vv. 1447–49)

[By this death you have humbled me
Down to hell; I have felt its bonds,
And then by grace you have unbound me.]

Ten is the number of perfection, appropriate to the final appearance of divine light. Marguerite's self-description from the earlier *Vision nocturne* returns here, but in a new and happier context:

O Charité, au Seigneur ententive,
En ta brebis *pis que morte* et perie
Tu as usé de ta bonté naifve;
J'ay ferme espoir. . . .

(vv. 1456–59, my emphasis)

[O Charity, in accord with the Lord,
On your sheep worse than dead and perished
You have used your sincere goodness;
I have firm hope. . . .]

The final tercet suggests the heavenly version of the beloved conversation with a brother: it is not silence, as scholars have suggested, but a chorus of praises for God by "la fraternité / De tous esleuz" (vv. 1462–63) [the brotherhood of all the elect]. United once more not as carnal siblings but as a brotherhood of the elect within the "Dieu tout en tous" (v. 1464) [God entire in all of them], brother and sister will replace their arguments with a unison in and about God. The theme of a song in unison as symbolic of the relationship of souls in a state of blessedness appears also in *L'inquisiteur* (v. 292), where the singing children "s'accordent d'une voix ensemble" [sing together with one voice]. Gerson's *Canticordum* dialogue (1966, 117, 126), with explicit reference to Plato, discusses the difference between the discord of the worldly soul and the concord of the blessed. Marguerite was undoubtedly aware, if not of Gerson's dialogue, at least of this central Platonic notion. It is only the scattered multiplicity of this world that can support dialogue. The conversation with her brother is one of discord and disagreement, which must ultimately give way to a unison in which the identity of souls with each other and with God has made dialogue impossible. But the alternative to dialogue is not silence.

Gender may be an issue in the *Vision nocturne*, where two young females surprisingly discuss theology,[58] but it is not a special focus of attention there. It is even less an issue in *La navire*, not only because the traditional male-female roles are restored as the blessed brother tries to counsel and console his troubled sister but also because the whole thrust of the discussion is one to which gender has become irrelevant. Marguerite, like many medieval women mystics, identifies herself as human rather than female and seeks to move from the problematic human flesh to the liberated spirit (Sommers 1995, 177). The potential implication that the flesh is represented by the woman while the spirit is represented by the man is overcome both by the sexless way in which the body is discussed and also by the failure of François to persuade his sister fully. Only the divine light that replaces his ghost at the end of the poem allows real healing to begin. François himself reiterates that whatever good qualities he had were God's doing and not his own. Just as the *Heptameron* discussants conclude that man and woman are alike worthless and in need of God, so here too, without an explicit gender war, the same conclusion is amply implied.

Moreover, as in the earlier dialogue, the speakers are not entirely themselves. Abel Lefranc (1969, 116–17) comments on the oddity of François urging Marguerite to evangelical ideas that he had persecuted during his lifetime; it is her ideas that come through his mouth. Any evangelical urging between brother and sister must have gone the other way and, one might add, with as little success. But François is indeed not himself anymore, just as Charlotte does not speak like a small child. Both have become the residents of heaven and as such the spokespersons for a heavenly truth. Perhaps, just as Marguerite had used a child to indicate that the truth comes from God and not from our human wisdom, so too she used her brother in a similar way: if he is saved, as she fervently hopes, then he will have the truth, even though it was not always his in the political world. His very change of view would indicate that these ideas come not from the earthly king and brother but from heaven itself. It is indicative of Marguerite's emphasis on human ignorance and incapability that within the dialogues only the dead are given a speaking position of authoritative knowledge. And even they are not effective without the ultimate gift of grace.

The dictates of drama, another dialogic genre favored by Marguerite, produce a different situation, in which living humans are enabled to speak for the truth, but from which Marguerite has removed herself as a participant. If the youthful evangelical preaching of the *Vision nocturne* resembles that of *Le malade* (1535) and *L'inquisiteur* (1536), the impasse and final revelation of *La navire* come closer to the late comedies *Sur le trespas du roy* (1547) and *Mont-de-Marsan* (1548). In *Le malade* the clear and sure preaching of the servant girl cures the sick master whom neither the learned doctor (of medicine but also, allegorically, of theology) nor the old wife with her traditional fund of recipes and superstitions can aid. The servant's stanzaic songs express a joy that differentiates them from the more prosaic verses of the older characters, who are as concerned about maintaining their authoritative standing relative to each other as they are about curing the sick. The sick man is definitively cured, just as the Inquisitor, in the play named for him, is definitively converted by the children whose joyful songs and games he had criticized as foolish and impudent. Indeed, it is the very youngest of the children, barely able to talk at all, who is most willing to engage with the Inquisitor and draw him toward an openness to hear the truths that the older children then expound. Human evangelical preaching is seen in both cases to be effective, and the plays deliver very clear notions of what is the right path.

The two late plays function rather differently. In the play on the king's death, the attempts of human characters to comfort each other fail completely, just as even the dead François himself fails to comfort his sister in *La navire*. In both dialogue and play, only a revelation of divinity at the end turns the sorrowing human conversation into a unison song of praise. Once again then, we have the shift from dialogue to unison, a shift that in the play is reinforced by a transition from French to Latin.

In the *Comédie jouée au Mont-de-Marsan*, Mondaine (Worldly) and Supersticieuse (Superstitious) come to Sage (Wise) to solve their opening debate; they do so in the manner of a pastoral contest or medieval debate between body and soul seeking a judge to decide their "cas" (v. 206). It seems at first as if Sage has taken over the role of the evangelical servant in her advice to both erring women, but we discover in time that her role is more limited. She enters with a praise of reason as God's special gift to man but is in turn reduced to uncomprehending witness with the entrance of the Shepherdess, whose seemingly senseless songs of joyful love resemble those of the children. The play leaves its readers famously uncertain as to where Marguerite's ultimate sympathies lie: with the sensible and evangelical Sage or with the irrational mystic lover.[59] The strong identification of Sage with Reason and her clear limitations of understanding, including the way that her remarks about the Shepherdess resemble those of the Inquisitor about the children before they succeed in converting him, all tend to work against too close an identification of Marguerite with Sage. Verdun Saulnier's observation (Marguerite de Navarre 1946, 243–71) about the connections between the Shepherdess's songs and Marguerite's own *Chansons spirituelles* adds further support to the idea that Marguerite is more than simply sympathetic with the attitude represented by the Shepherdess, who furthermore has the last words in the play. As befits the triumph of love over reason, the short lines of the Shepherdess's final song begin with an emphasis on the beloved as "ignoré" and "incognu" and end with an emphasis on the beloved as "amour" and "lumière," much like the ending of *La navire*.

The parallels between the figures in this play and those in the play on the king's death reinforce some of these implications. Securus is the rational figure like Sage; he offers, like philosophers, the virtuous examples of the ancients to encourage the mourner to be strong. Amarissima (Most Bitter), though less amenable to educative efforts than Mondaine, is like Mondaine readier than her more rational advisor to accept the message of Paraclesis, who takes the position of the Shepherdess both in the nature of her message and in her structural placement in the play, appearing at the end and confounding the others. Securus, being rational, has a harder time than the loving Amarissima, for example, in believing that the king still lives. Amarissima exclaims near the end that although reason was unable to console her, God has succeeded in comforting her by his promise of joy. Paraclesis is by name not simply another human but the Holy Spirit sent by God to the human heart. In the light of this play one might read *Mont-de-Marsan* as an expression of the greater importance of faith over the more limited human reading and reasoning rather than as an advocacy of mysticism versus evangelism. As in *La navire*, human conversations and consolations are ineffective; only a divine epiphany provides a resolution.

In both plays, the clear sense that the true path is known and that one can do certain things to advance along it—such as reading Scripture, doing good works with a true feeling of charity, and trusting in God—gives way before the possibility that nothing that really matters can be humanly or rationally accomplished. Yet as we cannot even choose to live in rapture like the Shepherdess, most of us, as Marguerite sees it, are left trying to be sensible and devout while doubting the efficacy of our own efforts and awaiting a gift of grace that might transform us into more ardent lovers of God.

If arrogant presumption of knowledge seems more associated with male characters (although Sage takes on certain characteristics of the Inquisitor in her reaction to songs of irrational love, she is not so vicious or proud) and superstition more with female ones (both in *Le malade* and in *Mont-de-Marsan*), the roles of evangelical and mystical—or intellectually and affectively oriented—piety are open equally to male and female characters because gender simply does not matter in these cases. It is in the realms of worldly knowledge that gender differences are manifest—in the struggle for medical authority, for example, in *Le malade,* between women as traditional healers and university-trained doctors. In the kingdom of spirit where all becomes one, differences of gender disappear. Whereas Marguerite seemed to be proclaiming her triumph over her opponents at the Sorbonne in her earlier work by setting a woman and children against established men, all four religious positions are represented by women in the final play. Gendered struggles for authority are effaced by the ultimate nothingness of the world. Just as dialogue will become unison, gender differences will vanish in an undifferentiated spirit.

I have digressed to include several plays in this discussion of spiritual dialogues because they function much like the dialogues, in fact more and more so. While the early plays still have some sense of setting and action, the later plays are chiefly speeches expressing particular attitudes. Whatever drama there may be consists in the interplay of ideas rather than of actions and in the relationships among attitudes rather than whole rounded characters. These works demonstrate the fluid boundaries of dialogue that will be further explored in later chapters: besides their close ties with letters and eclogues, we can see their proximity to plays, especially this sort of play of ideas.

Mont-de-Marsan, for example, resembles one of Gerson's dialogues between two hearts, Cuer Mondain and Cuer Seulet (1966, 112–39). Like the three women approaching the Shepherdess, the worldly heart ("on me repute ung saige mondain") sees the devoted heart ("ravie") as crazy or foolish and impractical; it cannot see the cause of the other heart's joy. Over the course of several days, however, the worldly heart receives a singing lesson: how to sing the heart's song, as Psalm 143 describes: "Deus, canticum novum cantabo tibi" is the "text" for Gerson's dialogue.[60] The worldly heart, says Gerson in his initial summary, must first become "raisonnable et espirituel; puis est parfait en bonne amour ardent, comme deifié & celestial" (112) [rational and spiritual; then it is perfected in good burning love, as one deified and celestial]. The mixed human and abstract quality of these speakers, the stages of the lesson from worldliness to reason and then on to a perfect love, and the emphases on love and a song of joy all resonate with Marguerite's work, whether she knew it directly or had received its influence indirectly through Briçonnet. Since Gerson was, in Gustave Lanson's description (1938, 163), "la plus grand gloire de Navarre avant Bossuet" [the greatest glory of Navarre before Bossuet], it seems likely that at least in the latter part of her life, as Queen of Navarre, Marguerite would have had some acquaintance with his work. If so, she saw no problem in transforming his dialogue into a drama. In any case, she herself used both forms to express similar ideas.

At the time of Marguerite's death, Olympia Morata was a remarkably well-educated teenager in Ferrara, the daughter of a humanist professor. Olympia's two dialogues were written separately but to the same friend, Lavinia delle Rovere Orsini.[61] The first was composed probably in 1550 when Olympia, still in Ferrara, had just married and was waiting for her German husband to make arrangements in Germany and then return for her.[62] Her previous few years had been spent in a desperate crisis involving the death of her father; the flight from Italy of his reform-minded friends; her dismissal because of increasing religious intolerance from the court of Ferrara, where she had served for years as a study companion for the duke's daughter Anne; and the consequent financial difficulties of her largely female family. This period of crisis had also aroused in Olympia a serious interest in religious thought and a reevaluation of her period as a humanist performer at the ducal court.[63]

Although there is no evidence that Olympia Morata had any knowledge of Marguerite, she may well have known either Valdés's or Ochino's works, or even both of them. Enmeshed through her father's interests and friends in a network of reform-minded Italians, she was an especially close friend of the reformist writer Celio Secondo Curione, who greatly admired Valdés and knew Ochino personally (Nieto 1970, 147). She mentions Ochino twice in her letters, once concerning his flight from Italy and later concerning his having to leave England as well. She was in Ferrara when he came there to preach and may possibly have heard him. The letter accompanying her second dialogue intriguingly mentions that she had previously sent her friend Lavinia "a dialogue of a certain learned and pious man." Her reformist notion of piety plus the fact that she omits his name indicate almost certainly a reformer whose identification might have proven dangerous to her friend. Olympia's letter, written from Germany after her marriage, comments happily on the freedom that her new homeland offers her to read religious books impermissible in Italy. Might the dialogue she transcribed have been one of Ochino's or Valdés's? One of Ochino's would have been much shorter and easier to send in a letter. Whichever text she might have sent to Lavinia, I venture to guess that she had at least been reading Ochino's dialogues, because her own work shares a number of features with his, especially his and her second dialogues.

The first dialogue is much more personal than the second. Not only do the speakers receive their own real names, but also the topics discussed are quite particular to Olympia's historical situation: her reputation as a learned woman, the way both men and women tried to discourage her from her studies by claiming that they would make it harder for her to marry, the wonderful husband she has found despite such negative prognostications, her discovery at long last of the spiritual dangers of her humanistic pursuit of glory, and her acknowledgment of the active intercession of God's protecting grace that has rescued her from her time of troubles. This dialogue is thus chiefly a kind of autobiography, but it is told by two people, Lavinia praising Olympia's diligence in study while Olympia herself belittles both her own accomplishments and the general value of those studies, lamenting her long ignorance of God and her previous apathy concerning the importance of religious matters. Through this discussion between friends, Olympia can work out with herself the conflicting claims of humanist learning and religious devotion.[64]

Olympia's resolution is presented not as her own finding but as Lavinia's advice: that she not abandon her classical studies completely but rather make them into the handmaids of religious study. Lavinia is thus given the role both of urging the more worldly Olympia toward religious studies and at the same time of praising and supporting her humanistic work. Olympia's gratitude to Lavinia is no doubt quite sincere. The dialogue is at least a tribute to her friend for general comfort and support during a time of crises. Lavinia had helped find financial support for some of Olympia's family members after the death of Olympia's father and Olympia's dismissal from the court. She had offered the adolescent Olympia an example of a woman both learned and married. She had certainly shared and quite probably encouraged Olympia's newly developing sympathies for religious reform. In short, she had been a real friend in need and, as an older and socially nobler person, a model and mentor. If the last section, consisting of a paraphrase of chapters from the Book of Wisdom, is really meant to be part of the dialogue and not accidentally attached,[65] then Lavinia is identified with none other than Solomon himself, a lover simultaneously of wisdom and of God. This would give Lavinia the authority of a male and a king as well as making her quite openly the vehicle for God's word.

The second dialogue was probably written in the following year, 1551, when Olympia was happily settled in Germany.[66] This time it is Lavinia whose husband is away and who may need the comfort of conversation with a friend. In both cases, then, we have not a clear teacher-student relationship but a friendship of two women. Yet these women are also in the act of persuading each other toward much the same goals as those addressed by male spiritual counselors.

Whereas the first of the two dialogues names the speakers Olympia and Lavinia and refers clearly to Olympia's particular real situation, the second dialogue, like Ochino's, combines specific historical identity with a broader quasi-allegorical agenda. The speakers are named Theophila and Philotima, or Love of God and Love of Honor, but they also in part represent Olympia and Lavinia. The letter to Lavinia accompanying this text claims that Lavinia will recognize her own concerns in some, but not all, of Philotima's: "ideo in dialogo aliqua quae tibi convenirent, et si non omnia, interspersi, ut videbis" (1940, 80) [and so in the dialogue I interspersed some things that are suited to you, although not everything is, as you will see]. Presumably Olympia intended for Lavinia to circulate the dialogue to other readers, who might identify with some of the other particular troubles *not* shared by Lavinia. Nonetheless, for Lavinia as reader, the bond of friendship between the two speakers expressed her real friendship with Olympia. For outside readers, the speakers are more generally identified by their allegorical names as two points of view.[67]

As in the dialogues of Ochino and Valdés, there is also an immense difference in social status between the historical persons here shown as advisor and advisee. Lavinia delle Rovere Orsini was by both birth and marriage a member of two of the noblest families in Italy; Olympia was the middle-class daughter of a professor, whose learning had earned her a service position at the ducal court. Had it not been for their living as two educated young women at the court of Ferrara, they might never have had any contact at all. Like Valdés and Ochino, then, Morata in this second dialogue is performing a spiritual service for a much nobler friend. It is not simply education that gives her this possibility, for both friends were well educated; nor is it a sense of having found a better religious understanding, for Lavinia was also a supporter of reformers and possibly more of an influence on Olympia than the other way around: at least that is how she is depicted in the first dialogue. But Morata was now in a moment of relative repose and reading as much as she could of the religious writings available to her in Germany. Lavinia, she feared, was more embroiled in daily anxieties and less free to nourish herself spiritually through reading, certainly less able to have access to the types of religious books that Olympia could find in Germany. Indeed, the religious situation in Ferrara had become much more restrictive as the Pope pressured the Este duke to crack down on heretics. Thus, like Gerson passing on to his sisters the benefits of his study, Olympia passes on to Lavinia the benefits of her own distanced and leisurely reflection and her own emotional cheer.

As at the opening of Ochino's second dialogue, so at the beginning of Olympia's second, one friend has come to comfort another who is in apparent distress. The novelty is that the spiritual advisor, both as Olympia and as Theophila, is now a woman—and a living woman, not a dead one visiting from heaven. Olympia indicates her need to justify her position by writing at the very end of her accompanying letter: "et considera iam, non quae tecum colloquatur, sed qualia et cuius sunt haec dicta" (1940, 80) [and consider now not who is speaking to you but rather whose and of what kind are these words]. She would later write similarly in a letter to Cherubina Orsini: "Non considerate che io sia una donna che vi avviso. Ma siete certa che Iddio con la sua parola pronunciata per la mia bocca benignamente vi invita a lui" (epis. 42; Morata 1940, 111–12) [Do not consider that I am a woman who advises you. But be sure that God with his word pronounced through my mouth kindly invites you to him]. Just as Philotima is and is not Lavinia, so Theophila is and is not Olympia. As in Ochino's volume, the dialogue between real friends is also a dialogue between God's word and the troubled soul.

We have seen a similar strategy in the dialogues of Marguerite, where attention is drawn to the word of God speaking through the human, rather than to the human as a source of authority. So too both women, while situating themselves within the dialogue, hesitate to identify themselves openly with the authoritative voice, even though they are ultimately writing its words. The claim that it is not I but God through me who speaks was a common one among female religious writers, especially those who transcribed (or dictated to scribes) their mystical visions or auditions. But even women, like Olympia, who were not seized with saintly raptures felt that they had found rather than invented the pious truths that they transmitted. As Augustine reiterated, all truth is God's; only the errors are our own. Indeed, like Marguerite, Olympia disparages not only female authority but any human authority, counseling repeatedly in her letter to Cherubina (1940, 112, 113): "Vi priego, per amor di Cristo, che vi governate secondo la parola di Dio e non secondo le opinioni d'omini" [I beg you, by the love of Christ, to govern yourself according to the word of God and not according to any opinions of men] and "la Scrittura sarà regola della vostra vita, non l'autorità di persona alcuna" [Scripture will provide the rule for your life, not the authority of any person].

Other factors besides transmission of God's words further contribute to the justification of the woman's role as advisor. For one thing, Philotima's husband, like Lavinia's, is away at the wars. Thus the man she might have turned to is absent. The same situation holds for Olympia's first dialogue, where it is Olympia's new husband who is out of the country and Lavinia who acts as the advising friend. The implication is that the absence of men has created a situation in which women must consult with each other. The situation becomes an excuse for a woman's writing and for a dialogue between women.

Another factor is the sheer genderlessness of Christian duty.

Cum et monere et moneri proprium sit verae et Christianae amicitiae et alterum libere facere, non aspere, alterum patienter accipere, non repugnanter, eo a me audacius es admonenda quo charior. (1954, 40)

*[Since it befits true and Christian friends both to advise and to be advised,
and to do it to each other freely, not harshly, and to receive it from each other
patiently, not defensively, the dearer you are to me the more boldly I may
admonish you.]*

Friendship, especially Christian friendship, not only permits the free expression of thoughts but thereby also requires the assumption of a certain benev-
olent authority, made tolerable by being mutual.[68] Thus Theophila and
Olympia both can take the initiative of offering unsolicited, though welcomed, advice; the situation of writing for a friend enables the boldness of
sending forth one's work without waiting to be asked. Her dialogue of general spiritual advice is set as a conversation between friends, sent in and as a
letter to that friend. Yet, as the problems addressed in it are only *in part*
Lavinia's, there is an implicit understanding that the text will be circulated
beyond its initial audience.

As in the dialogues of Valdés and Ochino to the lady of a noble and powerful family, the main thrust of the advice is to turn her away from worldly
concerns to spiritual ones.[69] Philotima, as her name suggests, is more completely and naively worldly than either Giulia or Caterina (or Lavinia, for
that matter), but the list of things she wants comes close to Caterina's list of
places in which she has looked for peace: fine foods, honor, beautiful fur-
nishings, and so on. Theophila then allegorizes these items:

Currus habere optamus, quibus hic in hoc tam exiguo vitae curriculo et
tam brevi invehamur, at currum quo in caelum, quo via longissima est,
vectae ascendamus, hoc est fidem habere, non optamus. Habitare laxe
et magnifice volumus, at in caelesti regno, quo nihil splendidius et
magnificentius esse potest, habitandi nullo afficimur desiderio. . . .
(1954, 42)

*[We wish to have carriages by which we may be carried in this course of life
that is so narrow and so brief, and we do not wish to have the carriage by
which we can be drawn upward into heaven, which is a very long way, that
is, to have faith. We want to dwell in a spacious and magnificent house, but
in the heavenly kingdom, than which nothing can be more splendid and
magnificent, we feel no desire to dwell. . . .]*

Like Ochino's interlocutors, Philotima wonders whether there is a way to
have both goods at once but is told that peace can never be found that way.
Morata, Ochino, and Valdés could all have had in mind Erasmus's comment
in the *Enchiridion* (1964, 58–59), which is based in turn on well-known pas-

sages of Scripture: "Ne velis temetipsum partiri duobus, mundo et Christo. . . . Duae tantum viae sunt. . . . Tertia nulla est. Harum alteram velis nolis adeas oportet" [Do not wish to divide yourself in two, for the world and for Christ. . . . There are only two ways. . . . There is no third. Of these two willy-nilly you must take one].

A new emphasis in Olympia's dialogue is on the brevity and insignificance of life as a goad to realizing the importance of attention to spiritual matters. Indeed she seems to have believed that the whole world would end very soon. For example, her letter to her sister warns her not to trust in "the appearance of this world, whether threatening or even smiling and flattering. For everything that you see, what is it all but a thin vapor, or evanescent smoke, or stubble or straw soon to be consumed by fire?" [huius mundi speciem, quantumvis minitantem, aut etiam arridentem & blanditientem. Nam quae cernis omni, qui sunt quam tenuis quidam vapor, aut fumus evanescens, aut stipula foenumque igni mox absumenda? (1580, 179)]. Or, as she writes to Lavinia: "Cito praeterit figura huius mundi" (1940, 99) [Soon the figure of this world shall pass]. Seeing the religious violence all across Europe as the raging of the Antichrist (e.g., 1940, 77, 98), Olympia wanted to prepare herself, her family, and her friends for the kingdom of God. The urgency of the situation not only permits but makes it imperative for her to speak.

Despite the abstracting or allegorizing tendency of this piece, which is shared with many of Ochino's, Olympia also makes room for the specifics of history, holding up as models both the contemporary Duke of Saxony and his wife, and the scriptural Queen Esther. Although Philotima's worldly desires are particularly female—focusing on embroidered cloths and tapestries, an elegant coach in which to visit her friends, and some cash with which to buy them presents—Theophila's inclusion of both male and female models for her female friend suggests the unimportance of sexual difference in matters of faith; yet it suggests this in a gender-conscious way as an encouragement to a woman who complains of being too weak for the demands of religion. Indeed, the male example is praised for suffering patiently through a series of unjust calamities, while the female Esther is praised for taking perilous action to save her people. Christian faith can make men patient and women heroic.[70] This possibility of heroism makes Morata quite unlike Marguerite, even though both shared basic religious sympathies.

Theophila's own gender is also clearly marked in her more worldly role. She leaves at the end of the conversation to attend to her housework, "nam ubi materfamilias abest, citius quod non facto est usus fit, quam quod facto est opus" (1954, 46) [for when the mother of the household is away, there is sooner need for what has not been done than for what has been done]. The phrase is adapted from Plautus's *Amphtruo* (504–5), where it is spoken about the need of a general to leave his wife and return to his camp. Household duties become the female version of male military duties,[71] and the pleasure of lingering with a woman becomes a conversational rather than a sexual pleasure.

Theophila promises to return soon, and Philotima expresses her eagerness for their next encounter. Like Valdés's dialogue, then, Olympia's ends with a promise of future conversations. The dialogue, both internally and externally, comes as a response to a perceived need to comfort and teach a female friend; but the reason for Theophila's departure calls attention to the femaleness of the comforter as well as of the needy person. It also calls attention to the learned Olympia's real need to balance her roles of writer and housewife. Even though the quoted passage from Plautus suggests that such conflicts between public duty and private pleasure are shared by both sexes, the sense of conflicting roles is not present in the men's dialogue writings that we have seen. The men who offer spiritual counsel are fulfilling their primary role; Olympia must steal unoccupied moments to do this. Thus too Olympia's accompanying letter seeks to justify her "leaving everything else aside" in order to "compose this dialogue" [Propterea licet occupationibus maximis distinear, relictis tamen omnibus, hunc dialogum tua causa componere volui (1940, 80)]. Her concern for Lavinia's well-being and her fear that Lavinia may be "beset with anxieties" and "consumed with cares" make this use of time for writing "permissible."

Women's adhesion to intellectual or spiritual concerns was often accompanied by a negation of themselves as female, emphasizing the genderless spirit rather than the gendered body as the site of identity. Gabriella Zarri (1994, 200) goes even further, seeing Olympia's early poem about her dedication to the Muses as the choice of male rather than female occupations: "I have abandoned women's things, the loom, the spindle and the baskets, and find delight only in the flowery field of the Muses and in the joyful songs of double-peaked Parnassus. Other women may appreciate other delights, but this is my occupation and my happiness."[72] While this early poem does seem to imply that Olympia felt she had left behind a normal female identity in her cultivation of writing, the second dialogue, written after the crisis that completely reordered her life and after her marriage, is remarkable in its insistence on the female identity of both speakers. Although the first dialogue refers to the assumption of those around her that she was giving up her chances for marriage by her intellectual work, she is now—in reality as well as in her text—the wife and homemaker as well as the writer and teacher, rather than having given up one for the other.

Whereas the dialogues of Ochino have always one clear teacher-student relationship, an interesting feature of Olympia's two dialogues when looked at together is that the roles of teacher and student are exchanged. The existence of the first dialogue, in which Olympia is the one learning while Lavinia speaks with her own authoritative voice, and possibly even with the voice of Solomon, makes all the more remarkable Olympia's assumption of the teaching and comforting role in the second dialogue, a year or so later.

In the posthumous volume of Morata's works, the two dialogues form a pair (possibly she herself recognized them as such) that implicitly contrasts contemplative and active work. Whereas the first dialogue focuses on a shift in learning from classical to Christian wisdom, the pursuit of which is praised for itself, the second dialogue focuses on the practical application of such wisdom to everyday life. In the first case, Lavinia casually walks in on Olympia at her studies, an activity that Olympia defends in at least two ways: that it is a morally good way of removing idleness; and that her inclination for it comes from God, who intends her to make use of her intellectual talent. In the second case, Theophila-Olympia actively seeks out a friend in trouble and goes to her with advice, both within the dialogue and beyond it. Thus we have shifted from learning as a pastime of the idle woman at home to the active uses of learning outside her own home. Esther is brought forward in the second dialogue as an example of a woman who, though living at a royal court, was willing to risk everything to save her people from persecution. The relevance to Lavinia, whom Olympia frequently encouraged to support the religious reformers against increasingly harsh persecution, would have been very clear to her intended reader.

Olympia's letters to women—that is, to former associates from Ferrara: the duke's daughter Anne (now married to the duc de Guise); Lavinia; Olympia's sister Vittoria; and her sister's employer, Madam Cherubina Orsini—continue the situation of one woman exhorting another toward a religious life that we find in both dialogues. The references to the need to bear one's cross, including her own nonexemption from tribulation; the emphasis on the brevity and instability of this life and the need to focus on the immortal life of the spirit; the encouragement to read Scripture and to pray for God's strengthening grace; and—most of all—the sense of the importance for women of reading Scripture and praying *together*, of conversing with each other and encouraging each other in the right way—all of these connect her letters and her dialogues.

The sharing of basic views and exhortations between Olympia's dialogues and her letters, which make up the largest bulk of her writings, demonstrates the close relation between these two forms for her just as for Marguerite. Indeed, her second dialogue was written at a time when warfare had caused her correspondence with Lavinia to be interrupted (1940, 79) ("perraro enim literae hisce turbulentissimis temporibus redduntur" [very rarely, indeed, are letters answered in these turbulent times]). Writing dialogue made up for this loss of two-way communication.

The relation of friendship between or among participants establishes a special tone. If Olympia thought of offering her counsel to the world at large,[73] she wanted first of all to offer it to her friend. For a woman seeking to avoid the censure of making herself too public, this sense of writing to and for one's personal friends provided a space between private and public. Moreover, Olympia knew that for her to take on the tone of authority, to preach, would be more readily acceptable if her audience were at least ostensibly female and someone whom she could encounter within domestic spaces.

Nonetheless, the personal quality and domestic site of these dialogues paradoxically reveal their literary ambition and have a classical model. Olympia's Ciceronianism is evident in a number of ways: the use of real persons as speakers, the inclusion of herself, the friendship among educated persons that gives rise to an intellectual conversation, the references to historical examples, and even some of the phrasing. Olympia was certainly well acquainted with Cicero's work and had written a defense of Cicero (now lost), as well as performing readings of Cicero at the ducal court. The combination of Ciceronian models with the dialogue of spiritual counsel is not surprising in a classically educated humanist turned religious reformer. Homer, Vergil, and Plautus join Cicero and the Scriptures in providing phrases—sometimes in Greek—for this conversation of educated females.

The domesticity and even specifically female concerns of both women in the second dialogue (Theophila must go home to attend to household needs, while Philotima worries about her husband and her ability to entertain her female friends in style) suggest that if Morata expected it to be applicable to, and read by, readers other than Lavinia, she had a clearly female readership in mind. Yet the combination of these female and domestic markings with the use of Ciceronian Latin is unique among women's dialogues and certainly expresses the attempt by Olympia to forge for herself (and her friend) an identity as simultaneously female friends and educated humanists.

Olympia Morata seems not to have had the sort of personal spiritual correspondence in her letters with men that Marguerite had with Briçonnet. Her last years in Italy were a time of terrible isolation, not of correspondence. Once married, she must have had many pious conversations with her husband and their friends, but these went unrecorded. Her Latin letters to various learned men after her marriage and move to Germany recount what has been happening to her, or invite translation into Italian of Luther's work, or urge the protection of reformers in trouble, but do not seek the kind of personal spiritual guidance that other women sought. Rather, despite her deference to the learning and devotion of male reformers, she feels sure of her own religious ideas and believes she has a religious duty through letters and dialogues alike to urge on others—especially women—to right living, the spreading of the "true" Christianity, and the defense of its martyrs. If the didactic certainty of her second dialogue is less appealing to us now than the expressions of uncertainty and discovery in the first, we might remember that this change was the product of a much greater happiness and assurance within Morata's life. In the first dialogue, she represents Lavinia as the source of guidance and comfort, perhaps as an act of gratitude for real support from her friend. By the second dialogue, she was now confirmed in her views, living happily with her husband, ready to turn from the consideration of her own personal problems to a more generalized perspective and to take up not the anxious role of seeker for counsel but the calm and helpful role of counselor.

Already in the fourteenth century, Francesco da Barberino in his *Reggimento e costumi di donna* (1318–20) had complained that certain religious women were acting as if they were "philosophers or teachers" and that other women were often readier to believe a female recluse than a master of theology.[74] The complaint demonstrates that at least for religious women there was a long tradition of teaching, not only other women but even men as well, and that at the same time, the role continued to appear inappropriate to some mainstream members of society. Without being a recluse or a mystic, Morata assumed for herself the right and even the duty to teach a Christian message. Nor was she the only laywoman of the sixteenth century to choose to do this through the form of dialogue.

One more, very different, example of spiritual dialogue written by a woman is the set of four dialogues on four days by Chiara Matraini, published in 1602 but probably written sometime between 1560 and 1581.[75] A Catholic writing in post-Tridentine Italy, Matraini takes a much more conservative approach to both the contents and the form of her teaching.[76] Her earlier years of a scandalous love affair and its resultant volume of *Rime* (first published in 1555) were followed by a period of intense religiosity in which, as Giovanna Rabitti observes, Matraini redesigned her own image, producing volumes of *Meditazioni spirituali* (1581), *Considerazioni sopra i sette salmi penitenziali . . .* (1587), and a very popular life of the Virgin Mary (1590).[77] The *Meditazioni* are already dialogic, following the example of Boethius. Lamenting a fearful dream of her own destruction, Matraini is addressed by her mind in a series of edifying conversations, each ending with a prayer and poem addressed to God. The *Dialoghi spirituali* shift from this Boethian model of internal dialogue to an external dialogue between two human beings.

The attachment to Mary appears strongly in the *Dialoghi spirituali*, which is set with its third day on the day of the Virgin's assumption into heaven (August 15); one of the two sonnets that end that day announces this event: "Hoggi . . . s'è alzata all'alta sua gloria infinita . . ." (1602, 60) [Today . . . she has risen to her high infinite glory . . .]. This poem also comes appropriately after Teofila's promise at the end of the third day to teach on the fourth how we may "salire al nostro desiderato, & infinito bene" (58) [ascend to our desired and infinite good]. Mary's ascension to "il sommo ben" becomes a model for our own attempted imitation. Each day ends with poetry, and since the work also begins with four sonnets by the author, the one canzone following the first day is actually the central poem of all the poems included, as well as being singled out by its form. It is a canzone to the Virgin Mary.

There is another clear sense of center halfway through the four days, that is, between dialogues two and three, where a sonnet describes the birth of Christ "Nel centro della notte, a mezzo il verno" (45) [In the center of the night, in the middle of the winter]. We can see at once, then, the formal influences of both Dante's *Vita nuova* and Petrarch's *Canzoniere*, the latter of which is explicitly cited within the dialogues.[78] The first and last poems of the text are not to Mary but to the "sommo Sol" [supreme Sun] or the "Principio sol, senza principio" [Sun that is the origin without origin], by whose light Chiara hopes to be made "bright," as her name signifies. In short, the lyrics provide a formally ordered framework within which the dialogues proceed.

The following list shows these formal arrangements more clearly:

Sonnet to Sol (poem 1)
Sonnet (poem 2)
Sonnet (poem 3)
Sonnet (poem 4)
Day 1
Canzone to Virgin Mary (central poem 5)
Day 2
Sonnet on birth of Christ: "Nel centro . . ." (poem 6)
Day 3 (Feast of the Assumption)
Sonnet (poem 7)
Sonnet (poem 8)
Day 4
Sonnet to Sol (poem 9)

There is also a certain symmetry to the volume as a whole, which includes three texts. The central *Narratione* presents Matraini as the student of a

celestial guide, who grants her a vision of eternal life. This scene of education is flanked by Matraini's efforts to teach: the dialogues with her friend's
son and the *Sermoni* (sermons or speeches) directed to academy members.
The three works in this volume, however, are of decreasing length, so that
this arrangement has nothing to do with a symmetrical amount of writing;
the *Dialoghi* dominate the volume.

Obviously there is no pretense here of offering the transcription of a real
encounter. The author is clearly in control of setting forth and arranging her
material, as befits its basically monological instructional content. She is also
ambitiously setting her work into a context of celebrated literature (Dante
and Petrarch) as well of spiritual instruction.

The dialogue begins without any narrative framework but includes some
information about the setting and speakers in its opening exchanges. Teofila
(Lover of God) is about to knock on the door of her neighbor and friend, the
historical Signora Cangenna, when the friend's son, renamed Filocalio
(Lover of Beauty), comes out and, explaining that his mother is not in at the
moment, invites Teofila to wait for her in the garden. Teofila engages Filocalio in a conversation that draws him to visit her on the next three days to
learn from her about the vices, the virtues, and the three steps that we can
take toward our salvation.

Matraini's audience is at least triple. Internal to the dialogues, it is Filocalio, the son of her real friend of many decades, Signora Cangenna.
Matraini had written two sonnets, printed during the 1550s, that address her
explicitly: one, "Quando formò di voi la bella figlia," celebrates the birth of
Cangenna's daughter; the other, "S'uguale avessi al gran dolor il pianto" (not
included in the revised *Rime* forty years later), laments to her friend, "fida
Cangenna mia," the violent death of Chiara's lover. This friend is also one
of the only two people to receive more than one of the *Lettere*, published
together with the *Rime* in the 1590s. In fact, in the 1597 edition the very first
letter is to her: addressing her as "cara compagna," it sends a poem and
accompanying gloss that the writer claims Cangenna has been asking for.
That sonnet encourages the soul, represented by the female Luna, to turn
away from earthly shadows and toward the sun of intellectual light, which
will enlighten her with "virtù conoscitive" [cognitive power] and "vera
sapienza, la qual rende perfetta la sua celeste contemplazione" (1989,
124–25) [true wisdom, which renders perfect one's heavenly contempla-
tion], a lesson much like the one offered to Cangenna's son in the dialogues.
In the 1595 edition of the letters Cangenna receives the second and also
penultimate letter, a consolation on the death of her only son, placed appropriately right before the final letter to Mary. (This letter is repositioned in
1597.) Presumably this son was the same one who is used as a speaker in the

Dialoghi. We do not know anything more about the identity of this woman or her family.[79]

Cangenna's son is a young man on the verge of deciding to set forth into a career of commerce: "ero quasi del tutto resoluto fra pochi giorni . . . andar solcando mari, passando monti, e trascorendo terre, per accrescer, & ampliar le nostre ricchezze" (15) [I was almost entirely resolved to leave within a few days . . . and go ploughing the sea, crossing the mountains, and traversing the lands, in order to increase and amplify our wealth]. Teofila, persuading him that wisdom is more valuable than wealth, becomes his teacher. She explicitly compares the two gardens, her neighbor's and her own, one with its fading material beauties and the other with its lasting intellectual ones. Humanist writers on education often turned to the metaphor of cultivation. Matraini's use of the image of the garden renders even her intellectual pursuits in the image of a private, domestic, female space.[80]

Filocalio's youth and his relation to Teofila as the child of a friend make him a fit recipient of what might be considered a basically maternal instruction. Indeed, Matraini had previously published a translation of Isocrates' oration to Demonicus, son of Ipponicus, concerning the manners appropriate to a noble young man; and she had later included in her volume of letters a letter of instruction to her own son that, as Rabitti has pointed out, draws heavily from Isocrates' discourse.[81] It includes, like the *Dialoghi*, a passage on the importance of study and the superior value of lasting knowledge to unstable wealth. Another of Matraini's letters addresses a different young man who has gone to study in Padua, encouraging his aim to study philosophy. Thus Matraini clearly had an interest in the theme of instructing a young man and encouraging his studies. On this first level the dialogue is simply a dialogic form for the kind of work accomplished also in a treatise and a letter. Writing to the son of a friend follows the model of Isocrates, although Matraini is quite willing to write also to her own son. The classical model allows her to be less personally maternal and more publicly a teacher, without transgressing the bounds considered normal for a woman.

Christine de Pizan defends the female as teacher of a male student at the end of her *Letter of Othea to Hector* (*Epistre d'Othea*): do not despise learning from a woman, for Augustine learned from his mother. The example she chose is amply packed, for Monica had the authority not only of a mother to her son but also of a Christian and thus a possessor of truth to the unenlightened. So too Matraini claims a double authority: as maternal substitute and as someone who realizes better than her pupil the nature and importance of divine truths over his more worldly knowledge.

The speaker or teacher in this inner core is not directly Matraini herself, but Teofila, whose name promises a safely pious kind of wisdom; and even though the friend named at the beginning is Matraini's real friend, we learn almost nothing personal about Matraini or her life other than her exemplary enthusiasm for study, virtue, and religious devotion. Teofila's name in fact is akin to that of Diotima and parallel significantly to the name of her pupil: Filocalio, as a lover of beautiful things, is at the beginning of the process that Diotima outlined; he must learn to rise from a love of beautiful things to a love of beauty itself, from goods to the Good, equated in Christian terms with God. Teofila, as her name implies, has made the ascent and can thus lead him as Diotima led Socrates. Indeed, the opening framework of Plato's *Symposium* includes a debate between its narrator and its addressee over whether it is better to lead a life of business affairs or to spend one's life devoted to philosophy. Thus Matraini's dialogue is a *Symposium* reduced to its opening frame and Socratic speech. In this mode, the text posits itself as a lesson for anyone worldly and presents its teacher simply as a happy, pious resident in the garden of good books. Platonism contributed an encouraging model to the female writer who wanted for herself the position of teacher rather than student.[82] Meanwhile Filocalio, his masculinity overriden by his youth, is given the role that is frequently the role of women in dialogues with an instructive male: while Teofila discourses at length, Filocalio asks questions and adds brief encouragements to her to continue.

The change of location from Filocalio's house on the first day to Teofila's on the following three days marks, without intruding in any heavy-handed way, the shift in the relationship of the two speakers, from their casual encounter at Filocalio's home to his intentionally seeking her out in her own text-sown garden with his newly desired goal of study. Through Filocalio Matraini envisions a reader who may think his main concerns lie elsewhere but who is open to being persuaded that she has something better to show him. This whole structure, with the worldly soul returning voluntarily for instruction in a better way of life, is analogous to that of Gerson's *Canticordum du Pelerin*. Whether or not Matraini could have read Gerson—it seems unlikely—she is following an established pattern for this type of work: first the teacher reaches out; then the student comes back for more. If we read the relation between Teofila and Filocalio as a sign for the relation between writer and reader, we find ourselves invited into Matraini's own space of learning and thought within the book, while the division into days ensures that it is our own active seeking for her wisdom that brings us back again and again to continue the reading.

In a second layer of readership, the dialogue as a whole is dedicated to the illustrissima signora donna Marfisa da Este Cibò Malespina, described in the dedication as "persona Reale per nobiltà di sangue" [royal through nobility of blood], to whom Matraini humbly offers her lowly gift, fearing to have been perhaps too bold in her selection of dedicatee but hoping in the lady's benev-olent recognition of the author's intended reverence. This relationship looks more like those in the spiritual dialogues of Ochino, Valdés, and Briçonnet in that it offers elementary spiritual education to a woman of much higher social status. In Matraini's case, of course, this status is in no way counter-balanced, for the author is not a member of the clergy who can offer certified wisdom on request. In this layer, therefore, Matraini has not been asked for counsel, as were the three men just named; rather Matraini takes the initia-tive of offering it—hence her concern about being too bold.[83] Still, as with Morata, the instruction remains between women.

At this level, Matraini is a woman holding out to another woman the allure of both book learning and piety. Matraini might have assumed that her patroness would share the book with other women in her entourage. Thus the single female dedicatee might in turn have drawn in other female readers or auditors. The instruction is simply offered as a gift or service, but it implies that Matraini does not wish to see herself as a lone figure, the unique learned female in her group. Rather she wishes to use her learning to draw other women into the pleasures of study. The dialogue makes very clear that study of this kind is not contrary to piety but indeed a help and means toward it. Describing learning as a private garden makes it inviting to a female who might have thought of learning as something connected with the public sphere and therefore inappropriate or at least unnecessary for her-self, the way it is often presented in male arguments about women's educa-tion. The private garden indicates that learning for Matraini and her female reader is intended ultimately as a path to contemplation and not to action.

Yet Matraini herself is taking a more active role in writing this book. She represents herself as leaving her own home and garden in order to seek out the home of her friend Cangenna. Matraini, like Morata, shows herself turn-ing learning into teaching by this literal leaving of home to seek out conver-sation with another. The publication and dedication of the book are a real-ization of that figurative movement out from home.

The third audience is the Accademia dei Curiosi, to which the whole book (with the *Dialoghi*, *Narratione*, and *Sermoni*) is addressed. The three pieces of the volume are all on the same theme: the importance of self-knowledge and the superiority of intellectual and spiritual concerns to more worldly ones. The "Narratione di alcune cose notabili" is dedicated "alla grand'Academia de i Curiosi" and the sermons "a i medesimi Curiosi." But the dialogues too are introduced by a letter "a benigni e curiosi lettori" [to kind and curious readers], an address that takes on a more specific meaning when we have become aware of the other two dedications. On the other hand, as there seems to be no information about this academy, it has been

suggested that the academy might be a fiction, representing in fact the "curious readers" of the book.[84] One of Matraini's letters asks for some objective
criticism of her work so that she may correct it before presenting it in public;
read it, she requests, as if it were the writing of one of your brothers "che
abbia a mandare i suoi scritti davanti ad una pubblica accademia di gran
literati" [who has to send his writings before a public academy of great men
of letters].[85] This seems to suggest her anticipation of a real audience. However, Matraini's *Narratione all'Academia de i Curiosi* describes the audience as
"nobilissimi e saggi lettori" (96), and the noun may support the hypothesis
that this "academy" is really Matraini's public readership.

Although the academy in either case was presumably largely male,
Matraini does not seem to have too high an opinion of this audience. For
one thing, there is no sign of the groveling humility that she expressed to
Donna Marfisa nor of any humility at all. Moreover, her letter to these
"curiosi lettori" just before the start of the dialogues is a detailed explanation
of the preceding sonnet "a lettori," an explanation that clearly expects very
little in the way of either imagination or understanding from its readers,
whether in matters of mythology or in basic science. It is very similar to the
sonnet and explication that the opening letter of her 1597 volume offers to
Cangenna. Matraini seems to see no difference between Cangenna and the
members of the academy as audiences for this kind of explication. Perhaps,
however, these explanations—that Cynthia is the moon, that the moon is
fullest when farthest from the sun, and so on—are meant less to instruct the
academic audience than to indicate her own basic knowledge and therefore
her right to speak and publish. In addressing an academy with a text that
invites one to study and to acknowledge the superior value of learning over
commerce, Matraini is not teaching something new to this group; rather she
is articulating the values already shared by an academic audience. Thus she
speaks not as an outsider but as one of them, not to them but for them, giving them the words by which they might encourage their own sons, if not
daughters, to pursue learning rather than money-making or at least to make
room within an active life for study and contemplation. She is offering, in
sum, to be a spokesperson for the educated members of her society.

In any case, these layers of audience indicate multiple functions for the
text, of which the instruction of children is only one. They allow Matraini
simultaneously to heed and blithely disregard the warnings of someone like
Lodovico Dolce, who, despite arguing for women's education, goes on to
admonish them: "non dee esser Maestra di altri, che di se medesima, & de
suoi figliuoli: e non le appartiene tener schola, o disputar tra gli huomini"
(1547, 18r) [she should not be a Teacher of others, except of herself and of
her children: and it does not suit her to run a school, or to dispute among

men]. Each layer seeks a more public audience, and thus, while the core places its author safely in a maternal role and private garden, its outer layer presents her—whether truthfully or wishfully—as an educated and eloquent participant in the public life of the cultured class.

Rabitti (1981, 157, 161–65) observes that Matraini seems to have remained fairly marginal to the limited cultural life of Lucca, partly because of her odd social status—neither noble nor courtesan—and partly because the Buonvisi, in whose palazzo the chief gatherings were held, were political enemies of the Matraini family. She did, however, participate in a network of connections surrounding Lodovico Domenichi, a friend of the Lucchese publisher Busdraghi who printed her works. Publishing and addressing her readers as a community may have been for her a way of redefining her social situation. The first of two prose pieces published with her *Rime* in 1555 (1989, 93–94) responds to a charge that since she is not noble, it is inappropriate for her to be studying and writing, especially about love. She replies, with the traditional Tuscan argument of the professional class, that true nobility comes from an "animo di virtù."[86]

In some ways, the dialogues resemble other instructive conversations that we have seen, but the work contains some features that make it hover between a spiritual and a more secular theme. Like Gerson's Cuer Mondain to Cuer Seulet, which Matraini would most likely not have known, Filocalio asks Teofila how she can be happy when she is usually alone and shut up out of the light, and like Cuer Seulet, Teofila responds that she has a spiritual company and an intellectual light that more than compensate for what the world has to offer. Her own garden is sown with writings and bears the flowers and fruit of virtue and wisdom. The description of her garden with its freedom from rough weather and its continual sweet breeze resembles Dante's description of the earthly paradise, but it is watered with the "fonte di Parnaso" rather than the streams of paradise. Inspired by these descriptions, Filocalio decides to change his plans from the pursuit of riches to "lo studio delle buone lettere." Matraini's phrase translates "bonae litterae," a standard way of referring to humanist writings. "Lo studio delle buone lettere" becomes interchangeable with "l'honorato studio delle buone scienze" (18) [the honored study of the good sciences] and includes the classical philosophers and poets along with Christian writers.[87] Dante provides one of the links here between religious and literary emphases.

The first two dialogues are more secular than the last two: in them Matraini explicitly cites Aesop, Pliny, Petrarch, Aristotle, Thales, Democritus, Propertius, Ptolemy, Socrates, and the famous inscription on the Delphic temple of Apollo, along with the Psalms and Wisdom (both in dialogue two).[88] The third dialogue, while still citing Plato, Aristotle, and Cicero (several times), adds Augustine, Isidore, "learned" Hugh, Gregory, and Bernard, as well as the Scriptures (not only the Old Testament David but also the New Testament Matthew). In the fourth, Gregory and Augustine stand alone beside scriptural quotation. This shifting cast of authorities fits the shifting topics of the four days—from praises of the intellectual life; through a description of the vices and virtues; and finally on to the steps toward salvation: humility, prayer, and confession. The process of learning begins with classical literature and philosophy and ends with Christian doctrine.

Matraini's opening sonnet reads as a confession of her past sinful errors and her recovery, thanks to the light of the divine sun, of the true way previously obscured by shadows. The second poem prays more specifically for liberation from "le nebbie . . . Dell'oscura ignoranza, e'l freddo verno / Della pigritia" (5) [The mists . . . of dark ignorance, and the cold winter of sloth]. These two terms are then echoed early in the first dialogue in a citation from Petrarch's sonnet (*Rime* no. 7):

La gola, il sonno, e l'otiose piume
Hanno dal mondo ogni virtù sbandita
Che per cosa mirabile s'addita
Chi vuol far d'eloquenze nascer fiume.[89]

(1957, 12)

This recurring criticism of ignorance and laziness sounds more like a humanist appeal to study and writing than a Christian appeal to pursue salvation, especially when its praise of eloquence is followed almost immediately by a reference to Apollo and the Muses. Those who persevere in traversing Teofila's garden of studies are crowned with Laurel or Myrtle and set above the stars by "honoratissima fama" (14), while the vile mud of "otio" besmirches those who close the eyes of reason and intellect. Yet these humanist praises of eloquence, learning, and fame are, as Teofila's name suggests, the introduction to instruction on salvation.

This account seems to merge the human and divine studies, and the humanist and religious aims, that Olympia Morata was at pains to distinguish. Morata had come to see her years of humanist glory at the Este court as a peril to her soul. Yet both she and Matraini end up refusing to reject their own learning and viewing it instead as a step in a progression. Morata's first dialogue with Lavinia tells how her devotion to intellectual pursuits was much superior to the devotion of most women to physical adornments and to repose; yet as much as these human studies surpass mere physical pleasures and sloth, so much also divine studies surpass the human, which, like physical beauties, offer only a quickly withering bouquet. God, who gave Olympia her passion for study, is described himself as the supreme orator who "impels our mind to wherever he will." The long passage from the Book of Wisdom underlines the notion that Solomon's desire for wisdom is good, repeating its superiority to the more material values of wealth and beauty and suggesting that an understanding of the cosmos leads to an appreciation of God's power and benevolence. Thus wisdom produces in its followers "the friendship of God." At the same time, the paraphrased passages of Wisdom that promise to Solomon "glory among people," being "held in honor," and arousing "the admiration of the powerful" celebrate the very aims of which Olympia has expressed her suspicion and rejection. However, one further scriptural phrase perhaps gives even these dangerous goods a more valuable purpose: "I will strike terror into the ferocious tyrants who hear me." If the admiration that Olympia has won among learned men (now living in Germany and Switzerland) and among her female friends in the ruling class can help—as her letters repeatedly urge—to spread the true religion and to defend religious reformers from the wrath of persecuting rulers, whom her letters portray as agents of the Antichrist, then perhaps even her years of glory at court may be turned to the service of God against the efforts of tyrants to repress religious reform.

Matraini has no such reformist agenda and does not share Morata's apprehensions about the self-glorifying dangers of her work. Rather Matraini wholeheartedly endorses the humanist appreciation of education and the humanist goal of fame. Nonetheless, like Morata, Matraini quotes repeatedly from the Book of Wisdom, indicating its importance in the relation of man to God. Both women take up the topic, shared by both Wisdom and the classical philosophers, of contrasting intellectual study positively with sloth and more material pursuits. Filocalio must first be lured from the pursuit of riches (beautiful adornment is too feminine a pursuit to ascribe to the young man, but wealth is similarly worldly and unstable) to that of human wisdom and the study of good books. The garden of knowledge ("terra dei libri, seminata di molte varie, e generose scritture" [earth of books, sown with many varied and productive writings]) offers undying fragrant flowers preserved both by the unchanging spring weather and by the eternal soil of ideas in which they are rooted ("per haver essi nell'immortalità fondate le lor radici" [12]).

Intellectual pursuit is advocated according to the principle of following one's true nature, for the nature of humans, as distinct from other creatures, is defined by the faculty of reason: "Naturam ducem si sequamur nunquam aberrabimus" (15); the use of Latin enhances the authoritative ring of this dictum, as does the prestige of Cicero's De officiis (1.100), from which it is quoted.[90] Cicero had gone on to note that this nature includes the mind or spirit as well as the body. The "nature" meant by Matraini is especially the rational or intellectual human nature, without regard to differences either of individual or of gender. The fact that it is a male whom she encourages to study only half covers the fact that it is a woman who finds such study "natural" to herself as well.

Like Plato in the *Republic*, or like Leone Ebreo in his Platonic *Dialoghi d'amore*, Matraini outlines a long ascending series of studies that she recommends to Filocalio: logic (to distinguish truth and falsehood); moral philosophy; natural philosophy; "rising to" mathematics, metaphysics, and finally theology.[91] Her own lessons to Filocalio do not fully embody this process, focusing chiefly on moral philosophy and then leaping to theology. Yet her continual praises of Pliny, Aristotle, Ptolemy, and their like make clear how important she thinks the "sciences."

The difference between learning and wisdom, a difference carefully set forth by Gerson and Valdés, is blurred by Matraini, who uses "scienze" and "sapienza" interchangeably. The Sun in her opening poems seems to be the divine light but is glossed in her letter to readers as "lo studio delle buone scienze" (8) [the study of good sciences], which can lead one out of darkness. "Studio" is both human study and the zealous pursuit of religious wisdom. "Dottrina" is both religious doctrine and scientific learning. Because God has made humans distinct by their rational, intellectual nature (15–19), "quel vero, e retto camino, che gli dimostra la ragione a tutte l'hore" [that true and straight path that reason shows him at every hour] is the one that "col favor della divina grazia, lo condurebbe al suo vero, perfetto, e felicissimo fine" (16) [with the grace of God, would lead to his true, perfect, and most happy goal], that is, a life of contemplation, both philosophical and religious (31–32): "in somma la vera, e perfetta felicità dell'huomo . . . consiste . . . solo nell'attioni dell'intelletto le quali si rivolgono intorno alla contemplatione della verità" [in sum, the true and perfect felicity of man . . . consists . . . only in the actions of the intellect, which center themselves on the contemplation of truth], in which "si uniscono con Dio, mediante il loro intelletto" (31) [they are united with God, through the means of the intellect]. "Deum agnoscimus ex operibus eius" (26) [We know God through his works]; therefore science leads to knowledge of the creator. Moreover, if we do not come to a knowledge of God, we cannot love him: "s'egli primieramente non è da noi conosciuto, noi non lo possiamo amare" (25).

This emphasis on knowledge and study is precisely what the Duchess of Camerino suggested she needed: describing knowledge as the servant of the will that carries the light before it, she proposed that one needs to know God in order to love him and that people in general fail to love him properly "perché di Iddio n'habbiamo poco lume e sì perché non si attende, non si pensa e non si studia . . ." (1985, 48–50) [because we have little enlightenment concerning God and also because people don't pay attention, don't think, and don't study . . .]. A program of study and contemplation, she proposed, would lead us to a better love of God. But Ochino (1985, 48–50) rejected this proposal as wrong, introducing the image of the pious old woman. Perhaps some women tended to place what religious men considered an excessive trust in the powers of education and intellectual activity. Women's general exclusion from these areas, however, would naturally have made them appear all the more infused with special promise—hence too women's recurring praises of wisdom.[92] Platonism, attractive to women for a number of reasons, would certainly have reinforced this emphasis on the importance of education and knowledge. The Platonist Leone Ebreo's widely read *Dialoghi* similarly assert that love, if it is not mere vulgar desire, must always be based on knowledge, even the love of God.[93] He too cites the Book of Wisdom in this cause.

After these rational studies have indicated the nature of the universe, and of the vices and virtues, three further steps are needed to draw close "al sommo nostro, e desiato bene" (61) [to our supreme and desired good]; Matraini's fourth dialogue defines them as humility, prayer, and confession. Here at last we might seem to have passed beyond the relevance of human learning; yet just as the dialogues begin with the importance of following one's true nature, they end maintaining the importance of understanding one's true nature: through humility, which consists in acknowledging our mortal and corporal condition; prayer, "per il qual l'intelletto nostro si viene a illuminar della vera cognition del sommo Dio, e di se stesso" (62) [by which our intellect comes to be illuminated by the true knowledge of the supreme God and of itself]; and confession, which is by definition a self-examination (67). The entire garden of varied human knowledge, then, leads ultimately to a knowledge of the self and God. Even in this ultimate consummation, the "knowledge" of God is still emphasized rather than an uneducated love.

So too the *Narratione* in this same volume begins with the appearance of a celestial lady who, like Boethius's Philosophy, promises to show Matraini "quella che sei, e dove habbi il tuo principio, & fine" (74) [what you are, and where lies your beginning and your end]. The central of the three *Sermoni* similarly opens with and develops the text: "Multi multa sciunt, & se ipsos nesciunt" (100) [Many people know many things and yet do not know themselves]. Although both texts lead the seeker of knowledge to a realization that the divine is beyond any human understanding, nonetheless, the *Narratione* blames ignorance as the cause of all evils (77) and leaves Matraini at the end capable of flying on her own—with the grace of God—"sopra l'eccelso monte della divina contemplatione" (96) [up to the top of the high mountain of divine contemplation].

Several years before writing these dialogues, Matraini had commissioned an altar painting for S. Maria Forisportam, in Lucca, in which she herself was depicted as the Cumaean Sybil pointing to the Virgin Mary foretold in the sybilline prophecies.[94] The painting contributes to our understanding of Matraini's own sense of her curious role in these dialogues. On the one hand, her discourse, like the sybil's, is validated by the Catholic truth that it indicates. On the other hand, she cloaks herself at the same time with a classical wisdom that stands outside the church, even while it shows itself to be compatible with and even in the service of that church. For although holy women, such as the several St. Catherines, might become the sought-out advisors of men because of their saintliness, Matraini seeks to offer her teachings as a secular woman, without possessing or claiming the status of holiness, simply because she has the education and intelligence to read, understand, and write on moral and religious truth.

At the end of the final dialogue, Teofila urges Filocalio to do everything for the glory of God. Thus, like Morata, Matraini sees intellectual studies as something that, if done with the proper attitude, can be put to the service of religion. In a sense, these dialogues embody that very purpose, putting Matraini's own studies to work toward the salvation of others and the praises of God and Mary and thereby simultaneously justifying her desires to read, to think, and to write.

Like Morata's second dialogue, with its mix of female concerns and Latin erudition, Matraini ends her educative dialogue, which is written in Italian although with occasional Latin quotations interspersed, by offering a "recipe"—a traditionally female gesture—in Latin, the language not of women but of the learned. This "Ricetta per la salute dell'anima" [Recipe for the soul's health/salvation]—take the root of humility, the rose of charity, the lily of purity, and the absinth of contrition; mix in the mortar of conscience; add the water of tears; cook in the fire of tribulation and patience— produces a "syrup" that cures the sick soul. Its ingredients have nothing to do with learning, but its Latin status requires an educated reader to make use of it. Thus the dialogue ends with the same melded interest in learning and in the soul's salvation that it has manifested all along. Moreover, like Morata's second dialogue with its references to housework and female activities, Matraini's final gesture presents the author as simultaneously female and learned. Thus it draws our attention to the fact that it is indeed a woman who is offering to teach us for our own good. As in Marguerite's *Le malade*, the traditionally female role of household healing is used metaphorically to naturalize the presentation of a woman teaching and preaching to a male, that is, composing and offering medicine for the health of his soul.

Matraini was most likely not aware of Morata's writings. Their religious differences meant that Morata was not an attractive writer for Matraini, and Morata's volume, printed in Basel, would probably have been difficult to obtain in Italy even for someone who wanted it. If these two women overlap in some particular attitudes and strategies, it may be because both shared the situation of being learned women, yet neither noblewomen nor courtesans, but members of a middle class from which an educated female was hard to "place" socially.[95] Both, therefore, wrote their dialogues ostensibly for a domestic audience of immediate friends and also for a nobler female who may have enabled their acceptance more widely. The opening letter of Matraini's first version of her collection of letters combines a praise of love with a defense of her own writing, linked explicitly to class identity (1989, 93–94):

> Ma perché vi siete premieramente sforzato di mostrarmi quanto dis-dicevole sia a donna non de' più alti sangui nata, né dentro i più superbi palagi fra copiose e abbondantissime ricchezze nodrita, andar continovamente il tempo consumando ne gli studi e nello scrivere, fuori in tutto dell'uso della nostra città, . . . vi dico che, quantunque io d'alto e real sangue nata non sia né dentro i grandi e sontuosi palagi, ne le pompose camere o ne' dorati letti nodrita, non però di ignobile famiglia né di poveri e bassi progenitori (come saper possiate), ma di chiaro sangue e di onesti beni di fortuna dotata, in città libera, e di grand'animo generata sono. Benché se con dritto occhio riguardar vor-remo (se alle dotte carte de' più famosi e pregiati scrittori fede alcuna prestar si deve), vederemo certamente che non l'antiquità de' sangui né'l soggiogar de' popoli, non l'oro né la porpora, ma l'animo di virtù splendido far l'uomo veramente nobile.

> [But because you first felt the need to demonstrate to me how blamewor-thy it is for a woman not born of the highest blood, nor raised within the most splendid palaces among copious and abundant riches, to go continually con-suming her time in studies and writing, completely outside the custom of our city . . . I tell you that, although I was not born of lofty and royal blood nor raised in great and sumptuous palaces, in pompous chambers or in gilded beds, nonetheless I was born in a not ignoble family, to parents neither poor nor lowly (as you can know), but of clear blood and endowed with the for-tunes of an honest wealth, in a free city, and with great spirit. For if we wish to look with a clear eye (if any credence should be given to the learned pages

of the most famous and prized writers), we will surely see that neither antiq-
uity of blood nor the subjugation of peoples, neither gold nor purple, but the
mind resplendent with virtue makes a human truly noble.]

There seems to be an implicit argument here about whether study is a luxu-
rious consumption of time, a consumption inappropriate to the middle class
though permissible to the upper class, or whether it is instead a kind of pro-
ductivity appropriate to the citizen of a "free"—that is, commercially rather
than aristocratically governed—city. It is noteworthy that Matraini feels
attacked not as a woman but specifically as a middle-class woman, unlike the
ubiquitously praised Vittoria Colonna or Veronica Gambara. Perhaps therefore both Matraini and Morata felt especially the need to make their learning useful. At the same time, Matraini's description of herself as "di
grand'animo" suggests the *magnanimitas* that Aristotle posits as the supreme
virtue of the upper class. Matraini aspires to social status through her intellectual ambition.

Both Morata and Matraini—though at different ages and in different
decades—made a turn from more worldly ambitions to a religious devotion
that they needed to reconcile somehow with their unabated love of learning,
a love that they felt God had given them. Both adopted the name "Teofila"
to indicate their personal religious devotion and to authorize their discourse
by association with God's word, thus simultaneously identifying with and
disengaging the individual self from the renamed figure who speaks for them.
Both expressed awareness of the need to negotiate the difficulties of writing
and teaching as women, even though both felt strongly—especially as
nonaristocrats—that their studies were a major source of their personal
value.

   Both even saw themselves as engaged in a battle under divine auspices:
Matraini argues that when God shines his light of grace, "non bisogna
chiuder gli occhi dell'intelletto . . . ne quando è tempo di combatter gettar
l'armi per terra, chi non vuol rimaner preso, o ferito, o morto" (47–48) [one
ought not to close the eyes of one's intellect . . . nor when it is time to fight,
should one throw one's arms on the ground if one does not want to be cap-
tured or wounded or killed]. Morata writes in exhortation to another woman,
"Non si dà la corona se non a colui che combatte" (1940, 107) [The crown
is not given except to those who fight]. The image of the soldier of Christ,
used explicitly by Morata and implicitly by Matraini, is of course a traditional one and possibly reinforced—at least in Morata's case, although the
book was popular with Catholics and Reformers alike—by the influence of
Erasmus's *Enchiridion militis christiani* (1501). But one should note as well the

continuing popularity of Catherine of Bologna's *Le sette armi spirituali* (reprinted in 1520 and 1550), in which a woman counsels other women on how to do battle against sin. The concept of spiritual battle enables women to participate in combat, which, as we saw earlier, was an image used to gender debate as male and to demonstrate the inappropriateness of women's participation. In the war for God against sin, even women may take up arms.

For both women, despite their religious difference, this means a readiness to turn knowledge into action. "Non in sermone est regnum Dei, sed in virtute" [Not in speech is the kingdom of God, but in virtuous action], writes Matraini, quoting from John (1 John 3:18) just as Morata had written (in an essay in praise of Mucius Scaevola): "Neque enim in scientia, sed in exercitatione atque actione et initium virtutis est et finis" (1580, 72) [For not in knowledge but in practice and action is the beginning and end of virtue]. Although Matraini makes contemplation the highest goal, both Matraini and Morata sought to feel active and to make themselves useful to a wider public in a way that was justified as the use of God's gift and as service to God. Both found dialogues a useful form, among other forms, for the expression and realization of this set of aims.

Spiritual dialogues tend to give very little in the way of a setting and narrative frame. They emphasize not the historical conversation of a particular time and place but rather the eternal truth in its combat with a more worldly perspective. To the extent that there is some setting, it may take on a symbolic cast: Marguerite's nighttime dialogue takes place simply in the dark world of time and mortality unlit by grace. The domestic spaces of Morata's and Matraini's dialogues simultaneously imitate the Ciceronian model and give the female speakers a safely and modestly "private" locus in their home or garden. The characters are specific but also representative of a much more general perspective: the human most broadly and the divine insofar as it can be articulated in human speech. They may inhabit simultaneously an allegorical name such as "Teofila" and an unconcealed historical identity. Even without allegorical naming, they may set themselves forth as a representative of humanity in its need for counsel. Yet despite this generalizing aspect, the dialogues derive a considerable energy from the intensity of the real, lived relationships and personal concerns that provoked them.

They also tend to fuse external and internal debates, much like Petrarch's famous dialogue with the ghost of Augustine. For Morata and Marguerite, the second speaker's real absence from the writer provokes a conversation that is simultaneously by two people and by one alone, talking to herself as if the friend or kinsman were near. The dialogue comes to fill a need for conversation with a trusted friend. It thus imagines with sympathy both speakers' points of view, even when one is clearly a corrective for the other. For none of these dialogues offers a truly open choice of alternatives; they aim to teach and persuade, even when the writer herself is the one in need of persuasion.

These dialogues are, moreover, a recurring site for discussion of the relationship between learning and spiritual wisdom. While Valdés, Ochino, and Marguerite emphatically downplay the need for much learning, advocating instead a simple and affective wisdom that is crucial for salvation, Morata and Matraini struggle with the role and value of their own learning, advocating its usefulness as either handmaiden (Morata) or pathway (Matraini) to a more religious wisdom. Writing for a learned readership, whether male or female, these two women felt a need to write in a manner appropriately learned and eloquent. Both cite Cicero and other classical authors along with the Bible. Their authority, as they seem to have seen it, comes from a combination of education and divine grace, with shifting emphases between those two.

Marguerite, whose emphasis is heavily on grace, presents herself in her dialogues only as the one in need of learning. Morata and Matraini, with a greater confidence in the value of their educations, offer themselves as teachers. Marguerite's self-presentation as student rather than teacher, even when she is the author of the words of both, is also possibly connected to the fact of her writing earlier in the century. In midcentury, Morata begins with a self-critical first dialogue and comes through her new reformist zeal to a more assured and teacherly position. Writing at the end of the century, when a career of both practical and spiritual instruction was becoming a new option for pious women not only within the convent but also in secular institutions,[96] Matraini is the most self-assured in her teaching role and most openly seeks the appreciation of a broad audience.

Besides the social changes occurring between the first and second halves of the sixteenth century, women who returned to the dialogue form at different times allow us a glimpse into their own inner changes. In these personal changes, we must not assume that for these writers increasing assurance was a sign of progress. While we see in the young Olympia's two dialogues a development from self-doubt to pious self-assurance, in Marguerite, who had a longer life of writing, we see a maturation from fairly clear and assured answers to a deep self-doubt, which must have seemed to Marguerite in her happier moments a step forward on the path toward the recognition of her own "Rien" and the "Tout" of God.

3 *Dialogue & Social Conversation*

Besides spiritual instruction, the two-person dialogue by women had another strong recurring use, best called feminist persuasion. Although not all of the secular dialogues by women are strictly devoted to issues that might be labeled feminist, most of them in fact deal with women's issues in one way or another. In both cases, the spiritual and the secular, we are often dealing not with a truly open and undecided argument but with an intent to change someone's mind. The women treated in this chapter are arguing for their own and other women's right to learn and to speak. Indeed, they are arguing in part for their right to argue.

Two methods combine in these women's dialogues, but one was more readily adaptable than the other. The first, associated with a type of learning from which women were generally excluded, is the *conflictus* or *altercatio*, a form that schoolteachers had long found lively and effective.[1] For Agricola humanist dialogue was disputation, and Le Caron similarly defined dialogue as "poetic disputation," that is, a mimesis of disputation.[2] It was a mode not surprisingly familiar to lawyers and thus to the women associated with lawyers. Since disputation was frequently a tool for education, the convergence of adversarial and educative functions implies some ambiguity in the relation between speakers and between writer and reader.[3] Eva Kushner (1982, 149), following the trail of the structuralist Vladimir Propp, has suggested that all relationships in dialogue can be reduced to two: "adjuvant ou opposant" [helping or opposing]. Obviously disputation implies a relationship of opposition while the educative dialogue suggests a friendly helping relationship.

Women were often in a similarly ambivalent relationship with their anticipated readers. On one hand, women often wanted to educate other women or men to change their attitudes in a way that would increase the options for women. On the other hand, knowing that feminist concerns would likely find a hostile audience in many readers, women writers could use the disputative dialogue to express all the usual and anticipated objections while still getting their own views heard. The presentation and authorization of speakers is part of a delicate negotiation between the writer and reader. Since the reader might often be expected to identify with the objecting speaker rather than with the advocate for feminism, there is in a sense a truly dialogic approach here even where there is an obvious preference for one side within the dialogue text itself; that is, the dialogue offers a way of getting the other side heard and of leaving the reader perhaps less certain than he or she was before.

As schoolmen expected to debate other schoolmen, so women most often had the opportunity to converse with other women. A number of women's dialogues use a female social visit as the frame for their discussions. We have seen in the previous chapter that Olympia Morata's dialogues are with her friend Lavinia: in the first, Lavinia seems to have dropped in on Olympia as she is studying among her books; in the second, Theophila has paid a visit to her friend Philotima at a moment when she is free from other duties. Matraini's dialogues similarly begin with her calling at the home of a female friend, although in that case the friend is out and her son becomes the participant in the conversation. Catherine des Roches's dialogue of Iris and Pasithée takes place during a visit arranged by their fathers. In the dialogue of Moderata Fonte, which we will consider in chapter 6, the group of women who gather for lunch "spesse volte si pigliavano il tempo e l'occasione di trovarsi insieme in una domestica conversazione" (1988, 14) [often seized the time and opportunity to get together for a private conversation]. This kind of framing is the female equivalent of humanist friends gathering in a garden for informal reflective talk: it is a realistic situation that can mix relaxed humor with frank and serious discussion. It has the asset of allowing women to argue freely because they are not trying to win against a man.

Another adaptable real-life model for women's participation in argument, even with men, is the witty discussions of salon life. Tullia d'Aragona and Catherine des Roches, considered in this chapter, were active members of such social gatherings, using them both as a means to learn and as a means to publicize their learning. Both wrote with the sophisticated wit of women experienced in salon conversation. Their writing reflects the tone necessary to keep a woman's arguments with men always on the edge between the serious and the socially entertaining. This engenders an ambivalent relation between speakers, who seek to persuade without offending and to amuse without conceding.

Although women were often advised to remain silent in the presence of men, certain men encouraged women's eloquence as an enhancement to the pleasures of a social evening. The Sienese Girolamo Bargagli, writing about the social entertainments of his city in his *Dialogo de' giuochi che nelle vegghie sanesi si usano di fare* (1982, 141–42), argues against the model of the silent woman and complains about women who are mute like statues, as if it were enough to be pretty. The ancients, he says, set Mercury next to Venus because beauty is enhanced by eloquence. Women who have to be begged too long to speak are tiresome: "E pensano che da purità d'animo proceda il non saper favellare tra gli uomini, ponendo alla dappocaggine il nome di onestà, quasi niuna donna si ritrovi onesta se non colei che parla solamente con la fante e con la fornaia" [And they think that not knowing how to speak among men comes from purity of mind, giving their mental poverty the name of honesty, as if no woman is considered honest except one who speaks only to the servant and the bakerwoman]. Those who say that women should not have learning and eloquence, argues his fellow Sienese Aonio Paleario, "impediscono e corrompono ogni buono e civile ordine di ben vivere" (1933, 76) [impede and corrupt every good and civil order of living well].

It is this cultured urban good life that Paleario celebrates, retrospectively mourning its loss since Siena's defeat and the oppressive empowerment of the Jesuits. His book ends with a praise of city life as the best environment for raising children who are well mannered and of noble character (1933, 103). He describes the frequency with which women of a certain class are likely to find themselves at parties, perhaps those following the meetings of the academies in which their husbands are involved; and while he considers it improper for them to recount novelle or discuss love songs "in mezzo delle ampie sale, piene d'uomini stranieri" [in the middle of broad halls filled with male strangers], he too does not want them standing mute like stones or dunces (77–80). It is a disgrace if a noblewoman knows how to converse only with servants and not with people of her own class. Conor Fahy (2000, 438–52) demonstrates the rarity of women's active participation in Italian academies; but Paleario is referring to less formal social events.

Bargagli, whose dialogue was published in 1572 but written most likely around 1563–64, records an occasion on which several women participated in a discussion comparing the tales told by men at an outdoor party of the Intronati. The telling of stories had ended with the raising of some traditional questions: which of the men in the stories had shown greater love, or greater restraint, or had lost more with the death of his beloved, or had received a better souvenir? In response to these questions, "contesero fra loro con tante leggiadria e vivezza d'ingegno che stupiti ne restarono quei che l'udirono" (1989, 229–30) [they debated among themselves with such charm and vivacity of wit that those who heard it were left in astonishment], wrote Girolamo Bargagli admiringly. The dialogue among women was clearly meant as an entertainment for the mixed gathering and, although it is presented as an improvisation, was quite possibly even prepared ahead of time as something like a dramatic performance. A similar entertainment in the French Académie du Palais was recorded by Agrippa d'Aubigné: Madame de Nevers and Madame de Lignerolles discoursed and debated on the excellence of moral and intellectual virtues, to the admiration of their audience (Le Gendre 2001, 16). While women were commonly warned not to argue publicly with men, Bargagli and d'Aubigné show women arguing with women before a mixed audience in a show of wit that, contained among women, does not threaten or compete with any man present. For Bargagli it is part of that "civil" or "urbane" good living that his fellow Sienese, Paleario, influenced by Castiglione, recalls nostalgically. For both Paleario and Bargagli, the dialogue as a written genre is connected to oral encounters in social life rather than to philosophers exchanging orations or correspondence.

Aonio Paleario's dialogue among four women, *Dell'economia o vero del governo della xasa,* written around 1530 and never published, is a totally fictive conversation at which he could not have been present,[4] since it takes place only among women; nonetheless, it involves real participants from noble or wealthy Sienese families that he knew well. Situating these aristocratic or wealthy women between men on the one hand and lowly women on the other, Paleario has the women themselves advocate a good education for girls, including the great usefulness of literacy and rhetorical skills as well as history and honorable authors both classical and modern. Since he was the humanist tutor in one of these households, we are not surprised to see him advocating the usefulness of a good education in history and rhetoric, but his inclusion of girls in these subjects, and his argument that these subjects are in fact of practical use to a woman, is a less expected position.

Women, Paleario advises, should not glory in their knowledge and show off in front of gatherings of men, asking and answering questions (this certainly sounds like a recommendation not to engage in learned dialogues with the other sex); yet a woman should know enough and speak well enough to defend her rights, for "quanti siano i danni di quei che non sanno dire le loro ragioni" (77–78) [how many harms do they suffer who are unable to speak for their cause]. The des Roches, like Christine de Pizan long before, could confirm the importance for women of being able to defend their rights in legal cases. Eloquence of this sort is presented as a practical part of women's traditional duties in maintaining the household.

Women can learn what they need, suggests Paleario, from reading books like Castiglione's *Cortegiano* and from conversation with family members and esteemed friends (1933, 77–79). They can learn these things also, we presume, from reading his own book. Since this is his only work in Italian, he clearly intended it to be read by a broader audience than his other writings, although political changes made it finally unpublishable. The speeches of its ladies offer an example of female eloquence that, because of its all-female audience, does not need to restrain itself as much as the decorously brief speech of women in mixed company, such as Castiglione's ladies. Indeed, the relation between older and younger women replaces in some important respects that between men and women at the court of Urbino. The older woman in the dialogue, like the esteemed friend, educated and well man-nered and knowing how to speak up for herself when necessary, is to be both model and tutor for the younger women. Exemplifying this idea, the two older women do most of the talking in the dialogue—which is chastely confined to a gathering of women—while "le nostre giovani," the teenage newlyweds, though invited to speak up if they disagree, chiefly listen and learn both the ideas and the eloquence.

Here, then, is a model for the education of young women through partic-ipation in social dialogues among educated and honorable ladies. Paleario's dialogue both embodies and advocates instructive conversation among intel-ligent women. It is similar to the function and model that Catherine des Roches would set forth in her educative dialogue between a wiser and a more ignorant young lady and to the long education that she received from daily conversation with her mother; and it is similar to the conversations that Morata enjoyed with Lavinia in reality and re-created in her writings.

The newlywed woman is advised by Paleario to be pleasant to the female relations of her husband and to find among them some women who can be real friends, women with whom she can "ragionando, leggendo, diportarsi" [enjoy talking and reading]. The word used for talking, "ragionando," con-tains the root of "reason" and thus implies rational conversation, as opposed to the false and empty "favolando" of which women were often accused. Paleario argues that the friendship of a cultured and honorable woman is a much better influence than conversation with corrupting friars! Nor should a lady be able to speak only with servants, washerwomen, and secondhand dealers, never raising their heads out of the mud of material needs (74–75). Paleario follows here as elsewhere the lead of Erasmus, whom he greatly admired. In Erasmus's colloquy *Virgo misogamos* (The Girl with No Interest in Marriage), a suitor attempting to persuade his beloved to marry rather than join a convent lists among the advantages of a secular life: "Et si quam videris matronam aut virginem egregie probam, ex eius colloquio fieri meliorem" (1969, vol. 3, 295) [And if you see some lady or unmarried woman of outstanding moral excellence, you can improve yourself by her conversation (110)]. This mentoring via female conversation is offered as common knowledge, not as something new or odd.[5] Paleario has developed the idea, however, by suggesting that these women will read good authors, perhaps together with other women, and talk about their reading as well as other things. He presents both the importance of rhetorical skills for women and the modeling of these skills by women for other women.

That this kind of education existed in reality as well as in theory can be illustrated from texts both Italian and French. Even in the fourteenth century Francesco da Barberino's *Reggimento e costumi di donna*, acknowledging the need of noblewomen for literacy, urged parents to hire a female teacher for their daughters in order to avoid suspicion or danger (Lenzi 1982, 198). Such female teachers must have been available, for he does not indicate in any way that finding one would be a problem. Marguerite de Navarre's sixty-seventh *Heptameron* tale recounts the life of a widow so admired by the women of la Rochelle that "volontiers luy baillerent leurs filles pour aprendre à lire et à escripre" (1967, 394) [they were glad to send their daughters to her to learn to read and write (1984, 504)]. Laura Cereta describes her own life, mentioning her education by "Foemine, consilio & religione electissime, credor, a qua erudienda, morum exercitiique disciplinam haurirem intentius" (1640, 147–48) [a woman highly esteemed both for her counsel and sanctity, whose learning, habits, and discipline I, who was to be educated, intently absorbed (1997, 25)]. Later, to avoid her languishing in idleness, her father sent her back to this admired female teacher: "liberalium studiorum praeceptrici me meae restituit" (150) [(he) soon sent me back to my instructress in liberal studies (27)]. We can think also of the experience of Catherine des Roches, educated by her mother. These schooling situations were certainly occasions for women to teach and model verbal skills to younger females.

Luisa Sigea, a Spanish humanist at the Portuguese court, having been allowed by the Portuguese Infante time to study in the royal library, composed a dialogue for her mistress in which she quotes copiously from both pagan and Christian sources; one clear aim of the dialogue, besides its appointed topic (whether the court life or private life is better), is simply—as her dedicatory letter indicates—to transmit a compendium of learned citations to the princess, whose life does not permit her so much study: "Utriusque sententiam sapientissimorum virorum dictis comprobare atque impugnare nitimur, paucis admodum ex Minerva nostra interpositis . . . ut, quorum doctrinam ab ipsis paene incunabulis voluimus, in medium proferamus . . ." (1970, 69) [We have striven to support and confirm both sides of the question with the words of the wisest men, mixing in only a few words from our own Minerva . . . so that we might make available the learning of those men that we have desired almost from our infancy . . .].[6] This is an example of a learned woman passing on part of her learning in dialogue form to another woman, whose studies she had been brought to court to assist.[7] While she can claim with proper modesty to have inserted only a few of her own words among those of wiser men, she has nonetheless produced a dialogue by a woman and between two women that runs to over a hundred pages of Latin. The copiousness of citations makes the dialogue for a modern reader rather tedious to read but is part of what Sigea announces proudly as an asset: her text will be a brief compendium for the princess of what can be found in the royal library. Janis Butler Holm (1991, 267) suggests that Vives's copious use of learned authorities conveys "the demonstration of apparent universals" and "immutable truths" shared by pagans and Christians alike; however, Sigea not only pitches these authorities against each other but even shows them in contradiction with themselves and usable for arguing both sides. Although writing in Portugal, she casts her two speakers as Italian women, the more worldly Flaminia from Rome and the more religiously minded Blessila from Siena, appropriately enough. I agree with Odette Sauvage (Sigée 1970) that Siena must be a reference to Catherine; here then is a case of a woman's dialogue aware of another woman's dialogue. Furthermore, Augustine's mother provides an explicit model for Sigea's own role as teacher although her own pupil is female like herself. My main point here in referring to Sigea's work, which is otherwise outside the geographical scope of this book, is to reinforce the notion of dialogue as offering to a female reader or conversational partner an otherwise inaccessible education. Women saw and seized upon that aspect of the genre.

If women could find among other women the opportunity for education and conversation, could they make use of these skills among men? Unlike Paleario, Bargagli does not rule out a discussion with mixed speakers. Indeed, near the beginning of his book (1982, 57), he quotes a member of the Accademia as saying: "Ma fra tutti i diporti che si possano a ricreazione de gli animi nostri ritrovare, quello della conversazione di nobili e virtuose donne par che sia il più bello e il più degno" [But among all the pastimes which can be found to give recreation to our spirits, that of conversation with noble and virtuous women appears to be the finest and worthiest]. In support of the good influence of such conversation he cites an odd pair of examples: Socrates (for his conversations with Diotima) and Cimone from the *Decameron* (5.1). Cimone is a seemingly uneducable idiot whose sudden love for Efigenia inspires him to acquire excellent learning. Thus the rude Cimone becomes refined, and the refined Socrates becomes even more elevated. The speaker goes on to say that it is because of these good effects that the founding member of the Intronati established "una certa pura e onesta dimestichezza con alquante nobili e belle donne della nostra città . . . donne d'alto intelletto. . . . Aveva la modestia del loro conversare e la bontà di quei tempi una tal sicurtà a ciascuno di loro acquistata, che continuamente e in ogni tempo eran soliti or una e ora un'altra di quelle donne di visitare, con quella libertà che a vedere una sorella si va oggi" (57) [a certain pure and honest familiarity with several noble and fair ladies of our city . . . ladies of high intellect. . . . The modesty of their conversation and the goodness of those times had gained such assurance for each of the men that they used to go frequently and at all times to visit now one and now another of those ladies, with the same liberty with which today one goes to see one's sister]. It was to entertain these ladies, who were not interested in continually dancing or playing cards, that the more intellectual games Bargagli describes in his book were brought into play. Thus we get a portrait of an urban social life that included proper women in its conversations and discussions, whether serious or playful. This same "bontà di quel tempo" is precisely what the Jesuits by 1559 would label a shameful corruption and seek to suppress, along with the suspected heresy of the academy members.[8]

Paleario's similar defense of women's participation in an urbane society goes hand in hand with his praise of a "città libera" [free city] in which the male citizens can actively participate (1933, 49–50). It also goes hand in hand with his Erasmian praises of marriage as a companionship between husband and wife. A reformer and ardent enthusiast of Erasmus, Paleario corresponded with Celio Secondo Curione, a close friend of Olympia Morata, just at the time that she too was in correspondence with him. Perhaps he heard about her, or vice versa.[9] In any case, both were members of the same reformist circles. His celebration of a "civil" society in which cultured men and women could feel trusting and free sets this Tuscan behavior against the corruption of Rome. There celibate priests and monks give in to their appetites and seduce men's wives, or worse. There fathers sell their daughters to the highest bidder without regard for the girls' happiness. There husbands, having lost "benigna loro natura . . . e la innata gentilezza" [their kind nature . . . and inborn gentlemanliness], treat even noble wives as servants and shut them up in the upper chambers (cold in winter, hot in summer) while feasting with prostitutes in the pleasanter rooms below (44–45, 53–54). But while the Romans are mere beasts, the Tuscans are superior in "umanità" (65).

Obviously many agendas are here interconnected.[10] But the descriptions of historical soirées where women might participate in the honorable and useful pastime of intellectual conversation, whether in their own homes or at more public gatherings, let us see one more aspect of the lives of at least some women that was conducive to their entering into a secular type of dialogue, either with men or with other women. We can see also the kinds of defense that could be mustered for this: that such activity is "human" when "human" is defined by reasoning and speech; that it is appropriate to distinguish the "lady" from her servants or the urban woman of culture from peasant women in the country; that it is a school for younger women in the skills they need to survive; that it is an honest recreation for men and women alike; that it turns marriage into the companionship God meant it to be; and so on.

The entertainment value made dialogue a good genre for debating—whether seriously or merely for amusement—the issues of women's equality with men; the appropriate education for women; and the ways that men and women should imagine and treat each other, in marriage or in other relationships. All of these are topics included by Paleario's group of women; they were issues that women took up as writers of their own dialogues, which they set as social conversation, whether among men or women or in mixed company.

The nostalgia with which Bargagli and Paleario wrote indicates that the social acceptability of such mixed gatherings was unstable over time. Indeed, whereas a salon life involving women flourished in France both in Paris and in the provinces, female participation in the famous salons of Italy tended to be restricted to less reputable women: poets whose honor was in question, such as Gaspara Stampa, or who were openly courtesans, such as Tullia d'Aragona and Veronica Franco. Court circles allowed more reputable mixing than urban salons; however, unlike Marguerite de Navarre, those women at the top of Italian society do not seem to have taken up the dialogue genre.

My first example of a female-authored dialogue derives precisely from the kind of salon entertainments, the dropping in of educated men on a witty woman, that Bargagli describes. This woman, however, was somewhat less proper than the ladies Bargagli had in mind: the courtesan Tullia d'Aragona. In 1542 a volume was published of the dialogues of a much-admired man of letters, Sperone Speroni. His *Dialogo di amore* includes the courtesan-poet Tullia d'Aragona as one of its speakers. Love, not surprisingly, is the main topic on which women, particularly courtesans, were presumed to have something to say. Five years later Tullia published her own dialogue on love, *Dialogo dell'infinità di amore*, in which she is again one of the speakers.[11] This pair of texts forms a dialogue of dialogues in which Tullia responds to Speroni's work.

Speroni did not make himself one of the speakers in his own dialogue; Tullia, by maintaining her presence as a speaker, inserts an authorial voice. Being a courtesan, Tullia is most interested in establishing the cultural and social (and thus also economic) level of her relationships with men. She is not concerned, like Olympia—or like Catherine des Roches, who is discussed later—with addressing other women or with teaching them, but rather with demonstrating to a male society how she would like to be perceived. This is sufficiently different from how they do perceive her, however, as to constitute what we might well call a feminist action, even though Tullia does not have women as a group at heart.

Referring several times to Speroni's text (as well as to other classical and Renaissance treatments of the subject), Tullia constructs in her own writing a very different role for herself. While admiring and respecting Speroni, she seems to have intentionally refashioned her image along more ambitious lines than Speroni allowed her. A broader feminist argument is also explicitly part of her agenda, making this dialogue not simply one about love.[12]

In Speroni's conversation, Tullia's opening lines—she gets the first word in both dialogues—welcome Nicolo Gratia or Grazia (a less known member of their circle) as the resolver of their difficulties. Grazia immediately comments on the mutual love of the disputants. The problem is indeed a result of their love: Bernardo Tasso (father of the famous epic poet, but also a poet in his own right and one of Tullia's many admirers) complains that Tullia praises him more than he deserves; he is therefore afraid that she is mistaken about him, or that she loves some idea rather than his real self, and that he will consequently lose her love: "par che ella tuttavia mi colga in iscambio, ed altri ami perfettamente, alla cui idea mi assimiglia" (1989, 1: 2) [it seems that she always takes me for another, and loves another perfectly, to whose image she assimilates me].

Tullia similarly complains that Tasso praises her more than she deserves and that she is afraid he will cease to love her when he realizes the truth, adding that she would rather be loved "sempre . . . quanto io dovrei, che troppo amata per pochi giorni" (2) [always . . . to the extent that I deserve, than loved too much for only a few days]. Both lovers thus express fear and jealousy, which they claim are inseparable from love. The other inducement of Tullia's jealousy is Tasso's imminent departure to serve the Prince of Salerno.

In sum, Tullia and Tasso are presented as a mirrorlike pair of lovers, while Signor Grazia comes, perhaps with an appropriate name, as the wise teacher to both of them. Francesco Maria Molza, another man of letters and poet of both Latin and Italian verses, occasionally joins in to help Grazia. Tullia is the main questioner although Tasso also speaks. Virginia Cox (2000, 388, 391) has pointed out that one of the major roles of women in dialogues by men is to ask questions that wiser men can answer. This is certainly Tullia's role here.

Grazia, with Molza's contributions, argues that jealousy is a defect rather than a necessary part of love; that although a man cannot compatibly love two women, he can compatibly love both his woman and his prince, duty, or honor; and that absence is good for love because it forces the lover to shift from a focus on the senses to a focus on the intellect as he or she thinks about the person who cannot be seen.[13] Thus a clear hierarchy is established between sensual and rational love, although both are affirmed as necessary aspects. This combination of the sensual and the rational in love's essential nature is pronounced by both Tullia and Tasso a monster, a sort of minotaur or centaur (13, 20). However, they come at this double image from opposite angles.

Tullia (6) protests:

Diteci in prima, come stia inseme ragione e amore; che già so io troppo bene, niuna gioia amorosa non potere esser perfetta, se ciascun senso non si congiunge al suo obietto, e si fa uno con esso lui. . . . Ma che da i sensi alla ragione faccia tragitto l'amore, io non lo provo per me, nè posso credere che sia vero; anzi a me pare, tanto esser maggiore e più fervente lo amore, quanto egli è meno dalla ragion temperato.

[Tell us first how love and reason can be together; for I know too well that no amorous joy can be perfect unless each sense joins with its object and becomes one with it. . . . But that love can pass from the senses to reason, I have not experienced, nor can I believe that it is true; rather it seems to me that the greater and more fervent the love, the less it is tempered by reason.]

When Tasso affirms that he does indeed love both her beauty and her virtues, Tullia reasserts the importance of physical presence:

Ma siate certo, che tutto che'l valor vostro sia in se molto, e degno obbietto d'ogni eccellente intelletto, tuttavia ogni'altra cosa è nulla alla vostra presenza, senza la quale mai non fia vero, ch'io mi rallegri.

[But be sure that however great your worth may be in itself, and however worthy an object of every excellent understanding, yet everything else is as nothing compared to your presence, without which I can never truly be glad.]

Moreover, she argues (7), if Grazia is right in defining perfect love as a union of the lovers, "quasi uno Ermafrodito" [like a Hermaphrodite], how can we be perfect lovers when you go off to Salerno?[14]

Tullia rejects the notion that love is a god, since it springs from the mortal sources of human beauty and human virtue. Thus it must also die when we die (14–16). Defining love as the operation established by God for the continuation of species (18), she maintains its contradiction to reason. Thus Tullia is firmly identified with carnal, sexual love and with the resistance of the flesh to accepting the sovereignty of reason. For her, human love is the same as animal love and utterly irrational.

Tasso, taking the opposite tack, comments about the centaur image of love, saying that he would rather think of his beloved as wholly divine than as half a horse (23). Similarly, Grazia concludes that Tasso's absence from Tullia will allow Tasso to write his famous love poetry, which will make both lovers and their love immortal. It is clear that Tasso's poetry is not going to emphasize the carnal side of love but rather to consist of the heavenly praises that worried Tullia at the start. The final image of the perfect lover as a Ganymede, raised from earthly to divine love, might well make a woman feel insecure, for we see how easily women can drop out of that picture altogether. Tullia is right to complain that it is easier for Tasso than for her to contemplate his departure from her. Her final observation is a stubborn protest that absence may be a good, but only if it is brief (41).

Tullia's role in this debate is defined in other ways besides her adherence to the physical. One is the open reference to her profession as courtesan. Grazia cites another writer's treatise in praise of the courtesan's life, while Tasso responds—perhaps ungallantly—with a negative view of its baseness and uncertainty. Grazia then tells Tullia that she should be pleased to be inscribed into a book like Plato's Diotima and adds her name to a list of famous literary courtesans: Sappho, Corinna, and Diotima (26–27). There are two assumptions here: first, that all these women must have been courtesans; and second, that Tullia needs to be written about in order to be famous because she cannot sufficiently write herself into immortality. Even though, like Sappho and Corinna, she has written her own poetry, she is compared most directly to Diotima and explicitly immortalized only by her appearance in another's writing. When the men then ask her for professional advice on how to make a woman return one's love, she answers like an appropriately passive and unintellectual female: "Io non so donna nata, la qual più ami di me, e meno intenda che sia amore ed amare . . . ma tutto ciò che io ne parlo, quale io l'ho letto o udito dir da qualcuno, tale il ridico" (28) [I don't know any woman born who loves more than I do and who understands less what love and loving may be . . . but all that I say about it is a restatement of what I have read or heard someone else say].

Although this may be a modesty trope, her passive role is further corroborated by what follows. Her subsequent discussion, suggesting that both male and female are lovers, produces a rebuke from Tasso: your role is to be the beloved, not to rival me as a lover, for that would be to "pervertire del tutto

la condizion delle cose" (32) [pervert the whole condition of things].
Whereas Tullia had been arguing that the lover always loves his or her own
image in the beloved, and lamenting that her canvas was not fine enough to
present a proper portrait of her beloved Tasso, Tasso insists that it is only the
male who bears this portrait of the beloved. The woman loves her own image
in the man, while he loves the good in her that he lacks. Her beauty makes
her the fit object of portraiture, while his strength makes him fit to bear the
travails of loving. If I had Tullia's qualities, says Tasso, I would be a Narcis-
sus.[15] As all actions have one of three aims, glory, pleasure, or utility, men
love for pleasure, but women for glory so that men may make known their
beauty, virtue, and courtesy. Thus women love themselves, while men love
women. The "lover" can only be male; the "beloved" is only the female
(32–35).

Tullia's presence in the conversation affects not only the contents of the
discussion but also its stylistic level. As Riccardo Bruscagli comments in his
introduction to Bargagli's *Dialogo de' giuochi* (1982, 19–22), the addressing of
games to a female public both indicates a debt to Boccaccio and also "serve
a indicare un destinatario identificato in realtà non tanto sessualmente
quanto culturalmente; serve a individuare un piano operativo non specia-
listo," a broad "schiera dei letterati" distinct from theologians, philosophers,
and lawyers, "un pubblico metaformicalmente 'femminile,' cioè proverbial-
mente digiuno di latino e di scienza" [serves to indicate a destinataire who is
really not so much sexually as culturally identified; it serves to particularize a
level of operation that is not for specialists, . . . a public metaphorically "feminine," that is, proverbially lacking in Latin and academic knowledge]. Speroni comments in his "Apologia dei dialogi" that the inclusion of an ignorant or uneducated person can be an effective way of providing contrast with
other more learned speakers, thus enlivening the dialogue (Kushner 1996,
59).

The talk in Speroni's dialogue is intentionally casual, without requiring
much learnedness in the reader or in Tullia. On the other hand, the language
remains polite throughout, neither ascending into philosophy nor descend-
ing into too common a vocabulary. The textual references are chiefly to
Petrarch's lyrics, which are treated as the authoritative Scripture on love,
and serve also as a model for tone and style. Trying to argue that love is
greater than reason, which is unjustly imposed upon it, Tullia begins to nar-
rate a myth about love's divine birth, acknowledging Molza as her model for
this kind of myth-making. Almost at once she is cut off by Signor Grazia, for
two reasons: he is afraid of the bad moral effect of her opinions on the "vol-
gari," and he ascribes to Molza, as a "vero poeta" [true poet], the special
"privilegio di dir menzogne e favoleggiare a sua voglia . . . però mentre voi

narravate le cose sue non interruppi la favola" [privilege of telling lies and fables at will . . . therefore while you were retelling things of his I did not interrupt the speech]. Tullia herself, however, has no power or right to enter the heavens with her own discourse (19). Accepting this slap, she drops her fable and gets to the point. She may be admitted into this dialogue, but her status within in it is clearly circumscribed. She may graciously ask wiser men for their opinions, but her own opinions are considered dangerous, and her attempt to imitate a "real" poet is mocked and halted.

Speroni's views on women come through clearly in his dialogue "Della dignità delle donne" (1989, 1: 46–63). While two men, speaking of "cose peravventura non vere, ma per la lor novità care molto ad udire" [things perhaps not true but enjoyable to hear because of their novelty], and "non a decider la quistione, ma a dilettar gli ascoltanti" [not to resolve the matter but to delight the audience], praise women as superior to men and protest the tyranny of husbands, the female speaker Beatrice degli Obizzi, speaking "divine parole," argues that servitude to the male is natural to women, who therefore enjoy it and—far from suffering—even glory in it. Women act well from habit rather than from understanding, and without the benefit of rational male governance, women readily decline to the bestial. Tullia may be taking on this whole broader attitude, although her attack focuses on the dialogue that gave her an opening by including her name.

Tullia d'Aragona's own dialogue announces its differences at once. When she welcomes Benedetto Varchi into her own already well-attended home, Varchi launches into praise of her salon as a place where there is always interesting discussion. She is the hostess, sought out and in control from the start. She is literally "at home" in this dialogue, not a patronized guest.

Varchi is a distinguished guest, a member of the Florentine academy, one of the better-known and well-connected men of letters of his day, to whom other writers often turned for assistance.[16] Tullia announces that Varchi may regret coming as he is going to have to listen to her:

La quale, oltra lo esser donna (le quali voi, per non so che vostre ragioni filosofiche, riputate men degne e men perfette degli uomini), non ho, come ben sapete, né dottrina di cose né ornamenti di parole. (1912, 187–88)

[not only as I am a woman—and you have some complex philosophical reasons for considering women less meritorious and intrinsically less perfect than men—but what is more, I do not possess either sufficient learning or verbal ornaments, as you are well aware. (1997, 55–56)]

The sentence pulls in several directions. On one hand, Tullia clearly rejects as suspect the male demonstrations—supposedly "scientific" but in fact subjective ("vostre") and mystifying ("non so che" implies their incomprehensibility)—of a natural female imperfection.[17] On the other hand, she confesses to the social handicap of her lack of learning. And yet, despite this handicap, she asserts her right to speak and be heard, even while acknowledging that men may not want to listen to her. Varchi is of course compelled to respond by denying any participation in the male devaluation of women and affirming his eager interest in her words.

Denigrating his own learning, he brings Speroni into the discussion in contrast to himself: "Io non mi voglio aguagliare in cosa niuna al vostro e mio dottissimo, leggiadrissimo e cortesissimo messer Sperone, né al raro ed eccellente valor del nostro signor Muzio; anzi voglio lor ceder, come è di loro merito e di mio debito, in tutto, salvo che in conoscer il pregio vostro" (188) [I don't want to set myself up in any way as the equal of our very learned, refined and gracious Signor Sperone, nor hold myself on a par with the exalted accomplishments of our dear (Girolamo) Muzio. Far from it: I wish to offer them the deference which is their due, and in every way I owe them, unless it be in the matter of appreciating your own worth (56)]. His praise of Speroni is turned into implicit criticism; Speroni is most learned but does not fully appreciate Tullia's own abilities. Tullia's admitted lack of learning comes to look like a polite rather than accurate statement as Varchi makes his similar humble self-denigration in comparison to their very learned friends. Of course, she would not have had the schooling of the males in her circle; but we will see that she has picked up quite a bit on her own.

Varchi mentions that both Speroni and Muzio have written praises of Tullia; yet he, though less eloquent, is even more admiring of her (188). Giuseppe Zonta in his notes (Tullia 1912, 362) expresses some embarrassment at the praises Tullia has orchestrated here for herself and suggests that Varchi, in editing the piece for her, must have added praises that she would not have written for herself. Possibly he did help her out in this manner, but Tullia repeatedly—in her volume of poetry as well as here—sought to position herself in the center of a circle of admiring intellectuals, whose praises legitimized her participation in their intellectual and literary exchanges. This position is important to the claims she is trying to oppose to Speroni's image of her. Georgia Masson (1975, 114–23) describes Tullia's ambition to establish herself in Florence as "the queen of an intellectual salon" and the publication of her *Rime* and *Dialogo* as a demonstration of "the rare gifts of poetry and philosophy" for which she had just been officially excused from wearing the yellow-bordered veil of a prostitute.[18]

When Tullia asks Varchi to clear up two questions that the company has been discussing, Varchi, rather than happily assuming the role of teacher, protests that he has come to listen and learn, not to teach. Finally he agrees to try to answer on condition that he will then be told in return some of the conversation he has missed (1912, 190). In sum, there is not a one-way student-teacher relationship as there was in Speroni's dialogue, but a set of equals who will instruct and learn from each other in pursuit of the truth.

The argument is truly developed jointly, not simply set forth by one speaker. After a while Tullia says: let me ask the questions for a change (208). Later Varchi expresses some uncertainty for Tullia in turn to resolve (217). Tullia gets another jibe in at men who hold forth too much. When she claims to know nothing but her own ignorance, Varchi identifies her as just like Socrates, the wisest of the Greeks. Tullia then quips (198): if you admire him so much, why don't you imitate him?

> Ché, come sapete, conferiva ogni cosa con la sua Diotima ed imparava da lei tante belle cose. . . . Fate il contrario di quello che faceva egli, percioché egli apparava e voi insegnate. (198)

> [*For as you know, he discussed everything with his friend Diotima and learned all manner of wonderful things from her. . . . (You are doing) quite the opposite of everything that Socrates did. Since he adopted a learning stance, whereas you're imparting lessons. (66)*]

But Varchi quips back: where do you think I acquired the little that I know? Indeed, it is Varchi in this dialogue who, like Tullia in Speroni's, claims that all he knows comes from what others have said or written (217). Tullia mocks him occasionally for a lack of practical knowledge (e.g., 207) and praises the value of experience, "alla quale sola credo molto più che a tutte le ragioni di tutti i filosofi" (204) [which I trust by itself far more than all the reasons produced by the whole class of philosophers (71)]. But this is not simply a woman's viewpoint, for Varchi immediately echoes, "Ed anche io" (204) [So do I]. Yet the value of logic itself is discussed and ultimately praised by both speakers as a very useful tool when not abused.

The dialogue between Varchi and Tullia continues as an equal exchange of compliments and bantering accusations, each taking a turn in questioning or answering and each, playfully but seriously, trying to win at their game of logic. Varchi laments that all women always want to win at everything. Tullia retorts that men use mystifying logic in order to win whether they are right or wrong (190, 191–92). She triumphantly catches Varchi in several contradictions, while he repeatedly resolves these contradictions by observing that the same words are being used for different meanings. Despite Tullia's disclaimer about her lack of learning, we are very quickly in the midst of philosophical vocabulary and references to Aristotle. Tullia mentions, for example, the efficient, formal, final, and material causes (195); distinguishes act and potential (216); and accepts a claim because it comes from Aristotle (219).

At the same time, Tullia flaunts her knowledge of the literature on love. Besides the references to Plato, Aristotle, Ficino, and Speroni, we find praises of Bembo's *Asolani* and, even more, of Leone Ebreo's dialogue, which Varchi compliments Tullia on having not only read but understood. Tullia here, for all her praise of experience, is not the carnal courtesan who cannot imagine what reason has to do with love. On the contrary, her discussion of love is immediately full of rational argumentation and philosophy while her profession is never mentioned. There is no need to create a casual language fit for unlearned women in order to include her in the talk. Nor need one restrict the literary references to popular poetry. She is able to talk books and logic with zest.

Her praise of Leone Ebreo's *Dialoghi d'amore* may be counterposed to Speroni's dialogue not only for its ideas about love but even more—or also—for the role it gives its woman speaker.[19] Although Sophia is not a historical woman, as her name indicates, and although she shares the general female role of asking questions in order to be taught by a more learned man, nonetheless she readily understands subtle philosophical analyses, does not balk at references to the ancient philosophers, is frequently able to make rational objections to Filone's comments, and indeed represents the very wisdom to which her lover Filone is so devoted. In fact, near the beginning of the first dialogue, he complains: "Io vengo, o Sofia, per domandarti rimedio a le mie pene; e tu mi domandi soluzione dei tuoi dubbi" [I come, O Sofia, to ask you for a remedy for my pains, and you ask me for solutions to your doubts]. She replies: "Non posso negare non abbi più forza in me, a commovermi, la soave e pura mente, che non ha l'amorosa volontà" (1929, 7) [I cannot deny that the sweet and pure mind has more power in me to move me than does the amorous will]. The male is the more passionate lover while the female is more interested in intellectual conversation. It is this image of the intellectual female that Tullia wishes to adopt for herself. She goes beyond even Leone, however, by equalizing the questioning and answering between the sexes.

Male authority, moreover, is under suspicion. The status of Petrarch as revered authority comes under attack along with sophistic logic. When Varchi cites Petrarch's verse, "un amoroso stato / in cor di donna picciol tempo dura" [Whence I know full well that the state of love / Lasts but a short time in a woman's heart], Tullia (201) responds:

Ma bisognava che madonna Laura avesse avuto a scrivere ella altret-
tanto di lui quanto egli scrisse di lei, ed avereste veduto come fosse ita
la bisogna.

*[Just think what would have happened if Madonna Laura had gotten around
to writing as much about Petrarch as he wrote about her: you'd have seen
things turn out quite differently then! (69)]*

Just as in her earlier phrase, "non so che vostre ragioni filosofiche," reasoning
is shown to be interested rather than truly universal (*vostre* ragioni), so even
the greatest love poet cannot know the whole truth about love but only his
own male point of view. Thus it is in the interest of a Socratic pursuit of
truth that women such as Tullia be allowed to speak up and participate not
only as students.

Tullia resists her identification in Speroni's dialogue with the subrational.
Her definition of love within her own conversation is not simply that of the
natural propagation of the species, as it was there, but includes the rational
aspect. For Tullia here distinguishes between animal love, which seeks generation and which she calls "volgar" and "disonesto," and a "virtuoso,"
"onesto" love, by which the lover seeks to be transformed into the beloved.
The animal love can accomplish its aim and cease, but the latter, more truly
human love can never fully accomplish its aim and thus endures (222). Love
as a desire to unite with the beautiful springs from the beauty "conosciuto e
desiderato nell'anima ed intelletto di colui che lo conosca e disidera"
(202–3) [knowledge and desire of beauty, both in the soul and in the intellect of the person who apprehends and desires it (71)]; that is, it requires the
intellect as well as the senses.

As with her comment about her own ignorance, Tullia takes her definition
of love from Socrates.[20] Perhaps she assumes that he learned it from Diotima
after all. In any case, she is not content to be the beloved object inscribed in
another's text; she can speak for herself. Diotima is here publishing her own
book on love, just as Laura is imagined publishing her own poetry.

The distinction between kinds of love raises the question about how to
classify homosexuality, which does not seek generation. This is a touchy
question for her to raise as Varchi was twice on trial for charges of homosexuality and was saved from punishment the second time (1545) only by the
intervention of Cosimo de' Medici. Possibly Tullia is giving Varchi a
response that allows him to sublimate his own recently suspect relationships.
When Varchi explains that Socrates' love for young men was not homosex-
ual in the physical sense but rather a desire to generate souls, not bodies, that
might resemble his own, Tullia inquires:

perché non si può amare anche una donna di cotesto medesimo amore; ché non penso giá che vogliate dire che le donne non abbiano l'anima intelletiva come gli uomini e non siano di una medesima specie, come ho sentito dire a certi. (229)

[I should still like to know why a woman cannot be loved with this same type of love. For I am certain that you don't wish to imply that women lack the intellectual soul that men have and that consequently they do not belong to the same species as males, as I have heard a number of men say. (97)]

Varchi's answer, that women can and should be and sometimes are loved in this manner, greatly relieves Tullia. "Racconsolata" is her word (229), as if she had been grieving at the exclusion of women from intellectual love. Not only had Plato and Aristotle assumed that only men could take part in this "amor virtuoso," but recently Speroni's dialogue, even while including her in its conversation, had again perpetrated just such an exclusion. By showing herself as seeking this kind of Socratic love and denigrating a merely animal love, she distances herself from the identity of base courtesan that Tasso had both pitied and blamed, replacing it with an identity as a member of Socrates' symposium, a salon not so different from her own.

As others join in the conversation near the end, the question arises, familiar from Speroni's dialogue, of whether lovers basically love themselves, whether all love is self-interested. This time both question and answer remain ungendered. All beings below the moon love themselves and their own interest first. If lovers are willing to die for the beloved, that is because they view this as better for themselves than living without the beloved (237–39). The issue is not turned into an assertion of male desire versus female narcissism, but into a distinction between human and heavenly love.

Finally one last stab is taken at Speroni's text. Two men begin talking about Tullia and how gracious she is to everyone. Lattanzio Benucci comments that many men who think she loves them are wrong. He comments on how lucky Tasso was in having Tullia's jealous love, as set forth in Speroni's dialogue; but Tullia replies that actually she and Tasso loved each other for their virtues and without any jealousy. Tullia ends the conversation by requesting them to talk about something other than "i casi miei" (243).[21] Clearly she is disengaging herself here from the role into which she had been put as ardent sensual lover of a particular man, present perhaps merely as his lover. Instead she circles back to the image she created at the start: a woman loved in her time by all the excellent men of letters or arms, a hostess whose house is sought out by princes and cardinals as an honored academy. In sum, she presents herself first and last as an admired member of intellectual society. She indicates that she can discuss general topics, about which she has been doing some reading, and not talk only about her own personal amatory experience. While the relationship between speakers is a friendly one within the dialogue, the dialogue itself takes on an antagonistic role to Speroni's preceding work. The references to Speroni's text, both explicit and implicit, that frame her dialogue indicate that hers is not only a joining in this game of love dialogues—although it certainly is that too—but also a critical response to the way she had been written about. It creates a dialogue of dialogues in which women—like the hypothetical Laura—write back.

A more "honest" but equally lively salon life was going on thirty years later in France, among women well acquainted with Italian humanist culture. The des Roches mother and daughter were a celebrated pair of intellectual hostesses in the town of Poitiers, which, with its university renowned especially in law, could boast of numerous well-educated professional men and men of letters. While Madeleine, the mother, twice married to lawyers, was described by a contemporary as the best-educated woman of only one language,[22] Catherine, the daughter, was learned in the classical languages as well as in French. She astonished her contemporaries by refusing all offers of marriage, asserting her desire to devote her life to her mother and her studies. Where the mother writes angrily about the impediments to her own education, the daughter gratefully enjoys the opportunity her mother has given her to devote her efforts to study. Her praises of her mother are part of a defense of her own choice of life.[23] It was a life that she not only enjoyed but wished for other women, as her writings make clear.

The des Roches's first joint volume, *Les oeuvres* (1579), includes a set of abstract debates, which I will discuss in chapter 5. Catherine's pair of dialogues in their *Secondes oeuvres* (1581) are entirely different.[24] Catherine's new interest in writing a realistic conversation among plausible human characters seems to have been due to the influence of Olympia Morata, whose name she mentions with praise in these very dialogues and whose volume of works she obviously knew. The first of the two dialogues offers examples both ancient and modern of learned women whose learning increased their virtue. The modern examples include three poets, Luisa Sigea, Laura Terracina, and Hippolyta Taurella, and one writer of more varied production, Olympia Morata.[25] The combination of these last two names indicates that Catherine was acquainted with the volume of Morata's works, which oddly includes at the end the epistolary poem of Taurella to her husband specifically mentioned in Catherine's dialogue.[26] The volume of Morata's *Opera omnia*, printed in Basel four times (1558, 1562, 1570, 1580), contains poems; letters; and, in all but the earliest edition, Olympia's two dialogues. These dialogues were, therefore, available to Catherine as models of a woman's humanist dialogue between female speakers.[27] Morata's influence seems to have come to Catherine between the writings of her first and second volumes.

The classical model for this more personal and seemingly historical writing, for Morata and others, was above all Cicero. Yet this classical model precisely allowed writers the expression of their own contemporary situations and perspectives, even while giving a classical authorization for this personalization. If Catherine's earlier material came from Plutarch, Plato, and Pliny, the later material came—like Morata's—from her own contemporary world and personal concerns.

It is particularly the first of Morata's dialogues, where the superior value of a life of study over the usual female life of frivolity is advocated, that seems to have provided a model for Catherine's own. Olympia's first dialogue opens with the image of Olympia studious among her books, the very self-image dear to Catherine. It defends and justifies this activity for women on several grounds. It also notes the resistance to it from both men and other women and their concern that the learned woman will turn away possible suitors. At this point in her life, Olympia had just married a man who admired her learning, so she could triumphantly dismiss such fears, happy to have attracted the right sort of man and not one of those who would prefer, as her critics kept arguing, a wealthy woman to a learned one. Olympia modestly deflects Lavinia's praises for her studious zeal and virtue and is admonished by Lavinia to turn from an emphasis on humanist learning, with its implicit goal of worldly fame, to a new emphasis on religious learning, with its reward of eternal life. By crediting Lavinia with an efficacious and virtuous influence, the dialogue presents one learned woman as a teacher of the other, encouraging her studies and leading her onward through such studies toward more spiritual concerns. Not only the topic but the model of a dialogue in which two female friends converse on a number of topics of interest to Catherine must have shown her how an Italian version of the dialogue genre could be put to use to further her agenda.

Although the des Roches saw the Protestant faction in France as the enemy, especially after the destruction wrought by the Huguenots during civil war in Poitiers, Catherine could on several grounds have overridden religious difference and identified with the vehemently reform-minded Olympia Morata. First, Olympia was herself a victim of religious civil wars, describing her family's sufferings vividly in the letters that Catherine would have read in the volume of Olympia's works. Several letters report how Olympia, her husband, and her little brother fled for their lives, barefoot and feverish, while all their possessions, including all her books and papers, were burned in the fire that swept through their city. Two of the des Roches properties were similarly destroyed by fire during religious war, although the family household itself was unharmed. Second, Olympia was, like Catherine, a middle-class learned woman, well versed in classical languages and texts and defending her learning on moral grounds as good for women. Third, she was writing as a woman to a woman, presenting a world of female bonding and mutual support familiar to Catherine from her own relationship with her mother. Reading Morata's dialogue as a learned woman of the sort to whom it was addressed, Catherine could respond to it with her own imitations and elaborations, which, however, she takes in a more secular and witty direction.

Catherine's dialogues are clearly connected with each other by both theme and speakers, for the two girls, Iris and Pasithée, who converse in the second are the daughters of the two men, Sevère and Placide, who argue in the first. How girls should be raised and how they should spend their time is the theme of both encounters. The fathers are free to meet on the street; but the daughters, like Olympia and Lavinia, meet indoors at Pasithée's home. Just as Olympia introduces herself in the first dialogue as busy with her books, so Pasithée is described by her father in Catherine's first dialogue as sitting alone in her room with "les belles sentences de Plutarque et de Seneque" (1998, 192) [the fine sayings of Plutarch and Seneca] as well as with musical instruments. As Olympia recalls the recurrent criticisms of her studies by both men and women, so both the father and mother of Iris resist the notion of allowing their daughter to read: the father, Sevère, because he thinks her incapable and, if not, fears reading will make her rebellious against men; the mother because she sees no need for her daughter to have an education that she herself never received. Placide defends the education of his daughter Pasithée as a virtuous occupation of idle time and a morally good influence. Olympia's reference to her talents and desires as God-given is omitted because the issue for Catherine has become not only whether she herself has been right in devoting her time to studies but whether women more generally should do the same.

Where Tullia took on male opponents (her argument with Speroni being deflected to her more mutually respectful conversation with Varchi), Catherine presents men and women in separate conversations. Showing this dispute among males is in itself a strategy for breaking down the claims that women's restricted role is the result of a monolithic agreement among men. It converts a conflict between men and women into a conflict between men, thus both defusing the woman's intervention and masculinizing the authority of her self-defense. Male anxiety is deflected by turning the debate into an argument among men rather than an attack on men.

The real reader, whether male or female, is expected either to identify with Placide and enjoy the mockery of Sevère or to be initially in agreement with Sevère and need Placide's combination of friendly reasoning and satiric jabbing to be persuaded to consider the alternative. The possibility of a hostile audience beyond the text and the presence of this hostile audience within the text, as well as the perspective of the male Placide, keep the argument within fairly conservative bounds, stressing that a girl's education will serve traditional values.

Yet Catherine's more worldly concerns relative to Morata become evident not only in the omission of God from her justifications for female study but also in the practical nature of the learning that Placide advocates: not only moral essays and Scripture but also a smattering of law and medicine for their needed application to a woman's life. The lengthy lawsuits in which Catherine's mother was involved had persuaded Catherine of a woman's need for some knowledge of law.

The question of how education will affect a woman's marriage is raised by both the fathers and the daughters, as in Morata's dialogue, but the two generations express slightly different aspects of the problem. Sevère does not question whether learning will drive away suitors, for he views marriage as something that he will arrange rather than something that the youngsters will choose for themselves. His worry is that learning will make a woman into a proud and ornery wife. Placide's counterargument is therefore that a learned woman will make a better, more obedient, reasonable, and loving wife. Placide points out that ignorant women are already proud, resistant, and capable of tricking their husbands, the things Sevère fears learning will produce. Moreover, he argues that education actually increases rationality; therefore men—like Sevère—who complain that women are subrational "beasts" (193, 196) yet refuse to educate them are creating their own problem.[28] Sevère has been punished for his own attitudes by finding himself irritatingly bound for life to "une sotte" (212) [a fool].

Iris's concern, unlike her father's, is not whether she will become a better wife but whether she will attract a husband at all, since the men she knows mock learned women (246). Pasithée therefore argues separately in the following dialogue, not that learning will produce a better wife but that it will attract a different and better type of husband, one more serious and thus faithfully affectionate. This is not a contradiction to her father's view but its complement. Just as Placide aims his persuasions at the concerns of Sevère, so Pasithée aims hers at the concerns of Iris, arguing that the activity of reading will (a) solve her problem of boredom (236); (b) reduce the scolding of her parents (236); (c) please her current beau, who has shown her a book (240); (d) create a lasting beauty unlike the fading physical beauties—to which a thwarted suitor has called Iris's anxious attention (241, 246); and (e) win a man who because of his own learning makes a better and more faithful lover (250). In sum, where the woman has been properly educated, suggests Catherine, both she and the sort of man attracted to her are likely to be better people, and the marriage is therefore more likely to be a happy one. Ultimately this is what both father and daughter wish for, though from different points of view.

Although Iris fears that learning will discourage her boyfriends, Pasithée urges her to reject her current suitors, who are satirically portrayed, and to wait for "Eucrit," "un homme discret" whose name means good judgment. He will be able to offer a marriage of affection and respect, such as Morata in fact enjoyed and celebrated in her letters. This argument resembles Morata's concerning the service that a woman's learning performs in discouraging men who seek merely physical or material goods and encouraging a man appreciative of mental qualities. Study by the woman will not frighten all men away, as people claim, but only ignorant men, and will attract a better, wiser husband.

I think Ann Rosalind Jones (1993, 219–21) goes too far in claiming that men in general fare badly in these dialogues, being the objects of Pasithée's and Catherine's satiric mockery. Both Placide and Eucrit imply by their presence that there are good men, whether good fathers or good husbands. Iris may be unable to win Eucrit's interest in her current condition, but he is presented as a desirable mate.

Iris's real problem in regard to marrying the right man is not only her own ignorance, however, but also her father's focus on material interests; he has therefore rejected the men his daughter likes in order to find a husband with money. He states quite frankly near the start of the fathers' conversation that he loves no one but himself and sometimes no one at all (188); he certainly shows no concern for his daughter's happiness. His primarily economic focus appears similarly in his response to the suggestion that women be allowed to read the Bible: "Vous mocquer. Apprendront-elles la Theologie, pour se presanter en chaire, faire un sermon devant le peuple, acquerir des benefices?" (199) [You're kidding. Shall they learn Theology so that they may present themselves in the pulpit, give a sermon before the crowd, and acquire a few benefices?]. Theology for him is merely a career. Placide needs to remind him that religion has value for the private person, not just as a source of income. The argument here, then, is not simply about the way to raise women but about the significance for both sexes of moral, intellectual, and spiritual values beyond the merely material. Catherine requires this pair of dialogues to address the problem of women's situation on both fronts and to make her case separately to two different audiences.

Jones (1993, esp. 217–21) has suggested that the dialogue between daughters subverts that between fathers; for while Placide argues that an educated woman will make a better wife, Pasithée suggests that women might be better off doing without men altogether.[29] One should note, however, that Placide already implies this possibility and that Pasithée, conversely, offers the possibility of a good husband in Eucrit. Placide, while seeking to assuage Sevère's fears, also fulfills some of his worst ones by indicating that learned women will either live honestly without a husband, avoiding love altogether, or will sweetly "gouvernent" their husbands: "Toutes leurs gentillesses ne servent pas à gaigner des Maris, mais font que sans en avoir, elles se déportent honnestement, ou en aiant, les gouvernent paisiblement" (216). By ending his catalog of learned women with a eulogy and lament for the "belle, chaste, et sçavante Diane," a name that while referring to a real married woman, Diane de Morel, certainly also evokes the goddess famous for living independently in a world of armed females and avoiding the sight of men, Placide summons up at the very end of the dialogue the image of the independent female: "O belle, chaste, et sçavante Diane, puisse ta vive lumier longtans eclairer les tenebres de mes propos . . . " (222) [O beautiful, chaste, and learned Diane, may your lively light long brighten the darkness of my discourse . . .]. His image of light in the darkness reinforces the connection with the lunar goddess Diana. He defines his aim for his daughter as one of nourishing her in a "chaste-gaie solitude" (217), where she will be happy with or without a man.

If Catherine des Roches read Morata's letters in the volume of her works—though the idea is present also in Morata's first dialogue—she would have known that Olympia did truly find a husband who valued her for the same qualities for which she valued herself and who enabled and encouraged her to continue her pursuit of study and writing even after marriage. In any case, despite Catherine's own rejection of marriage, Pasithée does not rule out the possibility of a happy marriage for an educated girl. Moreover, in arranging her volume for publication, Catherine repeated the pattern of the first volume by following her dialogues once again with an exchange of poems between Sincero and Charite. Their mutual love, including Sincero's praises for her reading and writing (1998, 263), illustrates the kind of affection possible between more enlightened persons. The chief differences between the two dialogues in this volume are caused by the addressees, who need to be brought by different means to the same conclusion: that women should be encouraged to read.

Although Catherine would not have known Matraini's dialogue, which was published two decades later (nor was Matraini likely to have known the des Roches's volumes), both share the justification of study as natural to any rational creature, rather than emphasizing, as did Morata, an uncommon individual desire implanted by God. Both des Roches and Matraini show how a teacher can arouse the natural curiosity even of people who have not previously had an interest in studies. This goes further than Morata's defense of her own intellectual pursuits and advocates awakening others to become appreciative of what education can offer.

Pasithée willingly takes on the role of female educator, adapting her strategies to the needs and perspectives of her pupil. Far from knowing Latin like Lavinia, Iris can barely read at all. She is not the hostile audience that her father represents; rather she is simply caught up in a traditional mode of living and unable to imagine clearly what the alternative might be. Moreover, she is the sort of person who wants life to be fun and is therefore not readily attracted by any kind of life that sounds too sober and difficult. Since this pupil is much more ignorant and flighty than Philotima, she is treated to songs, poems, and salon games rather than sermons and scriptural citations. Indeed, just as Pasithée does not go out to reach Iris but allows Iris to come to her, so too she spends much of the time, especially at first, listening to Iris and drawing her out so that she will know how best to address her; she does not launch into didactic speeches. Iris, from her own account, has never had anyone take her seriously enough to listen to her problems as she sees them. Pasithée finally diagnoses the chief problem as sheer boredom, which Iris's series of hapless flirtations has been an attempt to fill. Therefore Pasithée offers a lesson in self-esteem and the values of education rather than in piety. Yet she simultaneously fulfills her father's proud claim by using both her learning and these entertainments to support a conservative agenda: obedience to one's parents, chastity, and a willingness to stay in one's room rather than gad about.[30]

Catherine's two speakers have apparently just met, and their dialogue remains unresolved. Iris at the end is torn between her desire to hear more from Pasithée and her for the moment more pressing desire to rejoin her boyfriend waiting below. The spatial hierarchy is significant: Pasithée is "higher" than Eole; but Iris goes down, promising to come back up later. This reversal of the usual gender hierarchy repeats, perhaps, Placide's—to Sevère outrageous—claim that study is even more proper to women than to men: "Ces Philosophes avoient opinion que les personnes moins polues estoyent plus capables des disciplines. S'il est ainsi, les Femmes et Filles sont plus dignes des letres que les Hommes, pour estre plus sobre, chastes et paisibles" (192) [These philosophers held the opinion that persons less polluted were more capable of learning. If that is true, then women and girls are more worthy of letters than men, because they are more sober, chaste, and peaceable].

Unconvinced but intrigued, Iris promises to return for another conversation. Like Morata's dialogue of Theophila and Philotima, des Roches's second dialogue ends with a promise of further talk. We are left guessing whether Iris will be altered by repeated contact with her new friend or whether she will soon lose interest in this passing fancy and remain as she is. But we are induced to hope that she will change; that is, we are induced to see that she would be better and happier if she did. We are not required to see her actual conversion in order to be persuaded ourselves by des Roches's eloquent presentation.

But we also see how difficult it is for Pasithée to overcome the influence of Iris's parents. Significantly, the second dialogue begins with Pasithée's praise of inconstancy, for the "inconstancy" of Sévère (of which his daughter complains) is simply the possibility for change that has allowed him to be at least partially persuaded by Placide (224). So too, if Iris is as she is by fixed nature—as her father tends to think—nothing will help her; but if Placide is right that education actually changes people, then the possibility of change is to be welcomed and pursued. Of course the praise of inconstancy, like the assertion that learning is more appropriate to women than to men, is in the vein of Renaissance paradoxes and as such can be dismissed as witty virtuosity. Nonetheless, these claims contribute to the serious argument. Whether the audience for this dialogue is sympathetic or hostile, male or female, he or she is given to see the effects of the two kinds of upbringing in the behavior of the two girls. Anne Larsen (1999, 55–56) emphasizes the importance in the eyes of des Roches of a supportive family environment for women's development, set forth in the contrast between Catherine's own upbringing and the "dysfunctional" and discordant family life in which Iris has been raised.

Although Catherine has chosen mythical rather than either historical or allegorical names, Pasithée's advice to Iris resembles both of Morata's dialogues: a conversation between two friendly women at the home of one of them, and an argument that for women as for men attention to the mind is better than attention to physical and material goods. Whereas Olympia, however, repeatedly acknowledges like a good Protestant her own foolishness and vulnerability and thus her dependence on God, Pasithée seems quite self-sufficient and self-satisfied. "Decorez vostre Esprit de Vertus et de Grace" (246) [Adorn your spirit with virtues and grace], she says, without suggesting in the least that "Grace" requires divine action. This is a different sort of grace, the sort implied by her own name as one of the three classical Graces.[31] The model she offers Iris is not the biblical Esther saving God's people but the humanist Cassandra Fedele, admired and praised by the learned men of her time (246).

This sort of humanist admiration Olympia had experienced at the court of Ferrara and had abandoned as a kind of vanity perilous to her soul. The intellect may be better than the body, but for Morata it is still not enough. The image of fading flowers, which was used in a letter by the humanist Celio Calcagnini to praise Morata's cultivation of lasting beauties of the mind in preference to the ephemeral ones of the body,[32] is reworked by Morata in her dialogue to refer to lasting spiritual benefits in contrast with the ephemeral intellectual glory of her position at court. Both women seek an independent position that will allow them to pursue what they love, but Catherine feels capable of doing this with the support of her mother rather than of God.

Catherine's recommended readings, set forth in the fathers' dialogue, share Morata's classical humanism but not her shift toward a more religious focus. Both agree that women should read the Bible for themselves, but Catherine does not suggest the subservience of classical studies to a religious end. Her focus on this world leads to her recommendations of medicine, law, and music. Nor does she in any way indicate that her own talents or desire for learning are unusual or have a divine source; they are simply natural to the human animal with its rational faculty. Placide emphasizes this natural-ness (201, 217), in contrast to Sévère's notion that learning in women pro-duces either a monster (195) or a miracle (217). Only envy and fear keep this human nature from being allowed to develop in females. Thus where Olympia sees herself as unusual and her desire for learning as something peculiar to her and perhaps not for everyone, Catherine seems to feel that other women would be like her if only their situations allowed it. She is much more eager, like her mother, to attack the deprivation of education from which women suffer as a class. Olympia puts her learning to the service of God and the reformation of religion; Catherine puts hers to the service of feminist social change and the reformation of the way women are raised and thought about.

A prior model that may well have influenced both Morata and des Roches is Erasmus's *Colloquies*. "The Abbot and the Learned Lady," with its defense of women's studies, would certainly have pleased both women.[33] Moreover, Erasmus's "Coniugium" (Marriage) colloquy is a conversation between two women, one of whom gives advice to the other on how to reform her hus-band by being a good, patient wife, while her pupil-friend argues back but ultimately agrees to give this advice a try. Catherine des Roches knew at least Erasmus's *Adages*, published in Paris in 1570 (Larsen cited in des Roches and des Roches 1998, 28). What both Morata and des Roches added to this Erasmian precedent, whether they knew it or not, was a conversation between two women not primarily about their marriages but about their need for intellectual and spiritual development.

Erasmus said in his work on the instruction of boys: "at homines, mihi crede, non nascuntur, sed finguntur" (1969–77, 1.2: 31.21) [men, believe me, are not born but made]. Without education, men would be like wild beasts. Erasmus goes on to say that boys therefore might as well at an early age be reading bits of history or fables by the poets rather than being filled with and shaped by "the ridiculous tales of crazy old women, or learning and swallowing down the absurdities of some little woman" (1.2: 69.9–19):

> Quid enim obstat quo minus eadem opera discat aut lepidam ex poetis fabellam, aut festivam sententiam, aut insignem historiolam, aut eruditum apologum, qua cantionem ineptam, plerumque et scurrilem, qua ridenda delirantium anicularum fabulamenta, qua meras muliercularum imbibunt et ediscunt nugas? Quantum somniorum, quantum inanium aenigmatum, quantum inutilium naeniarium de lemuribus, spectris, larvis, strigibus, lamiis, ephialtis, sylvanis ac daemogorgonibus, quantum inutilium mendaciorum ex vulgaribus historiis, quantum deliramentorum, quantum nequiter dictorum, etiam viri memoria tenemus quae puelli a thattis, auiis, mammis ac puellis colo assidentes, et inter complexus ac lusus audiuimus?

> [For what impedes him from learning from the same work either a charming poetic fable, or a cheerful bit of wisdom, or a famous anecdote, or a learned narrative, rather than swallowing and learning an inept song—and many of them are scurrilous—or the ridiculous fictions of crazy old women, or the empty trifles of a little woman? How many dreams, how many inane riddles, how many useless nursery songs about ghosts, specters, phantoms, witches, vampires, incubi, woodland gods and demons, how many useless lies and vulgar tales, how many insanities, how many naughty sayings, we retain in our memory even as adult men that we heard as boys among the embraces and games of idle women, from nurses, grandmothers, mothers, and servant girls as we clung to their necks?]

Erasmus sets up a rivalry between the education delivered by a male teacher, full of useful truths, and that delivered by women, useless, even immoral, and untrue. History and moral aphorisms belong to the realm of men, silly songs and superstitious tales to the realm of women. Erasmus's project is to rescue boys from this pernicious female influence. The powerful and lasting effect of women's influence makes it all the more dangerous. The notion that women, like men, are made and not born is totally absent here, despite the influence of Thomas More and the example of More's daughters. Yet Erasmus urges repeatedly that learning be made fun for young boys through conversations and games that draw them through their childish interests into new areas of knowledge.

Catherine seems to agree with Erasmus concerning the shaping powers of education, though certainly not with his sentiments of scorn about learning from women, and she agrees also with his general technique of teaching through a kind of playing. She believes that by education she can alter the views and desires of Iris, or women like Iris, and change her from the sort of woman that Erasmus scorned into someone worthy of his respect. Her dialogue offers a kind of female school, with female teachers who can cite both the classics and Scriptures and who urge other women to read these texts. Iris exclaims as she is leaving, "Je viendrois tous les jours à votre école, si j'avois loisir!" (261) [I would come every day to your school if I had the leisure!]. The implication is that women, even those who seem frivolous, naturally find learning of interest if it is offered to them in a friendly manner. Anne Larsen (1999, 68; des Roches 1998, 50) connects this phrase with the observation by Estienne Pasquier in one of his letters, that the des Roches's salon was a "vraye escole d'honneur" [a true school of honor] from which all participants left "ou plus sçavant, ou mieux édifié" [wiser or better edified]. In both situations we have a learning that takes place through social conversation, as Paleario urged.

The learned female teacher may be better able than the male to make the female pupil feel capable of learning. Pasithée's presence as a model and her interest in helping Iris develop are just as important as the specific content of what she says. Like Pasithée, Catherine in both dialogues manages to maintain a playful humor along with Morata's serious didacticism. She is trying to teach her audience by engaging them in a delightful scene.

Madeleine Lazard offers, I think, too pessimistic a reading (1985, 114): "Mais elle [Pasithée] parle en vain et reste seule, comme Catherine, entre son luth et ses livres. Résignation désabusée et aussi constat d'échec: la solitude guette la femme qui tente par la culture de gagner son indépendance" [But she speaks in vain and remains alone, like Catherine, among her lute and books. Disillusioned resignation and also the ascertainment of being in check: solitude lies in wait for the woman who tries through culture to win independence]. This reading ignores both the real possibility that Iris will return to revisit Pasithée and Catherine's sense of community with her mother rather than of total isolation with her books.

This emphasis of both Morata and des Roches on the importance of bonds between women runs counter to a notion that has been expressed with regard to female lyric poets (Jones 1986, 80): "And although women poets occasionally open or close their collections with appeals to women readers, it is very rare to find them acknowledging or taking encouragement from other women poets. Their models and their judges are men." While this observation may be largely true, the importance of women writers for each other is an area deserving of considerable further attention. Certainly women, including poets, writing during the sixteenth century continually referred to each other as fortifying examples for their own enterprise.[34] Surely they had a considerable interest not only in knowing each other's names but also in acquainting themselves with each other's writings when possible. What a delight it must have been for Catherine des Roches to discover the dialogues of other women. As we shall see in chapter 5, she knew not only Morata's work but also Labé's. Given the wide range of forms and genres that she attempted, it is not surprising that she wanted to try out her own versions of both these models.

Catherine especially, in the unusual position of having had her education fostered by her mother rather than her father or another male family member, was particularly eager to claim the possibility of living in a world of woman-to-woman education and assistance. Her well-known refusals to marry in order to remain living with her mother and her recurrent poetic theme of Amazons or other women's communities (e.g., in the *Agnodice*) were part of an insistent desire, visible also in her second dialogue, to mark a separate female space within which one could see what a woman was capable of.

Placide in good humanist fashion stresses the importance of examples: the texts he recommends will offer women good examples to follow, and indeed his own discourse lists examples of women whose learning was combined with virtue and marital devotion. Pasithée is important as a living example for Iris, who otherwise cannot imagine the alternatives for herself. Both Catherine des Roches and Morata had the happy experience—unlike some earlier humanist women praised ambivalently as monstrous or miraculous prodigies[35]—of knowing personally other learned women with whom they could carry on intellectual conversation; besides her mother, Catherine addresses some of her poetry to a female cousin known to have written both verse and prose (des Roches and des Roches 1998, 70–71). Their dialogues both represent and encourage a system of women teaching women. If Catherine's dialogues were truly influenced by Morata's, then they also embody precisely the kind of female influence that they advocate.

In some ways Catherine is more conservative than Tullia. Her men and women converse separately, the men on the street, the women in one of their rooms. The male argues rationally; the female needs to be engaged more indirectly. In other ways, however, we can see how much more radical Catherine's project is than Tullia's. Where Tullia focuses on her own image from a combination of personal pride and the economic necessity to maintain her status as a highly cultured courtesan, Catherine focuses on the plight of young women more generally. Thus where Tullia uses her own and her friends' own names, Catherine makes her characters more general through names derived from descriptive terms or myth. Her argument attacks the entire traditional social system that leaves women ignorant and bored, using them merely as passive objects in a male-to-male negotiation for wealth. She tries to indicate that educating women will make both men and women happier, whether together or separately, and she has the audacity to suggest that women might even live very well without men. Yet, like Tullia, she remains amused and amusing as well as seriously engaged in her writing. Both women present a plausible social occasion for their speakers and write with the liveliness of real conversation. Writing is a way to capture the kind of exchange and influence possible for women in live social situations within a private home and to offer such exchange and influence to a wider audience, whose members are expected to confirm the rightness of their case.

4 Dialogue & Letter Writing

W omen's sense of the dialogue genre frequently drew from and gave back to the stream of correspondence. We have seen how for Marguerite de Navarre part of a real exchange of letters was reworked into a dialogic dream poem, turning a correspondence with the living into a dialogue with the dead. This written text paradoxically presents as an oral conversation what was originally part of a written correspondence. Yet the letters to and from Briçonnet filled in for his inability to be present in person at the time of her grief. The dialogue thus seeks an orality and presence not offered by correspondence. At the same time it fills in for the failure of conversation caused by the death of her niece. Writing and face-to-face speech substitute for each other in both directions.

Somewhat similarly for Morata, dialogue was composed in the context of an interruption of correspondence and sent in a letter complaining that she had not heard back from her friend. With correspondence made difficult by war, and having a strong desire to communicate with Lavinia, Morata wrote both voices. Implicitly she traces the sad trail from live conversation to correspondence to a written dialogue that fills in where the other two have failed.

Letter writing had long been one of the acceptable forms of writing for women. Women had practical reasons for writing to their husbands or children or to those who sought their intercession or assistance. Under the influence of humanism, the letter readily became a literary form in which women felt they could participate. Already in the fifteenth century, Latin letters by young humanist women were circulated among male readers. Laura Cereta, Cassandra Fedele, and Isota Nogarola even collected their letters into manuscript volumes as a kind of limited publication.[1] The humanism of women manifested itself in vernacular letters as well as in Latin, as with Helisenne de Crenne's published volume of *Epistres familieres et invectives* (1539), which will be discussed in this chapter. Besides these showpieces of learning and style, some women also collected the practical letters that they wrote in the vernacular to family members and friends. Olympia Morata's letters, mostly in Latin but some, to her sister, in Italian, were collected along with her other writings and printed repeatedly after her death in 1555. Chiara Matraini during her life published a similar volume combining her letters and poetry (1595, 1597). Madeleine and Catherine des Roches were the first women in France to publish a collection of their French letters, appropriately called *Missives* (1586), which had actually been sent as real letters and not invented for publication. These volumes usually included letters to women as well as men, displaying a network of literate connections across both genders. The sixteenth-century volumes of letters mentioned here are all by women who also wrote dialogues.

The humanist education of many of our women writers inclined them to look to letters as a model for dialogues of persuasion. Poliziano indicated the closeness of the two forms, citing classical sources for the idea that "Epistola velut pars altera dialogi" (Forni 1992, 251) [a letter is like one part of a dialogue]. This phrase was often repeated by other humanists in the course of the following century. Petrarch in his letters, both prose and metrical, had already made use of imagined dialogue with his addressee (Bernardo 1951, 1953), and other humanist letter writers followed suit. Carla Forni (1992, 251–59) suggests that the humanist link between these genres was based on their continual need for personal intellectual discussion and exchange. Poliziano, Sigonius, and others distinguished the two genres, however, by advocating the need for a more careful and polished style in letters, which are written with time for reflection, than in dialogues, which aim to convey the spontaneity of real conversation. Torquato Tasso, citing the examples of Plato and Cicero, proposed on the contrary that letters and dialogues should be written in the same polished style, especially as one is almost a part of the other.[2]

Since the humanist letter came to prominence well before the dialogue, the earliest efforts of women to make a dialogic use of the letter began in the fifteenth rather than the sixteenth century. The most literal embodiment of the enduring notion that letters are part of a dialogue can be found in Laura Cereta's letter to the fictionally named "Europa solitaria" (1487–88), which claims to be a response to Europa's letter about the joys of staying in the tranquil countryside instead of returning to town (1997, 123–28).[3] Cereta amply describes the sentiment of her friend as if referring to the letter received from her and then responds with counterarguments: that an "empty restfulness" is not to be preferred to a more active life of struggle among the troubles of life. By presenting both sides of the issue sympathetically, though clearly arguing for one side, she turns a letter into a dialogue between female friends on the relative merits of a more public or private life. The letter itself, hovering between public and private communication, well suits the topic of discussion. It also situates the correspondents separately in the town and in the country, while each argues for the superior benefits of the other's situation. Cereta thus presents as a letter a discussion between two young women about the options available to them and the goals they might have.

This same topic was, half a century later, treated in a full dialogue form by the Portuguese Luisa Sigea. In both cases, the dialogue is between two women, who compare the active and contemplative or public and private life in terms of the options available to women. Sigea, who was at court, argues strongly for a more private life, while Cereta, living the more private life of a woman at home, argues for maintaining an engaged life in the city rather than retiring to a quiet life in the isolated countryside. Since Sigea is at court, she can present her dialogue as a conversation between women at the court. Since Cereta is at home, she uses the letter form to connect herself to another female friend.

For Isota Nogarola, another fifteenth-century writer, a real exchange of letters became in itself a dialogue, as we shall see. Ludovico Foscarini, who suggested the publication of their correspondence as a dialogue, obviously shared the humanist view that the two genres were closely related, merely carrying on the conversation by paper rather than in person. In the sixteenth century, Helisenne de Crenne's invective dialogue consisted of a fictional exchange of letters between an estranged couple who no longer speak to each other. As with Nogarola, this exchange of letters is in itself the dialogue; but as with Cereta, the received letter is probably a fiction used as the spur to a response that is almost more essay than letter. Thus we will see that early dialogue writers among women demonstrate especially close connections between the two genres.

In a debate by Isota Nogarola and Ludovico Foscarini, "On the Equal or Unequal Sin of Adam and Eve," the law-trained Foscarini, who wrote his own parts of the debate, is both the opponent in a dispute and the teacher in an exercise to train Nogarola, whose intellectual abilities he clearly admired.[4] The fact that their topic is the relative sinfulness of Adam and Eve whets the disputative edge of their debate. Yet comments of mutual friendship and benevolence throughout the exchange temper this opposition with encouragement and suggest that Foscarini is simply helping Nogarola to sharpen her wits.

This dialogue, although published as a unit with a title, consists of an exchange of actually sent letters between the two debaters, and the speakers internally refer to their statements as written rather than spoken. Nogarola, for example, ends her first statement: "Haec ut tuae voluntati morem generem, scripsi, cum timore tamen, quia non hoc opus femineum est; sed tu pro tua humanitate, si quid inepte scriptum invenies, emendabis" (1886, 2.191) [I have written this because you wished me to. Yet I have done so fearfully, since this is not a woman's task. But you are kind, and if you find any part of my writing clumsy you will correct it (King and Rabil 1983, 61)]. Foscarini does indeed encourage her to continue writing: "et ne timeas et aude multa, quia plurima optime didicisti et doctissime scribis" (2.191) [and do not fear, but dare to do much, because you have excellently understood so much and write so learnedly (63)]. Actually he too apologizes for the clumsiness of his own writing and hopes in turn that she will improve it: "Atque ea si ineptissima erunt, tuo studio facies ingenio, virtute, gloria tua esse dignissima" (2.215) [And if what I have written is clumsy, by your skill you will make it worthy of your mind, virtue, and glory (69)]. If she fears her writing is "inepta," he suggests that his own may be "ineptissima." If she feels that he is merely being kind to her, he assures her that he is a true admirer of her abilities. Thus he establishes a parity between them.

Foscarini was indeed an enthusiastic, affectionate, and admiring friend of Nogarola, as his many letters to her attest.[5] Their friendship began when the Venetian statesman arrived in Verona as the new governor in 1451 and was sent a welcoming letter by Nogarola, who thus boldly took the first initiative in their acquaintance. She had by then been writing for at least fifteen years and had been already widely praised by contemporaries. Letters from Foscarini a few years later, sent to her after his move to Brescia, describe how much more he enjoyed the visits and conversations at her home than all the sumptuous public dinners and parties that his position forced him to attend. He describes their talking late into the night—in the presence of Isota's brother—and credits her influence with making him more desirous of a good and blessed life (epis. 56, 2.35–38). His immersion in worldly affairs makes him weep or become angry with himself when he compares his life to the detached and contemplative piety of Isota's (epis. 70, 71; 2.103–7, 108–11). He writes about their friendship: "Sit inter nos doctrinae, probitatis . . . [sic] morum contentio, quibus honestissimus amor coepit excrevitque nulla utilitatis spe, nulla voluptatis cogitatione, sed virtutis opinione; in his vincamus nec superari patiamur" (epis. 58, 2.53–54) [Between us let there be a rivalry in learning, in uprightness . . . of behavior, from which springs and increases an honest love without any intent of gain, without any thought of sensuality, but only with the expectation of virtue; in this (competition) let us be winners and not allow ourselves to be surpassed].[6]

Their discussion on Augustine's interpretation of Genesis had apparently begun as a conversation to be continued by letters. According to the letters that form the dialogue, it is ultimately his idea that she collect their letters together into a dialogic whole: "et quamquam apud alios haec mea dicta obscuritatis vitio laborarent, si apud te clarissimam accedent et prioribus tuis ac meis scriptis iungentur, apertissime fient, illustrabantur et radiabunt in tenebris" (2.215) [And although others may find that my writings suffer from the defect of obscurity, if you, most brilliant, accept them and join them to what you and I have already written, our views will become very evident and clear, and will shine amid the shadows (69)]. He sees the whole dialogue as better than its parts, and although he argues against her, it is the juxtaposition of arguments that will be most interesting and valuable. Each side helps to clarify the other; the statements do not make as much sense alone as they do within the larger context of give and take.

Indeed, he seems to suggest that she has won the argument, even if he has the last word. First, his humorous comment at the beginning of the third letter suggests that sexual identity rather than rational judgment is governing his position in the debate: "Subtilissime Evae causam defendis et ita defendis, ut, si vir natus non fuissem, me tuarum partium tutorem constituisses" (2.192) [You defend the cause of Eve most subtly, and indeed defend it so [well] that, if I had not been born a man, you would have made me your champion (61)]. Then the last letter presents his final points as "quae brevissme in diversem sententiam dici possunt" (2.211) [brief arguments which can be posed for the opposite view (67)] rather than as a view that he himself holds. Even if these indications are to be read as polite flattery, they still suggest that he finds the pleasure and interest of the dialogue in the repartee more than in the final persuasion to one side or the other. Similarly, he expects whatever outside readers this exchange may have—and he clearly anticipates such readers—to enjoy the clever parries and thrusts rather than to be seeking a final solution.

For Foscarini, a lawyer and a governor, interpreting and applying texts, whether laws or diplomatic documents, was a fundamental activity of his career. The dialogue with Isota is basically an argument over how to interpret the narrative of Genesis, and it begins—as noted in the long version of its title—in a disagreement sparked by Augustine's gloss on that text: "peccaverunt impari sexu sed pari fastu" [they sinned unequally according to sex, but equally according to pride]. In the process, the debaters cite Scripture, of course, but also Lombard, Ambrose, Gregory, and Aristotle.

Yet the topic also concerns the relations between the two sexes more generally. There is not always a clean distinction between spiritual and secular or even feminist uses of dialogue (we are talking about uses now, rather than formal types). We have seen, for example, how Olympia Morata's first dialogue combines the topic of the relative merits of humanistic and religious studies with the topic of a woman's choice of the intellectual life over the normal concerns of women. We have seen also how Matraini presents, along with her religious instructions, an implicit argument for the validity of women's engagement in learning, authoritative writing, and teaching. So too, because the presumed inequality of the sexes was based in part on passages from the Scriptures, religious arguments often enter into what are primarily secular attempts to present a more equalizing view of the sexes. Thus Isota tries to use the accepted notions of her day to argue that because Eve was weaker and less perfect than Adam, her sin was less, while Ludovico, although gallantly exempting his correspondent, gestures toward the continual deceitfulness of women toward men. None of these normative notions is challenged by either side except for the issue of women's intellect; and here we see some real ambiguities emerge.

The issue arises in the argument over the nature of Eve's sin. Isota argues that it was not pride, the worst of sins, but merely a temptation to pleasure, quoting from the Bible: "Now the woman saw that the tree was good for food, pleasing to the eyes, and desirable for the knowledge it would give. She took of its fruit and ate it. . . ." Thus even though the serpent may have tried to tempt Eve by saying that the fruit would make her "like God," that was not one of Eve's reasons for eating it: "Nec videtur id fecisse mulierem, quia dei similem se fieri magis crediderit, sed propter fragilitatem potius et voluptatem" (2.189) [Moreover, the woman did not (eat from the forbidden tree) because she believed that she was made more like God, but rather because she was weak and (inclined to indulge in) pleasure (60)].[7] Ludovico counters that her desire for knowledge was in itself an act of pride, both because "scientiae . . . arrogantes efficit" [knowledge . . . leads to arrogance] and because "Fuit ergo primus motus inordinatus appetitus appetendi quod naturae suae non competebat" (2.194) [The first impulse (of sin), therefore, was an inordinate appetite for seeking that which was not suited to its own nature (61)]. "Nec credidisset mulier, ut ait Augustinus super Genesi, suasioni daemonis, nisi propriae potestatis amor ipsam invasisset, qui rivus ex superbiae fonte procedit" (2.194–95) [Nor would the woman have believed the demon's persuasive words, as Augustine says (in his commentary) on Genesis, unless a love of her own power had overcome her, which (love is) a stream sprung from the well of pride (61–62)].

This notion, however—that a woman's desire for knowledge was a desire for something "not suited to her nature" and a prideful love of her own power—utterly contradicts Ludovico's own thoughts and feelings about Isota, whom he praises repeatedly for her learning and intellect and encourages to "dare to do much." Moreover, Isota was not alone in her female desire for learning; for her mother, herself a believer in the value of study for both sexes, had seen to the excellent education of at least two of her daughters as well as her sons.[8] Thus Foscarini can praise Isota as "Data nobis a summo deo, a sapientissima matre educata" (epis. 57; 2.43) [Given to us by God, educated by the wisest mother]. In fact, the whole dialogue is described by both participants as something they are continuing because it is "useful" to Isota, a kind of educative game intended to hone her argumentative and interpretive skills. Isota says she would renounce the fight against so learned an enemy except that "hoc certamen utile mihi esse cognoscam" (2.197–98) [I recognize that this contest is useful for me (63)]; Foscarini too says that he would abandon the fray, as her arguments are worthier of praise than of contradiction, but he is continuing "ne tamen coepta utilitate frauderis" (2.211) [lest you be cheated of the utility (you say you have begun to receive from this debate) (67)]. Foscarini, identified in the title as an "artium et utriusque iuris doctorem" [doctor of arts and both laws], would certainly have enjoyed this kind of educative debate, which would have been an important element in his own education. We can see the embarrassment of his conflicted position in the moments when he exempts Isota from general statements about women. We can see her own conflicted feelings as well in the moments where she suggests that what she is doing is "not a woman's task."[9]

Finally, we can see the importance, once again, of a real friendship in encouraging women's entrance into texts of intellectual discussion. In some sense, Isota is a speaker in a dialogue begun, ended, and encouraged by Foscarini. Yet she is writing her own part of the debate, and the whole dialogue was ultimately published under her name. It is not, like the dialogue of Gonzaga and Valdés, the recording of a prior conversation, because the conversation takes place as something written rather than spoken. Yet it is a record of an actual exchange of views by means of letters. This is a case in which the dialogue really has not only two participants but also two writers. The relinquishing of final control by either one results in a truly dialogic and unresolved debate.

The dialogue obviously circulated in manuscript form, for about ten years later the clergyman Matthaeus Bossus wrote to Isota that he had been recently reading it "cum voluptate sacra" [with holy pleasure] and was pleased by its combination of theology with "cultum eloquentiamque" [culture and eloquence].[10] Isota, who also collected many of her own letters into a volume, obviously had an interest in the preservation and circulation of her work.[11] The quality of her Latin was not only a source of pleasure to a reader such as Bossus but also part of Isota's demonstration that a woman could participate intellectually with men.

A century later (in 1563) a descendent of the Nogarola family, Franciscus Nogarola, published a revised version of this dialogue under Isota's name and offered it to a bishop of Verona who had just become cardinal, Bernard Naugerius. Franciscus obviously felt the need to make the work conform to a more normative model of the dialogue genre, and his changes reveal just how different Isota's dialogue is from that norm. He added at the beginning a narrative description of the setting: the governor of Verona has been invited to the Nogarolas' country estate; walking with Leonardo Nogarola, he comes upon Isota sitting with a book. Leonardo introduces his sister and remarks that he has another sister equally well educated. Praises of the site lead to Leonardo's observation that mankind lost true felicity with the fall. Isota then raises the question of whether Adam or Eve was the more to blame, and her brother suggests that this become a topic of discussion. The dialogue has thus been transformed into a Ciceronian country villa conversation instead of an urban exchange of letters. The word *oratio* recurs to label the speeches on both sides, for they are now spoken, not written and sent. The rural setting is emphasized by the inclusion at the end of the book of a Latin poem by Isota in praise of their country estate, a poem that Abel suspects was written by Franciscus (Nogarola 1886, 1: lvi). Franciscus, although referring to the book as "Isotae monumentum" [a monument to Isota], uses Isota as a means to induce the cardinal's respect for the entire Nogarola family, describing the intellectual value of all three siblings and the social status of their property holdings. The book is obviously intended to advance Franciscus's own interests by bringing him to the cardinal's attention.

Despite his pleasure at having such a distinguished family, Franciscus is not entirely sure how to deal with its learned female. He comments that Isota eagerly wrote down the words that were spoken that day in order to preserve the memory of the governor's visit ("ad tuendam clarissimi viri memoriam"); her writing thus becomes a mere recording intended to honor a male. The discussion is held not between her and the governor (who is identified as an ancestor of the cardinal and named Naugerius rather than Foscarini, implying that the two families have a long history of amicable relations) but between her and her brother as a kind of entertainment for their distinguished guest.[12] In this way Isota's honor is protected from the apparently embarrassing notion that she might have argued with a male in a more public relationship. Leonardo comments that his sister has been thinking about the topic for some time, thus explaining her ability to participate in a debate with learned men; her preparation puts her on an equal footing with men, who can compose impromptu arguments and speeches. Isota assures the men that she will participate not in order to appear clever but only because of her desire to ascertain the truth of the issue ("nec ad quaestionem argutias, sed ad veritatis statuendum iudicium"). The visiting governor ultimately calls a halt to the debate in order to preserve the benevolence between opponents and pronounces the results a draw. Augustine's analysis, which formed the heading of Isota's text, becomes the conclusion in Naugerius's mouth: Adam and Eve sinned unequally according to their own unequal natures, but equally according to the nature of their sin, which was pride. Indeed, Eve's pride was worse because, being less perfect to begin with, she strove to become like a god. Thus Isota's argument that Eve's sin was not a sin of pride and that her motive was not to become godlike but merely to eat a fruit that looked delicious—a carnal rather than spiritual sin—is dismissed. While seeming to create a balance between the two sides, Naugerius actually confirms the brother's position.

Franciscus's rewriting points up how different Isota's project was from the more conventional and male Ciceronian dialogue into which Franciscus transformed it. Its epistolary nature is lost. The governor's chief friendship is with Leonardo rather than with Isota. Isota is not permitted to argue with an outsider. Although Isota claims to be using the debate as a means to seek out the truth, we do not see the argument itself as a part of her intellectual training; the governor has no direct interest in honing her skills by this means. The roughness of a real-time trying out of arguments is smoothed into an exchange of prepared "orations." The whole activity has become a polite entertainment that can be offered as a gift from one male to another in the hope of recouping future benefit.

The link between letters and dialogue reappears, however, in the writing of Helisenne de Crenne. Helisenne was a well-educated provincial French woman and one of the very earliest women to see her own works into print. Her publications, beginning as early as the late 1530s, included a translation of the *Aeneid*'s first four books; a volume of letters; and, perhaps most famously, a long romance, *Les angoysses douloureuses qui procedent d'amours*.[13] The volume of letters, explicitly titled *Les epistres familieres et invectives*, which was published a year after the romance, shifted from the Latin of Nogarola's correspondence to the vernacular, although clearly following generic models established in Latin. It is within the set of invective letters that we find a dialogic exchange.

Actually the invective letter was a humanist but not a classical genre. Petrarch was the first to combine the Ciceronian model of classical invective oration with the equally Ciceronian epistle and to write both familiar and invective collections of letters, the *Familiares* and the *Sine nomine*. He borrowed from Cicero's Catiline orations for the opening of one of his invective *Sine nomine* letters.[14] The ease with which humanists merged the oral genre of oration and the written genre of epistle, both Ciceronian, indicates the overlapping of "spoken" and written text characteristic of the dialogue (as well as of the novelle collections and much of Renaissance lyric).

Petrarch was not only the originator but also the great establisher of the invective letter as a genre. At Petrarch's death, the library of his writings included an entire *Liber invectarum* as well as his *Liber sine nomine*.[15] The *De ignorantia sua et aliorum*, the *Invectiva contra Gallum quendam*, and the *Invectiva contra medicum* are all examples of Petrarch's invective letters; the last of these, although a treatise in four "books," is written from the start in the second person as a letter responding to the doctor's "inanem, sed ampullosam et tumidam plenamque convitiis epystolam" (1950, 25) [empty but swollen and bombastic and wine-bellied letter]. Helisenne loved this kind of exaggerated style, which one could indulge in and make fun of at the same time.

Jerome's widely popular *Adversus jovinianum* was another possible model for the invective epistle. Helisenne probably drew on Jerome for the idea of an invective letter attacking women and marriage. Juvenal's famous sixth satire on women may also have contributed to the tone and the arguments, although it is neither prose nor an epistle. Helisenne, however, drew on Petrarch for the idea of collecting invective letters, together with familiar letters, as a part of the humanist epistolary genre.

While the invective letter is not a classical genre, the notion of an exchange of invectives did have classical models. *Le grand et vray art de pleine rhéthorique*, first published in 1535 and reprinted by Helisenne's publisher, Denys Janot, in 1539, which Helisenne may have consulted (Mustacchi and Archambault in Helisenne 1986, 31), cites as its model for invective Cicero's Catiline orations. However, there also existed an invective attacking Cicero, *Declamatio in Ciceronem*, supposedly written by Sallust. Thus the idea emerged of a linked invective exchange. Petrarch was familiar with the apocryphal exchange of invectives between Sallust and Cicero (Billanovich 1996, 99, 109).

Erasmus, in his *De conscribendis epistolis*, includes the invective letter as a category, though he discusses it only briefly. He says that he is reluctant to use this form but feels it is important to mention as a possible weapon of self-defense in case one is maliciously attacked (1.2: 537.1–6). The examples he cites are all pairs of mutual invectives, some classical and some quite recent:

Demosthenes and Aeschines, Cicero and Sallust, Jerome and Ruffinus, Poggio and Valla, Poliziano and Scala (1.2: 536.23–537.1).

The notion that invective is part of an exchange, as a defense or counterattack against an initial invective attack, well suits Helisenne's use of it within the *querelle* between women and men and helps to explain why she included a letter supposedly by her husband—the only letter in the volume attributed to someone other than herself. Already her first invective letter is a self-defense against her husband's unwritten anger. His invective reply, which represents the whole tradition of male invective against women, is both the response to her and the provocation for her own further response. Helisenne thus expands the two-part exchange by adding a third letter. The genre of invective letter is thus made to converge with that of dialogue. As in the case of Isota, but perhaps more fictively, the exchange of letters ostensibly emerges from and continues what was originally a face-to-face conversation.

All of Helisenne's works, including the more medieval *Le songe*, deal with the problems caused by passion and the relations between the two sexes and do so in an interconnected manner.[16] The invective letters stage this issue as an epistolary debate between Helisenne and her husband.[17] Unlike Isota, whose work is induced, authorized, and given its setting by her male correspondent, Helisenne's female letter writer takes the initiative in provoking the husband's response, which she then encloses in a larger context of her own design. Her authority comes not from him but from her own learning (her ability to cite classical sources and historical examples), her eloquence (especially her control of tone), and her sense of righteous indignation. She needs no male to authorize her work, and certainly not the husband, whose authority and argumentation she denigrates.

The first or "familiar" part of the epistolary volume contains the usual humanist letters of advice and consolation to men and women on topics such as the death of a wife, the loss of money, and the male loss of standing at court or the female loss of reputation because of slander. Jean-Philippe Beaulieu (Helisenne 1995a, 16) has pointed out that there is a particularly feminine or domestic aspect to most of these letters, which frequently emphasize the duties of a daughter to her parents and offer the consolation of friends and relatives for personal losses. Most of these letters are one-way only, and it is easy to believe that the situations to which these letters "respond" have been invented as topics for a series of humanist essays. In this manner they resemble other humanist letter collections, including the letters of Chiara Matraini, published in Venice (1595) and Lucca (1597). Like Helisenne's letters, Matraini's address both men and women, including one nun, on a variety of topics that are announced in the letters' headings: consolations for the loss of a son or a husband, advice to temper one's anger with reason, exhortation to a young man to study, a description of some entertainments, generalizations about love, and so on. For both, the variety of topics and addressees is clearly an important aesthetic value. For both, the letters are brief essays either truly or feignedly elicited by events in the lives of their friends. Matraini's final letter, addressed to the Virgin Mary, was obviously never sent. Estienne Pasquier, whose "Lettres amoureuses" were published in 1555, commented openly that he saw little difference between fictive letters and the edited versions of letters that had really been sent to someone. For him the addressee was merely a pretext for treating a particular topic in the attractively supple form of the letter.[18] Jerry C. Nash, in the introduction to his edition of Helisenne's letters (1996, 21), notes that although Helisenne's letters are addressed to individual recipients, these persons probably never received them apart from the book: "Il est toujours question chez Crenne, non pas des divagations d'une correspondance ordinaire pour transmettre à quelqu'un des nouvelles ('lettre' personelle), mais d'une *narratio* de l'*ars dictaminis* bien réfléchie, bien documentée, et bien rhetorique ('epistre' littéraire)" [It is always a matter in the case of Crenne not of the meanderings of an ordinary correspondence intended to transmit news to someone (personal "letter"), but of a *narration* of the *art of letter writing* well thought through, well documented, and very rhetorical (literary "epistle")]. Thus even in the case of the one putative exchange of letters in the volume, we can expect that it is similarly staged. It merely expands into the format of exchange the implicitly dialogic nature of the humanist letter that claims to respond to particular news from a friend.

Helisenne's preface stresses the pleasures of variety of style as well as of topic, an aesthetic value frequently praised with regard to the letter genre. Both Matraini and Pasquier, for example, adhere more or less explicitly to this aesthetic. Erasmus heartily endorses it in the opening of his *De conscribendis epistolis* (1522), praising the epistolary genre as capable of infinite variety. In the interests of variety, therefore, the last four familiar letters of Helisenne's collection shift from rational advising to a more passionate tone as the letter writer confesses to being in love and includes a coded message to her beloved. Even these letters, however, which have been considered a reversal or disintegration of the views expressed in the previous ones, continue the basic moral perspective of both *Les angoysses* and the first nine letters:[19] that is, while accepting the possibility that feelings of love are too strong to be totally mastered by reason, Helisenne continues to reject adulterous sex as an immoral and dangerous action. They double the writer's position as the person both in need of moral advice and able to offer it. In that sense, they render explicit the self-enclosed nature of these supposed letters.

Near the end of the volume, after a new preamble to the readers, come five invective letters, including the exchange of three letters between herself and her husband and then a fourth addressed to other men who criticize women's writing. On one hand, these letters are clearly separated from *Les epistres familieres* by the new preface and are intentionally different in tone and style. On the other hand, they directly continue the issues of the familiar letters as Helisenne protests directly to her husband about her innocence of any adulterous misdeed and the unfairness of his anger, the very situation in which her familiar letters had asked a friend to intercede. It is now generally accepted that these letters are as fictive as the others and that she wrote all the letters herself, including the one ascribed to her husband.[20] Indeed, the book's title page follows the title with the phrase, "Le tout composé par icelle" [All composed by her], and there are stylistic reasons for believing that to be true. However, there is just enough basis in historical truth to make the correspondence at least plausibly real. Helisenne was definitely married and did end up separated from her husband, although probably the separation came after the publication of her letters rather than before.[21]

In this exchange, her husband attacks her for ruining her and his honor by writing a first-person romance about an adulterous love, which he assumes is a true confession of her guilt. Helisenne has several lines of response: a moral self-defense against the falsity of his accusations concerning her personal behavior; and a response to the issue of whether she should be writing and how her work should be read.

The moral defense of her personal behavior is supported by the familiar letters, although some readers have erroneously seen the two parts of the volume as incompatible. Beaulieu (1994, 11–12) argues that because of the confession of love in the familiar letters, Helisenne is clearly lying in the first invective letter when she denies her adulterous love ("son expérience de l'amour adultère").[22] She would therefore be offering her first invective letter as a virtuoso piece of arguing against a truth that she has already confessed even to her husband. However, Helisenne is instead playing the rather slippery game of considering that her restraint from consummating her love makes her still chaste. Her ninth letter to Clarisse urges her friend in love not to do anything that might damage her "honneur & utilite" (1995a, 81). Her tenth and eleventh letters then illustrate all the miseries and self-deceptions of love that she has warned her friend Galizia about in letter five; but she insists that the suspicions of her physical infidelity are unjust. The twelfth letter to a true friend celebrates friendship as a much happier and more reliable relationship, devoid of the continual fears and anxieties of passion, and urges this friend to intercede with her husband, persuading him of the injustice of his anger. The thirteenth letter, to the beloved, confirms that no actual adultery has occurred; she praises the beloved who "j'ay manifeste demonstrance, que nonobstant que ton desir soit quelque fois excité, si est il assiduelement mitigué de raison, arresté par bon advis, corrigé de discretion, & refrené de temperance" (1995a, 98) [I am pleased to have been able to show that if one's desire is occasionally stirred up, it can also be tempered with reason, arrested with good counsel, corrected with discretion, and restrained with moderation (1986, 71)].²³ She urges him not to do anything that would cause both their ruin.

Les angoysses similarly includes toward the end (3.8) the character Helisenne's thanks to divine Providence for preventing the lovers from succumbing to an adulterous sexual union. In this way it celebrates a combination of passion and physical purity that may seem either legalistic or sentimental but that is presented as the moral response to an ineluctable love. Similarly, in *Le songe*, which was later published together with the letters in her *Oeuvres*, Truth proclaims the lady within the dream—who had been eager to run off with her lover—chaste because their adulterous love was never consummated. This careful line between the expression of love and the rejection of adulterous action has caused interpretive trouble for the author with some of her modern readers as well as with her husband.

Helisenne's invective protests to her husband, "Et d'advantage tu crois que telle lascivité se soit en ma personne experimentée" (108) [You believe, moreover, that I really experienced the lasciviousness about which I wrote (81)].²⁴ She is denying here the charge of physical experience, which would indeed be "amour illicite." If her heart is chaste, it is perhaps because she has had the will to refrain from fulfilling an improper desire. For "si j'eusse esté en lascivité submergée comme tu diz, en vain tu fusse fatigué de me garder" (112) [had I sunk into lasciviousness as you so claim, you would not have succeeded in keeping me from it (85)]. Her final protest of "inviolable foy" [inviolable faith] suggests again her strict adherence to a physical fidelity to her marriage.

Along with this moral defense of her person, Helisenne defends her written work as literary and not autobiographical. The romance does indeed borrow obviously from other literature: Boccaccio's *Fiammetta* and *Filocolo,* and the *Roman de la rose,* for example. When Gabriel Dupuyherbault in his *Theotimus* of 1544 blamed the impudence of both Helisenne and Fiammetta ("Quid Helisennae, quid Flametae ignibus impudentius?"),²⁵ it is hard to know whether he considered them both characters or authors, but he was correct to associate the two narrating figures, even though one was authored by a woman and the other by a man. If he thought of them as authors, he was proving the folly of an autobiographical reading. Janet Altman (1986, 28) uses Helisenne as part of her evidence for considering sixteenth-century letter collections "as rudimentary autobiography"; but this is just what Helisenne is protesting against.[26] Through her letters she is presenting herself as a professional, educated writer, capable of addressing the situations of others, not as a woman able only to speak about her own emotions. As Jerry C. Nash (2000) has emphasized, she sees her work as fiction. These letters are written in an explicitly varied manner that demonstrates wit and skill in different styles.[27]

But Helisenne has also created the very problem of which she complains by repeating, from work to work and from genre to genre, a persona that readers might easily identify with the author. Marianna Mustacchi and Paul Archambault (Helisenne 1986, 5–6) suggest that the last four familiar letters turn the series into something resembling an epistolary novel as Helisenne, after advising a friend to obey her parents and suppress the love of which they disapprove, suddenly confesses that she too has fallen in love and then sends letters to a friend and to the beloved. As the friend has the name of a character in her romance, Helisenne perpetuates in the letters the confusion caused by her romance between her "real" voice and her first-person voice in a fiction, a confusion that has caused her the problems with her husband. One could read the letters as an autobiographical account corroborating her husband's fears about the autobiographical nature of the romance— although, as the character Helisenne dies at the end of the romance, there are certainly limits to the possibility of identifying the writer with the character.

Conversely, one could read this letter to a character as a flaunting of the fictionality of her written voice. Since men who wrote first-person narratives by lovesick women (Ovid in the *Heroides,* for example, or Boccaccio in the *Elegia di madonna Fiammetta,* both works Helisenne knew and drew on in her own writings) are clearly not confused with the characters in whose voices they write,[28] the mere replacement of the author by a female should not— Helisenne seems to be arguing—cause readers suddenly to read autobiographically. Following the romance with a letter to one of its characters may be a way of drawing attention to the fictionality of the letters as well. Helisenne's use of a nom de plume (her real name was Marguerite Briet), her taking that pen name from a famous romance ("Helisenne" is a reference either to Dido or to the mother of Amadis),[29] and her sharing the name with a character of her own creation all support the notion that she was forming a fictional first-person voice.

Her creation of personae includes her writing as an irate male. The participation of the "husband's" letter in the same invective strategies as the other letters supports the title page's claim that it was actually written by Helisenne. The rhetorical flourishes it contains, such as catalogs of classical examples and manipulative references to myth, certainly suggest that it is another sample of Helisenne's wit rather than a real letter from an enraged husband. Moreover, the first four invective letters all end in an identical manner, praying God to enlighten the recalcitrant reader or others with a similar need to be shown the truth.[30] Thus the four form a patterned unit on a focused topic.

Given the presentation of these letters as "all composed by her," the exchange with her husband forms an epistolary dialogue not unlike that of Nogarola and Foscarini, but more controlled by the female pen. Even though it is clear whose side Helisenne is on and what sort of attitude she wishes in her readers, she nonetheless does a creditable job of representing her husband's point of view—creditable enough to have convinced some readers that the letter is really his. He expresses surprise at her claiming to be hurt by him, saying that she has hurt him much more. He recalls the earlier days when he was happy with her chaste reputation and even trusted her to travel without him. He argues that it is not only dectractors or the evidence of her writings that has inflamed him, but "choses veues" (115) [things seen (88)], and reverses Helisenne's accusation: "tu . . . me veulx ascripre tout deffault & coulpe" [you want to make me the bearer of your guilt and blame (89)]. Perhaps most cutting of all, he argues that her pointing out the moral lessons of her romance with its warnings to ladies is a mere trick by which she can pretend to be good as a cover for her real interest in wallowing in erotic fantasies: "Je t'expose cecy, à cause de l'ingeniosité par toy excogitée, qui selon mon jugement d'aultre chose ne servira, que de prester faculté d'exhorter en secret, de perpetrer la chose que fainctement tu deteste" (116) [I know your ingenuity will ultimately serve no other purpose than to encourage other women secretly to commit what you pretend to loathe (88)].[31]

Helisenne must have heard criticisms like this and may even have worried that they might be true. After all, the effects of one's writings are always hard to predict, especially in a world where the circulation of manuscripts among friends had been replaced by the printing of books and where differences among readers, which Helisenne's letters amply set forth, made the effects of a book's diffusion impossible to control. Do not men's moralizing love stories contain some element of titillation? Might she be lying to herself about her own intentions? Helisenne's husband complains, "& si ne te debvrois occuper à me faire ung long recit, pour me donner intelligence, comment les personnes amantes sont aptes à excogiter subtilitez pour parvenir à l'acte venerien" (118) [I needn't listen to one of your endless narratives in order to understand that people in love are apt to think up any old trick in order to indulge in the veneral act (90)]. Is a long and detailed romance really justified by its short moral? Are Helisenne's protests and moralizations in part a rationalization to herself of a desire to write at length about amorous desire? Are they a self-deception as well as an attempt to deceive her public? If Helisenne invented this letter, she did not hold back from taking aim at what must have been her own most vulnerable point. In her temporary empathy with the husband's suspicions, as well as in her explicit anticipation of readers who would take different sides, she offers a remarkably "open" dialogue despite her own obvious preference for one set of views.

Controlling the design of the whole volume, Helisenne weaves the husband's letter into a context in which she is the clear winner. The preceding familiar letters demonstrate the moral and educated nature of her writing and her own physical innocence, supporting her first invective letter's opening argument that even the romance should be read in this same way: "Bien desireroye que souvent tu te occupasse à mediter, comment en plusieurs lieux de mes compositions je deteste amour illicite: & avec affectueux desir, Je exore les dames de tousjours le vivre pudicque observer, par ces remonstrances miennes" (109) [I should like you to consider the number of instances (in the romance) where I disapprove of illicit love. Haven't you noticed how often I plead with the women of this and any age to live decently? (82)]. This letter refers to itself as already a response to her husband's previous attacks, citing specifically some of the "oultrageux propos, que tu profere" (109) [outrageous statements you have made (82)].

The husband's reply, the second invective letter, confirms Helisenne's description of him as outrageous. He attacks not only her but women generally with such venomous violence as to demonstrate clearly the very irrationality that she blames him for—or that she sets us up to expect from "his" writing. Just as he has erred in jumping to conclusions about her behavior from the topic of her romance, so too he errs in rashly generalizing from one suspected example of women's behavior to the deceitful and lustful nature of all women. But of course his letter too is an example of invective, of which exaggeration is a strategic tool. Helisenne must in part have had some fun, however painful an amusement, constructing a typical misogynist invective within a context where she could then answer it and point out its failings. The husband's letter ends by repeating traditional warnings against marriage and exhorting men, with a list of classical examples of disaster, to avoid the fraudulent sex altogether.[32] Thus it lays claim to a male solidarity for its misogyny.

Beaulieu (1994, 7–19) sees the husband's letter as serving two instrumental purposes in the collection: presenting a "male" invective as a model for Helisenne to imitate and surpass; and, perhaps more important, allowing her own letter writing to shift from confessional or expressive to rhetorical or persuasive, in the process allowing her to draw systematically from the arguments and examples of the traditional defenses of women rather than con-tinuing to speak personally about her own experience. Thus it helps moti-vate her display of varied technique.

Helisenne's letter of response refutes the general attack against wom-ankind and marriage, which, she points out, was established by God. Like Morata and Matraini, she cites the Book of Wisdom, in this case to defend both the existence of good women and the literary strategy, shared by her romance, of portraying bad women in order to encourage others to be better. The theme of reason's struggle to assert mastery over sensuality cuts across all three letters, as the husband blames women for undermining male reason, while the wife accuses men of being irrational and then blaming women for it. Her counterattack becomes, like his, an attack on the other sex in general: men spend all their efforts in deceiving women and then blame women for being deceitful; men allow their sensual nature to overpower their rational-ity and then blame women for being irrational and lustful, and so on. Her ref-erences to "ce que tu dis" (125) [what you have said (96)] about women's self-adornment go beyond anything we have read in his preceding letter and seem therefore to refer rather to the whole tradition of misogynist writing that he invokes in his support.[33] The "you" is only partly her husband, then, despite the singular pronoun, and partly the whole male sex with its "inve-terée malice" (127) [inveterate ill will (97)].[34]

But besides responding to the arguments of his letter, she responds also to his claim of a unified male view by calling our attention to differences among her readers. For the end of the third invective letter shifts to argue that "tous hommes vertueulx me donneront ayde: car à ce faire raison le stimulera" (127) [Many good men too will come to my aid, for reason will urge them to do so (97)].[35] The preamble to the invective letters addresses itself to "dear friends and readers," implying that Helisenne has various readers in mind. Some are "friends," who will presumably give her a sympathetic reading. Readers who are not "friends" may indicate either the unknown public of a printed work or the actual enmity of the "readers" directly addressed by these invectives. Indeed, the first of the invective letters expresses the fear that her husband's hostility to her is so great that he will not read her letter at all.

Together with this preamble, the end of the third invective constructs an alternate male readership—of men who are rational, of "readers" who are also "friends"—and envisions an ongoing debate among men about the nature of women. Helisenne seems to hope that it may be more effective against people like her husband when men take up the argument on women's side; but she also hopes that her book will inspire some male readers to do just that. Thus she envisions the debate in her letters turning into a conver-sational debate between misogynist and more liberal men. The argument between hostile and sympathetic or "rational" men that Catherine des Roches would later depict within the text of the debate between the two fathers, Sevère and Placide, Helisenne imagines—and even advocates—taking place beyond her book of letters among its readers. By allowing that men are not all the same, Helisenne not only promotes the possibility of sympathetic male readers but also reinforces her claims about women: they too are not all the same and therefore not to be lumped together in generalizing misogynist attacks.

On the one hand, husband and wife form an intimate relationship within which correspondence is natural. On the other hand, this estranged couple tends toward representing men and women more generally and posits that relationship, at least frequently, as an enmity. While the familiar letters address both men and women, the invective letters address only men, except for the letter supposedly from her husband and addressed to Helisenne. Thus, unlike Laura Cereta, who aims one of her epistolary diatribes at a woman significantly named Vernacula and against other women of her ilk who disparage learning in females,[36] Helisenne uses the invective only for the male enemy, ignoring the possibility that other women might share those hostile views. Yet she is not simply enlisting the invective as a weapon in the war between the sexes, for part of her strategy is to deny to the husband the appeal to stereotypes or the claim that all members of the same sex can be assumed to be the same.

Indeed, the roles of herself and her husband reverse the usual gender identifications. Her side is identified as the side of "reason" against the errors of her husband's emotional and thus irrational thought process. Nevertheless, in the end she expresses the "timeur que remonstrances ne fussent suffisantes, pour extirper tes damnables opinions" (127) [fear that merely remonstrating with you would not be enough to root out your wretched opinions (98)]. "Damnable" is actually stronger than "wretched"; Helisenne has argued that her husband's attack on marriage is a blasphemous attack against a divinely established sacrament and that his attack on women in general is similarly a stubborn refusal to heed what the Bible says about good women. Thus both husband and wife warn each other that they will go to hell if they do not change their ways. Helisenne expresses here a fear concerning not only her relation with her husband, whatever that may actually have been like at the time, but also her larger project of changing male opinion about women so that women may be allowed to write, even about love, without being harassed and condemned: the fear is that reason may not be strong enough to overcome men's irrational anxieties and attacks.

The fourth letter advances this latter theme by "responding" to the attack on women's writing by someone named Elenot. This letter adds some valuable information about Helisenne's motivations and her construction of possible readers. She mentions the common moral excuse for writing: she wishes to avoid idleness. But she also acknowledges her great pleasure at the thought that "mes livres ont leurs cours en ceste noble Parisienne cité: Laquelle est habitée d'innumerable multitude de gens, merveilleusement scientifiques, & amateurs de l'amenité, doulceur & suavité, qui se retrouve en la delectable accointance de Minerve" (132) [my books are being published in this great city of Paris, which is filled with innumerable crowds of people who love science, elegance, leisure and culture—the graces that flow from conversing with Minerva (102)]. Her expression of pleasure at participating in the cultural scene may be part of a demonstration of how this is as natural to women as to men.

In citing a catalog of classical learned women who disprove the notion that women are unfit for learning, she adds one contemporary example: Marguerite de Navarre, who combines "la divinité Platonicque, la prudence de Caton, l'eloquence de Cicero, & la Socratique raison . . . la splendeur d'icelle à la condition femenine donne lustre" (130) [Plato's godlike wisdom, Cato's prudence, Cicero's eloquence, and Socrates' wisdom . . . her brilliance enhances all of womankind (101)]. Although Helisenne does not say as much explicitly, surely the publications of Marguerite's volumes in 1531 and 1533 played a major role in inspiring Helisenne to think of publishing books of her own. Although the catalog of ancient women of learning mixes pagan and biblical examples, Helisenne's admiration for Marguerite is expressed entirely in classical rather than Christian terms: "car je n'estime point, qu'au preterit jamais fut, ne pour le futur peult estre personne de plus preclaire & altissime esperit, que tresillustre & magnanime princesse, ma dame la royne de Navarre" (130) [For I believe that never was there in the past, nor will there ever be in the future, a loftier or more brilliant spirit than the most illustrious and distinguished princess, the queen of Navarre (101)]. Helisenne is impressed not by the queen's piety or mysticism or evangelism, but by her intelligence, her learning, and her eloquence. If Helisenne sees culture as something that flows "from conversing with Minerva," Marguerite is perhaps a particular Minerva from whose work Helisenne has felt the flow of exciting possibilities.[37]

Not surprisingly, Helisenne seeks similar qualities in her readers. She contrasts the Parisian readers "who love science, elegance, leisure and culture," and therefore enjoy her books, with the "ignorant, dishonest, wicked person" who is sure to give them "an unfavorable review" simply because he "won't have the ability to understand them" (102): "s'il ya une ignorante, scelere & maulvaise personne dans la prenommée tres inclite cité, qu'il fault, que devant ses aveuglez yeulx, mes livres s'offrent, certaine suis que bonne relation il n'en fera: car . . . si ne sera il en sa faculté de les entendre" (132). Rather, "bien vouldroye que mes livres fussent tousjours exhibez aux sca-vantes personnes" (132) [I like my books to be shown to competent people (102)]. For "gens d'esperitz" [men of wit] are self-confident enough to praise and encourage even what perhaps does not deserve their praise, whereas men who do not understand what they are reading are quick to jump to a ven-omous judgment that is even more undeserved.

The reader Helisenne addresses in this fourth letter is not, like her hus-band, someone personally offended or dishonored by her writing, but rather a generic male reader who thinks of women that "aultre occupation ne doib-vent avoir que de filler" (129) [their one and only pastime should be to spin (99)]. Ironically, Helisenne attributes their difference of view to her superior education: "Si tu avois esté bien studieux en diversitez de livres, aultre seroit ton opinion" (129) [If you were better read, your opinion would be different (99)]. It is only male ignorance of the long catalogs of learned and brilliant women, that is, ignorance of both history and literature, that can maintain this prejudice against women's abilities. Helisenne in no way shares the ear-lier Nogarola's plaintive apology that her writing is "not a woman's task."

Another issue may lie lurking beneath this argument and beneath her expectation of two sets of readers, the ignorant and the understanding. Helisenne's odd defense of Marot immediately after her praise of Marguerite implies evangelical leanings.[38] Other evidence supports the idea that Helisenne was a sympathizer with religious reform. One piece of evidence is her defense of marriage, which Beaulieu notes (Helisenne 1995a, 147) was a popular theme with reformers. Another is her reference to a literal reading of the Proverbs in defense of the good woman, for Anne Larsen (1990a, 559–74) has shown that a literal reading of this text as a model for women was a similarly reformist innovation. The attack on her "infidelity" may be in part a coded reference to religious disagreements, situating the husband on the side of corrupt medieval thinking. If so, hers would not be the only work in which a defense of women was used to signify a defense of religious reform. Francine Daenens, in a fascinating essay, has demonstrated that the women whose letters were "collected," or rather composed, by Ortensio Lando, apparently as an example of female eloquence, are all connected to the reform movement in Italy and may thus have offered a coded list of people in various parts of Italy who might be contacted by those of similar views ("L'autore mette qui a stampa una ragnatela di rapporti di solidarietà" [Dae-nens 1999, 203]). This suggestion is not meant to brush aside the arguments on the surface of Helisenne's text, for they express concerns that she reiter-ated in many of her works. But it may draw more careful attention to some of her words, which have religious implications that current translators tend to ignore. I refer, for example, to "damnable" as a description of her husband's attack on women and marriage.

Near the end of the fourth letter, Helisenne writes: "Je desireroys bien que ton vouloir fust de communicquer ceste mienne epistre, á gens de splendides & claires esperitz: pour ce que j'ay certitude qu'apres qu'ilz l'auroient bien considerées: ilz te feroient entendre que c'est une remonstrance qui pour ta salvation & utilité a esté faicte" (133) [I should very much like you to pass on this letter of mine to a few sound-minded, intelligent people; surely, once having read it, they would enable you to understand that if I am remonstrating with you, it is for your own good (103)]. Again, the published translation weakens the religious import of the original: her exhortation is not only for his good but for his "salvation."

Here once more Helisenne envisions a double readership: the sane, learned, and intelligent reader that she longs for; and the irrationally prejudiced and ignorant reader that she fears may also pick up her book: "Mais helas de douloureuse anxieté suis agitée, quand me souvient que de ta bouche abhominable t'ay ouy proferer, que affectueusement tu desirois de t'occuper á la lecture des angoysses . . ." (132) [A painful anxiety disturbs me, unfortunately, when I recall that you have let it be known with your loathsome, mincing words that you would like to spend time reading my *Angoysses* . . ." (102)]. Unlike the romance, for which she hopes for only the better sort of reader, the letter collection plainly seeks both types, and indeed the invective letters directly address only the worst kind. Furthermore, Helisenne imagines a dialogue outside and beyond her epistolary text in which better readers, whether male or female, will both discuss her book and continue her educative efforts to change the views of the ignorant. To the extent that her letter collection really addresses such better readers, she is urging them to join in the debate on her side. In short, she anticipates a spillover of dialogue from the text into reality and aims at having some real effect on the world.

Helisenne may have felt the need to write this dialogue about her own role as a writer and the meanings or effects of her romance to guide the readers of her works to take them in a better sense. As she writes to her husband, "Mais dis moy, qui te donne la stimulation de continuelement prendre les chose de la plus deterieure partie? Certainement par cela, tu fais indice, que la commotion de l'ame telement te trouble, que de tous vrays jugemens elle te prive" (108–9) [Tell me, what is it that always makes you consider things in their worst light? In doing so, you convey the impression of a man so disturbed as to be deprived of his true judgment (81–82)]. Caveat lector: when the writer's intentions are unclear, the reader is responsible for making good use of the text. A suspicious reading reflects more on the mental state of the reader than on the virtue or vice of the writer. By broadening the debate to include women's writing and rationality in general, however, she moves beyond her concerns about her own literary situation to a broader feminist concern.

We are certainly a long way here from the dialogue of spiritual counsel, but this eruption of violent exchange near the end of a series of advisory epistles demonstrates the close connection between correspondence and dialogue in the minds of humanist writers. It also indicates the potential dangers of the introduction of a real woman's voice into these dialogues, the expectation of resistance from men, and the need for women to defend their work. Following a series of humanist letters of moral counsel, this exchange, with its sharply different tone, nonetheless posits itself as similarly humanist and moral advice. The attitudes of men toward women are foolish and unjust, and the desire to change them is similar to the desire in the familiar letters to turn men and women from their emotion-driven responses to a more rational evaluation of their situations. In the recurring theme of reason versus the passions thoughout Helisenne's writings, the victory of reason is continually urged and is seen here as the best hope for women's vindication.[39] Although her invective to her husband provokes a similarly invective response, almost luring him into a display of emotional excess, the very vehemence of the invectives as a series, through their conscious participation in an established mode or style, paradoxically creates in the reader not a similar anger but a rational detachment that can both enjoy the wit or skill of these diatribes and critically consider the issues they set forth.

Chiara Matraini, near the end of the sixteenth century, published a letter that, like Cereta's on the country life, was clearly intended as *pars altera dialogi*. She had purportedly received a letter from Maria Cardonia describing a discussion in her house about the relative merits of arms and letters. Several *cavalieri* argued there for the superiority of arms, and Maria turned to the absent Matraini for a defense of the other side. Matraini wittily replies that she is hesitant to pit the force of her reason against such strong-armed knights but then launches into an effective counterattack. We are reminded of the broader cultural tendency to think of disputation as armed combat unsuitable to women;[40] Matraini's opponents may be armed males, but she responds armed only with a pen. Here a letter becomes the mediary between a supposedly live discussion and a written reply; the dialogue remains half oral and half written, calling attention to its hybrid nature and to the logical position of letter writing between conversation and the single-authored text.

Just as Helisenne used an epistolary dialogue to defend women's writing, so Matraini makes similar use of this debate by letter. The topic allows Matraini to associate the rational and rhetorical skills with a woman, in opposition to the brute force associated with men. Like Ovid, who identifies with eloquent Ulysses against brawny Ajax in their competition for Achilles' armor, Matraini can use the debate to praise her own participation in intellectual life. Just as the notion of spiritual battle enabled women to overcome the image of rhetoric as a battle fit only for men, so Matraini's pitting of pen against sword enables her to do battle in a way that distinguishes between a kind of battle appropriate only to men and one in which women can very well compete. Furthermore, as Helisenne presented her public argument about her own and women's writing as a domestic exchange of letters with her husband, and as Laura Cereta argued for a life of public involvement in a "private" letter to a female friend, so Matraini justifies her engagement in this argument by framing her response to the men as a reply to the female acquaintance whose letter has solicited her own.

The prevalence of a strong link between women's dialogues and the epistolary form may be understood not only through the explicit association of the two genres in humanist thought but also in connection to the situation of the women who wrote. Letter writing was more acceptable for women than participation in public gatherings or face-to-face meetings with men. Castiglione's preeminent model presents the conversation of educated persons at a court. But most of the women who wrote dialogues were not at courts; they were more likely to be living in middle-class homes. Thus Nogarola chastely addresses Foscarini from her brother's home; and Matraini, writing from her private house, projects herself as the absent participant in a salon discussion. This enables Matraini to avoid a direct confrontation with men in public, while nonetheless giving her the opportunity of refuting their views. Even Morata wrote her dialogues after her dismissal from court, not while she was there.

Thus the connections between dialogue and letter have a special function for women's dialogues, a function not relevant to dialogues written by men, who were eager to challenge each other face to face. The revision of Isota's dialogue by her male descendent from an epistolary exchange into a Ciceronian conversation indicates how particularly female was the application of what for humanists was a theoretical connection between the dialogic and epistolary genres. The women who used this form call attention to their physical isolation. Letter writing is their only link with distant friends or with the men whose views they wish to challenge. Therefore they imagine letters both as an extension of past conversations and as a means of making their intellectual presence visible in public discussions despite their physical absence. The range of ways and tones in which women developed the linkage of letter and dialogue indicates the exploratory nature of their contributions to the dialogue genre as they tried to find a way to make it work for them.

5 Dialogue & Drama

One important way in which the Renaissance dialogue differed from medieval debate was by bringing back from antiquity the use of realistic or even historical humans as speakers. In Italy this mode generally prevailed, apart from religious dialogues such as Ochino's of the Soul with Christ or Catherine's of the Soul with God. Two strands of development converged to reinforce this predominant Ciceronianism in Italy. One was the humanist dialogue of the fifteenth century, written by men of letters who intentionally took Cicero as their model for eloquence. The dialogues by Poggio, Bruni, Alberti, or even Pontano tend to be set in their own cities among their personal acquaintances, all men of letters and public affairs.[1] Their celebration of their own elite society of friends, along with the presentation of their discussions on various topics, is part and parcel of the Ciceronian model. The other strand comes from Boccaccio, who similarly picked a realistic setting near his own home and realistic, although renamed, members of his society as speakers. The garden setting of the *Decameron* merged with the relaxed settings of humanists conversing in their own homes and gardens and with the Ciceronian settings of a similar nature.

Castiglione, an important model for all subsequent dialogue writers, combined a Ciceronian source (especially *De oratore*) with a Boccaccian inclusion of women and jest.[2] Bembo's *Asolani*, contemporary in its conception with the *Cortegiano*, shared the same combination of Cicero and Boccaccio: the Ciceronian form of complementary discourses on a set topic by learned male friends; and the Boccaccian entertainment among friends of both sexes in a garden of the geographically real court of Asoli. A plausible realism, then, was firmly established, whether the dialogue was to emphasize didactic or literary intentions.

Italian women writers of dialogue, generally trained by humanists, tended to write in the Ciceronian mode. Certainly most of the Italian women whose work has been discussed fit that model: Isota Nogarola, Olympia Morata, Chiara Matraini, and Tullia d'Aragona. All include themselves as speakers along with other historically real acquaintances. They present their discussions as real or plausible conversations among real friends in their own hometowns. Matraini even makes use of the garden setting, at least for her first day. These women aim in part at celebrating those same personal relations that help them to define for themselves who they are.

In France, however, medieval traditions held on more strongly, producing an oddly mixed form of the dialogue. The models were not only Cicero and Boccaccio but also, or even more so, Lucian, the *Roman de la rose*, the medieval débat, and morality plays. Just as the Italians turned to Roman models, so the French turned somewhat to Greek but especially to earlier French models as a way of competing with the glorifying Roman-Italian identity. Lucian's dialogues of gods and humans representing particular schools of thought or types of behavior merged with the mixed human, allegorical, and divine characters of medieval *sottie* and morality plays as well as the classical gods and personifications of the *Roman de la rose*. The possibilities for satire surfaced both in Lucian's dialogues and in the medieval personification allegory of the *Roman de la rose* and the later plays.

The medieval debate among people and abstractions was combined in the sixteenth century with a humanist interest in certain topics of contrast: for example, fortune versus *virtù*, to take a widely popular example treated by Plutarch or in Platonic myths about Eros. Thus French humanist women produced dialogues that wavered between the humanist and the medieval, shifting forms in the course of the text. Helisenne de Crenne's peculiar *Songe* is one such example. Another is the dialogues by Catherine des Roches in her first volume of *Oeuvres* (1579). Their relation to Labé's *Débat de Folie et d'Amour*, which manages to convey a more fully Renaissance feel, merits consideration. Finally we will turn to Marie Le Gendre's *Dialogue des chastes amours d'Eros et de Kalisti*, which drew clearly from des Roches and probably from Labé as well. Together these dialogues constitute a particularly French female tradition of dialogue writing, tied to personification allegory and classical mythology in a way that Italian women's dialogues were not and thus distinct both from what we think of as the typical Renaissance dialogue and from what Italian women were writing.

These dialogues are not only more abstract than the Italian ones but also more dramatic. We have noted already the close ties between Marguerite de Navarre's dialogues and her plays. Her work may well have been an inspiring example for later French women. Helisenne knew the 1533 volume with

Marguerite de Navarre's *Dialogue en forme de vision nocturne*,[3] a work whose form bears at least some resemblance to Helisenne's *Songe*, where a heavenly female instructs an earthly one in a dream vision. Several of Marguerite's plays were published between the time of Helisenne's writing and that of the other women in this chapter. These included four religious plays; two comedies about love—one debated among entirely female characters, the other involving both men and women; and the enigmatic *Trop, prou, peu, moins*, a sottie on evangelical themes.[4] Helisenne's dream, although described as a set of "disputations," is both a morality play and a kind of masque and pageant; the dramatic quality of Labé's work has been frequently remarked; and Marie Le Gendre presents under the title *Dialogue* what is really an odd combination of sentimental narrative and drama, complete with scenes and interludes.

The influence of Lucian was better suited to this model than that of Cicero. As in Lucian's writings, the use of clearly fictional characters, including both humans and gods, facilitated a reconception of the dialogue in a more dramatic mode, with imagined scenes. A dialogue of Lucian's was even performed in 1441 at the Anjevin court in Naples (D'Ancona 1996, 2, 360). If Lucian did provide a model for French women, however, he remains completely unacknowledged in their dialogues. Even among French male dialogue authors, Bonaventure des Periers was perhaps unique in taking up this more dramatic and unrealistic style for his *Cymbalum mundi*, which, like Lucian, he cast entirely with male speakers. Most other male dialogue writers in France followed the Ciceronian form, including often long speeches among the learned. Meanwhile women in France pushed dialogue in the direction of drama.

Dialogue has an intrinsically dramatic potential. Although it tends to focus almost entirely on an exchange of words and not on action, the genre did occasionally include some reference to action, such as the women's playful attack on the misogynist Gasparo in Castiglione's *Cortegiano* (2.96).[5] Dialogues also frequently opened with a description of the setting, thus inviting the reader to imagine the scene as well as to listen to the conversation. Erasmus's colloquies, set among neighbors in their homes or on the street, drew intentionally and explicitly from Latin comedy and were meant to be acted aloud by boys in school. Indeed, his colloquy on marriage was translated into French in 1531 as "Comédie ou dialogue" (Lazard 1980, 155). Similarly, the dialogues in *Dialogi aliquot festivissimi* of Ravisius Textor, Erasmus's contemporary, which were meant, like Erasmus's, for recitation by boys in school, are occasionally labeled "comoedia" within the volume and closely resemble morality plays. Human types such as "three worldly fellows" or "flatterers" interact with characters named Death, Pleasure, Virtue, and

Reason. One of the dialogues labeled "comoedia" is a dialogue unusual in this collection for containing only human characters and domestic settings: a Youth rebels against his Father's desire for him to study and instead marries a Wife, only to discover that his marriage is becoming unhappy and that Father was right. However, another example labeled "comoedia" is entirely different and resembles a sottie: Moria (Folly) introduces a series of competitions between two liars, two deceivers, and two fools. Thomas Heywood published his translated selections from Lucian, Erasmus, and Ravisius under the title *Pleasant Dialogues and Drammas*. Dialogue was clearly seen as potentially a kind of drama for live performance.[6]

So too the drama of fifteenth- and early sixteenth-century France drew close to the genre of dialogue. Jean Jacquot (1964, 486) lists débats along with eclogues, farces, and interludes as brief dramatic forms that were popular in performance. In sixteenth-century Italy, *dialogo* was used to mean a one-act play (Borsellino 1976, 64). Aubailly has traced the development of French performances from monologue through dialogue and into sottie, observing that many of the morality and sottie plays are essentially dramatic dialogues with extra characters. The interactions among characters in a morality play are often a more lively presentation of what is basically still a debate between positions on a given subject. Marguerite's dramas are clearly an example of this, and their emphasis on words rather than actions has long been noted. Through human types, and later increasingly through the mix of human types and personifications, they present the rivalry of interests among different social groups or the conflicting values and attitudes of the world.[7] It is not surprising, then, that French women would have found the convergence between dialogue and drama a familiar and fruitful ground for working.

The conflict of reason versus passion and its connection to gender relations is the topic of Helisenne's *Le songe* (The Dream), first published in 1540 (one year after the humanist *Les epistres familieres et invectives*), reprinted the following year, and republished a number of times with the letters in her collected *Oeuvres*.[8] Thematically *Le songe* continues the work of *Les angoysses* and *Les epistres*. But if Helisenne's themes remain the same throughout the volume of her works, her use of genre changes from romance to letters to the imagined arguments of speakers in a theatrical dream.

This work draws its dialogic form from a very different set of traditions than her invective letters, although it claims to be closer in inheritance than it appears. This *songe*, as its title indicates, picks up the medieval genre of the lover's dream vision. The *Roman de la rose* is probably an important model here, for Helisenne's romance, *Les angoysses*, had already demonstrated her familiarity with that medieval text. As in the *Roman*, moral abstractions and symbolic classical deities argue for the allegiance of human lovers.[9] Yet Helisenne's text refers at the start to a humanistic model: Cicero's *Dream of Scipio*, "en la lecture duquel on peut veoir plusieurs disputations" (Helisenne 1977, P4r) [in the reading of which one can see several disputations]. Thus the form of a dream containing debates about love versus reason is presented as classical, even Ciceronian, just like the letters.

Humanist notions of the dialogue as "disputation" derived from and remained associated with a more medieval form of scholastic *altercatio*.[10] Dramatic disputation in Latin was a popular part of school exercises for boys, especially since the first decades of the century. Erasmus saw it as an engaging way of teaching good Latin and good morals simultaneously. The *Dialogues* of his contemporary Ravisius Textor (or Tixier de Ravisi) were basically morality plays for the students at his College of Navarre. Women, of course, would not have had access to the actors and audience of a school to effect the performance of their work. Helisenne, who knew Latin well enough to publish a partial translation of the *Aeneid*, chose to write in French so as to include a female audience not permitted into such colleges. While addressing moral issues, her lively scenes, complete with occasional stage directions, move us from the schoolroom or the debates of learned men to the theater of a female dreamer's mind.

Within the dream of Helisenne are three pairs of speakers: first a human lady and lover; then two classical goddesses, Venus and Pallas; and finally two abstractions, Sensuality and Reason. The dialogues form a sort of nested series, for the goddesses and abstractions directly address the lady and her lover, who become the witnesses and judges of their debates, their judgments witnessed in turn by the dreamer, who describes herself as similarly stimulated by love and who comments from time to time on the lessons she is receiving. Beyond this audience lies the readership and the historical author, whose prologue praises the use of literature and Scripture as mirrors for self-evaluation. In one odd intervention, Helisenne herself, who persistently intrudes as the narrator of the dream, appears to engage directly with Reason. Thus we find ourselves flowing between the conversation of humans and the debate of qualities that are obviously both personified abstractions and internal faculties or dispositions of the characters.

Although these characters make us feel more in the world of the *Roman de la rose* than of Cicero, Helisenne is clearly trying to merge two models by indicating a classical example of the instructive dream. Moreover, the initial description of the setting is filled with classical allusions to nymphs, naiads, and gods. Yet with an allegorizing use of classical reference, the lovely valley is compared to the one from which Pluto seized Proserpine, a warning about the potential fall into sin and return from Pluto's realm that will soon be staged.[11] One of the allegorical creatures that appears later on is drawn from the *Aeneid*. Helisenne's enthusiasm for humanism encouraged her to rethink inherited medieval genres in the more modern context of a classical revival.

Helisenne's earlier praise of Marguerite (in the fourth invective letter) for a combination of wisdom and eloquence suggests another model in this mix, for Helisenne shares with Marguerite the use of characters who represent a fixed point of view and engage more in verbal exchange than in action, yet who are set into a scene as if on stage. As in some of Marguerite's dramas or the *Vision nocturne*, there are one or two characters whose function is to be persuaded and spiritually changed by the exposition of another's views. Introduced on the title page as "Le Songe de ma Dame Helisenne, la consideration duquel est apte à instiguer toutes personnes de s'aliener de vice, & s'aprocher de vertu" [The Dream of my Lady Helisenne, the consideration of which is apt to provoke all persons to withdraw from vice and approach virtue], the dream stages itself as Helisenne's moral persuasion of the reader, represented through the persuasion of the lady by mythological or allegorical speakers.[12]

On one hand we are tempted to identify the lady in the dream—who, like the "I" of both *Les angoysses* and *Les epistres*, has fallen vehemently in love with a youth and lives under suspicion from her husband, to whom she maintains a merely physical fidelity—with the dreamer and possibly with the recurring persona of the writer Helisenne, although this identity remains uncertain.[13] On the other hand, as the person in need of persuasion, the lady is obviously us, the reader, while the figures of Pallas and Reason become the didactic author whose aim of teaching us virtue is announced with the title. So too the narrating "I" is both the producer and receiver of the message, while the dream itself is the text that the reader experiences moment by moment just as the dreamer experienced the dream. Identifications across the nested layers blur their boundaries as well as confounding a clear distinction between emitter and receiver.

Just as *Les epistres* contained an intentional variety of letters, so too within *Le songe*, a formal variety of debates takes place. The first dispute is within the lady alone: whether to choose the satisfaction of her desire along with perpetual infamy or sexual frustration along with chastity and honor. This internal monologue by a person divided between conflicting opinions becomes externalized as the lady is joined by her lover. In a reversal of typical scenes of seduction, it is the lady who declares her reckless desire to her beloved and the young man who argues for restraint out of fear that her husband may destroy them both. This is a perfectly human conversation, which includes expressions of joy at meeting, complaints about the husband's jeal-

ousy and a warning about the peril of sending letters, considerations of
whether they might be able to get away with their crime, and ultimately the
decision to think it over and defer action.

These first two disputes, internal and external, feel like scenes from a play.
Indeed, the scene begins with the entrance of the youth, in accordance with
a promise to meet his lady, and his prayer to Venus; then the lady enters and
considers her situation; at last she catches sight of the youth, and the two
engage with each other. In short, the several pieces are strung together into
a dramatic act with readily imaginable, and sometimes explicit, stage business. The act ends with the laments of the lover that love's service is too
cruel and unhappy, so that he wishes he could free himself from love.

This exclamation of despair provokes the next layer of the dream, as
Venus appears suddenly with Cupid in order to prevent the rebellion in her
ranks, while Pallas enters soon after in order to seize the opportunity to persuade the young man into her camp. Suddenly we have moved from a realistic scene between two humans to a masquelike scene in which symbolically
opposed goddesses vie for human allegiance. However, this debate is also
clearly an internal debate of the young man concerning the direction of his
future actions. Instead of repeating the inner debate presented by the lady,
Helisenne varies the form by turning to a dispute between classical goddesses.

Although we might expect Pallas to represent Reason, just as Venus is to
be identified with Sensuality, and although Pallas is identified as "la deesse
de prudence et de fortitude," her speech actually identifies her more
specifically with Learning. The young lover turns out to be a student, and
Pallas comes to defend her "amateurs de science." This debate between goddesses focuses on the persuasion of the youth, who must choose between his
sexual urge and his studies, each presented as a female object of possible
desire. The lady is, understandably, not interested in Pallas's speech—a
detachment that, we should note, distances her from the studious female
author. It is only the youth who feels the opposite tugging of these two goddesses, who lay into each other with a relish reminiscent of the invective letters.

There is clearly a playful delight in the rhetorical strategies of both sides,
through which we are made aware of the learnedness and eloquence of the
author herself and of her humanist interest in orations.[14] Cicero is indeed a
model for these arguers before their judge. The sheer delight in eloquence
felt outside the dream supports Pallas's argument against Venus's claim that
the choice of study is a choice of dreariness instead of pleasure, for Pallas has
her pleasures too. The youth is convinced to leave his horrified lady for his

books. Narrated stage directions indicate that the lady has drawn back from Pallas and moved closer to Venus, as the staging dramatizes the humans' reactions to these speeches.

Pallas's victory is aided by the theatrical entrance of two menacing symbolic figures in strange garb, whose identities she explains. One is the hideous *Inconvenient* (Trouble) and the other *Renomée* (A Reputation), based on Vergil's Fama, covered in feathers, tongues, and ears.[15] These entrances would certainly liven up a performance and contribute to our sense of witnessing a masque. But they also move us away from human characters or divinities in human form, introducing completely symbolic figures. The youth flees from their threatening approaches.

To comfort her unhappy protegée and punish her deserter, Venus now reverses the situation: the lady is cured of her love, while the youth is inflicted with renewed passion. This seems to be presented in a narrated dumb show, in which the youth returns only to be repulsed by the combined forces of the lady and Shame. At this point the youth disappears for good, while the lady becomes the primary object and audience of persuasive speeches in a morality play with personified speakers. Sensuality tries to persuade her to find another better man, while Reason seizes the opportunity of removing her from such dangerous desires altogether.

The contrivance by which this scene is made to follow as a consequence of the previous action is very weak; Venus's motives are a mere excuse for offering a new pair of speeches to balance the former pair. Nonetheless, the fact that Helisenne tried to make such a causal link is indicative: rather than merely offering a series of separate arguments to distinct audiences, as she had done in her letters, she is forging the causal connectives of a dramatic plot, in which divine interventions and sudden reversals have classical precedent.

Classical models, however, converge with Christian thinking. Unlike Pallas, who as a pagan refers to human studies as a path to virtue, liberty, and tranquillity, Reason at once refers to God, sin, repentance, and grace. The argument for the male was a rational choice, threatened by worldly concerns of trouble and reputation. For the lady the argument becomes religious, even though it is Reason who presents religion's teachings. Sin is equated with adultery against God, who is the only "parfait amy."

At this point a feminist argument creeps in, and we find an odd mingling of frame and content. When Sensuality protests:

O Raison: parquoy t'esforce tu tant de dominer en le sexe muliebre? Ne sces tu, que selon nature, ton domicille est plustost au sexe viril? Car

vulgairement la femme se regit & gouverne plus selon moy, & a sa fantaisie, que ne faict l'homme. Et comme chacun scet, la femme fut cause
premierement de peché. (T8v–8r)

*[O Reason: why do you try so hard to dominate within this female sex? Don't
you know that, according to nature, your domicile is rather the virile sex?
For commonly women rule and govern themselves more according to me,
and to her fantasy, than does a man. And as everyone knows, a woman was
the first cause of sin.]*

the words of Sensuality irritate the dreamer:

de ce que nostre condition feminine tant vituperoit: & pource stimulee
d'un excessif courroux, ne fis difficulté d'interrompre leurs propos: &
m'aprochant de raison, avec instantes prieres luy requis, que la verité
de ceste chose voulust exprimer. (T8r)

*[in that she so vituperated our female condition, and therefore stimulated by
extreme anger, I did not hesitate to interrupt their talk: and drawing near to
Reason, with insistent prayers I requested her to explain the truth of this matter.]*

The drama has been presenting the debaters as motivated by the events of
the story; but now we see the dreamer interrupting and explicitly requesting
Reason to discourse on a particular topic, a topic that readers of the previous
sections of Helisenne's volume would recognize at once as dear to the
author's heart. In short, the author's control of the play is revealed openly.
Yet instead of speaking in her own voice, she remains a member of the audience requesting a specific performance from the character on stage and thus
presents her case as the case of Reason itself. Since the dreamer is able to
rush up to the stage and call out to the speakers when they say what affronts
her, we seem to be watching not only a stage but an entire theater, including
an audience of one that can interact with the figures on stage. The dreamer
and her dream figures have become the characters in the wider dream of the
reading audience. Dialogues for public performance might involve a character who speaks from the audience; Aubailly (1976, 209–16) describes, for
example, a *Sermon du bien boire* in which the preacher is repeatedly interrupted and increasingly vilified by another character standing in the audience. This technique tended to be used in such performances for comic
effect, however, whereas Helisenne uses it in a very serious manner. She is
not undermining the authority on stage but appealing to it, not heckling the
preacher but urging her to preach in defense of women.

As Reason launches into her discourse on the comparative sin of Adam and Eve (the topic of Nogarola's dialogue), she begins to cite Augustine, Aquinas, Hugh, Gregory, and Cassiodorus, in a learned explanation of theological matters. Because both sexes are equally the image of God, an image based on their faculty of understanding, and because men and women are equally capable of glory in paradise, Reason concludes:

> pourquoy ne m'efforceray-ie nonobstant la fragilité, d'avoir domination en elle, & la corroborer de vertu? Certainement en ma force tant ie me confie, que de toy Sensualité sucumberas. (V4r–5v)

> *[why shouldn't I try to achieve domination within her, notwithstanding her fragility, and to strengthen her with virtue? Certainly I am so confident in my power that you, Sensuality, will yield of your own accord.]*

And indeed, Sensuality at once submits. A battery of church fathers has been summoned to defeat Sensuality's "petite estime" for women. Although both the dreamer and the audience for this debate within the dream are female, this argument is addressed in the real world also to men. Indeed, for Jean-Philippe Bealieu and Diane Desrosiers-Bonin (1999, 1166) Truth's certification of the lady's chastity together with Venus's reproaches against jealousy suggest that the husband of the letters may be one of the intended recipients of this text. The links with previous works in Helisenne's volume implicitly align Sensuality and Reason with the husband and wife of the invective letters, in a reversal of traditional gender roles; for Sensuality, like the husband, speaks undeserved but conventional ill of women, while Reason, like the wife, responds on behalf of the rationality of their sex.[16] Even when Sensuality refers to the "fantaisie" of women, Pallas's previous reference to the young man's having fallen in love "par fantaisie" has primed us to recognize that this is not chiefly a female problem. To posit the husband of the invective letters as a reader, however, makes sense only if we understand that husband as a representative of misogynist men more generally. Helisenne was not writing merely for private circulation in the family but for publication in Paris.

By this time the lady, who has been advised to strengthen herself with prayer, is far ahead of the youth, for she is headed for paradise while he is headed for school. However, this is a superiority that is also a conventional inferiority: that is, the male is getting a classical education while the female receives religious training. For all her own education and interest in the classics and their humanist revival (e.g., her translation of Vergil, her vernacular re-creation of familiar and invective epistles), and despite her defense of women's rationality, Helisenne seems to promote this conventional state of affairs. The most important worldly concern for a woman is her chastity, and the lady summons Truth to declare that she is indeed still chaste: "e porta tesmoignage, que nonobstant les detractions des langues pestiferes, si n'avoit la dame Chasteté corrompue: car de ce, la clemence divine par grace especialle l'avoit preservee" (X3r–4v) [and (Truth) bore witness that, notwithstanding the detractions of pestiferous tongues, the lady had not corrupted her Chastity: for divine mercy had saved her from this with special grace].

Now we get a final pageant of virtues. Chastity, Charity, and Humility appear as three beautiful women, and Reason promises that two more women, Diligence and Abstinence, will accompany the human lady. Truth also steps forward to present the lady to Chastity, and finally Peace, "more resplendent than any other" (100), joins the noble company. Each figure is presented to the lady by Reason with a long sermonlike speech. The dreamer has no need to add further moralizing of her own.

The lessons of this piece are as ambiguous as its dreamer's positions. On one hand, the obvious message is, as Pallas puts its: "si par fantaisie en amour tu es entré, par sapience tu en peux issir" (S4r) [if you have entered into love through fantasy, you can exit from it through wisdom]. Yet Pallas's success with the youth is very short-lived, for the irate Venus and Cupid swiftly make him worse than ever. So too Reason cannot even make itself heard to the lady until she has already begun to withdraw her love from the youth—again a situation brought about by Venus and Cupid. The forces of unreason are the most powerful, even though the advocates of reason seem to win.

What reason was unable to prevent, God's mercy has ultimately succeeded in preventing. This is not a Protestant or evangelical position like Marguerite's, that we are totally dependent on God, for Reason emphasizes the need for free will to work with God's aid; God's grace comes only to the already repentant sinner, and human efforts are favored by God. It is the combination that produces good results. What has saved the lady by enabling her to make that first effort is her disgust at the youth's mutability. Thus his virtuous choice, though seen by the lady as the demonstration of his fickleness, impels her toward her own redemption. In short, his love of studies is good for both of them. Yet women are urged not to study but to pray.

The dreamer narrates what she has seen: the visual is as important as the verbal. The various characters enter and exit; some of them seem to step out of a morality play and others to be part of a humanist interlude or masque. The final parade of virtues is a fitting dramatic conclusion to either form. In one last bit of theatrical magic, the splendid pageant vanishes, revealing a forest; then the dreamer, awakening, hastens to record the performance or dream. As she writes the ending, she renders no further judgment of her own.

The pageantlike triumph of virtues and heavenly Peace at the end of the dream are a clear enough conclusion.

The theatrical qualities of the text are mixed throughout with narrative framing and commentary by the dreamer-writer. On one hand, some of the longer passages, such as the initial description of the scene, would not be performable. On the other hand, intrusions by an "auctor" do not necessarily imply that a text was not intended for recitation aloud. One of Ravisius Textor's dialogues, concerning a rich man and his flatterers, is interrupted several times by a character named Auctor who addresses the audience directly in between the different dialogic scenes with their changing sets of speakers. As in Helisenne's text, Ravisius's moralizing conclusion is given not to Auctor but to Ratio (Reason). As this is one of the pieces meant for live performance by his youthful students, Helisenne might have imagined her own text being read aloud in parts, with the dreamer as one speaker. Yet, unlike Ravisius with his school, she lacked the social institution for such a performance. Hence she probably assumed that the work would be read rather than seen and heard.

The text is aimed at both male and female readers, since both the youth and the lady are addressed by its debates; yet since the dreamer is a woman, the female reader is clearly the predominant one, just as the lady is the dominant character within the dream. The youth has disappeared by the middle of the work, and we never find out what happens to his unhappily revived love; it is the lady's ultimate triumph that concludes the play. If morality plays brought characters such as Lust, Truth, and Peace on stage together with humans to demonstrate the redemption of mankind, usually represented by a male, Helisenne has focused on the redemption of a specifically female human and has even turned the workings of a morality play to include the teaching of a feminist lesson: that women's rational capacities are the same as men's. She has also used the traditional moralizing of her characters to display her own prowess in writing a variety of rhetorical orations and disputations. If eloquence is the expression of rationality, as it was commonly considered to be, then the author's display of eloquence is a further demonstration of women's rationality.

Obviously Helisenne trusts that her writing of both sides of these debates will be in the end an eloquent oration for one side over the other. We know from the start—from the very title—that the scales have been weighted, and the reader's female representative within the play is totally convinced. Unlike the resolvable conflicts of the debate, the unresolvable conflicts created by love render it a wretched condition from which, as the youth proclaims, one can long only to free oneself or die. Peace is the final goal of the dream, and the arrival of heavenly Peace is the ending for the lady within the scene. Lack of closure is not a positive value here. Yet the lingering ambiguities make perfect closure difficult to achieve beyond that inner scene. Helisenne preaches female piety and humility as a display of her own intellectual prowess and rhetorical skill. Simultaneously conventional and outrageous, Helisenne is the amorous champion of chastity, the impassioned teacher of reason, and the rational advocate of faith.

I have described Helisenne's piece at some length because it is not well-known these days; but this was not always the case. Besides the two separate printings of Le songe in 1540 and 1541, Helisenne's volume of collected works was published early and repeatedly: in 1543, 1551, 1553, 1555, and 1560. François de Billon, in the Fort inexpugnable de l'honneur du sexe feminin (1555)—the year of Louise Labé's publication—claims that Helisenne has brought honor to Picardie and that "Les Compositions de laquelle sont si souvent es mains des François se delectans de Prose, qu'il n'est besoin en faire autre discours" [Her compositions are so often in the hands of Frenchmen who enjoy prose that there is no need to say anything further about her (or them)].[17] Was her work known to dialogue writers of the following decades—Louise Labé, Catherine des Roches, or Marie Le Gendre? Quite possibly; for although they do not mention her, there are some suggestive connections. Certainly both Labé and des Roches had a general interest in other women's writing. Marie de Romieu, in her versified defense of women, "Brief discours: que l'excellence de la femme surpasse celle de l'homme" (published with her Oeuvres in 1581), names "Elisenes" and "Des Roches de Poictiers" side by side (1972, vv. 307–8, p. 21). In any case, later women writers seem to have pursued a similar direction in dramatized dialogue writing.

Louise Labé, like Helisenne, had surprising education and ambition for her social position. Although a solidly middle-class member of Lyon's commercial society, the daughter and wife of prosperous rope makers in Lyon, she learned Latin and Italian, possibly also some Greek, and hosted a salon that drew a number of well-known writers, so that she became friends with some of the most famous poets of her day, for example, Maurice Scève, Olivier de Magny, and Pontus de Tyard.[18] The preface to her Oeuvres complètes, published in Lyon in 1555, when she was in her thirties, urges other women to take up the pen, to embrace the pleasures and glories of writing and by their success to put men to shame. Her Oeuvres includes elegies, sonnets, and the Débat de Folie et d'Amour.

Although the Débat had a rich context of sources for its creation, Enzo Giudici (1965, 105) calls it "one of the most original works of the sixteenth century." The title suggests a medieval genre; yet Giudici denies the importance of medieval debate poems for Labé's work because those are more schematic and lack her "finezza e duttilità psicologica" (106) [subtlety and psychological pliancy]. Certainly her writing feels much more Renaissance than medieval. The use of Apollo and Mercury, who take up in a formal trial the debate between Love and Folly, has suggested to some Lucian and possibly des Periers's *Cymbalum mundi* as models for a dialogue of gods; but Labé's topic and tone are quite different from des Periers's (Giudici 1965, 108; Lauvergnat-Gagnière 1990, 55). The second of Lucian's *Dialogues of the Gods* seems to be a source for the fourth "discours" of Labé's *Débat;* but that is only one small part of her larger work. The *Asolani,* with its praise and disparise of love, and Erasmus's *Praise of Folly,* with its deification of Folly, may have contributed importantly to the contents of Labé's debate (M. M. Fontaine 1993, 289, 297); a French translation of *The Praise of Folly* had recently been published in Lyon (Sproxton 1999, 160). But her form and manner of presentation are utterly different from Erasmus's long oration. The sotties resemble Labé's piece in some ways: they sometimes feature a complaint brought before a judge who conducts a trial, and they tend to describe the powerful role of folly throughout the society. However, Folly, the Roy des Sottes or Mère Sotte, tends to be the judge and not the plaintiff or defendant. Morever, the emphasis of the sottie is usually on social and political problems of the time, involving the complaints of the working class against the abuses of the wealthy and powerful. Finally, the sottie uses the license of its foolscap to indulge in coarse humor and action.[19] Labé's work does none of these.

Lucian's imitators in Italy produced dialogues of paradoxical encomium that may similarly have formed part of Labé's inspiration. For example, the fifteenth-century Maffeo Vegio's "Disputatio inter Solem, Terram, et Aurum" [Dispute between Sun, Earth, and Gold] is a series of self-aggrandizing speeches before a divine judge. Gold, with the longest and winning speech, proclaims its power over the world and its motivation of all human actions. This proclamation leads into satirical portraits of lawyers, courtiers, priests, and other lesser professions. The dispute was first published in Paris in 1511 and remained popular during the sixteenth century. Speroni's "Discordia," published in 1542 and many times thereafter, bears a somewhat different resemblance to the *Débat:* in a paradoxical speech, Discord argues to Jupiter that she is wrongly blamed and is, in fact, natural and good. Mercury briefly appears to support Discord's claim, but she speaks at length on her own behalf. There is no opposing argument. Jupiter defers judgment until Discord can present her case in a proper order, which she is inherently incapable of ever doing. Labé could possibly have known either of these works. Nonetheless, her particular theme and the mixed manner in which she carries it out—partly dramatic with a series of scenes, partly forensic debate with advocates pleading on behalf of their clients before a divine judge, the whole introduced briefly by a narrative summary—are with good reason declared by Giudici (1965, 87–90) to be uniquely her own.[20]

In Labé's work there are five *discours*, or scenes. Four of these each have their own set of paired characters: scene 1: the encounter of Love and Folly; scene 2: the encounter of Love and his mother, Venus; scene 4: the encounter of Love and Jupiter; and finally, scene 5: the elaborate forensic arguments of Apollo and Mercury before an audience of the assembled gods. The central scene (scene 3) involves the entire cast of characters plus all the other gods, and in the final scene again this whole cast is present, their responses to Apollo's speech indicated in narrated stage directions. The five scenes divide into two "acts" on two days, the first three scenes taking place on the first day and the last two on the following day. Each "act" or day opens with a two-character scene and ends with the entire ensemble of characters on stage.

The *Débat* opens with a direct confrontation over precedence between the young male Love and the older female Folly: each insults the other while proclaiming his or her own superior importance. Attacked by Love, Folly causes his blindness. They decide to refer their case to Jupiter, and each selects an advocate for his or her cause. As Guylaine Fontaine (1998, 146) has noted, each scene has not only its own characters but also its own style: the aggressive insults in the first, the pleadings of Venus in the third, the more leisurely discourse in the fourth, and the formal oratory in the fifth. Although the fifth scene, with its competing orations, is much longer than the others, the playlike division into five reinforces the dramatic presentation of speakers without any narrative framework.

The opening scene contains numerous possibilities for stage action. First the two rivals try to enter simultaneously through the door, pushing each other aside. Their insults and shoving suggest the action of a comedy. Attacked by Love's arrow, Folly with a gesture causes Love's blindness; then she ties around his eyes the bandage that will not come off despite his and later his mother's efforts to tug it away. As with Helisenne's dream, we are invited to see as well as to hear. While not including a long introductory description of the setting such as we find in Helisenne's piece, Labé does share with Helisenne the indication of stage actions. Explicit stage directions encourage us to read this as a text for performance: "Folie bande Amour, et lui met des esles" (32); "Amour sort du Palais de Jupiter" (34); "Venus tache à desnouer la bande" (35). Although Pédron (1984, 190) calls this work an exquisite but unperformable piece of theater, Kupisz (1990) defends its performability; even the long orations of the fifth scene have plenty of features amenable to lively acting.

Labé's decision to shift this dialogue toward a directly dramatic presentation may be connected to the theatrical quality of Helisenne's dream. As with Helisenne's speaker pairs, an initial confrontation between two characters leads into a pair of orations staged before them by pagan deities who champion opposite sides, and more human interactions mingle with the conflicts of ideas. Love and Folly present abstract concepts; the motherly distressed Venus and the governing Jupiter function like people at a court; indeed, Venus enters less as the symbol of beauty than as the outraged mother of an injured son. Apollo and Mercury operate as opposing deities making their best rhetorical efforts to win a contest of persuasion. Without denying the relevance of a long tradition of male-authored texts for Labé's creation, I would like to add the possibility of a female-authored model as well. Indeed, Labé's work begins by staging the rivalry for precedence between a male and female.[21]

Although Labé uses no narrative framing, she has tied her scenes more tightly together into a narrative progress. Where Helisenne presents a series of parallel scenes loosely connected into a plot, Labé focuses on the development of one main action: the resolution of the initial brawl. Nonetheless, she is willing to digress, as in Love's explanation to Jupiter of how one can make oneself loved and why this is particularly difficult for men in power. Although the fifth scene's lengthy speech in defense of folly pulls the piece away from theater and toward a satirical social commentary, previous scenes—showing the concern of Venus for her son, her pleading with Jupiter for justice, and Jupiter's conversation with Cupid—feel like dramatic human interactions. The final debate takes on a liveliness of a different sort, verbally sparkling but more general and less personal. The first four scenes of this "play" have the function of setting up the debate, which then takes over as a separate kind of performance. The mix of scenes of relationship among humanly emotional characters and scenes of more abstract debate is very like the mix in Helisenne's piece, where the human emotional scenes set up the more generalized debate.

The consequence at stake in the trial is whether Love and Folly will be compelled to go about together, Folly leading the blind archer, or whether Love will be allowed to go free of Folly and regain his sight. Although officially Jupiter postpones his decision, he orders in the meantime that Folly and the still-blinded Love stay together. Thus for the time being Folly has won. The argument used to win Folly's case is the need of these two beings for each other. Without folly, no one would love; without love, folly would not seem so sweet and desirable. The possibility of a wise or rational love is rendered remote. Labé has no interest in offering religious love as a solution.[22]

Was it part of Labé's wit to reverse a didactic debate between love and reason into an officially unresolved dispute between love and folly—even into a tentative victory of folly? To accomplish this irresolution or this victory, Labé had to omit all reference to Christian religion. The play remains within the unified realm of the gods rather than including—with moralizing commentary—the humans they influence for good or ill. There is no ultimately authoritative voice, such as that of Reason in Helisenne's text, to sum up what we need to know. Jupiter, who might serve that role, disappoints the expectation of a final judgment on the case. The absence of religious reference or sermonlike preaching, the choice of a more purely dramatic presentation instead of a narrated dream vision, the unified Olympian world that is created, and the relative openness of Labé's debate all result in bringing her dialogue out of the Middle Ages and fully into the classical mode of the Renaissance.

The year that Helisenne first published her *Songe* was the same year (1540) that the first theater building was erected in Lyon. The public was being offered a combination of morality and mystery plays and farces. Although Helisenne's *Songe* comes close to being a morality play, the dramatic dialogue that Labé envisioned was not like anything appearing on stage. The presence of Folly as a character might suggest a connection with the sottie, which presented characters labeled "fols" or "sot" and engaged them in quarrels. Often the sottie is really a dialogue, sometimes even titled as such (Lazard 1980, 54).[23] However, the sottie tends to delight in stupidity and crudeness, which Labé never touches.[24] In distinction from the all-too-human nature of sottie characters, Labé's Folly is situated in a more Lucianic manner among the classical gods.

Helisenne's pageant would have required a stage with machinery for scenic transformations and special costumes for its realization, but that is something the author probably never expected to see, for the narrative framework around and within the dream implies a readership rather than an audience, and as far we know Helisenne was not involved in a group, such as a salon, that might have performed a recitation of her text. In contrast, Labé's piece, which is fully dramatized, could have been performed with no special costumes and minimal props as a reading in her salon. The narrative summary oddly published at the beginning of the *Débat* could have served as either a program or advance announcement.

Although we have no evidence that such a performance or reading ever took place,[25] a dramatic recitation of this sort could have been one of the events of a social gathering in a private home (M. M. Fontaine 1993, 286). Du Bellay wrote a dramatic epithalamium for the 1559 marriage of the Duke of Savoy and the Duchess of Berry, which he intended to have performed by the wife and three daughters of the middle-class but well-connected Jean de Morel. When the accidental death of Henry II caused the cancellation of that performance, the Morel family may have recited it in their own home, which had become a regular meeting place for courtiers and literary men (Nolhac 1921, 550). Whether the girls would have worn the costumes originally planned for them or merely spoken their lines, we do not know. Clark Keating (1941, 28) casts some doubt as to whether this household performance actually took place at all. Nonetheless, he confirms that Camilla, the oldest girl, was involved in recitations in her family's salon. Nolhac bases his suggestion on a manuscript in which Du Bellay recorded his directions for the performance, costumes and all. The Morel family must at least have rehearsed the work at home with Du Bellay in anticipation of their formal performance.

Brantome describes how Marguerite de Navarre "faisait jouer et représenter par les filles de la cour" (Marguerite de Navarre 1963, xviii) [had her ladies of court perform and present] the "Comédies" or "Moralités" that she had written. These were semiprivate performances, suggests Lazard (1985, 34), and not widely known.

A rather different example involves Madame de Retz, one of the few female members of the Palace Academy in the late sixteenth century, who took part with another female member in the performance of a debate about moral and intellectual virtues, which Agrippa d'Aubigné described with admiration in a letter to his daughters (Yates 1988, 32). This was not a play, but it was a debate staged as a performance. Amelie Mason claims, unfortunately without citing her sources, that the entertainments at the Hôtel de Rambouillet in the early 1600s included the performance of "little comedies," as well as Corneille's readings of his new plays (1891, 21, 15). The hostess of that salon, Catherine de Vivonne, having spent the early years of her life in Italy, was surely aware of the close association there between academies and dramatic performances during the sixteenth century.

The prologue to Grazzini's mid-sixteenth-century *L'arzigogolo* comments disdainfully on the difference between "academy members" who read their parts and professional actors "like us" who recite from memory (Scrivano 1966, 1024); this offers us a glimpse of an intellectual social group engaged in a reading, which obviously requires much less effort than a full performance. Salons were, in many respects, a less formal version of academies, more open to the participation of women. One of the most common functions of the salon, whether in Italy or in France, was the reading aloud or singing of recent poems and other writings by the members of the group. If Labé's associates did read aloud her *Débat*, they must have enjoyed the event, which could have been performed easily and amusingly. Its liveliness has made it one of the famous writings of the French Renaissance.

The des Roches's first joint volume of *Oeuvres* (1579) included one act of a play in rhymed couplets by Catherine, "La tragicomedie de Tobie," based on the Vulgate's *Liber Tobias*. Along with this clear sign of interest in dramatic writing, the volume presented a set of six dialogues by Catherine that, like those of Helisenne and Labé, are a mix of classical essay and medieval débat between objects or personifications. Where the drama drew on biblical history, the dialogues drew on more secular sources.

Labé's dialogue was certainly known to the des Roches, as Anne Larsen has demonstrated, for Madeleine des Roches published her first poems in a 1578 volume containing also Labé's *Débat* (Larsen 1987, 103, 115 n. 24).[26] Catherine's dialogues in the first volume of *Oeuvres* clearly borrow from Labé's and also, wittingly or unwittingly, share some features with Helisenne's. Like Helisenne's speakers, Catherine's shift between personifications and human lovers in a series of loosely connected parallel debates. But like Labé's work, the dialogues are presented in a completely dramatic form without narrative framing.

The dialogue of Old Age and Youth, which is the least well constructed, seems also most closely related to the medieval debate poem. The argument of Hand and Foot, however, clearly derives from another tradition: the famous Roman anecdote, recounted by Livy, about the parts of the body that grumble over having to feed the stomach but come to realize their dependence on its function.[27] Here Catherine's humanist love for the classics is evident. The conversation of Fortune and Virtue draws its topic from another humanist favorite: Plutarch's moral essays on "The Fortune of the Romans" and "The Fortune of Alexander," which consider whether virtue or fortune is more responsible for Greek and Roman greatness. Plutarch was, besides Plato, one of des Roches's most used sources among both ancients and moderns.[28] Catherine's dialogue of Beauty and Love could have drawn its material from any number of Renaissance dialogues on love or from the endless sonnets that share their themes. It harks back as well to medieval exchanges of poetry between lover and lady. As a female and male pair Beauty and Love are readily identifiable with the human pair Charite and Sincero, whose exchange follows directly and ends the series. Thus, besides finding a mix of classical and medieval sources, we are led through abstractions into human characters.

Rather than being connected into a plot, the whole set of dialogues offers a series of formal and thematic variations on a basic pattern familiar from Labé's *Débat*. They tend to begin with an aggressive confrontation between their two disputants, who sometimes allow a third party to adjudicate their dispute. In most cases, the resolution is precisely that the two need each other and thus must go together willy-nilly. The dialogues tend in this way to explore the nature of the relation between concepts that, like Love and Folly, are not necessarily in simple contradiction. Youth and Old Age are the most directly opposite and the most hostile, and their exchange of insults and boasts is without resolution. In the dialogue of Fortune and Virtue, Virtue seeks to combine with Fortune, who refuses to alter her proper character in order to become a predictable follower of Virtue. Thus the issue is, as in Labé's *Débat*, whether these two should work together or remain separate.

In demonstrating how many follow her and how few follow Virtue, Fortune argues just the way Labé's Folly does in calling attention to the massive foolishness of mankind. Ultimately Fortune does agree to join Virtue in prayers for the protection of Poitiers from further destruction by the Huguenots but stipulates that this is an isolated case of cooperation. The use of specific historical allusion diverges from Labé's model toward that of Plutarch's essay, with its reference to Alexander, in whose success both factors combine; however, the dramatized dialogue form is much closer to Labé's than to Plutarch's.

The mutual insult and complaint of Hand and Foot, and the concomitant listing of necessary services performed by each, get referred to a third party, Mouth, who points out to the disputants how necessary they are to each other. They are thus persuaded to work together in concord. Poverty and Hunger are similarly a necessary pair. Although each blames the other for her own bad reputation, they have been chained together by fate. Thus despite their desire to be free of each other, they are compelled to go off together in the end. Whereas persuasion brings Hand and Foot into accord, the force of necessity compels the union of Poverty and Hunger. Again we see the author composing variations on a pattern.

Catherine is generally explicitly Christian in a manner quite unlike Labé; in this regard she is closer in spirit to Helisenne. Youth and Age both refer to the Creator's power and will. Despite the classical source of the fable of Hand and Foot, Mouth similarly appeals to the natural order established by the Creator (223). Fortune and Virtue define themselves as the daughter and servant of the providential Christian God, whose work they both do with willing obedience and to whom they both pray.

In the dialogue of Poverty and Hunger, however, the classical setting contributes to bringing the piece closer than ever to Labé's model. Jupiter appears at the start as a character to whose party Poverty was heading, and other gods are named as attendants at the party, making Poverty and Hunger appear as inhabitants of the world of classical gods on a par with Venus, Mercury, and Apollo. Des Roches's opening line comes very close to Labé's as both describe, through the mouth of Folly or of Poverty, the desire of this goddess to attend Jupiter's party. Moreover, both goddesses are impeded right away by an encounter with a hostile and belligerent Cupid who refuses to recognize what he owes to her.[29] The closeness of these openings, calling us to see the two dialogues in relation to each other, induces our awareness of how Labé's lighthearted theme of foolish love has become the much grimmer theme of the poverty and hunger affecting war-torn regions of France.

Both Labé and des Roches use their characters' speeches to offer satirical portraits of various types of people. Labé's Apollo—though his intent is not to criticize but to demonstrate love's power—sketches the behavior of men and women in love, with borrowings from Ovid's Art of Love about the varieties of dress and hairstyle created to allure; but the really biting satire comes with Mercury's praise of Folly's power. In the final section of the dialogue kings and courtiers, philosophers and astronomers, military men, lawyers and judges, and all the rest of the world who admire such fools, are portrayed in all their foolishness by Mercury's wit. Similarly, near the end of des Roches's dialogue, Hunger describes courtiers, bankers, judges, lawyers, and merchants in brief but biting terms as she considers where she might get a meal. Both writers see their particular topic as a way of addressing at the same time much broader concerns. In this regard both works come close to the sottie, which regularly included a satirical review of the various classes and professions (Aubailly 1976, 313). Whereas Labé's theme has a timelessness to it, however, des Roches is more focused on the historical realities of her day. Labé seems content merely to laugh at the ubiquitous follies of mankind, whereas des Roches indicates at times an interest in trying to change things.

For example, the insertion of a feminist criticism against men who think that women lack reason is Catherine's addition to a topic that might seem remote from such concerns. However, both her dialogue and Labé's, treating abstractions as people, emphasize the gender of the speakers: the older female Poverty or Folly is scorned by the young male Love. When Poverty explains as rational her decision not to challenge Love's hostility to his own mother, Hunger responds, "Si dict-on communément que les femmes abondent en parolles, et manquent de raison" [Yet it is said that generally women are abundant in words and lacking in reason]. Poverty replies, "Qui dict ce propos sinon des hommes lourds et grossiers?" [Who says such a thing except for gross and uncultivated men?], and launches into a tirade against such men (230–31). Prudent speech is ascribed to women, imprudent blabbing to men. Poverty claims that she can point to a modern as well as an ancient example of female prudence, and although she refuses to reveal the name, we can guess that it is Catherine's mother. Hunger wishes to honor her by staying away, but Poverty is sure that this woman "sçait commander à toy et à toutes autres passions" (233) [knows how to dominate you and all other passions]. Thus the hunger and poverty effected by war become an occasion for praising a woman's power of reason over passions. The gendering of Poverty and Love suggests an identification of the male with sensuality and excess, of the female with prudence and restraint. Whether or not Catherine knew the work of Helisenne, they are making a similar argument and using similar techniques.

Des Roches's dialogues are part of an ensemble, and evoke each other through shared allusions. Youth, for example, compares her dispute with Age to the dispute between Hand and Foot, although humorously she misses the point of that anecdote.[30] The dialogue of Poverty and Hunger ensures the connectedness of the whole set by referring both backward and forward. It shares two details with the earlier dialogue of Fortune and Virtue: a reference to the civil war in Poitiers and a comment—attributed to Madeleine des Roches—that Virtue and Fortune are needed both together. It also looks forward to the dialogue with Love, as Poverty, picking up the Platonic myth of Love's parentage, complains that her son refuses to abide in her company;[31] in the later dialogue Love will repeat this reference to "ma mere Penie" (246). The repeated associations of Age with ugliness connect the first dialogue by contrast to the fifth, with its figure of Beauty. Youth's reference to the values of pursuing philosophy (194–96) connects her to the studious Beauty as well, while the pair of poems that Age and Youth recite in turn at the end of their dialogue anticipates the shift from prose into an exchange of verse between Charite and Sincero at the end of the dialogue set. These are not merely separate pieces, then, but a series, in which the change from abstract to human speakers is a part of a network of variations.

The dialogue of Love and Beauty is once again about whether the two must be coupled or whether Beauty can find a refuge free from the importunities of Love. Physis or Nature orders them to stay together as they need each other, for neither is honored without the other. The opening with its emphasis on Love's bandaged eyes reinforces the link with Labé's text. Although this image was certainly common, Beauty's question, "Pourquoy donc portez-vous ce bandeau sinon pour cacher l'imperfection de vos yeux?" (247) [Why then do you wear this blindfold if not to hide the imperfection of your eyes?], brings it more specifically into connection with Labé's scene. So does Beauty's insistence, like Folly's, that all of Love's force derives from her. A recurring theme from Labé, both in this dialogue and in that of Virtue and Fortune, is that of blindness and guidance. Fortune's final statement is "il vaut mieux estre guidée par un clair voyant, que de conduire un grand nombre d'aveugles" (217) [it is better to be guided by one who sees clearly than to lead a large number of the blind]. Beauty rejects Love's escort, saying, "Pensez-vous que je vueille estre guidée par un aveugle?" (247) [Do you think that I want to be guided by a blind man?].

As in the previous dialogue, Catherine's personal feminist concerns are given voice. Beauty in the end gains one place of respite, not in the convent (explicitly rejected) but with Pallas and among her books, "mon temple de franchise" [my temple of freedom]. Des Roches could have taken the idea directly from her own life. The judge, Physis or Nature, is herself a female (both disputants call her "ma mere"), and she aids Beauty's request in clear response to the critics of Catherine who considered her rejection of marriage unnatural. This mother is undoubtedly one last reference to Catherine's own mother, praised in two of the preceding dialogues, and to the maternal support that has enabled Catherine to live as she wishes. Love addresses her the way a suitor would address the parent of his beloved, asking her for Beauty's hand, while Beauty begs her mother not to grant his request. The solution is for Beauty to be offered a refuge where she can be free from Love, who waits hoping that she will eventually emerge. As in the preceding dialogue, we are in the combined contexts of the realm of classical gods and of des Roches's historical situation. Classical deities can readily be used to express features of des Roches's life.

This dialogue is the most dramatic of the set in the sense that it suggests a certain amount of action by characters in a scene. The temple was a common element in Renaissance backdrops, often used as the site for a concluding marriage. For Catherine, it becomes the site of a refuge from marriage. Yet religion as a defense against love is explicitly rejected in favor of the defense offered "par les livres, par les ouvrages, et par les yeux de la Meduse" (250) [by books, by works, and by the eyes of the Medusa], that is, the Medusa that appears on the protective shield of Pallas.

Catherine's clear identification with Beauty leads us into the final dialogue, which is quite different from the others. In this dialogue the abstract Love and Beauty become the human characters Sincero and Charite. While both names together make almost an anagram for Catherine's own (they form "Catherine Rocis"), and while both characters are her invention, at the same time Charite is more closely linked to Catherine herself, in both name and gender.[32] Charite's name evokes three meanings: as an imperfect anagram for "Catherine"; as one of the classical Graces; and as the Christian *caritas*, opposed to *cupiditas* or lust. Thus it sums up Catherine's mingling of historical, classical, and medieval frames of reference.

Sincero, meanwhile, is presented as an imagined lover.[33] Her preface states explicitly:

> Ils diront peut-estre que je ne devois pas escrire d'amour, que si je suis amoureuse il ne faut pas le dire, que si je ne suis telle il ne faut pas le feindre; je leur respondray à cela, que je ne le suis, ny ne feins de l'estre; car j'escry ce que j'ay pensé, et non pas ce que j'ay veu en Sincero, lequel je ne connoy que par imagination. (182)

> *[They will say perhaps that I should not write about love: that if I am in love, I should not say so, and that if I am not, I should not pretend to be; I will reply to them that I am not in love nor pretending to be, for I describe what I have thought and not what I have seen in Sincero, whom I know only through imagination.]*

This defense of her writing resembles Helisenne's, who claims in her letters to her husband that he is mistaking for autobiography work that has derived from her readings: "& pource (non que par experience je le saiche: Mais comme en l'exercise literaire j'ay compris) en parleray" (1995a, 111) [I shall, therefore, speak of love (not because I have learned this through experience, but because literature has taught me to understand) (1986, 84)]: in sum, I will write what I think rather than what I feel, what I have learned from the literary tradition rather than from personal experience.[34]

Moreover, as Helisenne ventriloquized an irate husband, Catherine ventriloquizes a perfect if rather conventional lover. Although des Roches goes on to compare her creation of this perfect lover to Castiglione's of the perfect courtier, thus implying a dialogic source for her dialogic work, her dialogues are nothing like Castiglione's. Instead of a historical cast of characters in a plausibly real conversation, des Roches presents explicitly invented human figures speaking in ways that do not resemble realistic conversation. What she offers is rather the presentation of relationships among ideas or positions in a vivacious manner. Yet Catherine's persistent references in the first five pieces to her own real situation in Poitiers pull her writing slowly away from a more abstract model to something more immediately personal. The humans of the sixth dialogue hover between representative types and autobiographical participants. Charite listens to Sincero's myths and flatteries, even encourages him to tell them to her, but remains detached and skeptical, pointing out his contradictions and finally requesting him to be quiet for a while. So too Beauty pointed out the contradictions in Love's claims that she should trust his oaths when he is a self-confessed deceiver. Both dialogues, then, offer witty deflations of male rhetoric by the female. Marie de

Romieu's "Bref discours de l'excellence de la femme" includes similarly mocking imitations of men's wooing speeches (vv. 149–80); since she mentions the des Roches later in the same work, she was probably aware of Catherine's ventriloquisms and, as a female reader, enjoyed them enough to make her own version.

Sincero's persistent request for Charite to assume the role of his guide, on earth and toward heaven, allows des Roches to use the phrases of neoplatonic love both to set the lady in a truly authoritative position and also to make fun of men who claim to need such guidance. At the same time, however, Catherine explicitly remarks on the continuing male control over discourse. When Sincero claims that her beauty raises him to the heavens, she replies: "Je croys plustost que par la faveur de voz propos vous portez mon nom au Ciel, Sincero, et que vous l'en raportez quand bon vous semble" (256) [I believe rather that by the favor of your words you carry my name up to Heaven, Sincero, and that you will carry it back down when you feel like it]. Male writing about a woman, while seeming to exalt the woman's reputation, has also the power to ruin it. Men praise women, but only when it suits men. Thus Charite both buys into the discourse, insofar as it enables her to tease Sincero, and simultaneously rejects it as the expression of male rather than female power. Men are free to say what they wish, unlike herself, who has been told by critics that she should not feign: "vous pouvez feindre sans etre repris" (256) [you can feign without being scolded]. The chief freedom for women lies in not believing what men say: "je puis seurement vous ouyr sans adjouter beaucoup de foy à vos parolles" (256) [I can surely hear you without granting much faith to your words].

In similar openness about the problematic relations of women to discourse, Charite responds to Sincero's elaborate praises by indicating the dilemma of women, previously discussed by Castiglione as well: if she rejects his flatteries, she seems to be inviting further insistence; yet if she says nothing, she seems to accept them.[35] The way to disarm this dilemma is to spell it out. This requires a female speech that breaks out of the manipulative alternatives set up by men and speaks about the discourse itself rather than responding to what men say.[36] Catherine's dialogue does just that.

Given the quickness of men to read women's writing as autobiographical, the dehumanizing of speakers—by the use of personifications or mythical figures and by putting the human speakers as a pair in a series of nonhuman speakers—was a means for these women to distance the work from the historical author and allow ideas to speak as if on their own. Yet none of these three writers wanted to efface herself completely; all three were eager for recognition. Thus we find a wavering between more and less recognizable stand-ins and the weaving of variations across debates with differently distanced speakers.

All three writers considered so far linked their dialogues to other writings in a volume of *oeuvres*. Just as the relationship of Sincero and Charite largely parallels that of Love and Beauty in the preceding dialogue, so the dialogue of Sincero and Charite overflows into the sonnets and songs that continue their wooing and response through poems addressed to each other. These two characters, partly fictional and yet anagrammatically signaling Catherine's own voice, connect the dialogues fluidly to the rest of her volume rather than allowing us to see them as a neatly separate piece.

Besides the many real exchanges of sonnets between men and women in the sixteenth century, Ovid's *Heroides* had established a model for the single-authored exchange between a pair of lovers.[37] Other male poets had also invented the replying poems of their female addressees. Petrarch's *Rime* no. 359 imagines Laura's reply from heaven. More dangerous because *in vita*, Lattanzio Benucci's *capitolo* to Tullia d'Aragona is followed by his own "Risposta a se stesso in nome della medesima Signora Tullia" [Reply to Himself in the Name of That Same Madam Tullia].[38] Catherine takes over this writing of exchanged verses from the perspective of the other gender and attaches it as the lyrical continuation of a dialogic form begun in prose.

This feature too may reveal the traces of Labé's volume. Both writers begin with a prefatory letter, then offer their dialogues, and then shift to poetry.[39] Labé's first elegy seems to link itself to the preceding dialogue by beginning:

Au temps qu'Amour, d'hommes et Dieus vainqueuer,
Faisoit bruler de sa flamme mon coeur

(1981, 129)

*[At the time when Love, vanquisher of men and Gods,
Made my heart burn with his flame]*

thus shifting from the impersonal debate about Love to the personal experience of it, as well as from prose to verse.[40] Catherine's dialogue of Love and Beauty already contained ample material from the sonnet tradition—that Love's bow is made from the beautiful lady's eyebrow, his darts from her glances, and so on. Therefore the transition from prose into sonnets is rendered smooth by the presence of the poetic conventions already within the prose. We have noticed already the links between the gendered debates of Helisenne's *Songe* and those of her previous letters. These writers repeatedly manifest the porousness of dialogue to other forms, such as the exchange of letters or verses.[41] If Catherine does less to develop the dramatic aspects of the genre, her dialogues were reworked not long after into a more fully theatrical form.

The dialogues of Catherine's first and second volumes, probably Labé's, and possibly Helisenne's as well inspired yet another female writer of dialogues, Marie Le Gendre, Dame de Rivery, whose *Dialogue des chastes amours d'Eros et de Kalisti* was published together with her *L'exercice de l'âme vertueuse* in Paris in 1596 and again by a different printer in 1597.[42] This noblewoman, about whose life almost nothing is known, had been recently widowed when her volume appeared, as her sad poems to her husband, also in the volume, make clear. Besides these poems, *L'exercice*, dedicated to the Princesse de Conty, contains twelve moral dialogues on topics such as reason, modesty, reputation, friendship, ignorance, passions, true honor, and so on, with reference to classical texts and examples. These straightforward pieces, a collection of commonplaces lined up in support of one view, suggest a woman sure of her traditional values. Her dialogue similarly makes very clear what its lessons are; it is not a work of ambivalences or open discussion but rather a much livelier and more original presentation of topics similar to those of her essays.

The first edition of the *Dialogue* is dedicated to François Le Poulchre, Sieur de La Motte-Messeme (1547–97?), a nobleman, retired military captain, and staunch royalist, whose father had served at the court of Marguerite de Navarre. To pass the time after his retirement, he composed, and dedicated to the king, a long history of the recent French civil wars in tedious verse, including many personal reflections and judgments. A few years later he continued his moral, political, and scientific reflections in a volume entitled *Le passe-temps de M. de la Motte-Messemé*, printed by the same publisher, Jean Le Blanc, who would print Le Gendre's dialogue just one year later.[43] This work is full of references to the classical gods and philosophers. Le Gendre refers to Le Poulchre's "doctes oeuvres" [learned works] and calls him "mon père," while he responds to her as "ma fille d'alliance," assuring her that her work has no need of his protection. Colette Winn (Le Gendre 2001, 15–16) notes that through Le Poulchre's participation in the Académie du Palais, Marie Le Gendre could have known about the moral discussions and discourses that formed part of its activities and that bear a close resemblance to the essays of *L'exercice*. Some noblewomen even attended these events. The name Kalisti in Le Gendre's dialogue is obviously in part a play on Le Poulchre's name, since *kalos* is the Greek and *pulcher* the Latin for "beautiful." Curiously, this identifies him with the female beloved rather than with the male. It implies moreover that Le Gendre herself is the male Love attracted by his Beauty. But this flattering identification in the dedication has little bearing once we are within the text.

The genres of dialogue, essay, narrative, and drama converge in this *Dialogue des chastes amours*. Like Helisenne's *Songe*, Le Gendre's dialogue combines a recurring narrator with a series of dramatic scenes. On the one hand, *Dialogue des chastes amours* seems more like an actual drama than Helisenne's piece, because it keeps its characters on a more unified level of reality and brings them repeatedly into dialogue in varying combinations rather than introducing new speakers with each scene. On the other hand, some of the narrated material more resembles part of a sentimental romance or moral essay than a play.

The narrator opens the text with general observations about the human emotions, of which love is said to be the most natural. She makes the traditional distinction among three objects of love, the honorable, the useful, and the beautiful; but for her all three are good, and love of beauty the best. One loves

l'honorable, pour la foelicité que nous recevons d'estre loués, et exaltez sur le commun; l'utille, pour l'exceder en preéminente autorité, et obvier à l'indigence: et le beau . . . pour la delectation qu'il aporte à nos sens interieurs par le rapport des exterieurs. (2001, 117)

[the honorable, for the happiness that we receive from being praised and exalted above the common run; the useful, in order to exceed in preeminent authority and to avoid poverty; and the beautiful . . . for the delight that it brings to our internal senses by means of the external ones.]

Le Gendre shares Helisenne's, Labé's, and des Roches's interest in being praised and standing out above the crowd. Utility is associated with the acquiring of authority rather than with the pursuit of wealth; thus it too is perceived as desirable. The love of Beauty is raised out of its sensual basis by considering sensual perception a mere means to something internal and immaterial, a neoplatonic attitude.

Her positive evaluation of all three kinds of love is quite remarkable given the historical background of this topic. Aristotle's *Ethics* 8.2–4, without being initially negative about a love or friendship based on utility or pleasure, nonetheless considers such a relationship impermanent (because focused on accidentals) and thus inferior to one based on the goodness of the person loved. Evil men love only for some gain to themselves and are thus incapable of the best love. Aristotle's discusssion thus drives an ever wider moral wedge between the two "ignoble" kinds of love and the one true and enduring kind. Boccaccio's *Filocolo* 4.43–46, in an argument based on this passage from Aristotle but transferred into the setting of a romance, praises only the honest love of friends unequivocally; the pursuit of utility is condemned harshly right away by both speakers, and the delightful love of pleasure and beauty is reluctantly dismissed as dangerously deluding and destructive.[44] Note also Foscarini's epistle 57, cited earlier (chap. 4), which rejects any notion of loving for reasons of either utility or pleasure, emphasizing a love based on virtue alone. Le Gendre follows up Aristotle's notion that one can love with two kinds of love at once by introducing the new notion that a combination of all three is actually the best. This opening moral essay, much like the earlier essays in the volume, becomes a prologue to the story that follows.

The two main characters who appear on the scene, Eros and Kalisti, are clearly an imitation of Catherine des Roches's Love and Beauty. Le Gendre's potentially puzzling use of the word "dialogue" in her title emphasizes the kinship to des Roches's dialogue. Le Poulchre had been present in Poitiers during the Huguenot siege, whose miseries he describes from the Catholic viewpoint. He was therefore personally acquainted with the des Roches and includes them in his *Passe-temps* in a list of contemporary women whose knowledge he admires. Marie Le Gendre is also in this list (Mouton 1931, 279). Most likely, therefore, it was through Le Poulchre that she became acquainted with the volumes of the des Roches. This might be one reason for her having dedicated this particular work to him. He would be a reader able to recognize her borrowings.

Like Catherine des Roches's Love, Eros woos his beloved, while Kalisti listens for a while "pour simplement passer le temps, & non pour vous croire" (124) [simply to pass the time and not to believe you]. As Catherine's Beauty fled from her suitor to Minerva's temple, so Kalisti flees to the Palace of Sophie (Wisdom). As Love appealed for help to Nature, who is partly suggestive of Catherine's own mother, so Eros appeals to Sophie, the mother of Kalisti, with whom she has some very human mother-daughter interactions. The influence of des Roches's work on Le Gendre's is undeniable. However, where des Roches left her Beauty unwed, Le Gendre ends her dialogue with a wedding to which the gods are invited. Apparently, having herself been married (Berriot-Salvadore 1990a, 462; Winn in Le Gendre 2001, 23), she did not see marriage and learning as incompatible activities for a woman. Indeed, married love becomes for her the ideal love that can combine all three kinds enumerated at the start: the honorable, the useful, and the delightful.

Le Gendre's interest in the education of girls along with boys, an education based on capabilities rather than gender, is manifest in the brief glimpse of the school of Minerva, whom they find "en son cabinet où elle enseignoit toutes sortes de sciences à ses Nimphes et chevaliers selon qu'elle recognois-soit leurs esprits en estre capable" (156–57) [in her study where she was teaching all sorts of sciences to her nymphs and knights according to what she recognized their intelligence as capable of]. Just as Pasithée, in Catherine's second volume, entertained herself chastely at home with her studies, so Sophie advises Kalisti to avoid Eros by staying at home and entertaining herself with the activities and company of Sophie and Minerva.

Lured out by Curiosity, represented as a woman intervening on Eros's behalf, Kalisti finds Eros lying in wait for her, just as Catherine's Love promised (or threatened) to lie in wait for Beauty to emerge; but when Kalisti flees at once to her mother, Sophie surprisingly offers to accompany her daughter back along with Curiosity, for in the company of Wisdom Curiosity cannot do harm and can lead us to learn things that are pleasing: "d'assez agreable accez et conduict à la cognoissance de choses qui plaisent" (154). Like des Roches, then, Le Gendre defends learning for women partly on the basis that they are capable of it and partly on the basis that it will actually protect them from falling into error and vice. As Sophie says to her daughter, without Sophie (or Wisdom) Kalisti is in grave danger, but together they are invincible (135–37, 145–47).[45] Moreover, like Labé, Le Gendre adds pleasure as a goal of learning that is not to be disdained.

Catherine's superposition of abstractions and humans is also a feature of Le Gendre's work, although the humans glimpsed through the abstractions do not in any obvious way refer to Le Gendre herself (or our almost total lack of knowledge about her may blind us to any such references that might exist). In some very human scenes, Sophie scolds her daughter for fixing her hair and for showing signs of interest in Eros, warning that Eros is not to be trusted even when he claims to be seeking an honest marriage and that Kalisti's honor is at stake: "il faut prendre garde que . . . il n'invente des ruses pour vous attraper dont la superficie soit vertue et l'interieur (vrayment) ruze" (146) [you must be on guard that he isn't just inventing ruses to catch you, which have the surface appearance of virtue but the interior (truly) of deceit]. Much of Sophie's advice is plain maternal advice to an adolescent daughter. With affectionate obedience Kalisti, like Catherine, praises her mother as her best instructor and example. Winn (Le Gendre 2001, 38–39) notes that the mother is a much more active and important character in this work than in Catherine's, while the daughter is much weaker to the attractions of love and less decisive about what she wants.

In other scenes Sophie evokes not Catherine's mother but Labé's Folly, for she bandages Eros's eyes so tightly that he cannot see. It seems odd that

Wisdom should have the same effect on love as Folly, but her blindfolding is less permanent. Where Folly was acting in self-defense, Sophie claims to be protecting her daughter from Eros's excessive passion. She is also testing Eros, who comically begins in his blindness to reveal his true feelings and give the lie to his former expressions of good intentions, complaining of Sophie's obstructions to his desires. As Kalisti comments: "Vous ne parliez pas d'elle, voyant clair, comme vous faites maintenant que vous estes aveuglé" (140) [You were not speaking about her when you saw clearly the way you are speaking now that you are blinded]. The allegorical intent is only too clear; but the presence of Labé's text seems evident in this bit of stage action as Sophie, an older woman like Folly, ties the bandage tightly around Eros's eyes only to have him complain bitterly about her.[46]

The scenes form a unified action that expands Catherine's dialogue into a multiscene play full of movement on the stage. We see Eros speaking to Kalisti, lamenting alone after her departure, seeking out her mother, talking again to Kalisti while blindfolded, trying to see her when she ventures outside, and finally accompanying mother and daughter to the house of Minerva for the wedding. In between we see Sophie watching her daughter for signs of love, scolding her, warning her, helping her, offering to accompany and chaperone her, and ultimately happily accepting for her daughter a suitor whose intentions have become honest. The final exit by all to attend the wedding of the two main characters is a typical conclusion to a comedy. Yet the fact that the couple is Love and Beauty and that the wedding guests are classical gods, Muses, and Graces creates the effect of a masque as well as of a human comedy.

The central scene, a conversation between Eros and Kalisti in her mother's home, comes closest of all the scenes to a traditional dialogue on the nature of love and its relation to wisdom. Winn has observed that Le Gendre does not immediately equate the love of beauty with a wise kind of love, thus tempering neoplatonic love theories with a bit of realism. But this move is already part of the whole tradition of love dialogues since Castiglione's. Placing the debate in the mouths of a male and a female speaker is also a frequent feature of the traditional treatment of this topic, from Leone Ebreo to Tullia d'Aragona. This scene, no doubt intentionally central in its placement, upholds the "dialogue" title of the piece. Framing this conversation, however, with scenes that include the young girl's mother adds the realistic social concerns of female life. Love is not merely something abstract and philosophical; and male desires, no matter how loftily phrased, are subject to honorable female suspicion.

Among the possible signs of Labé's influence on Le Gendre, Evelyne Berriot-Salvadore (1990b) cites the humorous undercutting of neoplatonic notions that beauty will automatically inspire a wise love, the combination of allegorical and realistic qualities in the speakers, the natural quality of the dialogue, the dramatic framing of the dialogue, and the presence of the gods as witness to the relationship between the two main characters. While she concludes that the evidence for Labé's influence on Le Gendre remains uncertain, Winn (Le Gendre 2001, 36) remarks that "sans doute" Marie Le Gendre knew Labé's *Débat*, suggests echoes of Labé's writing in Le Gendre's poetry (99, 106), and proposes that Kalisti's comments about Eros draw from Apollo's speech on love in Labé's *Débat* (141). Like Labé, Le Gendre avoids any Christian reference, leaving her message thoroughly within a context of classical gods.

Yet Le Gendre's recognizably theatrical ending combined with explicit moralizing resembles the end of Helisenne's *Songe* more than the dialogues of either Labé or des Roches. So too does the interspersing of narrative comments among these theatrical scenes. Like Helisenne's *Songe*, moreover, the entire dialogue addresses both sexes, but primarily females. This is clear from the explicit message that ends the work: that dishonest desires are brief at best and cause shame, and that girls should imitate Kalisti in order to triumph over passion and win honor and glory. It is quite possible that Marie Le Gendre knew both Labé's and Helisenne's writings as well as Catherine des Roches's.

The position of Le Gendre in relation to the scenes she sets forth is that of a detached and authoritative commentator. Both Helisenne and Catherine at least suggest their own disguised involvement in the scene, Helisenne by writing in the first person and becoming a participant in the discussion, and Catherine by referring to her mother and presenting a character whose name is an anagram for her own. Le Gendre and Labé remain completely outside the actions they present. Le Gendre, however, frequently makes generalizing moral comments about the action, careful to steer the reader's reception of the work.

Despite the presence of narrative moments, the theatrical qualities of Le Gendre's piece go beyond earlier dramatic dialogues in the construction of a unified and concluded plot that resembles that of a romantic comedy. The inclusion of stanzaic poems and songs by Eros at various points has the function of theatrical interludes between the seven scenes of action.[47] For the most part, Le Gendre's piece could actually work as theater if some of the narrated scenes were treated as interlude dumb shows.[48] For example, between the fifth and sixth scenes, Curiosity lures Kalisti outside, where she is frightened to see Eros and retreats into the palace to seek her mother, while Eros makes gestures of despair (148). Some narrative passages indicate performable actions: for example, Kalisti's disdainful exit (126), Eros's sudden burst of tears (133), Sophie's tightening the bandage over Eros's eyes before excusing herself and exiting (138). Other narrative passages (135, 145) indicate characters' thoughts and would be unperformable. The final brief scene in Minerva's chamber is entirely narrated, but its wedding announcement is so typical of theatrical endings that it bridges both genres. Moreover, this could once again be treated as a dumb show: Minerva greets the three main characters and then sends Mercury to bring in Hymen for a recognizable marriage ceremony. This silent action could be accompanied by a singing of the sonnet that follows: how Eros has been ensnared in his own nets and happily yields to his captivity.

The prose essay that serves as a prologue and the prose moral lesson at the end, along with the other less readily performable narrated passages, suggest that Marie Le Gendre—like Helisenne—expected this work primarily to be read rather than seen and heard. It is a work for the theater of the mind, a dialogue to be imagined as a series of lively scenes and relationships rather than read as an abstract discussion of ideas. Nonetheless, since it requires only a few actors, it might have been used also for an in-house production among friends, perhaps a staged reading with the narrator as one part. The preponderance of female characters (all except Eros, whose youthfulness could readily be played by a young woman) and the expectation of a female audience support the possibility that a few female friends and family members could have produced this work for their own delight. The costumes would be simply normal clothing. The changing scenes—a meadow, a room, another room, the outdoor surroundings of a palace—are mentioned in the text and would not need, in a private reading, to be physically created, although a more ambitious performance could use a backdrop for the outdoor scenes and the furniture of the Rivery home itself for the indoor ones. Le Gendre offers a work more refined and sentimental than the comedies and farces of the French public theater, a play for honorable young women to enjoy and be guided by.

I have tried to suggest that there is in France a female dialogue tradition that is quite different from the dialogue writing of Italian women as well as from that of men. The word *tradition* implies that the similarities among these writings are not entirely due to chance. Marie Le Gendre was certainly influenced by the dialogues of Catherine des Roches and probably also by Labé's and Helisenne's. Catherine des Roches herself clearly knew and drew from Labé's work, whose satiric wit she imitated happily along with many details from Labé's *Débat*.

Besides the clearly established knowledge of Labé's work by des Roches and of des Roches's work by Le Gendre, it is also quite possible that any or all of these women knew the work of Helisenne de Crenne, which was published repeatedly from the 1540s to the 1560s. Helisenne in turn praises Marguerite de Navarre as her inspiration, the same Marguerite that François Le Poulchre boasted had held him as a baby; Marie Le Gendre would not have been allowed to forget about her. Marguerite de Navarre's own interest in dramatic dialogue and dialogic drama, which I discuss in chapter 2, provided a strong initial model for this French female tradition. Thus these French women writers are much more interconnected as a group than the Italian women who wrote in the dialogue genre but who seem to have been unaware of each other's work. The French writers openly aimed at and expected female as well as male readers. The signs of their influence by and on other women show that those expectations of a female readership were fulfilled.

Besides knowing each other's work, these French writers shared an interest in developing the theatrical qualities of the dialogue genre. The dialogues in Catherine's second volume of works, which I discuss in chapter 3, continue to push the dialogue toward theater. The scene between two girls implies considerable action along with speech: Iris keeps running to the window to look for her boyfriend, and Pasithée introduces song and dance into the conversation. Larsen (des Roches 1998, 40) describes these dialogues as "proches du théâtre lu" [close to theater for a reading audience]. They show Catherine's increasing interest in presenting a lively and fully human action. Her dialogues between fathers and daughters also come closer to the works of the other three writers discussed in this chapter in another important way: these French women all linked dialogues among different characters into an ongoing dramatic narrative. This development moves beyond Erasmus's separate scenes; only des Periers's *Cymbalum mundi* does something similar. The dramatic structure of the women's dialogues is enhanced by suggestions or descriptions of action and by the incorporation of widely used dramatic elements such as a theatrical finale: a pageant of celestial virtues, a judgment before the assembly of gods, a wedding in the presence of gods and Graces. Le Gendre even includes interludes of song between her scenes and at the end of the play.

One feature of the tradition, shared more with French drama than with humanist dialogue, is the oddly heterogeneous nature of the speaking characters. For Helisenne, humans are addressed by pairs of gods and personifications. For Labé, two gods similarly perform as advocates in parallel with a conflict between personifications, while other gods act more like human characters. For Catherine des Roches, disputes between personifications fade into human conversation in a gradual metamorphosis, and a historical identity can coexist with an allegorical figure such as Physis or Beauté. With Marie Le Gendre we find ourselves watching classical gods and abstractions that feel very much like human beings. The simultaneous or parallel figures of different degrees of reality and abstraction look back as much to medieval as to humanist sources. The series of dialogues among similarly heterogeneous characters that comprises the *Roman de la rose* mingles with sottie and morality plays, débats, Italian comedy, and other Renaissance dialogues as elements of a conglomerate inspiration.

Perhaps it seemed more permissible to write a dramatic dialogue among characters who are clearly fictional than to write the sort of Ciceronian recorded conversation that would present the author speaking in her own voice in a female or mixed company. Nonetheless, that Ciceronian form is what the contemporary Italian women were writing. One might argue that the French carefulness was a result of the writers' unanimous intentions to publish, unlike Nogarola or Morata. However, Nogarola certainly circulated her dialogue, and Matraini clearly aimed for publication. Neither of these Italians sought to conceal her role as a speaker, even in a dialogue with a male. Tullia d'Aragona as a courtesan positively sought publicity through publication, but even the "honest" Italians did not shrink from it. Were the French women simply more modest? Catherine des Roches sought publicity for her work under own name; yet even her most autobiographical dialogues are put into the mouths of objectified characters. One might argue that the theme of love, which drama encourages, made honest women reluctant to speak in person. Yet Labé, who was willing to publish remarkably amorous verse in her own name, wrote her dialogue as a distanced dramatic fiction. In sum, the cultural difference seems less a matter of personal modesty than of genre and generic models. The difference, I suggest, has to do with the proud identification of Italians with classical Rome and the French rival preference for medieval and recent models that were French. I suggest furthermore that these French women were eager to build on specifically female models, a move consistent with their expressed desire to improve the possibilities for other women to learn and exercise their literacy.

Unlike most of the dialogues written by men, these female-authored dialogues include a preponderance of female speakers. Although female speakers were most likely to be used in men's dialogues concerning love, these women's dialogues include a wide variety of female roles: from Wisdom to Folly, from Beauty to Hunger and Poverty. When they discuss love, they tend to warn women against its dangers and advocate either avoiding it altogether or channeling it into marriage. Labé accepts it as a necessary folly. But love is certainly not the only theme on which women converse.

Besides discussing love, these writers share a certain feminist agenda: the defense of women's intellectual and moral equality with men and the advocacy of women's education. This agenda appears in Helisenne's *Songe* in the dreamer's unhappy request to Reason and Reason's reply. It reappears in the diatribe of Catherine des Roches's Poverty against misogynists who consider women irrational and in Beauty's preference for studies over love. The issue returns once again in Le Gendre's text, both through the significant presence of the female characters Sophie and Minerva and through a reference to Minerva's school, where boys and girls are educated together according to their abilities. While love is a recurring topic of these writings, their authors insist on the possibility for women to be rational. As a countereffort to the traditional association of women with sensuality, three of the dialogues connect their young females with characters such as Reason, Wisdom, and Minerva. They portray women with books and girls in school, advocating that females be allowed the same right as males to educational pursuits. Furthermore, they encourage women's study both as an aid to moral wisdom and as a pleasure.

The same three dialogues show women supported by other women in these concerns. Thus Helisenne's Reason supports the dreamer's protest against the misogynist view of women's irrationality; des Roches's Nature supports her daughter Beauty's desire to study rather than marry; Le Gendre's Sophie, while spending time with her own friend Minerva, assures her daughter that curiosity and learning are a useful pleasure not to be shunned.

Might these female bonds of support, or the salons in which at least Labé and des Roches were known to have regularly participated, have created the social conditions for at least private performances? It is possible that some of these texts were at least read aloud in the social and literary gatherings that we know occurred in some of their authors' homes, but there is no hard evidence for it. The inclusion of passages of description and narrative in the texts of Helisenne and Le Gendre suggests the expectation of a reading audience, although, as I have pointed out, their writings could be made to work in performance. In any case, all four women saw to the publication of their works for the mental theater of their unknown readers.[49]

Furthermore, for all these writers, dialogue is set into a volume with other texts with which it is thematically linked. Thus not only do speaker types shift from one conversation or debate to the next, but form itself changes in a formal variation on recurring themes that overflow into or from letters, essays, romance, and poetry. The very fluidity and permeability of the dialogue genre are repeatedly on display. These French women were experimenting with the form and its possible connections to other genres and especially its potential for dramatic development. Certainly des Roches and Le Gendre—possibly also Labé—were doing this with an awareness that it was an experiment in which other French women had similarly been engaged.

6 Many Voices

T wo women, one French and one Italian, wrote fully polyphonic dialogues: Marguerite de Navarre, whose *Heptameron* tales (written in
the 1540s and published in 1559, ten years after her death) are inter-
laced with vivacious discussions among their ten narrators;[1] and Moderata
Fonte, whose *Il merito delle donne* (written in 1592 and published posthumously by her family in 1600) is a Renaissance dialogue in the most familiar
sense.[2] These women, unaware of each other's writing, drew on the same two
major models for their quite different works. The earlier of these was Boccaccio's *Decameron*, with its ten narrators, both male and female, sitting in
their villa garden and entertaining each other with tales. Boccaccio even
includes occasional hints of discussion following some of these tales,
although the hints are never developed enough to allow us to hear much of
what was argued. The women, who outnumber the men and initiate the
entire country sojourn, have a remarkably equal role with that of the men:
they fully share in telling stories and in ruling one day each. Beholden to
Boccaccio as well as to the ancients, Castiglione's *Il libro del cortegiano* was
the other major influence on both women. The range of topics, sliding grace-
fully one into another; the witty banter adorning a discussion of serious issues
from differing points of view; the presence and participation of women
(though on less equal terms than in the *Decameron*); and the combination of
historical reality and nostalgic idealizing in its setting (these features also
demonstrating its kinship with the *Decameron*) all made it an attractive
model flexibly usable for any subject. Marguerite de Navarre and Moderata
Fonte both made use of the convergence of these models to open up discussion on feminist and other serious issues. The women's strategy here was to

rework an accepted form in such a way as to make possible some radical implications. They enhance at every turn the sense of a real openness to doubts, the sense that various differing voices may all be right or wrong to some extent and that the consequent possibilities for internal confusion may be wiser and healthier than an assurance that turns out to be unjust. On the other hand, there are fundamental differences in their ultimate goals for these methods.

The combined model of Boccaccio and Castiglione appealed especially to women writers for several reasons: (1) the focus on male-female relations, (2) the inclusion of women in the discussion, (3) the display of a variety of views, and (4) the presentation of the entire discussion as an entertainment or game.

1. Both works give a major place to questions about proper relations between the sexes and to the possible range of action for women's abilities. The *Decameron's* varied examples and the jests among the narrators offer more than one view of these topics. As a result, critics have argued equally for understanding Boccaccio as a feminist and as a misogynist.[3] But most important, the very existence of evidence in both directions opens up precisely the possibilities for this kind of continuing discussion among the members of the audience both inside and outside the text. At one moment Elissa offers the conventional view that men are the "head" of the human body and that women cannot successfully do anything without them (I.intro. 76). At another moment, Neifile, choosing Filostrato as the first male ruler for the following day, quips: "Tosto ci avedremo se il lupo saprà meglio guidar le pecore che le pecore abbiano i lupi guidati" (III.concl.1) [Soon we shall see whether the wolf knows how to lead the sheep better than the sheep have led the wolf]. Rational head of the sensual body or appetitive wolf destroying its innocent victims, the double perspective remains unresolved. The final tale of Griselda, the one most popular in the Renaissance and most disturbing to modern readers, raises blatantly the question of wifely obedience to a tyrannical husband's outrageous demands and does so at the rhetorically strongest place in the volume. The possible though muted connections between the behavior of this tale's Lombard tyrant and the politically canny cruelty of the contemporary Visconti pose the analogy of domestic and political power relations.[4] At issue are the limits both of the virtue of patient submission (how much is it right to accept?) and of the uses of power (how much is it right to demand?).

So too in *Il libro del cortegiano* Giuliano's speeches on the ideal lady of court and cynical retorts from the misogynist Gasparo make the question of women's role in society a major focus, with an added emphasis on the polarization of views. The issues raised in this discussion game were serious enough in the real world: How much education should a woman have and for what? Could women have a right to political power? How should a woman interact with men so as to combine adorning male life with maintaining female honor? Is the game of chaste love-service really possible to keep up?

It may not have escaped early readers that Castiglione's fourth book combines, like the Griselda story, two topics not explicitly connected but potentially analogous: relations between the sexes and those between the courtier and prince. When if ever may the courtier disobey his prince? What if the prince is in error or ordering something unethical? That, we recall, is precisely the problem of Griselda, whose husband is also a ruler. Joan Kelly (1984, 42–46) has suggested that the power appearing as service, which characterizes the courtly lover's relation to his lady, works as a metaphor for the courtier's actual or at least desired relation to his prince, who must similarly be manipulated by flattery to serve the interests of the courtier.[5] Certainly there is truth to this observation. A more subversive issue, however, lurks simultaneously within the opposite analogy: given the real power of prince and male, when can a subordinate—courtier or wife/daughter/sister—rightfully disobey? And how can the subordinate manipulate the superior while maintaining an appearance of subjection?

Even though Castiglione does not draw out this potential implication of his fourth book's combination of topics, he makes amply clear the political aspect of relations between the sexes. Giuliano, for example, is mockingly accused by other men of defending women in order to advance his own interests by winning the favor of the duchess (3.11).[6] This same notion surfaces in the *Discorsi* of Laura Terracina (1549) and in Moderata Fonte's *Il merito delle donne*: men who praise women do so for their own glory and advantage; therefore, a real defense of women must come from women themselves.[7] In sum, Castiglione established a strong link between this literary form and the "quistione delle donne"—maintaining a certain openness to debate rather than an ideological closure on the topic—and also plainly politicized the conception of woman's social role, which becomes a matter of humanly negotiated functions rather than of divinely or naturally given essences.

The whole notion of constructing, by committee, as it were, the ideal courtier and lady implied the possibility of seeing women's role as defined by social consensus rather than by nature and therefore as something that could be argued about and changed.[8] The popularity of the work as a guide to readers aspiring to make themselves more courtly in behavior and self-presentation endorsed this notion of the consciously malleable self. Furthermore, since the courtier's function in turn is to aid, via advice, manipulation, and representation, in the construction of an ideal real prince, we are made to see how identities are formed under competing social pressures. All of this was immensely useful to women seeking to question and possibly alter the prevalent conceptions of "woman."

2. A second useful feature of these models was Boccaccio's inclusion of women on two levels: among his narrators, where he inserted at least fictively female voices into the discussion without setting aside the voices of men; and among his readers—that is, not only the audience within the framing narrative but also the readership addressed directly by the author. The address to and inclusion of women are connected with Boccaccio's use of the vernacular.[9] Although both Marguerite and Fonte make reference to the classics, their most direct inspiration comes repeatedly from more recent vernacular texts.

Since Boccaccio dedicates his book to women alone in their rooms (although he circulated the text among male friends), he can simultaneously present a range of reader-writer relationships: his own self-mockingly seductive relationship with female readers, the sympathetic friendly advice of an ex-lover speaking to troubled lovers, and the group of female voices speaking through their scribe to other women within a domestic space. The doubled framework (a narrator telling about other narrators) and the mixed company, both at the author-reader level and within the gardens where the tales are initially told, blur the distinctions between private and public, indoors and outdoors, private female society and society more generally.

This confusion between domestic and public modes helped later women, such as Fonte, address the public while claiming to be speaking only to an intimate circle of female friends. Indeed, as a respectable woman in Venice, Fonte was, like any respectable woman there, physically absent from public life. A contemporary admirer, Sansovino, remarked that Fonte was "extremely learned in all disciplines, as far as one can gather (for to tell the truth, no one can actually claim to have seen her in person)."[10] She could not, like the literary courtesans of her city, mingle openly with males in a salon. Virginia Cox notes that even her writing was an anomaly for respectable Venetian women of her time.[11] The private visit among women offers Fonte both a realistic and a proper setting for her conversation, while her act of writing this conversation made it—with the help of her male kinsman and "agent"—available to a male as well as female readership.

Moreover, Boccaccio's women share not only in telling tales but also in ruling the group, selecting the topics and the order of speakers. They have, at least in the framing narrative, an implicit equality with the men in their abilities as both administrators and articulate narrators. Castiglione, like Boccaccio, set his conversation among a mixed group of men and women.

While it is true that the women say little and that the whole discussion about them is carried out among men (Kelly 1984, 30–36), nonetheless the discussion takes place not only in the presence of women but at their command. Giuliano may be merely theorizing when he cites Plato's statement that women can be educated to rule as capably as men, but in fact the center and leader of cultural—if not political—life at this court of Urbino is the duchess; and it is she and Emilia who set the general tone for behavior there. It is these women who, as evidence of their governing wisdom, seek some entertainment both for themselves and for the energetic males around them. They may request that men provide the speeches, but they also have and use the power to silence unwanted discourse (1.9) and to reject even those proposed games that everyone else likes (1.11) in order to choose one of their own preference. Thus, although Kelly calls their role "merely decorative," we must be careful not to underestimate the participation of the females present at this gathering. In the *Decameron* women speak as freely as men, and the women who imitated Castiglione tended to merge that model with Boccaccio's, making their women more vocal as well. The mixed group in both books implies at least that such tales and discussions were meant for women as well as for men. In this regard we are far from the Platonic or Ciceronian dialogue among males alone.[12]

3. The very genre of multivoiced conversation requires a variety of viewpoints, including some that might be less socially acceptable. The aesthetic pleasure of playing off different voices against each other is clearly related to the rich flourishing of polyphonic music at this time; a sixteenth-century writer even makes the connection explicit, referring in his *Dialogo de' giuochi* (1572) to the act of building upon a cantus firmus of male-female relations "il contrappunto di tutto il discorso" [the counterpoint of the whole discourse].[13] The maintenance of an overall harmony might require a balance among the parts. However, the depiction of a certain speaker as outrageous or extreme also allowed a writer to include statements that might well amuse or provoke a reader despite their rejection by the other speakers within the book. For example, Boccaccio's Dioneo, self-defined as the crow among swans, creates a space for bawdy humor; Castiglione's Gasparo, labeled as cynic, can try his worst to undo the idealism of Giuliano or of Bembo while they in turn maintain their positions in the game, despite responses from the others that imply that those positions are either extremely misogynist or excessively idealistic. In this way even ideas rejected by the group as wrong nonetheless get said and recorded for the reader's private consideration. There is some leeway here for the treatment of these radical voices as objects of humor or of serious consideration. Expected reactions of the audience can similarly be given voice by one or more speakers, thus making possible some

process of argument with the reader while avoiding the problems of situating the reader outside and against the text.

This arraying of different points of view, within which radical options can be included, proved extremely useful for feminists. In addition, the open-ended nature of Castiglione's discussions and the absence of either Boccaccio or Castiglione as speakers from the conversations they claimed to be recording allowed the writer to conceal her own views or indeed to remain undecided. As theorists have observed, polyphonic dialogues are much more likely to remain open than diphonic dialogues (Le Guern 1982, 145). In sum, the multiplicity of voices provided for the writer both a protective cover and a means of arguing either with the reader or with herself.

4. Working hand in hand with this mechanism for simultaneously proposing and hedging unconventional ideas was the notion of game. Boccaccio and Castiglione offer their entertainments within a special time and space apart from the normal working day. The game has its rules and its limits, within the containment of which a special freedom can be allowed.[14] This framework proved immensely useful rhetorically to women as well to men.[15] The game makes uncertain the sincere convictions of the author or of any of the speakers, while putting in play even outrageous ideas. Thus Speroni emphasized this aspect in his defense of his own dialogues when they came under attack concerning their orthodoxy.[16] For women it provided an excuse for writing at all: the daily duties have been attended to, and writing is merely a pastime preventing idleness. Marguerite's narrators are compelled by a flood to pass the time away from their normal duties. Fonte's women are enjoying a friendly visit but will soon go home to resume the duties that await them. Thus the space or time of a game allows women to step outside their normal roles and enter into discourse.

A variable of the game framework is the extent to which it may allow or hinder the transfer of its contents to the normal world. Coding statements as mere play can relegate them to the status of a joke or entertainment not intended to alter real social relations. To avoid this blockage, some "lines of flight" or strategies of "deterritorialization," as Gilles Deleuze and Félix Guattari call them, must be opened from the game structure to the structures of normal social life.[17] The status of the dialogue genre, which presents itself as the record of a real conversation while framing that conversation as a game in a garden or salon, contains already just the ambivalence that allows for slippage between enclosed game or text and social reality, if the writer wishes to make use of it. For his or her text is in a liminal status between the game recounted and the world for which it is recounted. If it is offered as recreation to the reader, the game space may be carried over into the historical world, but serious things can also be said through jest. Thomas Greene

(1979) writes about the *Cortegiano:* "We think normally of a game as a detached figure against a background of the serious, the non-ludic, but in this case the ground becomes the content of the figure" (177); "The game really becomes a contest between the community's will to understand itself, to examine and know itself, and conversely its will to protect itself from excessive knowledge, in order to function politically and socially. One way to gauge the threat to the social surface at any given moment is to note the presence or absence of laughter. It is extraordinary how many speeches are introduced with the participle *ridendo*" (180). We shall see that a certain ambiguity in the jesting or serious nature of the speakers' statements and of the writer's project is one of the genre's recurring features.

Marguerite de Navarre's *Heptameron* very clearly combines the models of Boccaccio and Castiglione. Starting as a collection of anecdotes and tales, the work probably began after 1546 to take shape as an organized system of tales connected by discussion among courtiers.[18] The reference to the *Decameron* as paradigm is explicit early in the prologue (1967, 9–10); Castiglione is not mentioned by name but is evoked by the decision of members of a court to entertain themselves with discussion as well as by the recurring theme of neoplatonic love. The tale collection becomes embedded in an ongoing conversation, with each story evoked to illustrate a point in the discussion. What Marguerite took from both these models was more the framework than the specific contents: an exchange of tales and comments among people of the same social circle yet of different perspectives and values. None of her tales nor the ensuing discussions repeats material from the two Italians, and she takes up a number of issues that are completely absent from their works. I shall discuss her work and then Fonte's, following the outline of the aspects of Boccaccio's and Castiglione's writing that these women found useful: the discussion of gender relations; the use of multiple voices, including women's, and of varied viewpoints; and the ambiguities between the withdrawn space of a game and real society.

Relations between the sexes are a major theme of Marguerite's book. Replacing Boccaccio's seven women and three men with an equal five and five, Marguerite seems thereby to enhance a sense of impasse.[19] Hircan, while clearly based in part on Boccaccio's Dioneo, goes beyond Dioneo's prescription of pleasure for all and advocates violent rape, to the horror of the women (34). Saffredent repeats the justification of rape the next day, again to a horrified female response (142). The discussion following tale 12, in which the duke of Florence is murdered by a gentleman whose sister the duke seeks to possess, divides according to the sexes: the men argue that the gentleman is to blame for betraying his lord, while the women maintain that he did well to protect his sister from such a brute. The issue of political tyranny—when can a gentleman rightly disobey his political master?—merges with the issue of male tyranny over women, especially through rape. A less blatant but nonetheless analogous form of tyranny emerges in tale 9, in which the mother supports her daughter's marriage to an affectionate and honest gentleman while the father's family insists on a wealthier candidate. The denial of the girl's happiness in favor of her economic usefulness to the family is associated with male power, and her sexual life belongs to the father to sell. Again the discussion follows gender lines (although the tale is told by Dagoucin): the women feel sorry for the loss of "honneste amitye," while Hircan and Saffredent support each other in the notion that God has given men the command over women, whose wishes are therefore not to be respected.

The sense that men and women live by completely different codes and are almost different species is absent from the *Decameron* but appears here repeatedly, particularly in the mouth of Parlamente. She says of women:

> celles qui sont vaincues en plaisir ne se doibvent plus nommer femmes, mais hommes, desquelz la fureur et la concupiscence augmente leur honneur; car ung homme qui se venge de son ennemy et le tue pour ung desmentir en est estimé plus gentil compaignon; aussy est-il quant il en ayme une douzaine avecq sa femme. Mais l'honneur des femmes a autre fondement: c'est doulceur, patience et chasteté. (301)

> [Women who are dominated by pleasure might as well call themselves men, since it is men who regard violence and lust as something honourable. When a man kills an enemy in revenge because he has been crossed by him, his friends think he's all the more gallant. It's the same thing when a man, not content with his wife, loves a dozen other women as well. But the basis of the honour of women has a different foundation: for them the basis of honour is gentleness, patience and chastity. (1984, 396–97)][20]

The notion that only women live by Christian values, while men live by a code of honor directly opposed to Christ's teaching, is stated even more explicitly by Parlamente at the end of tale 26, where she responds to the male claim that women's concern for their honor is a form of pride:

> si nous pechons par orgueil, nul tiers n'en a dommage, ny nostre corps et noz mains n'en demeurent souillées. Mais vostre plaisir gist à deshonorer les femmes, et vostre honneur à tuer les hommes en guerre; qui sont deux poinctz formellement contraires à la loy de Dieu. (221)

[if we sin though pride, no one suffers for it, and neither our body nor our hands are tainted by it. But all your pleasure is derived from dishonouring women, and your honour depends on killing other men in war. These are two things that are expressly contrary to the law of God. (305)]

A woman's love, she says elsewhere, "bien fondée sur Dieu et sur honneur, est si juste et raisonnable" (174–75) [rooted in God and founded on honour . . . is so just and reasonable (253)], whereas that of most men is founded on "plaisir" [pleasure] and full of "malice du cueur" [evil intentions (254)] against the good of women. In Parlamente's tale 42, furthermore, the men encouraging the young prince in his pursuit of an honest and socially inferior woman tell him: "que ce n'estoit poinct son honneur de n'avoir sceu gaigner une telle femme" (292) [it would be a great dishonour to fail to vanquish a woman of this kind (387)]. However, the prince, appreciating the virtue of his beloved, ultimately decides to leave her alone, thinking all the better of her. Here, as in Parlamente's tale of Amadour and Floride, the "honor" of men and that of women are not only different but directly pitted against each other.

The famous tale of Amadour and Floride, told by Parlamente, turns the ideal male and the ideal female into inevitable enemies, as Amadour's honor requires the violation of Floride's. Moreover, as Floride bitterly points out, the emphasis on chastity has been impressed on women by the very men who then seek to subvert it: "Et où est l'honneur, dist Floride, que tant de foys vous m'avex presché?" (73) ["And what," she replied, "has become of the honour you preached about so often?" (141)]. Deborah Losse (1982, esp. 81–84) has noted the disappointment of women with men in many of the *Heptameron* tales. The reader shares this disappointment, she adds, because we are introduced to both male and female protagonists as perfect, but in the long run the man cannot maintain this perfection. Under the pressures of lust, he degenerates into a brute or demon. The paradox is that a perfect love requires virtue as its object, a virtue that is defined as opposition to love's desires: "Mais Floride creut trop plus son conseil qu'il ne vouloit" (65) [However, Florida took his advice too seriously (133)].[21] It is the contradictions in our own internal desires that generate these incompatible social codes and values.

If Parlamente is the main spokesperson for a major rift between the sexes, her husband, Hircan, is one of the supporters of a view of men and women as essentially the same. This similarity is revealed not in social codes but in the flesh and its desires: "Si leur honneur n'en estoit non plus taché que le nostre, vous trouveriez que Nature n'a rien oblyé en elles non plus que en nous" (220) [if their honour were unstained by the fact as ours is, you would find that Nature has no more forgotten anything where women are concerned than she has where we men are concerned (305)]. Only social constraint makes women not dare to take the pleasure they desire (220). His response to his wife's claim that the love of men and the love of women differ runs:

Voylà doncques une raison, dist Hircan, forgée sur vostre fantaisie, de vouloir soustenir que les femmes honnestes peuvent laisser honneste-ment l'amour des hommes, et non les hommes, celle des femmes, comme si leurs cueurs estoiest differens; mais combien que les visaiges et habitz le soyent, si croy-je que les voluntez sont toutes pareilles. . . . (175).

[*"If what you are maintaining," said Hircan, "is that an honest woman can honourably abandon her love for a man, but that a man can't do the same, then it's just an argument made up to suit your own fancies. As if the hearts of men and women were any different! Although their clothes and faces may be, their dispositions are the same. . . ."* (254)]

Simontault tries to resolve this debate with a shift into religious registers: "pour faire conclusion du cueur de l'homme et de la femme, le meilleur des deux n'en vault riens" (175) [To put an end once and for all to this question of the difference between the hearts of men and women, I say that the best of them is good for nothing (254)], a sentiment that is echoed several times throughout the book.[22] Even Hircan himself, following the pious lines of Simontault's comment, seeks to spiritualize his argument for the equality of all humans before God: "la nature des femmes et des hommes est de soy incline à tout vice, si elle n'est preservé de Celluy à qui l'honneur de toute victoire doibt estre rendu" (254) [both men and women are by nature inclined to vices of all kinds, unless they are preserved by Him to whom hon-our for any victory is due (345)]. But this resolution is not allowed to stand, pious though it may be, and the argument erupts anew as the woman-hating Saffredent begins a tale soon after by saying: "nonobstant, mes dames, qu'il ayt esté dict parcydevant que le vice est commun aux femmes et aux hommes, si est-ce que l'invention d'une finesse sera trouvée plus prompte-ment et subtillement d'une femme que d'un homme . . ." (272) [For, Ladies, although it has been said earlier that vice is equally shared by men and women, it is in fact women rather than men who will the more eagerly and craftily devise acts of cunning (364)]. Thus even what looked like an ortho-dox closure to the argument does not succeed in closing anything for long.

Through her narrators' discussions on the nature of similarities and differ-ences between the sexes, Marguerite arrives at a social rather than natural understanding of these differences. To see the differences between men and women as fashioned purely by social codes—and on this Parlamente and Hircan seem to be in agreement—is to find in alterable social constructions gender differences that do not "naturally" exist. Hircan's solution is the sexual liberation of women; Parlamente's is the Christianization of male culture. Marguerite allows a certain sympathy for both points of view;[23] Hircan's indication of the self-serving nature of Parlamente's argument about love is a moment when Hircan is not simply the horrid beast nor Parlamente the purely correct.

The deconstruction of what we thought were clear categories can be enlisted to undo quick judgments in matters pertaining to women. For example, is the wife who corrects the foolish last will of her husband in tale 55 doing good or ill? She is disobeying her husband's wishes, but then she is sure that her husband was wrong and that she can see more clearly what is proper. Moreover, he is dead; his will was an attempt to spend not his own money during his life but the money of his family after his death and to spend it erroneously in the foolish thought that a belated contribution to monks might counterbalance his sins. Traditional advice insisted that the wife obey her husband even when she thought that he was wrong. But this wife does not go along with such notions; or rather, without disobeying the letter of his will, she finds a way to do what she wants after all. Thus she can pretend to adhere to traditional norms while actually seizing control of the situation for herself. There is a socially significant struggle over economic control here between the surviving wife and the dying or dead husband. The issue of economic power, like so many others, is left dangling as the ensuing discussion veers into other directions; but at least it is raised, along with the link between power in the family and economic control. Also made clear is the conflict for women between the social imperatives to do what is right for the rest of the family and to obey even a stupid husband.

The important contribution of the *Heptameron*, however, is not so much the offering of specific programs for social change as the recognition that change is possible; that the categories invented by the human mind are not natural distinctions but can all be reconceived. The many voices of the text, whose unfinished state seems almost (though unintentionally) symbolic, are used continually to reopen the possibilities for a healthy confusion.

Since the very codes that structure the society are an incompatible set, these conflicts render uncertain how characters and actions should be judged. Of this problem there are innumerable examples. When Rolandine, who has been reproved for her austerity, is then blamed for developing friendship with a male, she protests in perplexity at this no-win situation (159). Other tales and discussions debate whether a woman's cold reply to suitors is a sign of virtue or of sin: perhaps hypocrisy or pride. The danger of virtue altogether is that it paradoxically entails the sin of pride unless we acknowledge that we are virtuous not by our own power but by God's (see, e.g., tales 18, 26, 30, 34, 52). But the sin of pride is indistinguishable from the social virtue of a concern for honor.[24] Men too are affected by these contradictory codes. Is the man in tale 18 an example of virtuous patience or of stupidity or impotence, the perfect lover or the perfect fool? Is the husband of tale 36 demonstrating virtuous prudence and concern for the family honor or cruel malice and vengeful anger? The husband in tale 70 kills his wife as an act of just punishment for her malicious destruction of others; but then he fears that this act of justice is itself a sinful murder and, burying her in an abbey, goes on a crusade to set himself right with God. Like Rolandine, he stands to be blamed whatever he does. If we cannot distinguish good from evil, virtue from sin, how can we know how to act? The narrators' arguments over these definitions are not concluded but only abandoned.

The conflicts are not only between people but within them, in the contradictions by which both men and women try to live. These contradictions derive not only from external social codes but from the ambivalences of internal desires. As Lodovico Canossa observes in Castiglione's *Il libro del cortegiano* (1.13): "Non solamente a voi po parer una cosa ed a me un'altra, ma a me stesso poria parer or una cosa ed ora un'altra" [not only can you think one thing and I another, but I myself may sometimes think one thing and sometimes another (28)]. This inner ambivalence shows up repeatedly in the mixed or uncertain motivation of characters within the tales, even though the tales are told in order to contribute to the discussions ostensibly unambiguous examples. Love is especially easy to combine with other desires. Both lover and queen in tale 3 seem to be acting from this mixture of motives: they are certainly driven by a desire for vengeance on their spouses; yet the queen, considering her suitor's declaration of love, surprisingly comes to "cognoistre que ce qu'il disoit proceddoit du profond du cueur" (24–25) [to realize . . . that he was speaking from the depths of his heart (86)], and sincere affection seems to blossom along with their calculated use of each other. The wife in tale 8, taking her chambermaid's place, takes pleasure equally in maintaining her husband's fidelity and in tricking him. Rolandine's young man demonstrates real affection and consideration for her, yet he has in mind as well the advancement of his own honor and wealth that would result from this alliance (160, 162–63, 172). Similarly, the Count of Jossebelin keeps his sister at home unmarried both because he loves her more than any other woman and because he does not want to lay out the money for her dowry (tale 40). Sometimes the narrator gives us alternate motives as if unsure which is the right one: for example, "mais elle ou cuydant trouver mieulx, ou voulant dissimuler l'amour qu'elle luy avoit portée" (383) [perhaps because she hoped for a better match, or perhaps to hide the love she felt for the man (492)].

Where the tales do not offer a statement of motivations, the discussants infer a conflicting variety of them. The discussion following tale 5 questions whether the valiant ferryboat woman avoided the advances of her passengers because of chastity and honor or because she found the friars unattractive. Similarly, one of the discussants following tale 38 suggests that the good wife who won back her husband by fixing up his mistress's abode was actually trying to encourage him to stay away so that she could see her own lover. The "perfect" lover of tale 19 may truly have turned his worldly love to God or may have turned monk out of melancholy and despair, an act of dubious virtue.

Again, this sort of disagreement about how to assess the characters occurs not only between members of the narrating group but also within individual members; thus occasionally the narrator's introductory or concluding remarks seem bizarre in relation to his or her own tale. Tale 10 is introduced as a story "à la louange de l'homme" (54) [in praise of the man]; yet it conveys Amadour's failure both as a perfect, honorable lover (since he ultimately resorts to attempted rape) and as a successfully predatory male (since even this aggressive effort is foiled), concluding instead with the praise of Floride's virtue (83). Parlamente, in tale 40, after elaborately demonstrating that Rolandine's aunt is in her rights to marry the man she loves—since she is legally old enough to decide for herself, since her brother has been neglecting her needs, and since she has married the very man that her brother wished aloud she could marry—astonishingly ends by declaring that the tale is an example of the importance of obtaining the consent of one's kin before marriage.[25] Oisille's additional comment that "cest exemple est suffisant pour leur donner plus de reverence à leur parens" (277) [(this) example would be enough to make them show more respect for their parents and relatives (371)] seems ludicrous, given the negligence and criminal error of the brother, who, having murdered his sister's husband, imprisons the sister in order to prevent her demanding justice from the law for what is explicitly labeled his "crime." Tale 16 similarly is narrated with great sympathy for the woman, and from her point of view, only to end with the narrator's condemnation of her despair at ever obtaining her husband's love. The opening of the tale paints the husband as a villain: he rarely spends the night at home; never speaks to his wife, much less shows her any sign of friendship; and does not even pay for her proper upkeep. He ignores the warnings of his friends about the consequences of his behavior. Yet in the end, it is the wife who takes the blame. An honest woman must be patient forever; nothing the husband does can justify her infidelity. The expectations that were set up for us by the apparent sympathies of the narrator are all undone.

Saffredent offers two incompatible readings of his own tale 26.[26] At first, surprisingly given his usual remarks, he classifies the honest woman as "saige" [wise], leading to a "mort glorieuse et louable" [glorious death that we should all admire], while the more carnal woman is "folle" [wanton] and "honteuse et infame" (219–20) [disgrace (and) shame (304)]. Yet a moment later he reverts to his usual style, blaming the

> saige femme, qui, pour se monstrer plus vertueuse par dehors qu'elle n'estoit au cueur, et pour dissimuler ung amour que la raison de nature voulloit qu'elle portast à ung si honneste seigneur, s'alla laisser morir, par faulte de se donnner le plaisir qu'elle desiroit couvertement. (220)

> [*wise woman, who, for the sake of showing herself outwardly more virtuous than she was in her heart and for the sake of covering up a passion which the logic of Nature demanded she should conceive for this most noble lord, goes and allows herself to die just because she denies herself the pleasure that she covertly desires!* (304)]

We are back to the question of virtue or hypocrisy, and Hircan launches into a tirade against women who treat men cruelly in order to enhance their own glory. Kupisz (1981, 384–85) has noted several surprising comments from Parlamente herself: for example, when she rejects a wife's exemplary patience with her husband (1967, 268).

The narrators surprise each other as well as us by their inconsistencies. When lusty Hircan concludes tale 35 with the pious sentiment that women should not trust in their own strength but should rely on God to protect them from lust, Parlamente responds, "Je suys bien ayse de quoy vous estes devenu prescheur des dames; et le serois encores plus si vous vouliez continuer ces beaulx sermons à toutes celles à qui vous parlez" (260) [I'm glad to see that you have started to preach for the ladies. I'd be even happier if you would kindly continue to preach these fine sermons to *all* the ladies you address! (351)]. Simontault, making a comment very similar to Hircan's after tale 56, draws a surprised response from Oisille: "Comment, Simontault? dist Oisille; je ne pensois que vous sceussiez tant de bien!" (352) ["Well, Simontaut!" said Oisille. "I did not know that you were capable of such good thoughts!" (455)]. When Geburon, usually the defender of women, follows tale 68 with a remark denigrating their ability to act wisely when in love, Oisille again notes her surprise: "Geburon, dist Oisille, vous saillez hors de vostre bonne coustume, pour vous rendre de l'opinion de vos compaignons" (397) ["Geburon, you are departing from your customary excellent sentiments," said Oisille, "and joining the ranks of your companions" (509)].

Marguerite's world is one of continual surprises and inconsistencies. For her the genre of conversation opens up the vision of unresolvable differences, within the self as well as among selves. This opening permits the acknowledgment of views that one might generally prefer to suppress, including some that subsequent editors, fearful of the religious authorities, did suppress. The recognition that contradictions lie within us and not just between us makes the possibility of resolution all the more remote, but so too the validity of fixed viewpoints—other than God's—all the more questionable.

The word of God becomes an authority to which women can appeal against the human authorities, secular as well as spiritual, to whom they find themselves subjected. The very existence of several discordant authorities— reflected in the incompatible appeals of the arguing narrators—opens a space for women's self-assertion.[27] Rolandine is perhaps the best example of a woman within one of the tales taking advantage of such conflicts:[28] "Quant à la Royne ma maitresse, je ne doibtz poinct faire de conscience de luy desplaire pour obeyr à Dieu" (162) [And as for my mistress the Queen, my conscience need not be troubled if I displease her in order to obey God (240)]; "Et voylà qui me faict parler sans craincte, estant seure que celluy qui voyt mon cueur est avecq moy; et si ung tel juge estoit pour moy, j'aurois tort de craindre ceulx qui sont subjectz à son jugement" (170) [It is this which makes me speak fearlessly, for I am sure that He who sees my heart is with me, and if such a judge (is) in my favour, then indeed I would be wrong to fear those who are subject to His judgment (248)]. The appeal to God's judgment turns the queen herself into a "subject." Similarly with regard to the combined anger of the queen and her father, Rolandine asserts: "Mais j'ay ung pere au ciel, lequel, je suis asseurée, me donnera autant de patience que je me voy par vous de grands maulx preparez" (170) [But I have a Father in Heaven, who, I know, will grant me patience enough to endure the evils which I see you preparing for me (249)]. God is conveniently both a ruler and a father who can take the place of human ones and who can be identified with the woman's individual conscience.

Yet, although Scripture may be the monologic word of God—the "touchstone," as Parlamente calls it (303–4), for all other truth claims—its interpretation is not free from the arguments generated by differences in human understanding. This may be especially true in the case of feminist issues. For example, we find in tale 67 a woman who, abandoned on an island with her husband, serves him as confessor and priest at his death. Saffredent objects in

the subsequent discussion: "Si vous avez bien veu l'Escripture, dist Saffredent, sainct Pol dist que: 'Apollo a planté, et qu'il a arrousé'; mais il ne parle
poinct que les femmes ayent mis les mains à l'ouvraige de Dieu" (394) ["If
you have read Scripture properly," said Saffredent, "you will know that Saint
Paul wrote that Apollos planted and that he watered, but he says nothing
about *women* lending a hand in God's labour" (505)]. Parlamente quickly
rebuts this appeal to the well-established notion that women should not be
active in preaching and confessing: "Vous vouldriez suyvre, dist Parlamente,
l'opinion des mauvais hommes qui prennent ung passage de l'Escripture pour
eulx et laissent celluy qui leur est contraire. Si vous avez leu sainct Pol
jusques au bout, vous trouverez qu'il se recommande aux dames, qui ont
beaucoup labouré avecq luy en l'Evangille" (394) [You're as bad as all the
other men who take a passage from Scripture which serves their purposes,
and leave out anything that contradicts it. If you had read everything Saint
Paul says, you would find that he commends himself to those women who
have laboured with him in the Gospel (505)]. Longarine deflects the direction of the conversation with a "Quoy qu'il y ait . . ." (394) [Be that as it may
. . . (505)], thus leaving a contentious contemporary issue undecided. Parlamente's view is reinforced, however, by her additional comment soon after
that most husbands are such beasts that the woman in the story probably did
not notice much difference between living with her husband and living
alone among wild animals after his death (1967, 395; 1984, 505). This reversal of the traditional male-female hierarchy, here associating women with
human reason and men with animality, reinforces her emphasis on the legitimacy and capacity of women speaking for the church.[29]

Her argument is further supported by the presence in the framing narrative of Oisille as the one who reads and explains the lessons from Scripture
each morning, a role for which she is certainly more suited than any of the
men present. Marguerite herself comments on how well Oisille performs this
function: "A quoy elle s'acquicta si très bien, qu'il sembloit que le Sainct
Esperit, plain d'amour et de doulceur, parlast par sa bouche" (421) [So well
did she deliver the reading that the Holy Spirit, full of sweetness and love,
seemed to be speaking through her mouth (535)]. This can be seen as part of
a general defense of women's more active role in the church.

The discussion of this topic surfaces again in an argument about why
women are not normally allowed to act as confessors. Oddly it follows a tale
about a woman who has a whole series of lovers (tale 49). The pivot is the
issue of keeping secrets: in this case the woman is able to remain secretive
while the men who love her are not. Simontault, defending the traditional
view that men are really much more able than women to keep matters
confidential, brings in as evidence: "Et, par ce, a l'Eglise, comme bonne

mere, ordonné les prestres confesseurs et non pas les femmes, parce qu'elle ne peuvent rien celler" (322) [That is why the Church, as a good mother, has ordained that priests, not women, should be confessors, because women are incapable of concealing anything (422)]. It is Oisille, significantly, who offers an alternate interpretation, reversing the moral hierarchy between men and women:

> Ce n'est pas pour ceste occasion, dist Oisille, mais c'est parce que les femmes sont tant ennemyes du vice, qu'elles ne donneroit pas si facillement absolution que les hommes, et seroient trop austeres en leur penitences. (322)

> *["That," said Oisille, "is not the real reason. The real reason is that women are such great opponents of vice that they would not grant absolution as easily as men, and the penances they imposed would be more severe." (422)]*

Dagoucin returns the conversation to a flippant tone by commenting that if women were as harsh to those confessing as to their lovers, sinners would all die of despair. As before, the issue is not pursued; it is simply brought forth and then left dangling. The presence of multiple voices allows for the radical suggestion to be presented side by side with traditional views. Yet the traditional views are placed in the mouths of the two most misogynistic men, while the two most undoubtedly virtuous women hold the opposing side. The lack of conclusion keeps the issue alive for further discussion while protecting the author from any decisive statement that could be condemned and cause her personal trouble.

As we have seen, the focus on women and relations between the sexes carries over even into topics of religion. Reformation issues and feminist issues are inextricably intertwined by their shared questioning of hierarchies of human authority. Tale 44 makes fun together of the two most common butts of traditional novella humor: friars and women. Despite his wife's anger, the husband rewards a friar who explains that the sure foundation of his order is the folly of women. Yet the ensuing discussion undoes this complicity among men and this silencing of a woman by raising the question of whether women should believe what friars and preachers tell them or instead apply their own best judgment based on their knowledge of the text of Scripture. Preachers who are truly Christian are few and far between, asserts Parlamente.

> En bonne foy, je pensois, dist Ennasuite, que nous fussions tenuz, sur peyne de peché mortel, de croire tout ce qu'ilz nous dient en chaire de

verité: c'est quant ilz ne parlent que de ce qui est en la saincte Escripture ou ilz alleguent les expositions des sainctz docteurs divinement inspirez.—Quant est de moy, dist Parlamente, je ne puis ignorer qu'il n'y en ait entre eulx de très mauvaise foy . . . et . . . ne vouluz croire en parolle de prescheur, si je ne la trouve conforme à celle de Dieu. (303–4)

[*"But I thought," said Ennasuite, "that we were bound on pain of mortal sin to believe what they preach to us from the pulpit?" "Only when they speak of what is in Holy Scripture [said Oisille], or adduce the expositions of the divinely inspired holy doctors." "As far as I'm concerned," said Parlamente, "I can't overlook the fact that there have been some men of very bad faith among them . . . and . . . I have refused to believe these preachers, unless what they say seems to me to conform to the word of God." (399–400)]*

Parlamente presents God's word as if it were clear and direct; nevertheless, the real issue here is not God's authority versus the preachers' but the relative authority of preachers versus laypersons, especially women, who wish to interpret the Scripture for themselves. The inclusion of women equally in the group of courtiers holding these discussions implies sympathy for an inclusion of women equally in the broader cultural discussions of social and religious issues.

This rebellion against the human (male) authorities who expound Scripture is further endorsed by Simontault, despite his subsequent attack against women confessors; for he offers next a tale to demonstrate that "une femme bonne, doulce et simple" (304) [a nice, gentle, simple woman (400)] is perhaps not the ideal really to be desired since such a woman is much easier to deceive. Paradoxically, just as the humanists were trying to argue, the conservative role of good wife may be better performed by a woman with some independence of judgment than by the docile ignorant creature men think they want. In Simontault's tale it is a husband who deceives his simple, trusting wife; but there are plenty of other tales in which it is precisely men of the church whom women must not trust, even when they are performing their duties in church as confessor (e.g., tales 22, 33, 41).[30] Parlamente's suggestion that women ought to resist what they are told by the authorities and interpret Scripture for themselves comes in the wake of misogynistic humor; thus it may pass itself off to some readers simply as an opposite extreme. Yet the continued return to these themes of women's role in religion, and the continued placement of these themes in the mouths of respectable and devout speakers, must have encouraged many readers to take them as potentially valid.

In sum, the possibility for argument even about Scripture and the authority of the church enables the assertion of feminist views. The presence of traditional views side by side with more radical ones, the slippery shifts from
these assertions to other topics without the achievement of a conclusion,
and the general sliding between jest (even misogynist jest) and earnest all
practice what the reformers preach: that is, they leave to the individual
reader or listener to judge what is right. Thus the very strategy of writing a
polyphonic dialogue with equal voices supports the feminist and reformist
antiauthoritarian claims. The reader must judge, however, not by capricious
subjective standards or personal desires but by "bonne foy," a humble desire
for the Good and the True, however confusing these may be to ascertain.

The *Heptameron* seems on one hand to argue for social changes of attitude
toward women: for example, for a recognition of women's moral strength and
for an acceptance of women in unconventional roles such as preacher or
interpreter of Scripture. On the other hand, the faith in any social reform on
women's behalf may actually be undermined not only by the devout sentiments that all effective action is God's and that the most important goal is
individual salvation but also on a more earthly plane by bottomless self-suspicion and the restless compulsion to undo all settlements. Thus, for example, although Nicole Cazauran (1976, 254–55) argues quite credibly for the
importance of married love to the whole group of narrators—and thus to
Marguerite too—as the only kind that can reconcile the laws of Nature and
of God, the project of producing a happy marriage is rendered impossible by
the recurrent notion that calm and stability in themselves provoke unrest.
For example, concerning the faithless husband of tale 54, Ennasuite remarks:
"Mais l'on dict que toutes choses se peuvent endurer, sinon l'aise" (344)
[they say that people can put up with anything except comfort (447)].
Dagoucin, narrating tale 37, similarly explains that husband's reason for
infidelity as "trouvant l'honneste repos insupportable" (266) [her husband
became dissatisfied with their quiet, respectable life (358)].[31] Longarine
begins the very next tale with another roving husband and a general comment on "la fragilité des hommes qui s'ennuyent de manger bon pain" (270)
[the fragility of men that they soon tire of bread which is good and whole-
some (362)]. So too love relations outside marriage have their internal limitations in the unstable nature of man: tale 16 ends with the happy union of
lovers at last, only to add a suddenly bitter comment:

> Et, comme si la volunté de l'homme estoit immuable, se jurerent et
> promirent ce qui n'estoit en leur puissance: c'est une amityé per-
> petuelle, qui ne peult naistre ne demorer au cueur de l'homme. (132)

[*Thereupon, they solemnly swore, as if the will of man were immutable, an oath that they could never keep. Perpetual love was what they promised, perpetual love that can neither have birth in the hearts of men, nor have its abode therein (208)*].

The ultimate problem is not external but internal contradictions, the human impatience not only with injustice but also with happiness and peace. Just as a repeatedly suggested solution for the conflicts between men and women is to eclipse them in the vast difference between humans and God, so all human systems of whatever social value exist ineluctably in the realm of confusion and contradiction, from which the way out for Marguerite is ultimately not through social reform but through faith and grace. Marguerite's devout belief in the transcendent, however, never gives her the feeling that she or any other human can speak for God. Rather, within the human arena, faith confirms the distrust in husbands and priests, but it confirms as well the distrust in oneself.

The battle between men and women allows each to voice suspicions of the other and to indicate the inner contradictions of each position. In this sense it is not simply an argument about social issues but a mutual consciousness-raising about self-delusions. The tales and discussions about love and marriage share in observing that feelings are unreliable: that love does not last, that its motives are multiple rather than pure. But reason is just as unreliable. Parlamente's description of a neoplatonic ascent through perfect love ends with the sudden acknowledgment that unless God opens the eye of our faith, the whole process will get us worse than nowhere. Thus she proposes and undermines her own neoplatonism within one speech (151–52). Without faith, the human animal can understand nothing. Our reasoning is in danger of causing our damnation. Virtue too is unreliable; as it comes from God rather than from ourselves, it is most likely to fail us when we feel most self-assured.[32] Thus Longarine comments that we are lucky when God allows us to fall into a sin that wakes us up to "la lepre d'infidelité cachée en nostre cueur" (254) [the leprosy of faithlessness hidden within our hearts (344)]. Faith itself is uncertain, our own infidelity lurking unrealized like a latent illness in the heart.

Giselle Mathieu-Castellani (1992) has suggested that the process of unmasking is the main focus of Marguerite's book.[33] But it is an endless process, for we are compelled to doubt ourselves continually, finding assurance only in a God who may or may not grant us his grace. The very process of self-suspicion provokes the humility that alone can draw us toward God.

This constant self-suspicion requires a divided self. It is no wonder then that Marguerite returned repeatedly, in the *Heptameron* and in her plays and some of her poems, to forms that diffuse the writing subject into a variety of disagreeing speakers. Multiple voices allow Marguerite to acknowledge her own multiple and perpetually restless thoughts: "Since each of us was several, there was already quite a crowd."[34]

Also useful to Marguerite was the notion of a separate space and time within which her words could serve as a game. Yet just as this game takes place during the building of a bridge to the outer world, so too Marguerite's text enhances at every turn the confusion between inside and outside the text, between game and earnest living, between fiction on one hand and two kinds of truth on the other: the truths of history and of Scripture. This confusion encourages the opening of the game to reality, making impossible its neat enclosure and dismissal. Indeed, Marguerite seems to do everything possible to break down neat binaries and create a space of confusion from which altered structures might emerge.

The prologue is full of these "lines of flight" or "deterritorialization," continually reconfiguring whatever structures or borders seem to have been established. The discussions among the assembled group do not limit themselves to the hours of the game but spill over into their evenings and mealtimes (Winn 1993b, 93–94). Philippe de Lajarte (1981, esp. 401–8) has pointed out how Marguerite opens with a reference to herself and her writing—"que je veulx escripre" (1)—only to set up instead of herself a group of narrators, who claim that they will realize the project intended but left undone by Marguerite and her circle at court. Then they will present the written text of their oral narratives to that court circle as a gift. Thus Marguerite will be the recipient of the text rather than its author. Furthermore, the opening tales refer explicitly to Marguerite and her family as characters. As Lajarte (1981, 404, 408) puts it, the lines between history and fiction run both ways; each produces the other. Marcel Tetel (1981, 449) has noted the continual alternation between the telling of fictions and the relative reality of the discussions; but one could just as easily turn the case around, for the narrators, whose discussion is a pure work of fiction, establish the rule that their tales must be historically true.[35] Thus the prologue's comment that this book will differ from Boccaccio's by including only historically truthful tales (9)—even if not a strictly reliable claim—not only implies the possibility of a transference of ideas from game context to real life but also contributes to the confusion as to which is which: "true" tales have feigned tellers in a fictional frame. The actual mix of historical reference and literary borrowing in the tales blurs even the supposedly explicit opposition between historical and fictitious narrative, rendering unclear the status of many stories.[36]

In the other direction, the relation of these tales to scriptural truth is likewise problematic. Lajarte (1981, 411–18) sees an opposition between the two types of discourse as one of the central structures of the work. Certainly there is evidence for this position. The day is divided between mornings of reading Scripture and attending Mass, and afternoons of telling stories. The morning Mass represents serious business, the tale-telling mere entertainment. Scripture, as its very name asserts, is written and fixed, whereas the tales and discussions are oral. Lajarte adds to this a distinction between the hierarchized monologic discourse of religion—God's word, transmitted through the explanations of Oisille and received without argument by the rest of the group—with the horizontal dialogic secular discourse, produced among equals and infinitely arguable. Other pieces of support for the opposition between these two modes can be added from the text: for example, Oisille's polarizing admonition "de jamais ne mectre en doubte la parolle de Dieu et moins ne adjouster foy à celle des hommes" (356) [never cast doubt on the word of God, and even less give credence to the word of men (460)].

Yet at least as much evidence exists for blurring the distinction. Scripture in this setting is something read aloud and thus received orally by the group; and the tales, though oral initially, are to be written and presented—indeed have already been written as we receive them. Moreover, the tales are to be brought back to court as souvenirs from a pilgrimage instead of the usual statuettes and beads. The narrators' journey in the mountains is seen as a stage en route to the kingdom of God when, in their prayer of thanks to God for saving them, they continue by asking God "parfaire le voiage à sa gloire" (6) [that their journey might be finished to His glory (65)]. The secular trip to baths and back to court thus not only has an unexpected detour to a religious site (the monastery at which they stay) but includes in any case the spiritual goal of salvation beyond this world. Furthermore, Oisille, in recommending a spiritual pastime, refers to their situation—both in the wilderness and in the world—as "en ce desert" (8) [in this wilderness (67)]. Traditionally the wilderness is the site of our anticipation of God's kingdom. This suggests that the tales, though proposed initially as mere entertainment for those stuck in a rural area, are not only brought back from the goal of a pilgrimage but are also part of the voyage to that goal.

Nicole Cazauran (1976, 283) cites with approval Raymond Lebègue's phrase: "*l'Heptaméron*, un attrape-mondains" [a trap to catch the worldly]; she herself calls it an "introduction à la vie dévote" (292) [an introduction to the devout life], arguing for the very close connection of the afternoon's tale-telling to the morning's scriptural readings: both offer matter for meditation on the dangerous error of placing one's trust in human works or virtues and on the need for God's grace. She takes the following comment of Oisille, with which she notes that no one in the narrators' group disagrees, as a statement of Marguerite's purpose for the tales:

> les maulx que nous disons des hommes et des femmes ne sont poinct pour la honte particulliere de ceulx dont est faict le compte, mais pour oster l'estime de la confiance des creatures, en monstrant les miseres où ilz sont subgectz, afin que nostre espoir s'arreste et s'appuye à Celluy seul qui est parfaict et sans lequel tout homme n'est que imperfection. (317)

> *[when we recount the evil doings of the men and women in our stories, we are not doing it in order to bring shame upon individuals, but in order to remove the esteem (and) trust placed in the mere creatures of God, by means of displaying the sorrows to which those creatures are subject, to the end that our hope may come to rest upon Him who alone is perfect and without whom all men are but imperfection. (416)]*

This reading draws the *Heptameron* close to Marguerite's other writings, thus offering a unified vision not only of the tales and discussions but also of Marguerite's entire opus.

Lebègue's phrase makes sense when we recall that there is a double goal to the narrators' journey: the baths, an intended goal; and the monastery, an initially unintended one. In case we think there is a simple polarity here of secular baths versus religious monastery, we are led to consider that the baths, which have a long literary tradition as a site for sexual license, are described as truly healing while the monastery is a place of illicit sexual unions (1, cf. 282). Marguerite's movement from bath to monastery may be already in part a reversal from Boccaccio's *Decameron*, where the narrators meet in church and proceed through a pair of gardens to an isolated pond where they bathe. That pond is coded both for erotic enticement and for purity, the narrators' most distant remove from the sickness and corruption of town. Furthermore, Marguerite adds another opposition between a good monastery and an evil one. All these features quickly confound any neat binaries between the spiritual and the secular.

As baths are linked by ancient tradition to sexual license, the bath-monastery pair is soon mirrored in the pair of rejected suggestions for how to pass the time: in meditation on Scripture or in sexual pleasure. Tale-telling, however, becomes a kind of compromise between the two, though both activities continue in the margins of the text: through Oisille's readings and through the activities of the married couples among the group, mentioned explicitly at the beginning and ending of the fourth day. Thus the tales and discussions cannot stand only in opposition to religious discourse but must also be seen as in some sense akin to it. Their human discourse is a meeting point for the extremes of spiritual and carnal occupation. We have conversation instead of prayers, but also conversation along with prayers instead of sexual games. Indeed, the narratives of the New Testament, from which Oisille's readings are taken, are referred to as exemplary "comptes" (370) [tales]. So too Duval (1993) observes that the word "nouvelles" refers both to the tales and to the "bonne nouvelle" of the New Testament.[37]

Both scriptural and novella traditions merge in Geburon's string of phrases: "Je n'ai jamais veu, dist Geburon, mocqueur qui ne fut mocqué, trompeur qui ne fut trompé, et glorieux qui ne fut humillyé" (332) ["I have never seen," said Geburon, "a mocker who was never mocked, nor a deceiver who was never himself deceived, nor arrogance that was never in the end humiliated" (433)]. The novella's recurrent theme of the trickster tricked becomes one with God's promise of humbling the proud and raising the humble. Similarly, both God and Amour are separately credited with causing the disparities between how people appear and how they act. For God, as is frequently repeated, "par les choses foybles confond les fortes" (185) [chooses the weak things of the world to confound the things which are mighty (265)], and "eslit les choses basses, pour confondre celles que le monde estime haultes et honorables" (21) [Often does He choose that which is low, that He might confound that which the world places high and considers worthy (82)]. Thus a weak female, even one from the lower classes, can overcome the ruses and threats of the more powerful. But so too the erotic Amour, in dealing with his "fidelles," is seen to "faire tous les jours miracles, comme d'affoiblir les fortz, fortisfier les foibles, donner intelligence aux ignorans, oster les sens aux plus sçavans . . . et en telles mutations prent plaisir l'amoureuse divinité" (202) [(delight) in constantly working miracles—strengthening the weak, weakening the strong, making the ignorant wise, depriving the most learned of their wisdom. . . . Turning things upside down is what the god of Love enjoys (284)].

In a further confusion of territorial demarcations, we learn within two pages that the monks have not heard the bell ringing for vespers because they have been listening to the stories and that the narrators have not heard the bell ringing for Mass because they have been deep in contemplation of Oisille's reading from the Bible (156–57). This crossover simultaneously relies on a sense of oppositions and erases them, as monks and worldly nobles become indistinguishable in their activities. Presumably the monks stand to learn—and need to learn—as much about proper belief and behavior from the tales and discussions as the narrators from their readings and discussions of Scripture. Comic and even farcical narrative (such as tale 55 or 34) leads easily into theological argument.

In sum, if the intertwined tale-telling and dialogue are originally set up as a game to pass the time, and distinguished from more serious occupations, the boundaries between play and earnest are continually transgressed. But they must be, for as the "wilderness" is both the separate space of play and at the same time the space of all historical time, the game is in a sense the whole human world and the earnest is the divine. The desire to acknowledge God's ubiquitous presence and to "vivre le Christianisme évangélique dans la société aristocratique française" (Bideux 1992, 308) [live an evangelical Christianity in French aristocratic society] ensures the necessity of those transgressions.

Playful and religious discourses both have their limits too, and we are warned with the same breath against foolish belief in all tales and in all supposed miracles (246). Parlamente, reinforcing Simontault's warning later on, urges hesitation of belief, "pource que le vray et le faulx n'ont que ung mesme langaige" (359) [for truth and falsehood speak the same language (463)]. She is talking specifically about true and false lovers; but if we think of the friars who use religious language for wicked purposes, her sentence holds as well to describe the relations of religious and secular discourse, or indeed the whole problematic of getting at truth, historical or spiritual, through human language. Both scriptural readings and tales are embedded in discussions, whether these are presented to us or left offstage. Those conversations are a repeated effort to understand what use to make of what the group is hearing. The frequent response to the recurring impasse or perplexity of these conversations is an announced resignation concerning human blindness and a hope for salvation by a divine power that we can never understand.

Despite Marguerite's obvious piety, the uncertainties of her text, conveyed not only by the arguments within it but also by the very status of the discourse itself, make this one of the most open of women's dialogues. On one hand it challenges the reader to make sense of it in any number of ways; on the other hand, it humbles the reader into a sense of the human incapacity to determine any truth at all without God's grace. On one hand, it argues for the acknowledgment of women's capabilities; on the other hand, it demonstrates not only how confused and contradictory our social codes are but also how confused and contradictory are our own inner selves and our own desires, and how difficult to know. Despite the serious feminist arguments by some of its members, the group's general resignation in the face of their own polyphony does not lend itself to arousing social action. It tends instead to urge us to constant prayer.

Unlike Marguerite, Moderata Fonte in *Il merito delle donne* (The Worth of Women) neglects the transcendent to emphasize social and economic reform.[38] The daughter and wife of lawyers, Fonte was interested in laws, governance, and human justice. The multiple voices of her book focus directly on the faults of men and the consequent problems for relations between men and women. This time all the speakers are female: seven women as in the *Decameron* (a text to which Fonte several times alludes).[39] Whereas the seven *Decameron* ladies feel a need to bring along some men because "Veramente gli uomini sono delle femine capo, e senza l'ordine loro rade volte riesce alcuna nostra opera a laudevole fine" (I. intro. 76) [Truly men are the head of women, and without their government rarely does any of our work turn out in a praiseworthy manner], Fonte's omission of men indicates her disagreement with such sentiments.

Similarly, whereas Marguerite, disclaiming rhetorical skill, modestly refused to describe the scenery where her narrators gather, commenting that it would require a Boccaccio to do it justice ("qui estoit si beau et plaisant qu'il avoit besoin d'un Bocace pour le depaindre" [10]), Fonte, ambitious to be considered a rhetorically skilled writer herself, launches into the most detailed description of setting in any woman's dialogue. The presence of the description is in itself an argument for the eloquence and sufficiency of women; the details of the landscape offer further symbolic support for her agenda, as we shall see later.

Marguerite moved to equalize the male and female sides, allowing them to attack each other on even ground. She used the limited sphere of a game to create space for the equality of all participants: as Hircan says at the beginning, "au jeu nous sommes tous esgaulx" (10). Fonte does away with male participation altogether, creating a female space for women to speak in freedom about the abuses perpetrated by men. Nonetheless, despite a potentially one-sided perspective and despite the tone of us versus them, a wide range of positions is still presented. This allows the text both to offer radically feminist statements and to hedge them with reassuring and containing measures. It also allows us to see, as in Marguerite's work, conflicting assessments among and within the women themselves.

The seven women of *Il merito delle donne* represent various stages of life as well as various points of view. Adriana, chosen as queen of the seven, assigns three of her companions to say all the ill they can about men while the other three are to defend men. The division of sides neatly balances adherents from different stages of life. The youngest, Verginia, still unwed and initially full of idealism, is one of the defenders of men, although by the end of the two-day conversation she is not sure that she wants to marry at all. Her conversion to a separatist position, however, is swiftly countered by her mother's persuasions at the end of the book. Throughout the conversation Verginia, who has little experience of her own, tends to utter views based either on appearances or on things she has heard and is described by the others as naive. The other unwed woman, Corinna, is on the attacking team and staunchly refuses ever to marry. She is the most learned of the group and is encouraged by the others to hold forth on various scientific topics as well as to recite her own and others' verses. She is also described as *dimessa*, that is, a member of a new kind of post-Tridentine religious institution arising in the Veneto for women who wished to live a pious and celibate life without entering a convent. These women often dedicated their time to assisting young women "in pericolo" (i.e., in danger of losing their honor because of poverty) and instructing them in religious doctrine. Thus they opened the way for the development of a female teaching career, which in the following century would become more widespread (Zarri 1994, 212–18).[40] Corinna does at times take a rather teacherly attitude toward the other women, who are eager to share the fruits of her learning. Her instruction, however, seems remarkably secular despite Fonte's use of the term *dimessa*.

Lucrezia and Cornelia are both married women, and like the maidens, they take opposite sides of the argument, Lucrezia—as her namesake, the ideal wife, suggests—defending men and marriage, while Cornelia wishes that men would all just go away and let women live on their own altogether.

The two widows similarly tend to take opposite sides on the issue of marriage, though they are more likely to agree about the faults of men. Adriana, Verginia's mother, defends married life as better than its alternative, which is to remain shut up in one's parents' or brother's house, living a life of much greater restriction than that of a wife. Yet she offers her own two husbands as examples of how worthless men are: the first ran after servant girls, and the second wasted the family money on gambling. Men simply have no self-control but allow themselves to be run by their appetites, insouciant about the harm they are causing their families. Leonora, the young widow in whose house and garden the whole discussion takes place, is grateful to be free of married life and claims she would rather drown herself than remarry (1988, 21), though even she at the end surprisingly admits that she might eventually reconsider should one of those very rare good men show up.

Finally there is Elena, the newlywed just back from her honeymoon, and happy so far, although the others cause her anxious thoughts about the future. She too tends to defend men and marriage, although like Verginia she is considered naive and inexperienced by the older women. Thus, although the sides seem balanced, experience tends to speak worse of men, whose defense comes more generally from the idealistic young.

Not only has Moderata Fonte balanced the two sides, but she also allows them to persuade each other into tentatively changing positions, thus registering some uncertainty within a given stance. For example, Verginia is swayed by Corinna and Cornelia to decide against marriage, while her mother's counterarguments persuade Leonora not to rule out the possibility of a second marriage in the future. Thus a sense of give and take on the issue at hand pervades the entire work. These speakers are not simply representatives of fixed positions, as they tend to be for Marguerite, but humans capable of changing their minds in a discussion among friends.

Various factors sway the balance now this way and now that. The allotment of sides by Adriana ensures debate regardless of the speakers' real views, although they do also seem to be speaking according to their true thoughts and feelings. The attackers speak first; second, the defenders of men utter their objections. However, since their objections are then responded to in turn, we are left with a double statement by the attackers, sandwiching and undoing the defense. This puts the attackers in a rhetorically strong position. Nonetheless, the defense is there, maintaining a sense that other views exist and that not everyone agrees with what is being said.

Another factor in favor of the prosecution is the biased status of examples. Usually the attackers offer general statements, with an occasional example to prove the rule. When the defenders offer a counterexample, however, it is rejected as an exception. For example, Cornelia blames fathers who do not see to the welfare and happiness of their daughters but who act as if only their sons were their own beloved children deserving of education and inheritance. When Elena objects that her own father has always loved her dearly and has taken pains to find her a good marriage, Corinna answers, "uno non fa numero" (28) [one swallow does not make a summer (1997, 62)]. Similarly, when Corinna attacks brothers who keep their unmarried sister at home as a servant while making use of her dowry money for their own purposes, Lucrezia protests that there do exist affectionate brothers such as her own, who have treated her better than their own daughters. To this Corinna replies, "Iddio qualche volta mostra dei miracoli" (29) [God on occasion performs miracles (63)]. On the one hand, this dismissal of counterexamples as mere exceptions seems to favor the prosecution. On the other hand, the fact that members of the group can point to their own male kinsmen to refute the general charges suggests that the experiences of the group have indeed been mixed and that good men not only exist but are known to more than one of them.

Fonte herself knew more than one example of helpful males in her family. Orphaned during her first year, she was raised by her grandparents; her grandfather, seeing her quick intelligence, encouraged her education. Later, when the girl with whom Moderata had been raised almost as a sister was married, the husband, Niccolò Doglioni, allowed Moderata to join her companion in their home. There he not only continued to encourage her writing but even introduced it to the public.[41] It was he who arranged her marriage and also saw to the publication of *Il merito delle donne* after her death, adding to it his own encomiastic account of her life.[42] Thus Fonte had reason to acknowledge with appreciation the existence of kindly kinsmen. She even includes explicit praises of Doglioni and her husband in the mouth of Corinna:[43]

> tra gli altri io ne conosco il Signor Gio. Nicolò Doglioni, spirito gentilissimo e che oltre le altre sue singolar virtù, ha per propria dote una bontà e lealtà incredibile, il che di raro in uomo avviene. (84)
>
> [*One whom I know personally is Signor Giovanni Niccolò Doglioni, a man of great refinement and one who, in addition to his other remarkable talents, has been gifted with incredible kindness and loyalty (things rarely found in men). (132)*]

Even this moment of praise indicates that Fonte felt her situation to be lucky rather than common.

Husbands come off much less well than fathers and brothers. Not only has Lucrezia's dead husband been enough to make her rejoice at her widowhood, but even the twice-married Adriana admits that both her husbands were terrible. The defense of fathers and brothers thus ultimately contributes to the wholesale condemnation of husbands as illegitimate and irrational tyrants who treat their wives worse than their dogs. When Verginia expresses early on her reluctance to marry, her mother answers: "A questo, figliuola mia io sarei del tuo parere, ma li tuoi zii hanno deliberato che io ti mariti per la gran facultà che tu hai ereditata, la quale alcuno non ti può usurpare" (17) [When it comes to that, my dear child, I'd be quite happy to respect your opinion, but your uncles have decided you must marry, because you've inherited such a fortune and it needs to be in safe hands (48)]. The argument here is ironic, that to protect one's wealth one must lose it to a husband; but it is men who have made the decision. Both mother and daughter are powerless in relation to these uncles. This sentiment of Adriana's cuts against her argument at the end of the book that marriage is better than a single life. Even there, however, we have not so much a praise of marriage as the claim that it is the lesser of two evils.[44]

Conservatively, Adriana counsels dealing with a brutal, jealous, or unfaithful husband by humility, patience, and silence, in the hope that he will eventually appreciate one's virtues (170–71). But when Elena offers the same counsel earlier with regard to the general project of the book—instead of complaining about men let us be silent and perhaps they too will change their style—Leonora replies brusquely:

> Si è taciuto pur troppo . . . e più che si tace, essi fanno peggio, anzi per mover il giudice a dar giusta sentenza bisogna dir liberamente la verità e non tacer alcuna delle sue ragioni; che se per caso uno doverà aver dinari da tale che non si curi pagarlo ed egli si tace, colui che non ha discrezione, non lo satisferà mai, ma se parla, se dimanda, se si querela al giudice, ecco che pur tardi, o per tempo vien satisfatto. (140)

> *[We've already done too much keeping quiet in the past . . . and the more we keep quiet, the worse they get. On the contrary, in order to move a judge to pass a just sentence, one needs to speak out freely, not suppressing any argument that might support the truth. If a man needs to reclaim some money from a person who has refused to pay him and he keeps quiet about it, the unscrupulous debtor will never give him satisfaction, but if he speaks up, if he brings the case, if he complains in front of the judge, then sooner or later he will get back what is his by right. (199)]*

The hypothetical case is very much to the point, for the prosecution considers that men owe a debt to women that they have unjustly and intentionally ignored—thus the book's title, meaning "the merit of women" and implying "what women rightfully deserve." Even the financial aspect of the debt is not irrelevant, for this book places unusual emphasis (among feminist texts of the Renaissance) on the issue of property rights: inheritance, dowry, control of one's own money and goods. Men are repeatedly accused of unjustly taking over women's property (e.g., 69), an issue enhanced by the setting: a house and garden that widowhood has restored to a woman's control.

When Verginia asks plaintively, "Then are we to love no man?" Cornelia responds by comparing men to lottery tickets: among "thousands" there are "eight or ten" tickets worth a good sum (43–44). If history has recorded examples of good men, it is because they are so rare that they are worthy of note; similarly, history has recorded negative examples of women because these too are monsters rather than the norm. Besides, such women were made bad by importunate men, whereas men are bad all by themselves (51–52). When Corinna tells a romance about the origins of the unicorn, Leonora notes that the men in this tale are actually better than the women; "'Fate conto,' rispose Corinna, 'd'aver udito una favola'" (111) ["Ah, but you have to remember," said Corinna, "that what you've just heard was a fairy-tale" (166)]. The humor of the reply counteracts its cynicism.

Despite the many bitter comments about men, certain factors also work in their defense. The women unanimously praise certain professions, naming lists of contemporary local men famous for their talents in science, law, medicine, and letters. Even Corinna joins in offering her praises of these professionals and of the prince and magistrates of Venice, perhaps to demonstrate that the women are not only critical but also capable of praising men who prove themselves useful. The works that she cites by some of these men may have been Fonte's sources for much of her scientific information and may therefore offer a reading list for other women. Meanwhile the only list of praiseworthy contemporary women celebrates quite conventionally women who combine beauty and virtue. There is, it is true, a list of classical women known for their patriotic deeds and poetic talents as well as for chastity, peacemaking, and love of their kin (62–68). Since these are given as examples of the qualities for which men should love women, the implication is that such qualities still persist and ought still to be admired rather than repressed. Nonetheless, Corinna's presence as a learned woman does not lead to the acknowledgment and listing of other recent or contemporary learned and literary women such as those offered by other women writers,[45] even though sixteenth-century Venice certainly had its share of female poets, painters, and musicians.[46] The group's complaint about male opposition to the education of women (168–69) may serve as a partial explanation for this absence.

While on the one hand uttering a call to women to rise up and reclaim the liberty and honor that has for so long been usurped by men (169), on the other hand the learned Corinna modestly pretends at times that some unnamed gentleman has written the verses really composed by her, as her friends are able to guess (e.g., 152). Internalized norms of modesty prevent even Corinna from laying claim to the skills she actually possesses. Women of power and talent appear to have flourished chiefly in the ancient past, just as men who know how to be true friends are said to exist mainly in ancient examples and not in the contemporary world (77–78). While Marguerite's appeal is to Christian ideals, Fonte's appeal is more humanistically directed toward an idealized classical apex of full human accomplishment, when women could take public action and men could honestly love.

Besides their celebrations of useful male talent, most of the group express a wish for harmonious relations with men. Even Corinna, again, joins in the wish for peace and harmony between the sexes, although the once-married Leonora pessimistically doubts that men's wickedness could ever be in harmony with female goodness (158–59). When fathers and brothers are accused of not bothering to arrange suitable marriages for their female kin, marriage is thereby implied to be desirable and a suitable marriage at least possible. Indeed, the praises of local women of virtue and beauty mention their happy marriages to worthy husbands.[47] Leonora's cynicism is thus corrected, and she herself allows near the end that a good marriage may be possible.

Leonora, challenged by the group to give the speech that she would make to men if she could, has rhetorical reasons for stressing the possibilities of a better relationship even if experience has made her doubt its real chances. Indeed, the striking feature of her speech is its ambivalences, as she tries to present her case for women in terms that will appeal to men, whom she positions as simultaneously the judges and defendants in a trial. This unfair situation reappears (140) when Leonora argues for the importance of speaking out and telling the whole truth if you want justice done; Corinna replies to her example of trying to collect a debt, "Ma se'l giudice dovesse egli dare, non so se vi desse la sentenza in favore" (140) [But if it were the judge himself who was the debtor, then I'm not as sure as you seem to be that he would give the sentence in the plaintiff's favor (199)]. Leonora, in short, has what Cicero called a difficult audience. She begins by appealing to men to listen as impartial judges rather than as interested parties.

Until now, she argues, you men have continually done us wrong and put us down ("sempre avete cercato di abbassare ed offenderci" [132]), who were made by God to be your companions and not your slaves. Yet who loves and serves you better than we? "Però deh carissimi ed inseparabili amici, tutte le leggi divine ed umane vi fanno nostri, come noi siamo vostre. Deh fateci buona ed amorevol compagnia" (134) [So hear our plea, dearest friends and inseparable companions, for you belong to us by all laws, both human and divine, just as we belong to you. Come, be good and loving companions (191)]. Love us for our patience, humility, and kind service, as you ought, and we will be "più che mai per l'avenir amorevoli e soggette, per amore però e non per forza" (134) [we will love you . . . we will pay you that due to a husband—we will even regard you as our masters, not through obligation, but through love (191)].[48] Thus if you men will judge in our favor, you will be judging not against but for your own interest (1988, 132–35; 1997, 189–92).

The appeal to men is that women who are happy will be willingly "subject" to their men. Moreover, men are to love and respect women for precisely the qualities that express this subjection: humility, patience, loving service. The request, however, is more radical than it appears, for it asks for a fundamentally reconceived relationship between men and women in which women are considered fully human, so that daughters and sons, wives and husbands, sisters and brothers, are equal in their legal rights and help each other mutually out of equal affection and esteem. The words "istimare" and "stima" recur in varying forms throughout Leonora's speech.

The doubleness of Leonora's speech is implicit in its very presentation. It is a speech for the ears of men, yet it is delivered in the presence only of women. It is a public and formal address, yet delivered only privately in Leonora's own home. Leonora claims that her eloquence would probably falter if she were really to have the occasion of making this speech before a male audience; yet the eloquence is carefully written in a book that might well come before male readers. Thus Fonte again and again both makes the radical gesture and contains it, hoping, like Leonora with her artful rhetoric, to win an audience that may well be hostile. The case is made; the judgment, however, remains pending.

Among the multiple voices of this text, one must consider Moderata Fonte's own, which opens the narrative with other double gestures. The occasion for the group's meeting is the celebration of Elena's recent marriage. Yet the site for the meeting is the property of a widow who praises her own recently acquired freedom from marriage and the control it gives her over her own wealth. Leonora's ability to support herself demonstrates the thesis propounded by Cornelia that women can perfectly well live and manage financially without men, who steal the use and control of women's money (169). Moreover, Leonora's property has been embellished and bequeathed to her by a maiden aunt who detested men and marriage. Thus it does not even come to her from men but rather through a totally female network. The garden with its flowers, fruits, and fountain is not only a traditional locus amoenus, reminding one of the *Decameron*, but also like a paradise precisely for its exclusion of men (21). Its formal perfection suggests that women are not a wild nature or *materia* in need of the forming governance of men; rather, they can by themselves generate the proper balance of luxuriance and control.

The central fountain is carved with figures that honor Chastity, Solitude, and Liberty, while warning against Simplicity (the moth burned by the seemingly attractive candle) and against the Falsehood and Cruelty of men. The women naturally begin complaining to each other about men, thereby suggesting the topic that Adriana as queen sets for their ensuing discussion. Give honorable and experienced women a space with solitude and liberty, suggests the fountain, and the topic of men's treachery and cruelty will naturally emerge from the silence under which normal conditions keep it hidden. Is this fountain at the center of the scene, silent yet visually eloquent, a marker for Fonte herself as the silent *fonte* of this written text?[49] If so, its message would imply a bitterness possibly reinforced by Corinna's linking of intellectual pursuits with the avoidance of men and marriage.

It has been suggested by Adriana Chemello, Paola Malpezzi Price, and Margaret King that Corinna, who certainly speaks the most and who is urged to write a book, comes close to being the mouthpiece for Fonte herself.[50] Chemello, however, sees no trace in the text of the tensions in Fonte's life between her intellectual and literary ambitions on the one hand and her duties as wife and mother on the other (Fonte 1988, xix). Corinna's refusal to marry, however, may well be one such trace. Chemello notes that between Fonte's early works and *Il merito* fell ten years of silence (xvii–xix), precisely the years in which Fonte was being a wife and bearing children. Corinna seems convinced that her pursuit of learning and her avoidance of men go naturally together. The wonder is that Fonte, unlike so many other Italian humanist women, did manage to write again within her married life; most others either fell silent or picked up their old studies when widowhood left them free to do so.[51] Beatrice Collina (1989, 154), resisting the identification of Fonte with Corinna, suggests instead that she is "un po' tutti i personnagi del suo dialogo" [a bit of each of the characters of her dialogue]. In sum, the same question arises as for Marguerite—whether to see one of the speakers as a special mouthpiece for the author or whether to see the author dispersed through all her speakers. Inclining toward the latter view allows us to see the use of multiple voices as a means to express the author's own ambivalences. In any case it is significant that both Fonte and Marguerite have hidden their own thoughts behind a multiplicity of other speakers, unlike most of the writers of two-person dialogues, who make their identification with one side clear.

Fonte's introductory praises of Venice not only participate in the tradition of local writers praising this queen of cities but also join in the implication of a mixed set of values. More conservatively, the passage demonstrates total respect for the social and religious hierarchies:

in somma questa benedetta città è favorita da Dio di ogni sorte di beneficio che si possa desiderare, perchè teme sua divina maestà ed e religiosissima e ricognitrice dei doni celesti; e dopo Dio è devotissima e obedientissima al suo Principe, il qual (acciò nulla manchi a sì felice e ben ordinata Repubblica) in bontà, prudenzia e giustizia non ha chi l'agguagli. (14)

[In short, this most fortunate city is showered by God with all the blessings anyone could desire, owing to the fact that the people are so God-fearing and

*devout, and so grateful for all of God's gifts. And next to God, it is devoted
and obedient in the highest degree to its ruler, the doge, who (just so that
nothing should be lacking to such a happy and well-ordered Republic) is unri-
valed in his goodness, prudence, and justice. (44)]*

These praises of God and prince are followed by praise of the city's noble
families, to which our virtuous seven ladies belong. However, the qualities
that make Venice great are explicitly freedom ("libera come è il mare"),
peace, and equity, even among her different races. These are the values fundamental to Fonte's appeal on behalf of women. If Venice can offer a life of
freedom, harmony, and justice to its variety of male citizens, why not also to
its women, especially if these values are what give the city its fame and glory?
Indeed, since the name of Venice and the various words for *city* are female,
while the sea that surrounds, protects, and provides for Venice is male, the
statement that the city is as free as the sea implies an equality across genders.
The traditional image of Venice as a female, combined with the traditional
praises of Venetian freedom, becomes an element in the case for granting the
women of Venice their own freedom and esteem.

Within their conversation the ladies repeat the praises of their city and its
government, but the new context gives it new significance. The passage follows closely on the heels of Leonora's speech about the need to speak out in
order to win justice for one's case (140–42). Moreover, it is followed immediately by Leonora's disgusted comment:

Che avemo noi a far vi prego con magistrati, corti di palazzo e tali dis-
viamenti? Or non fanno tutti gli uomini questi offici contra di noi? . . .
Non procurano per loro in nostro danno? Non ci trattano da forestieri?
Non fannosi proprio il nostro mobile? (143–44)

*[What on earth do magistrates, law courts, and all this other nonsense have
to do with us women? Are not all these official functions exercised by men,
against our interests? . . . Do they not treat us as though we were aliens? Do
they not usurp our property? (204)]*

Conventional praises have suddenly taken a radical turn indeed. If the gov-
ernmental structures of Venice are to live up to their reputation for justice,
they must hearken to the case these women bring.[52]

The final moves, like the praises of Venice and its ordered society, gesture
alternately toward rebellion and containment. A long set of narrative stanzas by Corinna blames Juno (motivated by her sense of being slighted as a
result of people's worship of Cupid) for the world's turn from love to avarice

and pride. Although the text has all along associated kindly love with women, and avarice and pride with men, this ballad switches the genders and blames a goddess's jealousy for everybody's trouble. The move picks up an earlier suggestion by the defenders of men that the attackers are speaking from envy. Not from envy, they reply, but from truth and a sense of justice. It is men who envy and therefore deprive us of what we deserve (27).[53] Juno is, of course, not a human woman and not, for the Christian Fonte, a believable goddess either. We have here nonetheless a potential acknowledgment of the female jealousy of male power after all. Yet the association of the divine male power with love advocates precisely what these women want from their men: a return to the unity of maleness with loving kindness. It is as if men are here accused of having fallen into the female Juno's vicious errors, from which they are recalled to the male Cupid's love. As with the examples of classical friendship, an ancient golden age is explicitly evoked to which man is implicitly urged to return. The rule of avarice and arrogance is not the given nature of things, but an error that has been made and can be undone.

The form of the verses and the theme of Juno's jealous anger with regard to Venus's son suggest that these stanzas are a kind of small epic concerning the conflict between the rule of Pride, Avarice, and Envy and the idyllic rule of Love. In it the forces of cruel Juno succeed in destroying the power of Love, at least within the hearts and minds of men. The song ends by addressing women, urging them not to trust in men, for women's virtues and beauties now inspire men's self-serving deceptions rather than their honest love. Women are urged instead to devote themselves to higher studies by which they can immortalize themselves to men's shame. The desire for a restored harmony with men yields to a rivalry between the sexes and an appeal for more women's voices to make themselves heard.

Yet even here Fonte cannot take a final stand; rather, she immediately qualifies this song's ending with Elena's comment: "'Con tutto questo,' disse, 'e con tutto quello che finora abbiamo udito, mi credo pure che concederete, che si possi ritrovare alcun di buono tra gli uomini.' 'Lo concedo,' rispose Leonora" (181) ["But in spite of all this, and in spite of everything we've been hearing, I'm sure you must still be prepared to allow that there is some goodness to be found in men." "Oh, I'm happy to allow it," replied Leonora (258)]. The text thus continues to waver back and forth between challenging and conciliatory gestures, between the prosecution and defense in this ongoing trial.

The conversation is framed at beginning and end with comments about its audience and purpose. The audiences and therefore also the aims are multiple.

Near the beginning Lucrezia urges Corinna, because of her learning, her avoidance of "fallacissimi uomini" (18) [those falsest of creatures, men (48)], and her pursuit of the "virtù" that renders one immortal, to write a volume for "le povere figliuole che non sanno ancora discernere il mal dal bene" (18) [poor simple girls who don't know the difference between good and evil (49)]. The "virtù" here seems to include both learning, with its expression in writing, and moral virtue. The former use of the word implicitly advocates education for women, a topic to which the ladies return (168),[54] while the latter urges the avoidance of men, who are the cause of women's sin. Lucrezia, namesake of that famously chaste wife and defender of men within this conversation, both encourages a learned woman to teach other women the value of education and the dangers of men and yet also limits the prospective volume, like the conversation itself, to a female audience. The dialogue itself, as Cox has noted (Fonte 1997, 10), seeks through its discussions of an encyclopedic array of topics to contribute to the education of its women readers as well as to advocate such education.[55] The education it offers its women readers, like that it endorses, combines scientific, practical, and moral knowledge. Women with such an education will not only realize the threats posed by men but will also have increased their own female capacity for independence, an independence exemplified by both Leonora and Corinna.

At the end of the book, a rather different purpose and audience are proposed. There Leonora, defending herself against the suggestion that she has offended men, responds:

Anzi . . . c'hanno causa di onorarmi e favorirmi, perché tutto quello in somma ch'io ho detto, non è stato per offender i buoni, ma per convertir i cattivi, se essi mi udissero; di che dovriano anzi avermene obligo, poiché non ho detto per odio che lor porti, ma per zelo di carità e per la compassion che mi fanno molte tribolate donne, che io conosco, le quali si trovano mal satisfatte, chi di padre, chi di fratello, chi di marito, chi di figliuolo e così di ciascuna sorte di compagnia d'uomo con cui pratica e vive. Poiché molti avendo solamente questa mira, per tale indebito abuso che son fatti superiori alle donne, né pensando più oltra, par loro che sia lecito di usarci ogni sorte di tirannia e crudeltà; ma restando con ciò avertiti del loro errore forsi che potriano emendarsi. . . . (182)

[On the contrary . . . men have good cause to honor me and take my part, for when it comes down to it, nothing of what I've said has been intended to offend good men; rather, it's all been directed toward converting bad men—

if only they would listen. So they should be grateful to me, really, since I haven't been speaking out of any hatred for men, but rather in a spirit of charity, and moved by the compassion I feel for the many suffering women I see around me, one made unhappy by her father, another by her brother, another by her husband, still another by her son and so on across every relationship one person can have with another. For many men see this world in a blinkered way, and are so thoroughly convinced by the unwarrantable fallacy that they are created women's superiors, and so incapable of seeing past this lie, that they believe themselves fully justified in treating women as tyrannically and brutally as they like. But if they could be persuaded of their error, they might just change their ways. . . . (258–59)]

For her the audience is male, not female, and the aim is to change men's attitudes. Just as Catherine des Roches addressed both male and female audiences in a combined effort to improve women's lives, so both Lucrezia and Leonora see the book as helping to improve the social conditions of women either by enlightening women or by enlightening men.[56]

Almost immediately, the queen calls an end to the discussion, referring to it all as a day's entertainment and reminding the reader that the speakers on both sides were faithfully obeying the rules of the game she had commanded. By setting up the debate as a game and reminding us at the end of that status, Fonte renders these women unaccountable for the opinions they have delivered. The dismissal of examples of good men, for instance, may be taken as a witty retort, more humorous than serious. When later a series of puns on grammatical terms is used to insult men and praise women (139), they reestablish that we are involved in a mental game. Thus the distinction of seriousness from entertaining banter is not always clear. The reminders that we are observing a game form a gesture of containment that fails, however, to negate entirely the seriousness of the pleas we have heard. Indeed, the three expressed purposes may help to make each other possible, the playfulness allowing serious statements to be voiced, while the direct address to women allows an indirect address to male readers.[57]

The multiple voices of the text suggest the possibility for multiple readings. Take this as a game if it disturbs you, or as the idle chatter of women recorded for your amusement. Or take it seriously in at least some part, if not all: perhaps the most radical speakers are an extreme; still there may be some suggestions and complaints that seem reasonable. Or take it as a radical manifesto, written in full seriousness, with whatever rhetorical framing might encourage its reading. Certainly the zeal with which Fonte hastened to finish this work before her imminent and fatal childbirth suggests a seriousness of intent rather than an aim of mere entertainment. But the attacks on men are simultaneously serious and witty. The presence of these different women easily allows for and expresses the presence of varied intentions, one quite contained, one more socially radical, and one somewhere in between. It also distances all these aims from Fonte herself, who offers no explicit reason of her own for recording this "domestic conversation."

The game of subversion and containment continues to the very end. The conservative direction of the queen's closing remarks, with her reference to "entertainment," is reinforced by Leonora's comment that even she might some day remarry after Verginia has been appropriately taken care of and by her reference to Adriana's defense of marriage as "saggi e santi ricordi" (183) [wise and holy reminders (259)]. But the final brief song before the women's departure advises us that women are the adornment of the world and that men cannot live without their aid. This plays one final reversal on Lucrezia's earlier contribution to the argument for marriage: that women need men's help for their physical and legal defense in this imperfect world (172, 240). Indeed, the song stresses the *mutual* need and love between the sexes, combining the ideal of a harmonious relation with the sense of the equality and mutual recognition that such a relationship requires.

The very last sentence sends the women all home, some to their husbands, some to homes that are totally female spaces. There is no closing commentary by Fonte herself, just as there is no final judgment reached in the case that has been argued by the seven women. The multiple spaces of these women's lives are the last indication we receive. There has been no journey out of town as in Boccaccio's and Marguerite's works; yet there is a kind of journey relative to the fixed setting of Castiglione's court. These women move between the world in which they live with men and a totally female space. That female space is beautiful and free, unlike their lives among men. Yet the effect of this separate space is not simply to predicate an essential femaleness apart from maleness, although certainly much of the debate is given to just this kind of statement; rather, within this space seven quite different women emerge and acknowledge the diversity of their experiences and desires. The topic of the game may be defined as men against women, but the game itself sets women against women in a discussion on the value of men and marriage and on the positions of women in society. As we have seen in the *Heptameron*, so too here, the conflicts between radical and conservative views exist among women, even within women, as much as between women and men.[58]

Both Marguerite de Navarre and Moderata Fonte use multiple voices to express a real and unresolved multiplicity of feelings and views. Neither issues statements in her own voice; rather, both distance themselves from their texts, Fonte even more than Marguerite: for she has placed between herself and her readers not only her seven speakers and a fictional writer (Corinna) but also her nom de plume, her historical name (Modesta Pozzo) remaining entirely absent from the volume. Fonte's speakers giggle that fortunately no one can hear what they are saying, for men would surely mock them (16–17). Her book thus claims to have no real authority and no real audience either. Marguerite's book, to be presented to her as its recipient and reader by the narrators she has created (9), finds a similarly self-enclosed existence.

In both works, prevailing ideas emerge from the group, yet the writer herself never appears to lay claim to these messages; instead she encloses them in a game fraught with disagreements. The gamelike nature of these conversations is emphasized by the separate and unusual space in which they occur. These games, however, not only fence out the real world but also invite it in, as the ongoing unresolved discussions compel us to become involved in thinking through their matters for ourselves. Each writer thus seeks through a conversation from which she is absent to lure us into consideration of the issues that seem to her most important. The polyphonic form opens itself to the inclusion not simply of "the woman's voice" but of multiple women's voices and perspectives in the larger conversation of literature and society.

It is worth noting that the differences between Moderata Fonte and Marguerite de Navarre run parallel to those between Catherine des Roches and Olympia Morata, discussed in chapter 3. Unlike the dramatic dialogues of the previous chapter, therefore, these differences have nothing to do with being Italian or French and everything to do with the social situation and religious inclinations of the writer. The Italian Olympia and French Marguerite are both adherents of evangelical reform. They share a strong religious belief in the absolute need for God, with whom the most astonishing virtue and heroism are possible and without whom nothing will work. Their common emphasis on the vanity of worldly values and their common desire to convert the worldly induce in both a serious intensity and a style that weaves scriptural wisdom with human discourse. Both women lived for years at a politically and culturally powerful court without having been there as children, and both manifest a fairly detached and critical eye for its dangers. Neither is interested in describing its festivals; both focus on its perils to the soul. Marguerite may allow jokes and banter, but just as a sense of the world's imminent end pervades Olympia's later writing, so the *Heptameron*'s repeated message of the worthlessness, even viciousness, of human nature on its own has inclined some readers (e.g., Mathieu-Castellani 1992, 234) to note Marguerite's "pessimism." Neither writer, of course, would think her attitude pessimistic; quite the opposite. The disillusionment with mankind is accompanied by a joyful faith in God's ultimate victory. For both these reform-minded women, all earthly activity takes place under the eye of God and as part of the great battle between God and sin.

Catherine des Roches and Moderata Fonte, on the other hand, share a social context of lawyers' families in a city with thriving intellectual discussions and salons. Both remain Catholic and basically uninterested in discussing matters of religion. They turn for their models to the classics, read with the admiring eye of humanism, as they argue rationally for social justice to women. They too seek to enlighten others, but to bring them to an acknowledgment of women's need for education, appreciation, and independence, not for God. Examples of injustice are offered not as a revelation of ineluctable human nature but as a corrigible defect, an unnatural state of affairs. It is not that they are irreligious but that religion in no way displaces their sense of the importance of this world's arrangements for human happiness. They advocate the possibility of such happiness through intellectual development and either economic independence or a more equal relationship in marriage. They allow songs and poems to enter their discussions, pleasant demonstrations of their versatile skill. Their own happiness with learning emanates from their learned characters as an attitude of cheerful and virtuous self-confidence, which is represented as the object of admiration by other women and as a goal for other women to achieve.

Nonetheless, the diphonic dialogues of Morata and des Roches present a stronger sense of right and wrong sides of the discussion, while the polyphonic dialogues of Marguerite and Fonte are better able to complicate the taking of sides and thus to invite the reader into truly thinking through the issues rather than to persuade him or her to agree with one speaker. Both Marguerite and Fonte fragment the authorial voice in a way that indicates the contradictions and ambivalences among and within women and, in Marguerite's case, within the human condition more generally. In both works, no position is ever allowed to remain fixed. Each seeming closure is reopened by the next contributor. The use of the dialogue as game permits the inclusion of women's voices. At the same time, the writers turn this playful conversation to some very serious topics. They use the complexity and instability of the conversation genre to present quite radical views and to open up new possibilities for their societies. These serious issues, whether secular or spiritual, are shown to require the participation of women's critical thought and its expression. Both internally and externally, the dialogues enact that participation.

7 Cross-threads

I will try in conclusion to follow some of the threads that have woven their way across the fabric of the main discourse and to pull together issues that may have been scattered in the consideration of texts one by one. I will also try to step back and address some new issues that require a general survey of the field. What real relationships made possible the dialogic relationships of these writings? Who can speak to whom, and how? What are the sources of authority for women's speech? What topics do they turn to repeatedly or avoid? In other words, how do these writers imagine their own interaction with existing discourses? From where do these dialogues draw their energies and their conceptual frameworks?

The women who wrote or spoke in these dialogues were usually learned women. Most of them knew more than one language and had access to books. Even Tullia d'Aragona, who probably knew only Italian, had access to both classical and contemporary ideas either through translations or through her contacts with learned men. Some of the dialogue writers were members of the nobility or even royalty: Isota Nogarola, Giulia Gonzaga (if Valdés's dialogue truly records her voice, she can be considered partially its writer), Marie Le Gendre, and Marguerite de Navarre. Education had long been considered a practical necessity for women in the ruling families. One writer, Tullia d'Aragona, was a courtesan, educated (as Agnolo Firenzuola notes of courtiers) more by conversation than by serious study; education for the courtesan was a way of raising her status, her clientele, and thus her income. Many of the dialogue writers, however, were middle-class women. Since the dialogue is a humanist genre, many of the women who wrote dialogues were associated with humanist parents, husbands, or friends. Some, such as Olympia Morata, Moderata Fonte, and Catherine des Roches, came from professional families of scholars or lawyers. Others, such as Chiara Matraini and Louise Labé, were married women from commercial families. Helisenne, somewhere between the middle class and pretensions to rank, was the wife of a country squire. All were unusually well educated for their class and well connected with a publisher or with other men of letters.

The Renaissance dialogue, despite its classical and humanist roots, rapidly developed into a vernacular genre of conversational language. Our writers therefore had various linguistic models. Two of the Italian humanists wrote in Latin: Isota Nogarola and Olympia Morata. This choice of language did not necessarily imply addressing their work to men; Morata wrote in Latin to a learned female friend. Given the use of the vernacular in men's instructive dialogues to women (e.g., Valdés's, Ochino's), it is noteworthy that Morata chose Latin for similar spiritual instruction addressed to a female. The other women all wrote in the vernacular even when they knew Latin well—as many of them did.

Morata's work all along seeks to combine her classical learning with her strong religious sentiments; thus she translated psalms into classical Greek meters and wrote even the dialogue of spiritual instruction in a primarily Ciceronian form. She was in fact the first woman to write a classical Ciceronian dialogue: in Latin, with constructions and phrases borrowed from Cicero and other ancient writers, set among real acquaintances in a moment of leisure, and including herself as a speaker. Even the opening of her first dialogue, in which Lavinia finds Olympia at her studies, resembles the opening of Cicero's De finibus III (ii.7), where Cicero comes across Cato sitting in the library with books piled around him. Like Cicero's dialogues rather than Plato's, Morata's dialogues are a lively way of setting forth truths already decided on, rather than a heuristic means of discovering truth.

Helisenne, while sharing Morata's humanistic interests and well acquainted with the Latin classics, preferred to re-create them in French. She was among the first to write in French the genre of invective epistles derived from a Latin tradition. This choice displays the same concerns as her translation of Vergil and her attempts to produce an illustrious Latinate French. Claude Colet, who obtained Helisenne's permission to publish in 1560 an edition of her works with the language rendered somewhat simpler and clearer, actually suggested that Helisenne had chosen a Latinate language in order to ensure herself only educated readers: "[Elle] avoit usé d'un tel stille, pour ne vouloir estre entendue, fors des personnes plus doctes (en frustrant par ce moyen celles de mediocre sçavoir)," a theory that he supports with the statement from her fourth invective about her wish to avoid ignorant readers.[1] Colet's letter indicates that his request for a simplification of some of her language comes from women readers who wish to read Helisenne's texts but have not had the access to Latin that would enable them to decipher her neologisms. Thus Helisenne's *illustration* of the language came up against her desire for female readers and forced a compromise.

Catherine des Roches, taking ideas from Livy and Plutarch, similarly turned them into vernacular texts, but without Helisenne's stylistic artifice. She dramatized into lively conversations the materials that she had found in classical essays or narratives. For her the classics were a source of ideas rather than of forms, whereas for Morata the reverse had been true.

The use of French was not only a way of appropriating classical grandeur for France; it could also indicate a connection with medieval forms. Marguerite's plays, Helisenne's *Songe*, Labé's *Débat*, and Catherine des Roches's earlier dialogues all set forth speakers that represent ideas rather than historical persons. Their evocation of medieval débats or personification allegories aligns their use of French with the sense of developing a long national tradition rather than of turning to newer Italian models.

Meanwhile, the Italians, Morata and Matraini, used speakers who either are or openly imply a connection with historically real people. Even Fonte's seven women, without being specifically identifiable, are plausibly presented as realistic persons and not as the mouthpieces for abstractions. The group of women who gather at their friend's home would naturally have spoken to each other in Italian and not in Latin; indeed, only one of the speakers is learned in the way the author herself was. Thus realism combines with an evocation of Italian vernacular literary models (Boccaccio and Castiglione) to determine Fonte's language. Matraini could perhaps have opted to educate her young man in Latin; but his interest in commerce suggests that even he may not have the prerequisites for a university education. Eager for education themselves, women often saw their role as making their learning broadly available for others without formal education. This meant favoring the vernacular.

Women chose to participate in a broader culture than that of the highly educated elite even when they were part of the elite. For Marguerite de Navarre the vernacular was already the language of her spiritual correspondence with Briçonnet, as it was of other spiritual dialogues addressed to women; her continuance of the vernacular into her own spiritual dialogues with the dead was reinforced by the models of both Dante and Petrarch, who had used the vernacular for conversations with the dead Beatrice and Laura, women who, like little Charlotte, would not have known Latin. For the *Heptameron,* the novella genre demanded a vernacular treatment,[2] and the model of the *Decameron,* converging with the courtly discussions by Castiglione, provided further support for this choice of vernacular language. Yet

Marguerite explicitly rejects the Latinate constructions and rhetorical polish of Boccaccio in favor of a plainer style. She is not seeking, like Helisenne, to show off her writerly skills by means of elaborate linguistic display but to produce a work conducive to humility. In short, women had a number of reasons for choosing to write as they did: in Latin or the vernacular; in a vernacular that is elevated by Latinisms or one that is left in its normal, local, conversational usage.

The dialogue genre frequently offered a format for discussing just these linguistic issues: Alberti's *Famiglia* takes them up in the introduction to his Book 3, Gelli's *I capricci del bottaio* on days four and five, and Castiglione's *Cortegiano* on the very first day. Other dialogues were dedicated completely to this topic of choosing which language to use and what level of style: Bembo's *Prose della volgar lingua*, Machiavelli's *Dialogo sulla lingua*, Trissino's *Il castellano*, Varchi's *Ercolano*, Speroni's *Dialogo delle lingue*, and so on. Even Cicero framed his *De finibus* by pointing out proudly how the speakers manage to express various philosophical ideas just as lucidly in Latin as the Greeks did in Greek. Yet while men wrote numerous dialogues arguing the merits of the use of classical versus vernacular and discussing how the vernacular should be written, women did not directly treat the topic of language at all. They neither defend nor apologize for their choice of language, nor do they comment on questions of style, despite the variety of their consciously selected styles. Even those most self-conscious of language, such as Helisenne, do not comment on it. Fonte's only mention of grammar is to create a joke, not to discuss language in any serious way. Language was a tool that women used, often with evident pleasure, but it was not in itself an object of their discursive attention. Men sometimes excused their use of the vernacular by reference to female participants or an unacademic male audience. Women, even when they had to choose in which language and style to write, did not explain their choice.

Are these women's dialogues chiefly of interest to cultural history or also of aesthetic value? This depends, of course, on one's aesthetic values. Some readers prefer the lively wit of Catherine des Roches and Louise Labé to the impassioned but sometimes awkwardly expressed self-examinations of Marguerite; others find in Marguerite a psychological complexity and passionate spiritual engagement preferable to a more polished writing and worldly wit. Fonte interests us more in her moments of anger than in her more formal complimentary lists of contemporaries worthy of praise; yet the language of social compliment was important to most writers of the period and would probably have marked her more readily to contemporaries as a knowing and acceptable writer than her bleaker observations about social relations. We currently tend to prefer the lively banter of the courtesan Tullia to the self-consciously Latinate expressions of the humanist Helisenne. Yet for Helisenne, her Latinate French was an *illustration* (in Joachim Du Bellay's sense) of vernacular prose, not far in style from the letters of Briçonnet; both clearly offered their elaborate diction for the reader's pleasure.[3] Helisenne's Latinized language, difficult as it may have been for some contemporary readers, has a playful charm as well as a forbidding aspect. There is certainly a great variety in style from one writer to another and sometimes even within one writer's work. There is also a difference between the women who aimed primarily to win literary acclaim (e.g., Helisenne or Labé) and those for whom style was in the service of religion (e.g., Morata or Marguerite). By its nature, dialogue seeks to engage us in the flow of an interesting conversation; most of these works are in that way successfully engaging.

Conversations imply relationships. If we consider the personal relations important to these women's writing, we see a mix of male and female connections. For the earliest, Isota Nogarola, her relationship to Foscarini, though brief, was invaluable to the production of her text. It was a relationship that she sought out by taking the initiative to write to him. Yet even Isota was not too early as a woman writer to find a community of similar women. Her aunt had been one of the trailblazers of female education and writing, and her widowed mother had been the one to arrange for the education of her two daughters by a well-qualified tutor (King 1994, 313). In sum, both male and female models and encouragements were available to her.

In a very different social circumstance, the courtesan Tullia focused on the connections that would bring her most benefit. Obviously, given her profession, this meant focusing mostly on men. Although her mother had been an important influence in launching her career, other women, except for the women in the ruling Medici family, are not mentioned at all in Tullia's writing. Learned men such as Benedetto Varchi, to whom she could appeal for help in improving her writing and whose friendship she could then use to enhance her own cultured status, were the most important. Yet her dialogue wittily and impudently challenges the very men with whom she curries favor.

Helisenne, about whose personal life we know very little, also engages in a brief epistolary debate with a male opponent, but this is not the friendly rivalry of Tullia with Varchi and Benucci. Setting up her own husband as the representative of traditional misogyny, Helisenne portrays their vituperative relationship in a context of letters to both men and women, within a volume published for readers of both genders. Helisenne apparently did not need her husband for her own development; on the contrary, he is presented as an obstacle to her writing. Not all men, however, are such foes. Her friendship with her publisher, Denys Janot, may have enabled her to become acquainted, sometimes even before publication, with the works he was printing. Certainly his enthusiasm for publishing her writings year after year must have been a great encouragement.[4] Yet she does not openly acknowledge this relationship or its importance for her. Instead, within an argument for women's abilities, she praises Marguerite de Navarre as her most inspiring example.

Labé hosted an urban salon culture that mixed women with men yet dedicated her book to a single female, just as the des Roches would later address their parts of their joint volumes to each other. The prefatory letter of Labé's volume, immediately preceding the dialogue, speaks quite exclusively to "us" women. At the same time, the end of Labé's dedication indicates that without the encouragement of men her volume would not have been published (Losse 1994, 27). Thus Labé both seeks to encourage a female intellectual community and at the same time acknowledges the importance of male support for her own stepping out into print.

Olympia Morata owed her education to her father and his male friends, to whom she openly expresses her gratitude, and was happily encouraged to continue her studies and writing by her husband, whom she also praises affectionately. She was well aware that men had made her education and her continued life of reading and writing possible. Yet she was inspired in her dialogues by a learned female friend and benefactor, whom she wished to repay with whatever benefit she could offer in return. Certainly both gratitude and concern manifest themselves in her two dialogues with Lavinia. Her interest in the possibility of a friendship with another learned woman takes precedence, at least in the dialogues, over her generally positive relations with men, which appear in many of her letters. Her complaints are not against a male world that shuts her out but rather against those men and women who think that a woman should focus on her looks and dowry. The dialogues focus on the importance of female support for a woman's intellectual and spiritual development. It is as a woman to another woman that she speaks in both dialogues, whether recording her own conversion of values or urging another woman to follow this same path from worldly to spiritual concerns.

Similarly, Moderata Fonte, educated by a brother and a grandfather and encouraged in her work by the husband of her closest female companion, presents in her dialogue an entirely female group that revels delightedly in the opportunity to talk freely without the presence of men. Willing to acknowledge men's assistance in her own life, she allows her speakers to defend some men from the accusations leveled against men in general but reiterates that supportive and appreciative men are relatively rare. Although indicating that male readers might be expected to read the written version of this female conversation, she states as well an intent to write for the benefit of women, who need this kind of female support against the injustices perpetrated by the men in their lives. These two sets of readers, male and female, are expected to take quite different lessons from the text, although both lessons work to the same end: the improvement of life for women. Fonte, in short, sees her role as a writer as one that enables her to speak not only to women but also on behalf of women to men. The worlds of men and of women remain distinct, however, both importantly part of her life, but separately, as indeed Venetian society dictated.

Catherine des Roches, educated unusually by her mother, lived with her in an intensely close relationship of mutual support. She wrote her dialogues, like Fonte, equally for other women and for the males who controlled their lives. Like Labé and unlike Fonte, however, she had access through the soirees at her house to more public conversation with men. Although fathers and daughters converse separately in two dialogues, Charite and Sincero spar wittily together in another. Their chaste flirtation and intellectual rivalry reflect Catherine's own careful relations with the men who attended her salon. Their attraction to her needed to be neither yielded to nor entirely discouraged; either extreme would have broken off the possibility of further conversation. Ultimately, however, Catherine des Roches does not seem to have felt that she needed men to make possible the life of learning and writing that she wanted for herself. The letters of dedication by mother and daughter to each other present their volumes of writing as the product of their mutual and enclosed devotion.

Chiara Matraini again presents both male and female relationships as important to her work. Like Morata, she wrote in the context of a longtime female friendship, presenting her dialogue with the child of her friend Cangenna; yet this child is a male on the verge of adulthood. Thus she excuses her address to a male as the unintended substitute for a female with whom she had meant to speak. Similarly, she dedicates her work to a possible female patron yet addresses her text as well on a different level to males in the academy or among her readership. For des Roches and for Matraini, the single close friend is female; the collective audience—salon or academy—is male. Female conversation is more intimate; but desire to find honor in a more public realm requires forming a relationship with men. The collective nature of the male at the same time preserves the female's independence, preventing her from becoming merely someone's mistress or protégée.

Marguerite de Navarre's close ties with her brother and his accession to the throne obviously made this relationship one of the most important in her life. She benefited as well from her personal and written interactions with the bishop Briçonnet. Yet she does not necessarily associate authority with men alone. Her correspondence with a bishop is put into the mouth of a girl. The *Heptameron* narrator, Oisille, who seems to have at least some connection with Marguerite's mother, Louise, takes on the role of spiritual leader as efficaciously as any priest. Indeed, Marguerite, like Isota, owed her education to the arrangements made by her mother. Louise also added instruction and an example of her own, speaking to her children in Italian and Spanish to complement the Latin they were learning from their teachers. Marguerite owed to her mother's enthusiasm for Italian culture her own early acquaintance with the writings of Dante and Petrarch (Jourda 1930, 23–27). The debating courtiers of the *Heptameron* exchange their views on explicitly equal terms. The dialogue with her departed brother is not only for Marguerite's own benefit but for that of any Christian, mingling intensely personal laments with public ceremony. Marguerite's "is an empowered voice, used to speaking out and to being heard" (Losse 1994, 34). As a queen Marguerite expects both men and women to listen and can address her reader without concern for gender.

These women's connections with men were important, but their connections with women were also significant. They wrote for an educated audience, yet that audience was not solely male. Many of these women invited other women into the conversation through dedications or dialogic addresses; some of them—such as Labé, des Roches, and Fonte—hoped furthermore to produce a wider audience among women by advocating and encouraging their education and even their writing. Morata and Matraini composed their dialogues specifically for female friends and patrons, although anticipating further readers as well; other dialogues were intended for audiences at least including women: Marguerite's court, Labé's salon, Helisenne's Parisian readership.

Wanting to be read by women, these women were also interested in other women's work. Some of these writers pay explicit tribute to previous women's writing: Catherine's acknowledgment of Laura Cereta, Cassandra Fedele, and Olympia Morata, for example, or Helisenne's of Marguerite. We know that Marguerite was aware of and drew from the dialogic *Miroir* of Margaret Porete, realizing that it was by a woman whether or not she knew her name.[5] Catherine des Roches reworked in her dialogues both larger patterns and smaller phrases from the *Débat* of Louise Labé, and both are likely at least to have been aware of the publications of Helisenne de Crenne, even though they do not mention her. Labé's comment in her preface (1981, 17), "Estant le tems venu, Mademoiselle, que les severes loix des hommes n'empeschent plus les femmes de s'appliquer aus sciences et disciplines" [The time having arrived, Mademoiselle, when the severe laws of men no longer prevent women from applying themselves to learning and the arts], indicates a general awareness of a number of other women with the potential to write and to publish, as Labé urges more of them to do. She seems not to feel isolated as a woman writer and is willing to urge women into accepting for themselves a more conspicuous role: "Et si quelcune parvient en tel degré, que de pouvoir mettre ses concepcions par escrit, le faire songneuesement et non dédaigner la gloire . . ." (17) [And if some woman reaches such a degree as to be able to put her ideas into writing, let her do it attentively and not disdain the glory . . .]. At the end of the century Marie Le Gendre wrote a dialogue between love and beauty that is obviously modeled on Catherine's and quite probably draws as well from Helisenne's and Labé's. Indeed, as I hope to have demonstrated, there was what one might call a female tradition of dialogue writing in France, in which women drew consciously from each other's writings quite as much as from ancient or contemporary men's work. But French women were sometimes aware of Italian women's writings too, as Catherine's references demonstrate.

Although the bonds of gender do not imply necessary agreement, the bonds of empathy between particular women were able to cut across differences of language, politics, and religion. Just as Vittoria Colonna and Marguerite de Navarre exchanged letters and poems with affectionate admiration for each other despite the fierce political and military divisions between them, so too Catherine des Roches could give a sympathetic reception to the work of Olympia Morata despite their religious differences in a world torn by religious violence.

By including women, addressing women, and acknowledging or borrowing from other women writers, by expressing awareness of their own situation as women, these writers show that women were not always seeking only the models and the audience of men. They desired not only inclusion in a male world but also the representation of a female world where, as in Leonora's garden or Philotima's or Pasithée's room, women converse among themselves and bring these women's conversations to a wider public. In sum, most of these women envision their work circulating in a society where both men and women read and where both male and female alliances offer important support.

The male-female binary that would exclude women from this kind of participation is strategically deconstructed by the recurrent presentations of arguments within one sex about the nature of the two sexes and their relationships. Thus the *Heptameron* shows men disagreeing widely on the nature of women and the ways men should behave toward them. Fonte shows a similar disagreement among women about the nature of men and the best ways women can deal with them. Catherine des Roches and Helisenne de Crenne either show or indicate arguments between more and less enlightened men concerning the nature and permissible behavior of women. These emphases on differences are obviously useful to any effort to create an opening for real change.

Did women's sense of authority or self-confidence increase over the century and slightly more that this study spans? There does seem to have been some change in the general acceptability of women's writing, as Labé's comment, cited earlier, indicates. We can see a move from the lessons and practice of Isota Nogarola to the teachings of Chiara Matraini. Helisenne de Crenne, among the earliest women in print, is more aggressively defensive of her writing against a real or anticipated attack than the more self-assured Louise Labé, Catherine des Roches, and Marie Le Gendre. Yet Moderata Fonte, at the end of the century, is more defensive than many of the earlier writers, in part because her secular project lacks the spiritual assurance of someone like Olympia and in part because she is making more radically critical statements about the social order. Her qualms therefore are less about the legitimacy of her writing at all and more about the reception of what she has to say. Males who advised against allowing women an education for fear that they would try to upset the social hierarchy could have pointed to Catherine des Roches and Moderata Fonte, both near the end of the century, as fulfilling their dire predictions. The one refused to marry at all; the other advocated greater social equality between the sexes and even financial autonomy for women.

For male writers the inclusion of women in dialogue was most likely to accompany a discussion of love, marriage, or beauty. Men gave women a voice of at least limited authority in such cases for three reasons: because it was assumed that female experience enabled women to speak on these topics; because it was presumably titillating to a male reader to "overhear" the "secrets" of women learning the tricks of dealing with men; and because Diotima remained the most important model for the female role: a priestess who can instruct even the wisest of men on the nature of love. Men expected their own conversations with women to be about love rather than about the more public or intellectual matters that they would take up with men; therefore, they often could not imagine what else of general interest women might be able to discuss.

Because the love dialogue as a form included several widely popular texts, and because some of these, such as Plato's or Leone Ebreo's, offered the possibility of woman's active participation in a moral and philosophical discussion, the love dialogue, especially the neoplatonic love dialogue, was a model that women could find useful. However, although men associated women's voices predominantly with the theme of love, women writers had necessarily a more complex relationship to this topic. They might avoid it (Morata, Matraini, Fonte) or find ways to distance it from their own voices (Marguerite, Labé, des Roches, Le Gendre). The only dialogue directly on love that includes the author as a speaker is by a courtesan, Tullia d'Aragona's *Dialogo dell'infinità di amore*; and as I have indicated, she uses the topic to argue for a more intellectual role for herself than that allowed her by Speroni's *Dialogo di amore*. In his dialogue, she is a flesh-bound lover; in her own, she discusses love like a philosopher, disavowing the particular passion that had been attributed to her. Apart from the courtesan Tullia, Italian women avoided the topic of love completely.

French women were more likely to take up the subject; nonetheless, when "honest" women treat the theme of love in their dialogues, they anticipate trouble and take measures of defense. Marguerite, whose group of ten aristocrats never tire of talking about love, treats it generally as an unhappy and dangerous experience, a thing to avoid rather than to pursue. The most "perfect" lovers end up turning from human love to God's love to find consolation for their misery. Helisenne de Crenne, in *Le songe*, announces immediately after the title that her aim is to show the defeat of sensuality by virtue and ends the dream with a religious pageant emphasizing the importance of chastity for the soul's peace. Her letters, which precede this text both chronologically and within the volume of her works, indicate that she was—or expected to be—vehemently blamed for writing about love regardless of the virtuous nature of the lesson. Labé takes on the topic of love in her *Débat* in order to make fun of it: Love's plight is his inevitable association with Folly. But Labé is not personally a part of this dialogue, which pokes fun at other people through the mouths of male classical gods. Her willingness to write in the poems that follow about sensual love in a more personal voice was unusual and contributed to evoking Calvin's doubly insulting epithet "plebea meretrix" [lower-class whore] (Giudici 1965, 72).[6]

The dialogue of Catherine des Roches most clearly influenced by Labé's *Débat* and sharing its socially satirical aspect has been redirected to the topic of Poverty and Hunger, hardly an erotic topic. Des Roches broaches the theme of love in her creation of Charite and Sincero but appends their exchange as the sixth in a series of dialogues on quite different topics. It follows a parallel dialogue in which Beauty flees from Love to the safe space of study, and it presents a female who is suspicious of amorous rhetoric. It is really this rhetoric rather than love itself that is the subject of the exchange. While Charite's name reminds us of Catherine's own, it also evokes the *caritas* that is opposed to lustful love. Moreover, des Roches explicitly frames the exchange with a declaration that the man is her invention of a perfect suitor, not somebody real or even realistic. Similarly, Marie Le Gendre deals with love through abstractions and reiterates a moral message throughout. Her introduction and conclusion both aim at married love as the ideal that can combine pleasure with honor. The reproaches that Catherine des Roches cites, or anticipates, for writing about love at all give a good indication of why women other than courtesans might have preferred to avoid this topic or to treat it with circumspection.

At least two factors may be involved in the difference between French and Italian women with regard to the possibility or impossibility of writing about love. One factor is social. French women had noticeably more social liberty to come and go in public spaces and to mingle with men. Italian travelers in France marveled at the presence of all kinds of women on the street and in shops, while French travelers commented in surprise at the absence of women from such places (Berriot-Salvadore 1990a, 191–96). Thus, for example, honest women like the des Roches could entertain many men in a salon at their home, whereas among the Italian women we have considered, only the courtesan Tullia was evidently participating with men in a salon society.[7] The second factor is literary rather than social. Italian women, writing in a Ciceronian vein, that is, with themselves and their historical acquaintances as speakers, were careful not to attract any possible blame in the all-important matter of chastity. French women, writing in a more fictional mode using personified or mythical speakers, without the directly identified presence of real women, could touch on the topic of love in a general and abstract fashion.

Most of the women who wrote dialogues wanted nonetheless to focus, at least part of the time, on something other than love: on friendship, on spiritual duties, or on the social injustice to women and what could improve their situation. They write frequently about education, both spiritual and secular. They emphasize woman's rationality, her ability to learn and even to teach, her moral responsibility—possibly superior even to men's. They frequently use a discussion of love strategically to stage a defense of women's rationality and education. They do not want to be the ignorant and sensual partner in a dialogue—unless it is a spiritual dialogue about humanity in relation to God and not about women in relation to men—but prefer to present themselves explicitly as fully rational and knowledgeable participants. As for beauty, women with an education learned, and repeated, the topos that beauties of the mind or spirit outlast those of the flesh. Men may have enjoyed the composition of dialogues in which lascivious women advise each other on how to look their best; women who could write had no interest in this topic at all.

Women therefore had to find for the female voices in their dialogues different sources of authority from the kinds of authority men were willing to grant them. Experience was indeed one basis, but not amorous experience.

Both Helisenne and des Roches claim, whether sincerely or expediently, that their knowledge about love comes *not* from personal experience but from their readings. Women call rather upon experience of life more generally, especially of marriage and family life. Thus the older women in Fonte's group of seven have clear authority relative to the younger ones; they speak from personal knowledge about the behavior of husbands and sons, while the youngest have only hearsay to rely on. So too among Marguerite's courtiers, the oldest, Oisille, has an authority derived from her age as well as from her piety; she is regarded as a kind of mother to the group. Matraini similarly gives Teofila authority over her neighbor's son in part because she is old enough to be his mother and has a maternal interest in his welfare. In a more humorous vein, Labé's Folly, as an old woman, lays claim to the unwilling respect of the young boy Cupid. Along with age comes widowhood and the relative autonomy that it brought to women. Fonte's Leonora, being a widow and economically self-sufficient, has a kind of authority equal to though different from the authority of the widow Adriana, who is the group's chosen leader. Leonora's ability to play hostess to the group in a home without men enables the dialogue to take place at all.

Religious experience is as important as the secular kind. Olympia speaks in Morata's first dialogue about her personal experience of God's loving care, which has given her the assurance to pronounce on the foolishness of her previous views. The dead Charlotte's personal experience of paradise gives even an eight-year-old the authority to correct theologians, not to mention her aunt. The rapture of Marguerite's shepherdess grants her an utter confidence difficult to convey to others lacking her condition. Male-authored texts of spiritual guidance for women represent the male writer teaching his female pupil with the authority of an official position in the clergy (Gerson, Valdés, Ochino). Women-authored dialogues of spiritual guidance obviously cannot make this claim; nonetheless, they attribute to the lay female an absolutely assured voice of authority, whether it is Marguerite's niece, the servant girl in *Le malade,* both Sage and Ravie in *Mont-de-Marsan,* or Theophila in the dialogues of Morata and Matraini. Their assurance comes not from believing that they personally have a special knowledge to offer or a special position in society from which to offer it, but rather from believing that they are transmitting a knowledge that has the full authority of God's word, or of the church, or of the long tradition of learned writing. They speak a truth that is external, objective, and that has been formatively accepted into their own mode of thought. If the truth is God's, then surely it can be uttered through a woman's voice as well as through a man's.

Another most common basis for female authority was learning. Obviously this was true for men as well. Castiglione (1972, 1.33) has Count Ludovico da

Canossa maintain: "Quello che principalmente importa ed è necessario al cortegiano per parlare e scriver bene, estimo io che sia il sapere; perché chi non sa e nell'animo non ha cosa che meriti essere intesa, non po né dirla né scriverla" [So, as I believe, what is most important and necessary to the Courtier in order to speak and write well is knowledge: because one who is ignorant and has nothing in his mind worth listening to can neither speak nor write well (1959, 54)]. Actually, Singleton's translation mutes the count's statement by adding at the end "speak nor write *well*." The Italian indicates that one cannot write or speak at all without learning. A lack of learning is equated with having nothing to say worth anyone else's hearing. This attitude clearly had much to do with the silencing of women as not worth listening to. It was therefore imperative for women to demonstrate their learning in order to justify their speaking or writing for a public audience.

Matraini is not only older than her pupil but also much more widely read; she can cite both classical and Christian sources to support her claims. So too Helisenne attacks her husband and other misogynists with an assurance that comes from learning, taunting him that if he had read more books—as she has—he would not say the erroneous things that his current ignorance has prompted him to say. Catherine des Roches draws constantly on the learning that she openly praises and pursues. It enables her Pasithée to become a teacher to the almost illiterate Iris. It further allows Catherine to represent the voice of a well-educated father mocking and advising more ignorant men. Lavinia's praise of wisdom and declaration of her long love for it give her the role of advisor to Olympia in Morata's first dialogue. Fonte's Corinna, the learned woman of her group, is openly admired by the other women, who not only encourage her to speak but urge her also to write a book for other less enlightened females. Fonte herself, slipping into their conversation discussions of various scientific topics, authorizes her own writing by this display. Even the courtesan Tullia, rather than relying on her amorous savoir faire, cites poets and philosophers in her argument with Varchi.

Besides sheer knowledge, the ability to produce rational argument is highly prized. It enables Nogarola to compete admirably with Foscarini, and Tullia d'Aragona's self-named speaker to keep even in dispute with her learned partner. It gives Placide the clear edge over Sevère, two men measured by a woman's pen. Similarly, Helisenne imagines the more rational male reader who will reprove and correct her less rational husband. The pleasures of constructing a skillful and persuasive oration hold prominent place in Helisenne's *Songe*, Labé's *Débat*, and the second part of Fonte's *Il merito delle donne* (Leonora's hypothetical address to men). Indeed, through Apollo and Mercury, Labé displays a dazzling knowledge of the forms and rhetorical tricks of forensic oratory.[8] Rational persuasion allows Morata's Theophila to lead the anxious Philotima little by little toward a more spiritual view of her own life and its aims. Marguerite's evangelical Sage of *Mont-de Marsan* both uses and praises rationality in her persuasive efforts to offer guidance to Worldly and Superstitious; reason is both her means and her goal for the others. No wonder that women's need for education is a recurring theme in these dialogues: women saw it as creating the possibility of an authoritative voice.

The widespread notion that women might serve through conversation as teachers for other women, or that a mother would naturally instruct her children, and the existence of salons in which some women might even have intellectual conversation with men, all offered real oral situations that fed the dialogue genre. They brought forward the notion that the dialogue might offer a kind of schooling for women, less formal than male schooling, but with due attention to history, philosophy, rhetoric, and even theology. Men generally assumed that women would be on the learning end of these conversations, but women—and some men—imagined situations in which women could present themselves as teachers: of a youth, of a female friend, eventually of a reading public. The writing down of such instruction created the possibility of a transition from domestic to public circulation.

For men, dialogue was usually conceived of as the casual conversations of leisure time, in opposition to the formal disputations of the schools. Castiglione's courtiers are playing a game and relinquish scholastic terminology because of the presence of women; indeed, the female presence signifies the very distance from professional seriousness of their discussion. Boccaccio's *Decameron*, with its mixed group of men and women and its protest that their talk in a garden differs from the arguments of schoolmen, is also a constant model for dialogue writers: "né ancora nelle scuole de'filosofanti . . . dette sono; né tra cherici né tra filosofi in alcun luogo ma nei giardini, in luogo di sollazzo, tra persone giovani benché mature . . ." (Concl. 7) [neither among the schools of philosophers . . . were they told, nor among clerics nor among philosophers in any place, but in gardens, in a place of recreation, among persons young though mature . . .]. This topos was continually repeated by male dialogue writers. Speroni's "Apologia dei dialogi" (1575) contrasts the playfulness of dialogues with the seriousness of demonstrative science, describing

> il sentiero delli dialogi, per lo quale noi camminiamo anzi ai giardini e alle vigne che ai buoni campi contemplativi; però quivi in vece d'orzo e di grano, il quale é fatto per nutricarci, son solamente con qualche nostro diletto fiori, frondi, erbe, ombre, antri, onde, aure soavi.[9]

[the path of dialogues, along which we walk rather as if to gardens and vine-yards than as if to the good fields of contemplation; for there instead of barley and grain, which is produced to nourish us, are only—to our delight—flowers, leaves, grasses, shades, caverns, waves, sweet breezes.]

The citation of Petrarch (*Rime* no. 303) identifies the dialogue both with the popular form of lyric poetry and with Petrarch's withdrawal from the world of business into the leisurely countryside where he could dream of chatting with Love and write his verse. The garden for all its delights is not the serious agricultural field of nourishing sciences.

How different is the perspective of women, for whom the university was inaccessible. For them dialogue was precisely school, and its pleasant garden offered the attractions not of decorative arts but of access to real learning. Nogarola's dialogue is an exercise that forms part of her training in dialectic; her male descendent recasts it as the entertainment of a leisure moment. Matraini's garden grows flowers of philosophy and science and leads the garden visitor along a path toward enlightenment and God. Sigea sees the dialogue as a way of conveying to her princess some of the vast learning contained in Portugal's royal library. Morata's and des Roches's dialogues between women, whether written in a more serious or more playful tone, express a similar desire to educate and enlighten the female interlocutor. Tullia inserts into her dialogue on love the very philosophical terms that Castiglione and Speroni had eschewed because of the presence of women—in Speroni's case, because of the presence of Tullia herself. For her, the salon discussion with learned men is her means of education as well as her means of professional advancement. It is the place where she can find an exercise more intellectual than usual, a place of strenuous performance and not of relaxation. For Moderata Fonte, although her group of women is more relaxed than it would be with men present, the insertion of discussions on the natural sciences and the women's praises for their learned member indicate a desire to use the form in part for an education of its women participants and readers—and a desire of the less educated women to learn from their friend—even when the subjects of learning are also turned to witty use in the attack on men. Perhaps it is in recognition of this different function of dialogue for women that Agnolo Firenzuola (1957, 65) reverses the traditional topos and has his female main speaker suggest: "raggioniamo di qualche cosa, che sappia più de le scuole dei filosofi che dei piaceri che ne sogliono apportar le ville" [let us talk about something that is closer to the schools of the philosophers than to the usual pleasures of country villas].

In this regard, the women are actually closer to Cicero than to more recent models. Cicero's *Tusculan Disputations*, set in a villa outside town, opens with Cicero's statement that he is now temporarily free ("liberatus") from his duties in the law courts and senate; yet he welcomes this free time as the opportunity to turn his thoughts to moral philosophy. The *De oratore*, set in the same Tusculan villa, happily contrasts the mood of this villa and its garden to that of the senate with its current political turmoil; yet here too, the speakers decide to imitate Plato's *Phaedrus* by making this rural retreat the setting for a discussion on rhetoric. (I, vii, 1.27–28). For women, whose duties tended to be practical housework rather than the senate, leisure similarly meant the opportunity at last for philosophical discussion.

Despite the sense that dialogues may offer a more serious kind of schooling for women than for men, one of the school-derived forms frequent in men's dialogues is completely absent from women's. Numerous male-authored dialogues consist of a series of orations, presented in rivalry with each other as if before an academic or judicial audience.[10] Plato's *Symposium* was probably the originating model for this form. Cicero's *De oratore* quite appropriately consists of long speeches in a rivalry between Crassus and Antonius. Even his *De finibus* pairs up long speeches by the advocate and then the critic of each philosophical school, with the aim not simply of showing both sides but of coming to a judgment. More contemporary examples include Vegio's *Disputatio inter solem, terram, et aurum*, Alberti's *Uxoria*, some of Erasmus's *Colloquies*, Bembo's *Asolani*, Bruni's *De avaritia*, Valla's *De voluptate*, and Pontano's *Actius*.

In fact, a number of these Renaissance works follow a similar pattern: two opposing views are then superseded by a third speech that (like Socrates' speech in the *Symposium*) introduces a more divine or religious perspective. Pietro Bembo's youths who present the woes and pleasures of worldly love are superseded by Lavinello's oration on a more spiritual love. Lorenzo Valla's Stoic and Epicurean are followed by the proponent of a more Christian view.[11] In Giovanni Pontano's *Actius* three speeches on various aspects of poetry are followed by a speech on the heavenly qualities of poetry, depicted as the mother of culture and religion among men and as capable of lifting men's spirits toward the divine.

Neither this specific pattern nor the more generic pattern of a series of competing orations is used by women. Women speakers neither rival each other's eloquence before a judge nor consider it entertainment to take turns giving each other speeches. No doubt one reason for this is that women were not, like men, so trained in the skills of oration that they considered it a game. Yet several of these women writers did know how to compose an oration. Fonte, who shows off her ability in this genre, limits herself to one, Leonora's, which in itself says what is needed without requiring or rivaling a counterdiscourse. Significantly, it is an oration addressed to men rather than to the other women. Leonora is not arguing with the women present but speaking for them to a hypothetical male audience, as if presenting the women's "case" before a judge. Helisenne's speeches by Venus and Pallas are in competition but again directed at a male, indeed at a student or scholar. Moreover, the speakers are not human women; their rivalry is, in a more medieval manner, between aspects of the soul rather than between individual humans. So too Labé's paired orations are delivered by male gods before another male god as judge. Folly, despite the Erasmian precedent, does not hold forth on her own account but yields the floor to her appointed male advocate. These exceptions seem therefore to reinforce the conclusion: writing orations is writing the speech of men.

In sum, women write long speeches when they are speaking as male characters. They give such speeches to their female speakers only when they are addressing men. It is an attempt to write like a man, in a way that men will find familiar. This does not prevent female authors from enjoying the opportunity to weave witty speeches; it merely prevents them from constructing a scene, so common among men and so improbable among women, in which realistic female speakers deliver orations to each other in a competitive series. Women writers present human women speakers who converse, who persuade each other with conversation rather than with lecturing, and who are prone to share the speaking time with their partners. The speakers are not rivals in eloquence, even when their author is attempting to win serious regard for her own eloquence.

Works that in some sense come close to the pattern of contradictions with a divine or at least higher-level resolution, such as we find in the *Asolani*, begin for women with a back-and-forth argument rather than a pair of orations. For example, Marguerite's dialogue with her brother can be seen in this way: the ultimate resolution of their shared quarreling comes not from a third speaker but from the bright light of heaven that overwhelms human discourse. This heavenly resolution is provided not as the aftermath to two long rival speeches but as the end of many exchanges and interruptions between the two speakers. On a more secular level, des Roches's Foot and Hand are reconciled by Mouth, who can offer a more totalizing perspective, but only after a dialogic interchange, not a pair of orations.

Rather than drawing on the scholastic model of competing orations, women's sense of the dialogue genre frequently drew from and gave back to the stream of correspondence. Laura Cereta presents as a letter to a female friend the discussion between two young women about a withdrawn life versus a more active one. For Isota Nogarola a real exchange of letters became in itself a dialogue. Helisenne de Crenne's invective dialogue consists of a fictional exchange of letters between an estranged couple who no longer speak to each other. For Marguerite de Navarre part of a real exchange of letters was reworked into a dialogic dream poem, turning a correspondence with the living into a dialogue with the dead. Morata composed her second dialogue with Lavinia in the explicit context of an interruption of their correspondence; having a strong desire to communicate with Lavinia, Morata wrote both voices.

Letters and conversations were both intended to offer instruction; but both were also an expression of friendship and one of its pleasures. The public seriousness of humanist epistles and the honest intimacy of talk among trusted friends found their combined way into the dialogues of women. Nonetheless, their writers imagine for themselves not only the intimate relation with a friend but also, explicitly, the wider circle of readers, male and female, who will carry on its discussions. Morata writes to her closest friend but expects her to share the work with other women. Helisenne imagines her letter being read by her husband, by the friends to whom he will show it and with whom he will argue about it, and finally by her book-buying public in Paris. Matraini's spiritual dialogue addresses the son of a personal friend, a noblewoman who might give the work some circulation or patronage, and the members of an academy who perhaps represent the wider reading public. In sum, the letter to a friend becomes the acceptable means for what is really a broader conversation. These dialogues are tossed like pebbles into the water with an often explicit sense of the widening rings moving out around them: the internal addressee, the dedicatee, the readers of the published book who will continue its conversations.

If dialogues are, in one direction, like an exchange of letters, in another they approach the enclosed fiction and speaking characters of drama. Particularly in France, women explored these theatrical potentials. Marguerite's dialogic thought found expression in plays as well as in poems and in the conversations between tales. Her plays are often conceived more as verbal exchange than as action and thus overlap with the dialogue genre. Her influence may have been significant for later French women in this specific regard, as it certainly was for their writing more generally. Helisenne de Crenne's *Songe*, like Marguerite's plays, put the speakers for opposing views into a series of dramatic scenes. She went further than Marguerite in occasionally describing action, costuming, and theatrical pageantry. Yet these dramatic scenes remain interwoven with narrative. Louise Labé created a five-part dialogue without narrative framing, set among the classical gods. Her work directly inspired the dramatic conversations among personifications by Catherine des Roches. Catherine's most playlike dialogue in turn inspired Marie Le Gendre's *Dialogue* to turn the same material into a full-blown play, with scenery, interludes, and a typical comic ending. This play, despite its "dialogue" title and source, could even have been performed privately.

In sum, women, seeking forms of dialogue that they could make fit their own situations and needs, pushed across the boundaries of the genre in all directions. Besides presenting dialogue as the record of a live conversation, they expanded the exchange of humanist or invective epistles into argumentational dialogues. They proposed their dialogues as a replacement for correspondence with an unreachable other. They moved dialogue, either partway or more fully, into the forms of theater.

Yet perhaps women's dialogues are after all not so different from some of their male-written counterparts. Valerio Vianello has argued that many of the men of letters who wrote dialogues during the Renaissance were seeking a newly defined social place for themselves, a place to which they had no claims by birth or wealth but only by their intellect and pen. Shifting away from their original courtly settings of personal conversation to the urban community of printed circulation, they sought to create a court away from court, an educated and cultivated middle class in which they could find the cultured exchange of an Urbino or an Asolo. Their circulation of dialogues both expressed and concealed "la voce dei circoli dotti angosciati dalla definizione di un'identità" (23) [the voice of learned circles anguished about the definition of an identity] and "ansioso di reclamare nella penna un mezzo idoneo per intervenire nella realtá" (Vianello 1993, 23) [anxious to reclaim through the pen a suitable means for intervening in reality].[12] One can readily say the same things about the educated women who sought a valid place for themselves in society as intelligent and literate persons and who saw in their ability to write a means to intervene in their own and society's reshaping.

Piero Floriani (1981, 26–27), considering the shift from a court-associated production of literature (e.g., Bembo) to the creation of an at least apparently more independent man of letters (e.g., Speroni), distinguishes between "*gentiluomini* letterati" and "gentiluomini *letterati*," that is, between men who considered themselves primarily "gentiluomini ornati anche del pregio della poesia" [gentlemen also ornamented with the asset of poetry] and "letterati puri che chiedono onore e pane in nome del loro lavoro culturale" [purely men of letters who seek honor and income in the name of their cultural labor]. The dialogue was seen by these latter men as the right means of giving form to their new social role and their relations to the rest of society, envisioned as a newly national vernacular culture (41, 118–19). Of the women who wrote dialogues, only Marguerite conceived of herself primarily as nobility further adorned by literature. The rest, predominantly middle- or professional-class, belong to Floriani's second category and derived their sense of worth quite clearly from their intellectual activities.

They sought thereby to renegotiate their status within society as something higher than the traditional status of women. Like Speroni, they sought on the basis of their intellectual role a kind of autonomy and authority that had not previously been thinkable.

Floriani (1981) points out that the new print culture allowed a sense of national audience and thus an increased participation of writers from areas previously on the periphery. One did not need any longer to be in Rome or Florence in order to feel connected with the intellectual world. So too most of these women wrote from smaller, even provincial, towns and from the seclusion of private homes, using their writing to connect them in imagined conversation to a much broader cultured community.

Just as Castiglione's discussion about an ideal courtier led to the inclusion of discussion about the ideal court lady, so in other male-authored dialogues, part of their writers' concern with establishing their own social position as vernacular writers finds expression in a conscious attention to the presence and limitations of female speakers. It is not surprising that dialogue, with its giving of voice to female speakers and its staging of the very issue of women's possible positions in relations of authority both with each other and with men, should have been a popular form for women writers. Unlike lyric, the form most widely used by women and until now the most widely studied, dialogue was neither too personal nor too narrowly conventional. Its undefined range of contents allowed women to address the issues that most concerned them, both social and spiritual. Its polyphonic form enabled them to look at these issues from several viewpoints. Its relation to epistolary exchange enabled some women to engage in an exchange of views with men, yet without leaving the modest enclosure of their homes to encounter men directly in the public arena. The dialogue's enclosed dramatic quality permitted women to project a discussion onto invented characters distanced from the female writer and to enliven it with song and action. Its rhetorical strategies of persuasion within a scene of familiar conversation allowed them to stage among women or close friends and family members a discussion of issues intended ultimately to include a wider circle of readers and participants. Thus through a variety of experimental manipulations, women found in the dialogue a way to join the cultural conversation.

Notes

Chapter 1

1. Guitta Pessis-Pasternak, in an interview cited in Wesling and Slawek 1995 (15).

2. *Polylogue* might be a more linguistically consistent term. See Zumthor 1978, 185.

3. On the influence of Cicero, see esp. Michel 1984, 9–24. Also see Cox 1992, 10–16, 31–32. On the attractions of Lucian to the Renaissance and Reformation, see Mayer 1973, 5–22, and Marsh 1998. The three names Plato, Cicero, and Lucian are invoked repeatedly by almost anyone writing on dialogue.

4. For distinctions between Platonic and Ciceronian dialogues in relation to Renaissance uses, see Vianello 1993, 9–10; Hirzel's discussion of Cicero (1895, esp. 463–64, 486–87, 491–92); Marsh 1980, 2–3; and—somewhat unfair to Plato—Kenneth Wilson's chapter "Platonic vis-à-vis Ciceronian Dialogue" (1985, 23–45).

5. Morigi ([1947], 25) calls his dialogues a monument to friendship among the social and intellectual elite.

6. Alberti's fifteenth-century *Della famiglia* repeats this statement.

7. Salvatore Caponato, in his introduction to the edition of Aonio Paleario's *Dell'economia o vero del governo della casa* (1933, 9–10), claims this to be the first work in which women discuss their own condition in contemporary society.

8. Italian editions appeared with high frequency until the end of the 1560s and then more sparsely toward the end of the century.

9. Translations from the *Colloquies* are Craig R. Thompson's (Erasmus 1965). See Berlaire 1978, 51, 53, 101; and Erasmus's recommendation of comic plays for schoolroom use (Berlaire 1978, 64–65). Cornelis Augustijn (1991, 171) cites Erasmus's own comment added to the 1526 edition of the *Colloquies*: "Socrates brought philosophy down from heaven to earth, I have brought it even into games, informal conversations, and drinking parties. For the very amusements of Christians ought to have a philosophical flavor."

So too, Speroni's "Apologia dei dialoghi" (1574) repeatedly describes the dialogue

253

as a "giuoco" and "scherzo." See the discussions by Francesco Tateo (1967, 226) and Jon Snyder (1989, esp. 123). Speroni is, of course, trying to defend his texts from a serious and dangerous attack by claiming that they offer merely the playful imitation of opinions rather than make any claims to truth.

10. Augustijn (1991, 165) cites one such phrase from Erasmus's foreword to the 1524 edition: that the colloquies aim to make "better Latinists and better men"; similarly "De utilitate colloquiorum" (3.741.20): "vel ad elegantiam Latini sermonis, vel ad pietatem."

11. See Elizabeth McCutcheon's statement (1992, 69): "Erasmus' attitudes towards and feelings about women oscillate and multiply, frustrating any easy characterization of either gender. No wonder that recent feminist critics find Erasmus inconsistent, ambiguous, and 'contradictory and complex.'"

12. Kelly's article, originally published separately in 1977, can now be found in her *Women, History, Theory* (1984, 19–50). Regarding the role of the court ladies in the *Cortegiano*, see esp. 30–36. Also on the topic of women in Castiglione's *Cortegiano*, see Finucci 1989, 1992; Saccaro Battisti 1980; Zancan 1983a; and Guidi 1980.

13. All translations are my own, unless otherwise noted.

14. On Erasmus and women, see Erika Rummel's anthology of selections, *Erasmus on Women*, including her introduction (1996); McCutcheon 1992; and Sowards 1982.

15. Cf. Erika Rummel's comment (1996, 174): "Erasmus pays tribute here to the learned women of his age, although one suspects that the heroine, Magdalia, is introduced for shock value rather than as an exemplary character." So too McCutcheon (1992, 71) suggests that Erasmus is more likely to destabilize or reverse traditional gender roles when addressing a male audience whom he is attempting to shame.

16. He later complained, in his first edition, that her unauthorized circulation of the work had compelled him to publish a proper version.

17. Although Paleario's dialogue remained unpublished, it represents views that were shared by others.

18. Virginia Cox's "Seen but Not Heard" is the first attempt to study Renaissance dialogues containing women speakers and to interpret "the silence to which, in the majority of dialogues, women speakers are reduced" (2000, 386). According to Cox (391): "The contribution of women speakers, in almost all mixed dialogues of the period, is reduced to that of regulating, stimulating or commenting on (usually briefly) the 'teachings' of their male interlocutors. This is acceptable conversational behaviour for women; anything more may be frowned on."

19. Circulated simultaneously in manuscript and print, *Asolani* was first published in 1505 and much revised for the second edition of 1530. The text cited is in Pietro Bembo's *Prose e rime* (1966).

20. Vianello (1993, 32) indicates that Bembo's Berenice may be identified with Veronica Gambara, but the *Asolani* does not make this explicit. As for the others, I have listed here the Italian examples, but he mentions also Hrotswith and Hildegard and Elizabeth, praising their writings as better enlightened than the stupidities (i.e., reformist writings) more recently coming out of Germany.

21. The title *Ragionamenti* simultaneously implies rational conversation and echoes the word from Boccaccio's *Decameron*, where Boccaccio claims to be passing on to other suffering lovers the "piacevoli ragionamenti" with which his friends had helped him when he was in love (Proemio 4).

22. Published in her *Les dernières poésies* (1896, 345–49).

23. Kushner (1996, 55) notes that the dialogue genre, while apparently representing a conversation among different speakers, often "unveils inner conflict, as is the case in Petrarch's *Secretum* and Marguerite's *Dialogue en Forme de Vision Nocturne.*"

24. For this reading, see Relihan 1993, 187–94.

25. For the antecedents and imitators of Petrarch's work, see Diekstra's introduction to *A Dialogue between Reason and Adversity: A Late Middle English Version of Petrarch's* De remediis (Petrarch 1968).

26. Somewhat different but akin, Lucian's use of personifications and figures from the world of the dead steers toward a mocking vision of the human world from somewhere just beyond its margins. Medieval debates could similarly stage a discussion of human society through the mouths and eyes of birds or animals. These figures are neither simply abstractions nor simply humans in disguise.

27. Although theorists (e.g., Le Guern 1982, 145) have observed that polyphonic dialogues are more readily "open" than diphonic ones, Petrarch's example shows that even a diphonic dialogue can be left in suspense without a clear resolution for one side or the other.

28. For a survey of this material, see Jordan 1990.

29. Eva Kushner (1983, 133) cites and qualifies the observations of Michel Le Guern. Giovanna Wyss Morigi ([1947], 12) suggested previously that dialogue is related formally to drama while being thematically more akin to the prose treatise. She distinguishes dialogue from drama in that an exchange of ideas in the drama serves the action, while in a dialogue they are the end in themselves; action in dialogues tends to be rudimentary at best and is not necessary at all (13–14).

30. Cited in Wilson 1985 (11–12). Wilson, however, finds the resemblance to drama "deceptive," arguing that the dialogue is focused on ideas rather than on the sensual world and is thus primarily didactic rather than mimetic (18–20).

31. See the very useful discussions and citations on this topic by Girardi (1989, 45–63) and Forni (1992, 215–27).

32. Ann Rosalind Jones (1990, esp. 104, 107) refers to "the dialogic layout of the *proposte/riposte* poems," describing Tullia's volume as "a hall of mirrors in which the woman and the men all bask in one another's reflected glory."

33. Rosenthal 1989, 227–57.

34. For example, Forni 1992, Marsh 1980, Kushner 1972. Kushner (1977) refers again to this categorization by classical model but adds some reservations: that it ahistorically separates dialogues written within the same context, for example. Nonetheless, it remains almost unavoidable to mention these three names. Forni's study devotes large sections to the separate influence of the three ancients.

35. For example, see the focus of Massebieau (1878) on *Les colloques scolaires.* Bénouis (1976) and Girardi (1989) define chapters by a thematic typology: religious, philosophical, scientific, and so on. Hirzel (1895) combines this with the authorial model method. Virtanen (1977, 2–3) divides his material thematically (philosophical dialogues, dialogues of love, dialogues of literary criticism) but also cites the typologies of other critics—for example, Herbert Read's typology according to the chief purpose of the work: dialogue of ideas, of wit, and of character or personality. Rather similar, unintentionally, is Morigi's indication ([1947], 17) that dialogues can aim at transmitting or discussing ideas, analyzing a psyche (as in Petrarch's *Secretum*), or offering social satire. Morigi organizes her material according to a distinction between dialogues with a primary emphasis on instruction and those with a primary emphasis on pleasure or

entertainment, although this distinction is at best one of relative weights. The latter category includes dialogues that celebrate the local culture (court or humanist circle) and those that are, conversely, satirical.

36. Eva Kushner's essays (1984, 151–67; 1983, 131–43) use the monologic/dialogic measure, defining this parameter according to the degree of liberty accorded to the reader in considering real alternatives; it is a parameter that allows her to distinguish the "Renaissance dialogue" as a kind separable from the more monologic dialogues before and after. Virginia Cox (1992) calls them open and closed forms.

37. Vianello (1993, 9) refers similarly to the two functions of speakers: "cooperatrice ed opposititrice"; but his own subsequent analysis is focused rather on issues of audience and context.

38. Godard 2001, 5, 7, asks whether dialogue is a genre at all and, while asserting that it is, calls it "un genre polymorphe, un genre-frontière."

39. For the citation to Erasmus, the first number after the volume refers to the page, the next to the marginal numeration.

Chapter 2

1. On this topic see Voss 1970.

2. See Favez 1937, 24–25. Many of Jerome's letters of consolation were addressed to women. Seneca's consolation to Marcia for the death of her son was as famous as Jerome's epistles. Favez comments (63): "Il semble parfois que les *solacia* ne soient qu'une espèce particulière de *praecepta*."

3. It had appeared in Bologna around 1475, in Naples in 1478, and in Venice in 1494; Venetian editions appeared also in 1504 and 1517.

4. Zarri (1994) contrasts these marginal groups with the earlier focus of devotional reading groups in princely courts and their closely connected monasteries.

5. Caretti's edition has put the letters into chronological order and thus renumbered them; but his edition includes a table indicating the correspondence between his numbers and those of earlier editions.

6. In his *Specchio interiore* (1540), cited in Zarri 1987 (140).

7. Marcus (1992, 58) comments that "specifically female 'scenes of writing' . . . were often communal rather than individual."

8. Girardi (1989, part 3) describes four types of spiritual dialogue: catechism, controversy, mystical dialogue, and the devout and learned use of leisure.

9. *Fioretti utilissimi extratti dal devoto dialogo volgare* (1530). See Zarri 1987, 134.

10. See, for example, the letters of Olympia Morata, as well as of the sainted Catherines.

11. Jean Gerson's *Oeuvres complètes* (1966, 158–93) is only a partial text. See also Gerson's *Opera omnia* (1706, 3: 805–29). Although some of the French works have been translated into Latin for this edition, this dialogue happily remains in its original French.

12. For other similar examples see pp. 170–71, 177–78, 278–79.

13. Similarly San Bernardino, a traveling Franciscan preacher in Italy contemporary with Gerson, declared that he wanted to make the women in his audience "predicatrici" who would transmit his teachings to their children, husbands, and other relatives (Lenzi 1982, 166).

14. Bainton (1992, 249) has pointed out that Vittoria Colonna repeats some of Ochino's preaching in her letter to Costanza d'Avalos. This is the same kind of passing on wisdom in which Gerson might well have imagined his sisters engaged.

15. Both Augustine and Boethius had a strong influence on Gerson's writings. Augustine is repeatedly a source, both explicit and implicit, for Gerson's ideas. Gerson's moral dialogue in Latin, *De consolatione theologiae,* is obviously paying its debt to Boethius in the title; at the same time it borrows from Petrarch's first eclogue the names of the two brothers (Ouy 1967). The *Dialogue spirituel* contains a minidialogue within it, in which Gerson speaks with the apparition of Virtue, a brief scene reminiscent of both Augustine's imagined encounter with Chastity and Boethius's much longer one with Philosophy. Gerson was clearly well aware of the traditions within which he was writing and of the interconnections among their various strands.

16. The sisters themselves refer to ideas expressed in "le livret qui se nomme Caton" (1966, 178).

17. Sald (1994, 26) offers a partial listing of the contents of the royal library, including Gerson. A more thorough catalog of the library in 1518 and again in 1544 can be found in Omont 1908, volume 1. See also Baurmeister and Lafitte 1992 for a more general description of the collection and its development.

18. Agnolo Firenzuola in his "Epistola in lode delle donne," defending his previous representation of women discussing philosophical matters, points to a pair of models: Socrates' Diotima and Augustine's mother, Monica, noting that Augustine "fa dare risoluzione a la sua santissima madre in più dialogi di cose importantissime di teologia" (194) [has his most holy mother give the answer in several dialogues to important matters of theology]. Augustine's mother is thus a recurring model for the inclusion of women in theological dialogue. De Montmorency (1970, 15–16) notes that Gerson's own mother was a woman of such piety that Gerson compared her to Monica.

19. Matusevich (1998, esp. 133–73) describes Gerson's pedagogic and "democratic" inclinations, that is, his desire to reach the many simple members of the faith. She points to his more school-oriented dialogues, such as the classroom scene of "L'ecole de la raison" (1966, 103–8, 109–11), in which the Heart and five senses rebel against the school lessons assigned by Reason and are reported on by Conscience. The playfulness of these brief pieces contributes to the effect of "plaisant" that Gerson ascribes to dialogues. De Montmorency (1970, 22) notes that because of Gerson's concern for the education of children (he taught poor children in the Cloister School even after becoming chancellor of the University of Paris) and because of his use of the vernacular for a number of spiritual works, he was called "le Docteur du peuple et le Docteur des petits enfants." For more on these aspects of Gerson see also Connolly 1928 and Combes 1963.

· 20. Carron (1991, 102) suggests that dialogue "remains fundamentally a performance of persuasion rather than a true instrument of persuasion. The reader is not convinced by the arguments of the exchange but through the representation of someone being convinced." I see these two things not as alternatives but rather as working together, at least in the writer's hopes.

21. Nieto 1970 (esp. 106–55) contains some excellent discussion of his dialogic writings, the dating of their composition, the nature of their religious ideas, and their relation to Erasmus's work, which Nieto sees as considerably less close than had been previously asserted. Nonetheless, resemblances in their thought remain evident. Cor-

nelis Augustijn (1991, 78) comments: "Erasmus pleads on several occasions for as simple as possible a summary of the quintessence of Christian faith." His *Ratio verae theologiae*, *Enchiridion*, and *Colloquia* all aim to provide this kind of elementary guide.

22. For Gerson, see, for example, the *ABC des simples gens* (1966, 154–57); the text here is only an outline.

23. Nieto (1970, 116) notes that Maria Cazella, a member of the important Cazella family, was among its readers.

24. Benedetto Croce notes (Valdés 1938, xxv–xxvi) that the *Alfabeto* was originally written in Spanish, that Giulia had it translated for her into Italian; only the Italian version, which was printed in 1546, has survived. On Giulia Gonzaga and her relation with Valdés see also Bainton 1971, 171–85.

25. His influence was much wider than this group, however; he was accused to the Inquisition of having "infectato . . . tutta Italia de heresia" [infected . . . all Italy with heresy]. For a more objective account of his influence, see Firpo 1987.

26. Cf. Gerson's *ABC des simples gens*; it is indeed much more elementary, catechetical, and one-way than Valdés's piece, which allows Giulia a large amount of thoughtful speech. But Gerson's work shows that the idea of this kind of title had been around for a long time.

27. So too Gerson recommends to his sisters the reading of Scriptures (*Montaigne de contemplation*; 1966, 24–25).

28. Girardi (1989, 197) notes that Valdés presents two different moments of a sermon's reception: the immediate, collective, and emotional hearing; and the later, individual, thoughtful reflection, which Valdés obviously encourages.

29. See De Montmorency 1970, esp. 46–50, 297. His volume also includes Gerson's Latin text as an appendix. The work was repeatedly printed together with Kempis's *De imitatione* between 1485 and 1526, and one manuscript seems to attribute the entire *Imitatione* to Gerson.

30. For information about Caterina Cibo, see esp. Bainton 1971, 187–98, 1992, 229–42; Feliciangeli 1891.

31. Information about the versions and editions of this text comes from Ugo Rozzo's introduction to Bernardino Ochino's *I "dialogi sette"* (1985).

32. Both published editions—the *Dialogi quattro* (Venice: Nicolo d'Aristotile detto il Zoppino, 1540) and the *Dialogi sette*, brought out by the same publisher in the same year—address the duchess.

33. Caterina was eventually barred by the pope from her authority over Camerino and spent the many remaining years of her life in Florence.

34. See chapter 1.

35. See, for example, the *Montaigne de contemplation* (1966, 19). Augustine is clearly a source for this opposition.

36. Gerson presents a similar passage, based on Augustine's *Confessions*, in *Montaigne de contemplation* (1966, 54).

37. Toward the end of the list some seemingly spiritual items are added, which, however, are clearly being lumped with the others as erroneous efforts. Thus along with food, jewelry, honors, and pleasures come, in order, learning, moral virtues, speculation concerning the truth, and attempted mystical contemplation of God. Rather, argues Ochino, the path to peace lies in eliminating one's desires and recognizing that God already is present within the soul (1985, 62–63).

38. Girardi (1989, 240) comments that Ochino's general austere abstractness,

which suits his message, produces "una sorta di trasfigurazione metafisica della scena colloquiale" [a sort of metaphysical transfiguration of the conversational scene].

39. Similarly Valdés observes (1938, 29–30): "Voi, signora, . . . vorreste che io vi mostrassi un camino reale e signorile per lo quale poteste arrivare a Dio senza scostarvi dal mondo, . . . disprezzare il mondo ma di tal maniera che il mondo non disprezzasse voi . . . parer bene negli occhi di Dio senza parer male negli occhi del mondo . . ." [You, signora, . . . would like me to show you a royal and noble road by which you may be able to arrive at God without detaching yourself from the world, . . . to scorn the world but in such a manner that the world does not scorn you . . . to appear well in the eyes of God without appearing badly in the eyes of the world . . .].

40. This title, as also the title of her similar dialogue on the death of her brother, *La navire,* is probably not hers but an editor's (Cottrell 1986, 36, 204). For the text of this dialogue, see Jourda's edition (Marguerite de Navarre 1926). Jourda also discusses the dating of composition (5).

41. See also Martineau and Veissière's edition of the *Correspondance* between Briçonnet and Marguerite (1979, 291).

42. Jean-Claude Schmitt (1994, 182) discusses medieval examples of conversations with ghosts of the dead. They are usually from purgatory and seeking prayers or Masses to speed their way through torment to bliss; but they also answer questions about the nature of the afterlife. Schmitt demonstrates how these answers adapt themselves to the current views and how these ghosts thus become "les instruments d'une politique ecclésiastique d'endoctrinement moral et religieux." Marguerite's niece, being in paradise, needs nothing from the world anymore; like medieval ghosts, she is a means of asserting current religious ideas, but Marguerite is not likely expecting her readers to take this apparition as a real event.

43. Atance (1974) emphasizes the radical nature of some of Marguerite's religious views even relative to other reformers.

44. Lefranc (1969, 38) suggests that the early plays were written after 1535, considerably later than the *Vision nocturne. Le malade* and *L'inquisiteur* were not published in the 1547 volume of her *Marguerites,* probably, says Lefranc, because of their open attack on Beda and his ilk.

45. Although the correspondence between Briçonnet and Marguerite never refers explicitly to Gerson, it does take up at several points the theme of "mendicité" (1975, 64, 70–71; 1979, 10–15) and refers to "la montaigne de haute contemplation" (1979, 47), themes and images that could have come from Gerson's writings.

46. See Pellegrini 1920, esp. 15–18. He lists verses from all three cantiche with clear echoes in the French. Robert J. Clements (1941) offers a more limited account of Dante's influence on Marguerite, questioning how well she knew his work and how important it really was for her.

47. Pierre Jourda (Marguerite de Navarre 1926, 2–3) indicates that she certainly knew both the *Commedia* and the *Trionfi.* Robert Marichal (Marguerite de Navarre 1956, 42) suggests that Petrarch rather than Dante may have been the major source for both the terza rima and other details of this dialogue, but obviously both works were drawn from for this dialogue. Carlo Pellegrini (1947, 19–38) indicates a number of specific echoes from both Dante and Petrarch; other suggested echoes are my own.

48. Pellegrini (1947, 30–32) suggests this.

49. See note 17, this chapter. Nor is it listed among the holdings of the d'Urfé library inherited by Anne de Graville, a member of the queen's court (Longeon 1973, 143–56).

50. Briçonnet and d'Angoulême 1975, 25, 30: "Parquoy vous prie avoir pitié de me voir sy seulle" and "au moigns je vous prie que par escript vueillez visiter. . . ."

51. Marichal has also suggested that the Briçonnet correspondence had just ended abruptly, perhaps because of Marguerite's increasing interest in Luther despite Briçonnet's objections (Marguerite de Navarre 1956, 12–13). However, other scholars, such as Gary Ferguson (1992, esp. 27) and previously Jourda (Marguerite de Navarre 1926), argue that Marguerite remained all her life much closer to Briçonnet's views and solidly within the Catholic church. Moreover, the editors of the correspondence, Martineau and Veissière, point out that the manuscript of collected letters ends in midletter, indicating a rupture in the transcription rather than in the original correspondence (Briçonnet and d'Angoulême 1975, 3). Whether other letters were lost or never written is unclear. A break in the correspondence itself would further enhance the notion that a loss of real dialogue provoked the production of dialogue writing. But the loss of her brother's wife and a very dear niece in quick succession is in any case a similar provocation.

52. Jourda in Marguerite de Navarre 1926, 4. However, Pellegrini (1947, 28) rejects Jourda's suggestion as unlikely given the circumstances at the time it was written.

53. Possibly she did not publish this poem until later because of the ire it would have aroused among her enemies in the Sorbonne and the trouble this in turn would have caused for her brother's political efforts as well as for the bishop.

54. Comparison of the two pieces—though sometimes only brief—can be found in Jourda n.d., 242–43; Jourda 1930, 583–84, 591; Robert Marichal's introduction to his edition of Marguerite's *Navire* (1956, esp. 10–16); Sommers 1995, 171–79; and Martineau-Génieys 1977, 523–67. Robert Cottrell (1986) discusses both poems at some length, but without much comparison between them apart from brief comments on p. 204.

55. Marichal (Marguerite de Navarre 1956, 64–67) speculates on why this work was not published: perhaps because certain statements or omissions would have caused religious trouble or perhaps simply because it was not ready when the *Marguerites* volume received permission to be published on the very day of François's death—though some shorter poems about his death did get included.

56. See Cottrell 1986, 216–18. See also the similar statement by Colette Winn (1993b, 88): "Logically, only silence . . . can possibly translate the final silencing of reason." She sees the dialogue ending with the mind's acknowledgment of its failure and thus an end of speech.

57. The use of symbolic numbers of verses occurs elsewhere as well in Marguerite's work. Cottrell (1986, 163–65) has indicated, for example, the significant use of thirty-three stanzas for the *Comédie du desert*: "Christological numbering schemes would seem to be the determining factor in the shape or form of large parts of the text. However, no allusions to this patterning or to the number three are made." He adds (195) that Marguerite similarly selected thirty-three of her forty-seven songs to include as the *Chansons spirituelles* in the volume of *Marguerites*, again undoubtedly with Christological significance. It is thus not unlikely that Marguerite was aware of the number of verses in the divine ending of *La navire* and that this number was intended to be significant.

58. Pellegrini (1947, 36) complains: "né si può trovare davvero di buon gusto il far discutere di teologia per centinaia e centinaia di versi dallo spirito di una bambina. . . ."

59. Abel Lefranc (1969, 112–13) identifies the Shepherdess with the "libertins

spirituels" whom Marguerite received at her court, causing a break with Calvin, who had criticized them. Lefranc sees Marguerite as identifying herself primarily with Sage while showing some sympathy for these *libertins*. Verdun Saulnier, in his edition of the *Théâtre profane* (Marguerite de Navarre 1946, 243–71), suggests a closer tie between Marguerite and the Shepherdess, noting that the Shepherdess's songs resemble Marguerite's own *Chansons spirituelles*. He notes also the echo in this play of Briçonnet's advice in his correspondence with Marguerite: that once reason has dominated sensuality, reason itself must yield to "extaticque et transcendant ravissement en absorbicion de tout desir de vie." An even stronger emphasis on Marguerite's mysticism comes from Jourda (n.d., 277); but Régine Reynolds-Cornell, in the introduction to this play in her translation of the *Théâtre profane*, describes the voice of Sage as "the voice . . . that Marguerite wants to be heard" (Marguerite de Navarre 1992, 186) and rejects Saulnier's suggestion that the Shepherdess represents " a mystic Marguerite" (188). Felix Atance (1975), reviewing some of the major positions in the debate, suggests that Sage's *ideas* represent those of Marguerite but that Sage's personality seems too cold, authoritative, and self-assured; Ravie on the other hand embodies the *attitude* that Marguerite prefers: a joyful, hopeful, and loving faith that does not try to impose its ideas on others. For Atance, the figure of Sage indicates Marguerite's disappointment with the increasing intolerance and rigidity of some of the leading reformers, whose ideas Marguerite nonetheless still supports; "le mysticisme effréné de la Ravie n'a jamais été son fait" (55). On the other hand, Jean Dagens (1963, 281–89) demonstrates Marguerite's knowledge of and enthusiasm for the mystical dialogue of Margaret Porete, "d'une femme, / Depuys cent ans escript, remply de flamme / De charité," explicit in the *Les prisons* (3.1315–17) and lingering implicitly in the theatrical dialogue between Sage and Ravie de l'Amour de Dieu. As usual, Marguerite is drawing from many sources at once; an earlier woman's dialogue, *Le miroir des simples ames*, is one of them: "Gentil Loing Près! Celle qui t'appela / Par un tel nom, à mon gré mieux parla / Que maint docteur qui tant a travaillé / D'estudier" (*Les prisons*, 3.1375–78). See also Simone Glasson's introduction to her edition of *Les prisons* (Marguerite de Navarre 1978, 45–53) on Porete's influence and (58) "Le dilemme entre la Sage et la Ravie la laisse encore indécise."

60. Differently from *Mont-de-Marsan*, Gerson's text makes the heart that is "seulet, en repos, et de tout ravi en Jhesucrist" (1966, 132) nonetheless reach out to the worldly heart with carefully aimed lessons.

61. They were printed in the 1562, 1570, and 1580 (identical with 1570) editions of her *Opera omnia*, published in Basel, but not in the original 1558 edition. Curione, who took charge of collecting and publishing her writings after her death, added new materials as they came to him after the first edition. A modern edition of most of her *Opere* (excluding her translations) has been edited by Lanfranco Caretti (Morata 1940, 1954), who has performed the very useful task of sorting the letters into a chronological order instead of the haphazard way in which they were originally published. However, he has left out the letters to Olympia and the poems in her honor, which help to form the social context for her own writing.

62. The first dialogue is discussed further in chapter 3.

63. For a more detailed account of her life and a broader view of her writings more generally, see Bonnet 1856—the fullest account. See also Bainton 1971, 253–67; and my "Olympia Morata: From Classicist to Reformer" (Smarr 2004).

64. There is a remarkable similarity in some respects between this text and the

autobiographical letter by Laura Cereta to her friend Nazaria Olympica more than sixty years before. Like Morata and in similar phrases, Cereta describes her shift from humanistic studies to more spiritual concerns (1640, 152–54): "Delectabar & ipsa quondam his studiis, nunc imitata primam causam, secundas in sua instabilitate posthabeo. . . . Oro igitur Te, ne inani hac agnitionis pompa fictata, ad ventura certo casuum promissu suspires. Suspirabis sanctius ad justum homnium [or: hominum] judicem Deum, in quo dum sperabis, eris semper adjuta. . . . Omnia manu Dei librantur" [I myself used to enjoy these studies; now because I imitate the first cause, I consider of lesser importance the secondary causes, because of their instability. . . . I beg you, now that you have tasted the vanity of foolish ignorance, not to long for the certainty of promised events. You will long more reverently for God, who is the just judge of men, and in whom, while you have hope, you will always find succor. . . . All things are balanced by the hand of God] (1997, 29). One woman advises another to turn from the vanity of human knowledge—after it has been experienced—to the certainty of spiritual hope. Olympia might have known Cereta's letters and, if so, her eye might have fallen on an addressee's name that was close to her own. My thanks to Diana Robin for sending me photocopies of this Latin text in both a manuscript and a Renaissance printed version.

65. The final section has always been published as part of the dialogue, and no one previously questioned this or noted its nature as biblical paraphrase. Holt Parker (Morata 2003, 103) now suggests that this "Hymn to Wisdom" is the *De Trinitate et Sapientia divina sermo* by Calcagnini, which is listed in the table of contents to his *Opera* (1544) but missing from that volume, and that it might somehow have been misplaced into the volume of Olympia's works. Parker does not seem to recognize, however, that the text is a biblical paraphrase that follows the original verses quite closely. The odd shift of Lavinia's pronouns from female to male makes me wonder whether this paraphrase was not initially appended to, or simply next to, the dialogue among Olympia's papers and whether Curione may have mistakenly thought that they formed one unbroken piece. In any case, the paraphrase is certainly appropriate to the dialogue's central theme and in that sense belongs with it in one way or another.

Caretti too seems not to have recognized the source of the last portion of this dialogue, for some of his textual emendations do not accord with the meanings in the biblical text; therefore I believe that Olympia's words are correct as they were. For example, Caretti (Morata 1954, 36) suggests *concitator* instead of *concitatior*, but the *mobilior* of *Sapientia* 7.24 makes clear that *concitatior* is intended. Similarly, Caretti (37) suggests that *sapientiam* may have been intended instead of *iustitiam*, but *Sapientia* clearly says *iustitiam*.

66. Caretti (Morata 1954, 11) suggests the autumn of 1551.

67. Caretti (Morata 1954, 12) suggests that the lonely pain of Philotima is that of Olympia in exile, a pain overcome by ardent faith; thus he sees the dialogue as an internal dialogue of Olympia with herself. This may be part of the picture; however, as her accompanying letter makes clear, she is thinking with concern about the state of mind of her friend. Caretti separates the letter from the dialogue, publishing them in separate volumes.

68. See also the delicate way that Eulalia, in Erasmus's "Coniugium," begins her corrective advice to Xantippe, by appealing to their friendship: "Mea Xantippe, permittis mihi ut liberius loquar apud te? . . . Idem ius erit tibi apud me. Hoc certe postu-

lat nostra necessitudo, ab ipsis pene incunabulis inter nos inita" (3.303.74–77) ["Xantippe, my dear, may I speak rather frankly with you?... You may do the same with me.
Our intimacy—which goes back almost to the cradle—surely demands this" (1965,
117)]. Morata may have had this model in mind, though her own real friendship with
Lavinia would have been sufficient to suggest this type of *captatio benevolentiae*.

69. The same basic theme holds true also of Luisa Sigea's Latin dialogue *Duarum
virginum colloquium* (written in 1552 but unpublished). As this work falls outside the
regions of Italy and France, I have not made it a part of the main discussion; however,
its similarities in some respects to Olympia's make it worth mentioning briefly. Sigea,
like Morata, was an unusually learned woman, a humanist's daughter, whose education
obtained her a position at the Portuguese court as companion to the princess.
Although Sigea herself could and did soon after leave the court for a private life, her
patron the Infante obviously did not have this option. Flaminia continues to argue
until the end, therefore, that one can live a devout and moral life at court, despite its
abounding corruption and vanity. At least Flaminia does agree with Blessila that pleasing God is more important than pleasing men, but she rejects her friend's retreat from
the world as a failure of public service, while Blessila fears that Flaminia remains dangerously blinded and entrapped by the webs of secular pleasures. Similarly, Olympia left
the court for a private marriage, but Lavinia, like Sigea's royal mistress, remained
bound by the demands of an aristocratic life.

70. One might observe that the contemporary historical figure is male, while
the female is drawn from the Bible; but for Olympia's sense of the possibilities of heroism for contemporary women, see Smarr 2004, which indicates the personal significance for her of the models of classical Roman heroism that she had absorbed as a student.

71. For other examples of Olympia's self-identification with military generals, see
my "Olympia Morata: From Classicist to Reformer" (Smarr 2004).

72. The original verses are in Greek. A facing Latin translation—by Curione?—
reads:

Sic ego foemina nata, tamen muliebria liqui,
Staminaque & radios, pensaque cum calathis.
Et placuere mihi Musarum florida prata,
Parnassusque biceps, laetificique chori.
Matronas alias rapiat sua quamque voluptas:
Haec mihi gloria sunt, haec mihi laetitia.

73. It is impossible to know whether Olympia ever intended to publish her own
works; her early death in any case prevented this. Letters, however, were frequently
perceived as something closer to an essay than to a private message and circulated
beyond their original recipient.

74. Barberino 1957, 202, part 15: "Se forse fossi conversa di chiesa, / non ti mostrar
filosafa o maestra"; 216, part 16: "In molte cose più femina crede / A una feminella, /
che sta rinchiusa in cella, / ch' a un che sia maestro in teologia; / E vanno per questa
stoltía; / ma più sicura è palese dottrina, / che d'una oculta, rinchiusa vicina." See also
Gill 1994, 73, 77. Gill's essay demonstrates how often male religious writing was aimed
at or influenced by women, who were the silent partners in its production.

75. See the entry "Chiara Matraini" by Giovanna Rabitti in *Italian Women Writers*

(1994, 243–52), which also offers a further bibliography. My thanks to Veena Kumar Carlson for sending me a photocopy of the text of these *Dialoghi spirituali*, published in Venice (Prati, 1602).

76. Giovanna Rabitti, in the introduction to her edition of Matraini's *Rime e lettere* (1989, xii) comments intriguingly: "non sono stati affrontati finora in modo abbastanza approfondito i rapporti della Matraini con il mondo ereticale: rapporti cauti ma significativi" and promises future work on this topic. Throughout her life, in any case, Matraini manifested a strong Catholic devotion to the Virgin Mary.

77. Rabitti 1994. See also Maclachlan 1992.

78. On the placement of canzoni among the other poems of the *Vita nuova*, see Singleton 1977. Matraini has perhaps merged the models of Boethius and Dante in her alternation of prose and poetry.

79. See Matraini's *Rime e lettere* (1989, lxv–lxvi, 67, 84, 121–25, 177–81, 328).

80. For the image of the garden in relation to humanist studies and books, see Bushnell 1996, chapters 3 and 4, which treat various versions of the gardening image: the pupil as plant or as soil, the text as plant, the text as garden, the whole education as garden. Her book is chiefly concerned with English humanism, but obviously humanist ideas were international. Dolce's *Dialogo della institution delle donne*, for example, associates Flaminio's education of Dorothea with, first, their view of a garden through the window and, later, their walking out into it. The garden, in this case, is Dorothea's, not Flaminio's, and represents Dorothea's own careful cultivation of herself and her children.

81. *Orazione d'Isocrate a Demonico* . . . (Florence: Torrentino, 1556); Rabitti 1994, 248. The letter to Matraini's son appears in her *Rime e lettere* (1989, 156–66).

82. The same model is referred to explicitly by Tullia d'Aragona in her dialogue, discussed in chapter 3.

83. As Alan Bullock and Gabriella Palange (1980, 254–56) note, two of Matraini's other spiritual works, the *Considerationi sopra i sette salmi penitentiali* and the *Breve discorso sopra la vita e laude della Beatiss. Vergine*, do indicate that she was requested to write these works. Bullock and Palange suggest that her volume of *Meditationi* might have inspired these requests. The first set of requests comes from "molte degne, e devote persone" (the dedication is to the Duchess of Urbino), the second from Matraini's own cousin, an abbess in Pisa. In the *Dialoghi*, published later than both of these, Matraini might have felt thereby emboldened to offer unsolicited advice.

84. Giovanna Rabitti (1994, 249) refers to this group as "a not otherwise identified 'Academy of the Curious.'" I share her frustration in attempting to find any information about this group. Paola Malpezzi-Price made the suggestion to me that the academy might be a fiction representing Matraini's readers.

85. Cited in Rabitti 1981, 152.

86. See the discussion later in this chapter.

87. Compare with Erasmus's comment in a letter thirty years after its publication: "I wrote the *Enchiridion* so that good letters might be of service to piety" (cited in Augustijn 1991, 54).

88. One can see by the kind of company in which Petrarch is placed the way in which Matraini regards him: as a classic and a moralist rather than as a writer of popular love songs. Even Propertius is treated as a source of moral wisdom.

89. Did Matraini know that this poem was addressed to a woman? Eduardo Magliani (1885, 60–66) claims that Leopardi in *Storia del sonetto italiano* observed that

its rhyme scheme and contents respond to a sonnet by Giustina Perotti: "Io vorrei pur drizzar queste mie piume / Cola, signor, dove il desio m'invita, / E dopo morte rimanere in vita / Col chiaro di virtude inclito lume. / Ma il volgo inerte, che dal rio costume / Vinto ha d'ogni ben la via smarrita, / Come degno di biasmo ognor m'addita / Che ir tenti d'Elicona al sacro fiume," and so on. Although I have been unable to identify the Leopardi source, the two sonnets do seem well matched. If Matraini was aware of this exchange of sonnets, she would have found Petrarch's encouraging reply to an aspiring female poet all the more relevant to herself.

90. Erasmus's *Convivium religiosum* (Godly Feast) includes high praise of Cicero's *De officiis* and other Ciceronian texts as "divinely inspired" and more consistent with Christian teaching than all the works of "Scotus and others of his sort" (1965, 65–66).

91. As T. Anthony Perry notes (1980, 12): "Leone Ebreo asserts that a rigorously intellectual preparation is necessary to reach man's highest beatitude. As a prelude to theology, the student must have studied logic, natural philosophy, and the sciences."

92. Besides Morata and Matraini, who cites Cicero on this topic as well as the biblical Book of Wisdom, there are further examples in Helisenne de Crenne and Catherine des Roches, who will be discussed in the following chapters.

93. See Leone Ebreo 1929, 9: "Tanto a l'amore quanto al desiderio precede il conoscimento de la cosa amata o disiderata, qual è buona"; 32: "il conoscere Dio . . . causa in noi immenso amore, pieno di eccellenzia e onestá: perché tanto è amata la cosa onestamente, quanto è conosciuta per buona"; Sofia: "E come si comprenderá l'infinito dal finito, e l'immenso dal poco? E non potendosi conoscere, come si potrá amare? Ché tu hai detto, che la cosa buona bisogna conoscerla, prima che s'ami"; Filone: "L'immenso Dio tanto s'ama quanto si conosce." See also Perry 1980, 10.

94. Rabitti 1981, 148. The painting was commissioned in 1576. If the dialogues were in fact written during the 1580s (though printed in 1602), this would place them roughly in the decade after the painting.

95. Matraini's publications usually present her as "Gentildonna Lucchese."

96. See Zarri 1994, 212–18. Also see the discussion of the *dimessa* in chapter 6.

Chapter 3

1. On the scholastic use of dialogues, see Massebieau 1878, Derwa 1974, and Bömer 1897.

2. Gilman 1993, 25.

3. Gilman (1993, 31) cites Diogenes Laertius's typology of all dialogues into broader versions of these two basic types: "training the mind" or "the winning of verbal contests."

4. Caponetto in his introduction (Paleario 1933) suggests, persuasively, that the Medici conquest of Siena, and the ensuing pursuit of both political enemies and heretics, created a sad and dangerous situation for Paleario in which wisdom dictated keeping the work unprinted, even though the beautifully written manuscript had been apparently intended as a clean copy for a publisher.

5. Note the difference between this view of the improving conversation of morally upright women and the view expressed in *De pueris . . . instituendis* about the nonsense that young boys learn from women. Women are seen as acceptable teachers for other females, but not for males.

6. Luisa Sigea's (Louise Sigée's) *Dialogue de deux jeunes filles sur la vie de cour et la*

vie de retraite (1552) has been edited and translated into French on facing pages by Odette Sauvage (1970). Unfortunately her dialogue remained unpublished until 1905; thus although Catherine des Roches was aware of a poem of hers, she could not have known—nor probably even known about—the dialogue. For more information about Sigea, see the introduction by Sauvage (9–63).

7. Both Sigea and Morata were humanists' daughters whose learning had earned them positions at court. Both saw their court experience as morally dangerous and used their positions to urge the more powerful women with whom they had contact to exercise their knowledge of the good amid the surrounding worldliness.

8. Riccardo Bruscagli, in his introduction to the *Dialogo de' giuochi* (Bargagli 1982, 16), calls the work "l'epitaffio di un progetto culturale." Paleario himself was later imprisoned and executed on charges of heresy.

9. One might wonder whether he even knew of her dialogues, since his, although set in 1531, was written much later: the manuscript is dated 1555, a few years after Olympia's dialogues were written but before they were published. Olympia apparently did not send copies of these dialogues to Curione, although she sent him other examples of her work, for his first edition of her *Opera* does not include them; only the second edition, for which additional material had been gathered, prints them. Therefore Curione may not have known them in time to communicate about them with Paleario. Nonetheless, even without this direct connection, the two writers shared similar friends and ideas.

10. Just one of these is the connection that we will see again between a defense of women against brute men and a defense of religious reform against the corrupt authorities of Rome.

11. Speroni's volume, brought by Daniele Barbaro to publication in Venice in 1542 in the shop of Aldus's sons, was frequently reprinted and also translated. The *Dialogo di amore* can be found in Speroni's *Opere* (1989, 1: 1–45). Tullia's dialogue was published in Venice by Giolito in 1547 and reprinted in 1552.

12. Rinaldina Russell in her introduction to the translation of Tullia d'Aragona's *Dialogue on the Infinity of Love* (which offers a good bibliography on both Tullia and dialogues about love) similarly observes that Tullia's dialogue is responding to Speroni's but sees the response somewhat differently. Russell agrees that Tullia rejects the image of herself as a courtesan "unrestrained in her loves and ever-resurging jealousy" and placed in opposition to a Bembian view but sees her offering instead the image of a more "'honorable' courtesan," a "virtuoso of love, who disputes the adequacy of both the spiritualistic and sensualistic views of love" (1997, 36, 32). Although of course love is a central topic of the dialogue, my arguments point more to issues of intellectual participation. English translations of Tullia's dialogue are taken from Russell and Bruce Merry's translation (1997).

13. The debate about whether it is better to see your beloved or to think about her is a traditional "quistione"; Boccaccio, for example, refers to it both in the *Filocolo* (4.59–62) and in the beginning of the *Filostrato*, where he repents his earlier judgment.

14. Actually Tullia herself traveled considerably, living for periods of time in Rome, Ferrara, Venice, Siena, and Florence. Some of her admirers were similarly transient and reencountered her in different places, as her poetry indicates.

15. This certainly implies that she cannot really love him.

16. Cellini, for example, sent Varchi a draft of his autobiography, asking him to

help correct and polish it. Like Tullia, Varchi was indebted to Cosimo de' Medici for personal favors.

17. A similar attack against the presumed objective value of male philosophy with regard to women is made by Helisenne de Crenne in her third invective letter; when her husband cites Socrates' criticism of women in general, Helisenne replies that Socrates was biased by his personal experience in an unhappy marriage: "Tu doibs croire que quand Socrates proferoit ainsi mal d'elles: il estoit de la condition des hommes ennuyez, lesquelz tout ce qu'ilz voyent de telle forme, similitude ou semblance, que cela que les attedie, il[z] jugent estre apte à causer pareil mal . . . ainsi c'estoit son ennuy & fascherie qui en cela le stimuloit de errer" (1995a, 123). Even the judgment of a famous philosopher, an advocate of reason, is subjective and swayed to error by his emotional experience.

18. See also Fiora Bassanese (1988, 299), who describes more generally the need of "honest" courtesans to mask their profession and enhance their status by producing a cultured and intellectual self-image.

19. See Russell's introduction to her and Merry's translation (1997).

20. As Russell points out (1997, 30), Tullia's views are also very close to Leone Ebreo's, whose dialogue she praises. But he in turn is drawing from Plato although also developing his ideas through combination with Aristotle's ethics.

21. Russell and Merry translate this as "my personal merits" (1997, 110), but it is more neutrally something like "my personal matters."

22. Joseph-Juste Scaliger cited in Schutz 1933 (650) and in des Roches 1993 (21): "la plus docte personne pour ne savoir q'une langue, qui soit en Europe."

23. See Larsen 1990a, 572. Her edition of the des Roches's *Les oeuvres* (1993) includes an excellent introduction and bibliography.

24. My deep thanks to Anne Larsen for making available to me a copy of these dialogue texts while she was still editing them.

25. This is the same Luisa Sigea who wrote a Latin dialogue for the Portuguese princess, but Catherine could not have known Sigea's unpublished dialogue.

26. "Mais que diray-je de cete Morata, qui receut meritamment du ciel le nom d'Olympe? Et comment representerai-je la reverence que je porte à la memoire de la belle, gentille et vertueuse Hippolyte Taurelle, de qui les plaintives Elegies, donnoient tant de plaisir et de peine à son mari absent?" (1998, 219). Anne Larsen in her notes to this passage and in her introduction (1998, 52–53) suggests that the des Roches may have known of Morata's work through Agrippa d'Aubigné, who attended their salon and who in a letter to his own daughters mentions possessing Morata's volume.

27. Larsen comments in her introduction: "La nouveaté de ce 'Dialogue d'Iris, et Pasithae' réside dans l'importance qu'il accorde à la voix féminine" (1998, 50). This is precisely what Morata's example offered.

28. "[E]stant guidées par les bonnes letres, elles ne voudront rien faire qui ne soit raisonnable. . . . Ceux qui ont un peu de raison / L'accroissent bien par la Science, / Mais elle quitte sa maison, /Aux maux que traine l'Ignorance" (1998, 193–94). And 216: "Mémes les plus farouches sont moderez par la douceur, la douceur devient grande par la Raison, la Raison par la Science, la Science par les Livres."

29. Clark Keating (1941, 63) argues that Placide's views are not Catherine's, because she herself values learning for herself and not in order to make her a better wife. Anne Larsen, in her introduction to *Les secondes oeuvres* (1998), proposes that

the truth lies in between: Catherine can believe that learning functions as Placide suggests, arguing thus against critics who think that education will spoil women for marriage, while also believing that it has value quite apart from women's role in marriage. See also Zimmerman 1999, 91–93. Zimmerman considers the second dialogue more daring than the first in establishing not only the moral usefulness but also the pleasure of learning.

30. So too Helisenne de Crenne's learned epistles repeatedly advocate dutiful obedience to one's parents.

31. Jean Tagaut, an Protestant physician associated with the Pléiade, published in 1550 and 1552 odes to a Pasithée, whose name, meaning either "universally divine" or "belonging to the gods," refers in fact to a nun (Campo 1998, 989). It is possible that Catherine was aware of these odes and even that she might have associated their chaste recipient with her own refusal to marry; but there is no way to know that, and the religious resonances present in Tagaut are absent from her writing. The use of this same name by Pontus de Tyard was more certainly familiar to her. Ann Rosalind Jones (1993, 215) suggests that Catherine was responding to Tyard's work by making her Pasithée a teacher rather than a pupil. See also Kushner in her epilogue to the same volume (1993, 281). Furthermore, Jacques Pelletier had addressed a poem, "Louange des trois Graces," to the des Roches (Diller 1936, 19), and Catherine might have happily accepted the identity of one of the Graces. Her use of "Charite," also one of the Graces, reinforces her use of the name of the Grace Pasithée. The name was in any case widely popular among Italian and French poets (see Vaganay 1935).

32. His letter to her can be found on pages 79–81 of the 1580 edition of her *Opera omnia*. Caretti's edition of Morata's *Opera* omits the letters and poems to her by other writers, which were included in the sixteenth-century editions that the des Roches would have seen.

33. George Diller (1936, 134) suggests this colloquy as a possible source for the dialogues in Catherine's second volume. Anne Larsen, in her introduction to *Les secondes oeuvres* (1998), notes that the dialogue between the fathers shares ideas with several popular works on women's role in marriage, including Plutarch's "Precepts on Marriage," which had been translated into French by Jacques Amyot (1572), and Erasmus's "Coniugium" colloquy, translated into French by Barthelemy Aneau (1541) as "Comedie ou dialogue matrimoniale." Both of these texts are available in Guillerm et al. 1983.

34. As just one example of a female poet who explicitly acknowledges her debt, Luciana Bertani dell'Oro's sonnet "A Veronica Gambara e Vittoria Colonna Marchesa di Pescara" concludes:

> Queste alme illustri son cagion ch'ogni arte
> tento, per tôrre a la mia luce l'ombra,
> sol perchè al mondo un dì si mostri chiara.

The sonnet is printed in de Blasi's *Antologia* (1930, 218) and reprinted with an English translation in Stortoni 1997 (132–33). So too Catherine des Roches's contemporary Marie de Romieu, in her versified defense of the excellence of women, "Brief discours: Que l'excellence de la femme surpasse celle de l'homme," mentions Marguerite de Navarre, Helisenne de Crenne, and the des Roches, as well as Colonna and Gambara.

35. See, for example, Poliziano's letter to Cassandra Fedele, published in translation in King and Rabil 1983 (126–27).

Chapter 4

1. Cereta's volume of letters was printed finally in 1640, Fedele's in 1636. See Diana Robin's introductions to her translations of Cereta (1997, 3) and Fedele (2000, 3, 7, 13); and King and Rabil 1983, 24. For an overview of women's letters in Italy, see Doglio 2000.

2. For citations and discussion on this topic see Vianello 1993, 14–15; Forni 1992, 251–59.

3. For the dating see Rabil 1981, 51. Rabil (104), suggesting that "Europa solitaria" may be Cereta herself, calls the letter "among the earliest soliloquies in the western literary tradition"; however, it seems to me closer to dialogue than to soliloquy, at least in the way it presents itself.

4. Published in *Isotae Nogarolae Veronensis opera quae supersunt omnia*, ed. E. Abel (Vienna and Budapest, 1886), it is more readily available in an English translation in King and Rabil 1983 (57–69). Quotations are from this translation. The issue of Eve's and Adam's relative sin is addressed briefly also in Fonte's *Il merito delle donne* (1988, 56; 1997, 93–94) as part of an argument against misogyny.

5. Abel's edition of her *Opera* contains also the letters *to* Isota, among them twenty-two from Ludovico. His letters frequently refer to having received letters or other writings from Isota, but unfortunately only one of her letters to him is apparently extant. Their correspondence continued until just before her death.

6. Percy Gothein (1943, 394–413) cites in Italian passages from their Latin correspondence; despite the indication by Gothein that he was about to publish these Latin texts as *Epistolarium Ludovici Fuscareni*, in *Fonti per la storia d'Italia dell'Istituto Storico Italiano per il Medio Evo*, they do not seem to be part of this series but were instead published in Abel's volume (Nogarola 1886). King and Rabil, in the introduction to their anthology *Her Immaculate Hand* (1983, 17), comment that Isota, after two years of writing to many humanists, stopped such correspondence. On the other hand, Foscarini's letters to her make clear that he continued to receive from her letters no longer extant.

7. I think "se fieri" should rather be translated "would become."

8. Isota's father had died when his children were very young. Rabitti (1994, 313) calls the mother's decision "a most unusual action on the part of a mother in a century when even noble girls rarely received a classical education." Isota was one of ten children, of which six were female; of the girls, however, only Isota and Zinevra were praised by contemporaries for their learning. Abel's volume (Nogarola 1886) contains some Latin verses by Zinevra.

9. Margaret King has argued that the messages Isota received even from her admirers—that learning was odd for a woman and only appropriate if she lived chastely and quietly at home—soon discouraged her from her efforts to participate in the more public cultural world. See King and Rabil 1983, 17–18; King 1976, 1978, 1980.

10. His letter is printed in Abel's volume as epistle 77 (Nogarola 1886, 2: 131–32).

11. See Abel (Nogarola 1886, 1: clvi–clvii) regarding her collection of letters. Abel mentions (1: clxx–clxxi) that an Italian translation of the dialogue was given as a wedding present to the Marchesi Spinetta Malaspina and Marianna Fumanelli in 1851.

12. Abel (Nogarola 1886, 1: liii–lviii) points out that according to a letter of Foscarini's their conversation took place in the presence of Isota's brother Antonio rather

than Leonardo, and that Leonardo, who is referred to in the dialogue as Protonatarius, did not receive this title until after Isota's death. Moreover when the governor from Naugerius's family was in power, Isota was still a young child. Franciscus was obviously manipulating the facts to suit his own purposes. Antonio had a military career, whereas Leonardo, as the author of several theological works, was a more appropriate relative to present to the cardinal.

13. Helisenne's romance, *Les angoysses*, appeared in 1538, the year of the unauthorized volume of Vittoria Colonna's *Rime*. Helisenne's volume of letters, *Les epistres familieres et invectives de ma dame Helisenne*, was published in 1539, the same year as the edition of *Rime* authorized by Colonna. Helisenne's letters were reprinted, either by themselves or with other of her works, in 1543, 1544, 1550, 1551, 1553, and 1560. For a bibliography of her works, see Mustacchi and Archambault (Helisenne 1986, 123–24); Beaulieu (Helisenne 1995a, 39–40); and de Buzon (Helisenne 1997, 43–76).

See the following discussion regarding the example set for Helisenne herself by the even earlier publications of Marguerite de Navarre, who, like Colonna, had the visibility and prestige to become a model for imitators. The two noblewomen were much more influential in opening the possibility of publishing to other women, partly because of their social position and connections and partly because of their unimpeachable honor and piety, unlike the problem of honor in which Helisenne, with her writing about love, became embroiled. All quotations from her letters come from Beaulieu's edition (1995a), and the translations come from Mustacchi and Archambault's (1986).

14. Billanovich (1996, 99–100) makes reference to the work of P. Piur, *Petrarcas 'Buch ohne Namen' und die päpstliche Kurie* (1925, 235); however, I do not find this information in Piur's book.

15. A letter from Lombardo shortly after Petrarch's death lists the volumes of Petrarch's writing; see Billanovich 1996, 576–79.

16. The first four books of the *Aeneid* are, of course, the Dido story. Interestingly, the eighth letter recounts the story of Dido, or Helisa (a possible source for Helisenne's pen name?), as a positive example of female fortitude in the face of an emotionally difficult situation. The situation cited is her husband's murder; her subsequent relation with Aeneas is completely omitted. The use of Dido as a model may seem odd given that the difficult situation for the recipient of the letter is precisely a love of which her parents disapprove; but the name Helisa refers us to Boccaccio's "corrected" version of this woman's history in his *De mulieribus claris*, in which Elissa kills herself rather than be forced to remarry. Dido's fortitude in preserving her marital chastity is meant to be a model for Clarisse's resistance to love. Our inevitable Vergilian evocation of Dido as the miserable victim of love's destructive powers implicitly aids Helisenne's lesson here about the dangers and miseries of giving in to one's emotions. The total yielding to illicit passion is consistently depicted by Helisenne as wretched and disastrous. See also note 29.

17. Mustacchi and Archambault (Helisenne 1986, 13) and Beaulieu (Helisenne 1995a, 32) similarly see these invective epistles as a kind of "dialogue épistolaire." See also Beaulieu 1994, 7–19.

18. Duchène 1971, 178–79.

19. See Beaulieu (Helisenne 1995a): her subjective narration of love experience "modifie radicalement sa conception de la morale" (14); the love letters are "dénuées de didactisme" (15); "Contrairement au roman, le didactisme et la confession, dans les

Epistres, semblent s'exclure" (26). See also Wood 1991, 146: "Letter Ten completely reverses the previous self-description, destroying her persona as a stable and mature personality capable of giving advice to others." Beaulieu and Desrosiers-Bonin (1999, 1158–59) break the letters into three "movements": a voice of public duty, a more affective voice, and an invective voice.

20. Janet Altman (1986, 27) seems to think that the correspondence is a real exchange of letters, referring to them as "missive" letters, that is, as letters actually sent; however, Jean-Philippe Beaulieu (1994, 7–19, esp. 17) argues that Altman's claim is difficult to prove and that it is undermined by the lack of significant stylistic differences between the husband's writing and the wife's. See also Nash's introduction to his edition of the letters (Helisenne 1996).

21. Mustacchi and Archambault (Helisenne 1986, 2) indicate that the separation is documented for the year 1552 and that if the letters are autobiographical, the couple could have been separated already by 1539; nonetheless, they warn against assuming that these writings are "merely autobiographical." Veracruysse (1967, 80) infers from documents during the early 1540s, including 1545, that the couple was still together then. He suggests that the separation must have occurred between 1550 and 1552, a full decade after the publication of these epistles. By 1552 Helisenne was living in Paris.

22. Her husband, in the second letter, accuses her of "artificielles & coulourées mensonges" (115) [artificial and colorful lies (88)].

23. Instead of "one's desire," the French says, more specifically, "*your* desire." The writer is praising her friend's restraint, rather than making a general moral statement, as the translators imply.

24. "En ma personne" means physically experienced in my body; the translator's "really" does not quite carry this same force.

25. Cited by Nash (2000, 378), who does not recognize the reference to Fiammetta.

26. Nash (Helisenne 1996, 15–16) refers to her work as "fiction autobiographique" but acknowledges that "Chez elle, le littéraire et le littéral sont parfois très difficiles à délimiter" [With her, the literary and the literal are sometimes very difficult to distinguish]. See also Nash 2000, 375, 378: "the first-person female narrator of these letters gives us good reasons to reject an autobiographical pact." Helisenne's letter-writing, Nash says, is "fictitious mimesis."

27. See the similar use of this mode by other women in response to invective misogynist tracts: e.g., several of the respondents to Swetnam in England at the end of the sixteenth century and the beginning of the seventeenth. The invective mode of Gratien Du Pont's misogynist *Controverses des sexes masculin et femenin* (1534) and Symphorien Champier's defense of women, *La nef des dames vertueuses* (1503), which he refers to as "invective contre les medisans des femmes," further demonstrates the long-lasting popularity of invective contributions to the debate about women. Juvenal's famous sixth satire may have been the founding text in this regard.

28. Although some scholars around 1900 seeking information on Boccaccio's life saw everything he wrote as autobiographical, their efforts seem sometimes absurd; in any case, it is certainly more difficult to identify Boccaccio in any detail with the female life of Fiammetta. Any such confusion of Ovid with the narrators of his *Heroides* is plainly impossible.

29. Beaulieu (Helisenne 1995a, 10) emphasizes that the *Amadis* source remains

hypothetical only, since the French translation of the *Amadis* was not published until 1540. However, the publisher was Denys Janot, Helisenne's publisher and friend, and it is quite possible that Helisenne had access to some of the texts he was handling before their actual publication. Nash (2000, 379–83) suggests an alternate derivation of the name from Helisa or Dido, as in her eighth familiar letter (to Clarisse), noting that Dido's name is associated with the meaning of "virago" or a woman doing manly works. This derivation, based on the version of the Dido/Helisa story in which she is faithful to her husband, might reinforce Helisenne's protestations of her own fidelity; at the same time the ambiguous reputation of Dido in the two surviving versions of her history similarly parallels the ambiguous situation into which Helisenne seems to have placed herself repeatedly. (See note 16.) Veracruysse (1967, 77) suggests less persuasively that "Helisenne" is derived from Lizanne, a character in *Roman de Perceforest* (1531–32). De Buzon (Helisenne 1997, 20–28) discusses various possibilities for the derivation of the name "Helisenne." Even if the Dido/Helisa derivation seems most likely, readers soon after might have associated the name with the mother of Amadis.

30. Most of her familiar letters similarly end with the appeal to a deity, in either Christian or classical terms.

31. Or more literally: "I am making this plain to you because of the ingeniousness that you have thought up, which, according to my judgment, will serve no other purpose than to lend the ability to exhort in secret the perpetration of what you pretend to detest."

32. Nash (1997, 380) suggests that Gratien Du Pont's *Controverses des sexes masculin et femenin* (1534) inspired Helisenne's invective exchange, supplying the "husband" with lengthy examples of misogynist diatribe.

33. She writes: "Pour certains utile ne te sera de dire que formosité femenine, avec force & somptuosité d'accoustremens, ne sont seulement choses vaines, mais tres dommageables" (123) [It is pointless for you to say that feminine beauty with its sumptuous dress is both vain and dangerous (94)]; and "quant a ce que tu dis de la curiosité femenine, en sumptueulx & riches accoustremens" (125) [As to what you have said about women's willingness to experiment in rich and sumptuous clothes (95)]. The only such reference in his previous letter, however, is the brief statement near the end: "O que infelices sont vos beaultez fardz & aornemens" (120) [How dangerous are your powdered allurements (92)].

34. She does write "ton" instead of "vostre," but the husband in himself represents the whole tradition that he has invoked.

35. A more literal translation than "Many good men" would be "All good men."

36. This letter appears both in *Her Immaculate Hand* (King and Rabil 1983, 85–86) and in Laura Cereta's *Collected Letters* (1997, 80–82). For a listing of the printed Latin edition and extant manuscripts, see the latter volume (3).

37. Mustacchi and Archambault (Helisenne 1986, 14) suggest that the praises of Marguerite may have also been an attempt to gain court patronage, a suggestion corroborated by Helisenne's dedication of the *Aeneid* translation to Francis I. This failed effort, however, is not incompatible with a real admiration for the opening of possibilities for women's publishing.

38. Nash (Helisenne 1996, 210) suggests that as Marot had also written a set of "epistres familieres," this might be a basis for Helisenne's reference to him.

39. I disagree with the conclusion of Diane Wood (1991, 150) that the persona of Helisenne evolves through the romance and letters: "From a timid beginning, she grad-

ually finds a voice. . . . When she gains her voice as an author in the *Epistres invectives,* she speaks forcefully about womanhood and literature." Given the publication dates of the two works, one year apart, and Helisenne's explicit interest in offering variety, does it make sense to speak about a process of maturation? Is the forcefulness of the final letters not rather a matter of generic style (invective)?

40. See chapter 1's references to Bruni's comment on why women should not learn rhetoric and to the comments by speakers in Bembo's *Asolani.*

Chapter 5

1. Some of Pontano's dialogues are more Lucianic, such as the "Charon," which takes place in the underworld, but most are set in Naples among speakers that the author knew personally.

2. Morigi [1947], 153–56.

3. Helisenne's praise, in her invective letters, of Marguerite and Marot together reflects the contents of the early volume of Marguerite's work, which included also the hymn translations of Marot. See also chapter 4 regarding her references to this pair of writers.

4. These were published in the 1547 *Marguerites de la marguerite des princesses. Le malade* and *L'inquisiteur,* although written earlier, were not published in this volume. In any case, the available plays included a variety of dramatic genres.

5. The women's statement during their attack, "Now you shall see whether we care if we are slandered," is strikingly relevant to the women's dialogues discussed in this chapter. The translation of Castiglione is Singleton's (1959).

6. On the close links of dialogue and drama, see Barish 1994; Girardi 1989, 45–63.

7. Aubailly (1976, 326) notes the increasing interest in the use of personifications during the late fifteenth and early sixteenth centuries.

8. Her *Oeuvres* were first published in 1543, with further editions in 1544, 1551, 1553, and 1560, all in Paris. *Le songe* was published separately in 1540 and 1541 before reappearing in her *Oeuvres. Le songe de madame Hélisenne de Crenne* has been edited by Jean-Philippe Beaulieu (1995a), with modernized punctuation and some modernized spellings. It has been translated by Lisa Neal (2000). I am citing the 1977 facsimile of the 1560 edition in order to preserve the original spellings.

9. The readily allegorizable nature of a conflict between Cupid or Venus and Pallas made these classical deities easy to absorb into a context of morally edifying personifications. Although most of Ravisius's dialogues focus on these human types and personifications, one introduces classical gods: a dialogue in which Cupid complains to Venus about Pallas's flouting of his power. Ravisius's students are urged at the end to seek Pallas's aid in avoiding the snares of love.

10. Gilman (1993, 20–26) cites definitions of dialogue as "disputation" by both Agricola and Le Caron.

11. Can we see here the influence of Dante's earthly paradise? Helisenne seems to have been acquainted with some Italian literature, but possibly not directly in Italian. The description of Venus, for example, with her transparent purple veil, seems derived from Boccaccio's *Elegia di madonna Fiammetta,* a work she had used also for her *Angoysses,* but probably in a French translation.

12. Helisenne's *Songe* is a good example of the type of dialogue described by Car-

ron as the staging of a persuasion, in which the reader is to be moved by seeing the process of another character's successful persuasion.

13. Beaulieu (1998, 26) comments that both Helisenne de Crenne and Marguerite de Navarre are much more conservative in this regard than Christine de Pizan, who makes many clear references to her actual biography, thus strongly identifying the dreamer of her *L'avision* with her historical self.

14. Beaulieu and Desrosiers-Bonin (1999) discuss Helisenne's uses of erudition in one of the only scholarly treatments of *Le songe*.

15. *Aeneid* 4.173–88.

16. Nash (1990, 40) and Losse (1994, 31) point out similarly that Helisenne's letters and romance reverse the characteristics of male and female, making the female rational and the male irrational.

17. Cited by de Buzon (Helisenne 1997, 9).

18. For information on her life, see O'Connor 1926, Champdor 1981, and Prine 1987. See also Anne-Marie Bourbon's excellent bibliography of editions, translations, and criticism in her edition of the *Debate of Folly and Love* (2000). The *Débat* has received considerable critical attention. Robert Greene made an incomplete translation as early as 1584, an indication that the work was soon known even in England.

19. See esp. Aubailly 1976, 280–463, for a review of the types and features of the sottie.

20. Malenfant (1998, 108), noting the copresent variety of generic models, describes the *Débat* as "un texte éminemment rhétorique dont on ne sait cependant plus à quel genre il appartient." Besides dialogue, comedy, and paradoxical oration, she cites (124, n. 9) Martinez's identification of other generic traditions: medieval debate, farce, narrative, mythological fable, satire, eulogy, and so on. But as Kupisz (1990, 137) notes, scholars usually call it a "dialogue."

21. See Larsen 1983, 46: "Folly functions primarily as Woman throughout the *Débat*."

22. See Malenfant 1998, 107: Labé "fait montre de sa capacité à argumenter dans des sens opposés sans chercher à conclure de façon dogmatique." Victoria Kahn (1985) traces a shift in the aims of dialogue from "practical judgment" leading to action in early humanism to a more self-contained literary contemplation of paradox in the sixteenth century.

23. See also Aubailly 1976.

24. For its lighthearted treatment of a sentimental subject, its wit, and its psychological insight, Kupisz (1990, 137–38, 140) joins O'Connor and Zamaron in comparing Labé's *Débat* to the theatrical works of Marivaux, making this a type of play two hundred years ahead of its time. The comparison is farfetched in many ways, but it calls attention to the wit, polish, and psychological subtlety of Labé's work.

25. Kupisz (1981, 144 n. 69) notes that a comedy of Folly and blind Love was performed at the royal court in 1616, but this was not necessarily Labé's text. Giudici (1981, 35) indicates that a television performance of Labé's *Débat* was broadcast in 1962, demonstrating its performability.

26. Larsen (1983, 43) observes that the *Débat* was more widely praised than Labé's other writings.

27. *The Early History of Rome*, 2.32. There is also a morality play in which Cul goes on strike to protest the disdain of the other body parts (Lazard 1980, 43), but Livy is

clearly Catherine's source. The earthy level of comedy in the morality play is beneath Catherine's style.

28. George Diller (1936, 178–95) offers an incomplete list of citations and references in the writings of both des Roches, but especially Catherine, who was the more bookish. Some of their many Plutarch allusions are listed on pages 188–91. See also Anne Larsen's notes to the dialogues in her edition of the des Roches's *Oeuvres* (1993, 1998). For the Plutarch essays referred to here, see the bilingual edition of his *Oeuvres morales*, 5 (1990).

29. Anne Larsen in her notes (1993, 228) affirms for this dialogue in particular the clear influence of Labé's *Débat*.

30. Youth uses it to maintain the superior or inferior value of different parts of the same body in order to support her claim that she is superior to Age even though they are both part of the same creation.

31. Labé too refers to Poverty as the "tresmauvaise compagne d'Amour" (83). But this is a traditional notion running through classical and medieval texts.

32. Sincero and Cariteo were also the self-chosen names of two famous Neapolitan poets and fellow academy members. The reference may imply Catherine's identification with sixteenth-century intellectual and literary activity and her awareness of Italian as well as French texts. But she has her own stronger reasons for choosing these two names.

33. George Diller (1936, 38–46) argues not only that Sincero represents Claude Pellejay but also that Pellejay probably wrote the sonnets of Sincero and collaborated on the dialogue. While Pellejay may indeed have been on Catherine's mind—as Larsen (des Roches 1998, 57; des Roches 1993, 30, 278) concurs—I see no evidence for his authorship of works to which she lays claim. If male poets could occasionally imagine a poetic response by their lady, Catherine could much more easily imagine how a male might write conventional sonnets of love. Christine de Pizan's *Cent ballades d'amant et de dame* is another example of this sort of dialogic sequence, in which a woman poet writes for both lovers, although there is no evidence that Catherine knew this work. See also Laura Terracina's love poems written in the male voice, for example, "Che gloria avrai, Madonna, o che vaghezza," included in de Blasi's *Antologia* (1930, 198–99).

34. Fontaine (1998, 134) discusses "la nature particulièrement 'fantaisiste'" of women's writings about love in the French Renaissance.

35. Anne Larsen in her notes (1993, 252) points out the source in Castiglione's *Cortegiano* (3.5).

36. See also Ferguson 1994, 143, regarding Marguerite's *Heptameron*: "The problem of how to respond to male rhetoric, a primary concern of the women *devisants*, often forms the subject of their discussions."

37. Carlo Vecce (1994, 229–31) discusses the *Heroides* as offering an entrée for a woman, such as Vittoria Colonna, to write her own verse epistle.

38. Francesco Bausi (1994, 284) observes: "il capitolo in nome e in persona di una donna è genere assai diffuso tra Quattro e Cinquecento, soprattutto in àmbito cortigiano."

39. See Charpentier 1990 and Weil 1990 on the relations between the *Débat* and the following poems in Labé's volume.

40. Anne Larsen (1983, 52) proposes that Mercury's speech forms a "bridge"

between Labé's dedicatory letter and her sonnets, tying together the separate pieces of the volume; for the self-created satisfactions of study and writing set forth in the dedication are contrasted with Mercury's description of the generally unrequited love of women, which causes them endless suffering, a suffering expressed soon after in Labé's lyric poems. In this reading Labé would come close to des Roches in suggesting that writing is more satisfying than amorous relationships.

41. Zumthor (1978, 184–85) points briefly to the connection of dialogue with lyric through the use of dialogue within lyric poems. On the use of dialogue in Petrarch's poetry see Bernardo 1953, 92–96, 109–11. Sara Adler (1988, 215, 217) discusses the dialogic arrangement of Veronica Franco's poetic exchanges with men.

42. An earlier volume of moral essays, the *Cabinet des saines affections* (1584, reprinted several times), was printed in 1595 under the name of Madame de Rivery but was attributed by François Le Poulchre to another woman, Claude de L'Aubespine, who Winn suggests was actually Claude's daughter Madeleine (Winn in L'Aubespine 2001, 12–15; Le Gendre 2001, 13–14). Winn, while declaring the attribution an unresolved mystery, has published the work under the name of Madeleine de L'Aubespine. See also the equally inconclusive discussion of its authorship by Warner (1999, 221–27), with a chart of its publication history (237).

43. *Les Sept Livres des honnestes loisirs . . . intitulé chacun du nom d'une des Planettes. Qui est un Discours en forme de chronoviologie [sic] où sera veritablement discouru des plus notables occurrences de nos Guerres civiles, & des divers accidens de l'Auteur. Dedié au Roy. Plus un Meslange de diverse Poemes, Elegies, Stances & Sonnets* (Paris, 1587). Le Poulchre also published *Continuation des honnestes loisirs . . . tendans a faire cognoistre la miserable condition de l'homme* (Angers, 1591). *Le passe-temps de M. de la M-M* was published in Paris by Jean Le Blanc in 1595. For an account of the life and work of Le Poulchre see Mouton 1931.

44. The scene of love questions from the *Filocolo*, which contains this discussion, had been translated into French as *Treize elegantes demandes d'amour* and published in Paris in 1530 and again in 1541; a French translation of the whole *Filocolo* appeared as *Le philocope* in 1542 and was printed eight times (Kirkham 2001, 16). Thus Boccaccio's discussion would have been available in French and in France to Le Gendre.

45. See also her essay "L'ignorance," earlier in the same volume (2001), where she blames people who think that ignorance protects a woman's virtue.

46. Berriot-Salvadore (1990b, 99–105), inquiring about the possible influence of Labé on later women writers, finds this scene a suggestive link.

47. The number seven could be an intentionally significant number, symbolic of the "chaste" nature of this love, mentioned in the title.

48. One bibliographer describes it rather as "un roman . . . en dialogues" [a novel . . . in dialogues] (Pauphilet, Pichard, and Barroux 1996, 735).

49. For a similar example in seventeenth-century England, one can consider Margaret Cavendish, who comments in the preface to her 1668 volume of *Plays* that having written many "Dialogues," she had "afterwards order'd them into Acts and Scenes" (Ballaster 1996, 276). Tomlinson (1992) discusses Cavendish's mixed feelings about the possibility of performance for her plays, a possibility that she desired but thought unlikely and that she felt she was further undermining by publishing the texts. See also Barish 1994, 22–26, on the increasing interest in closet drama during the late sixteenth century in Italy, in accord with Aristotle's notion that performance is an unimportant aspect of drama.

Chapter 6

1. An incomplete version appeared in 1558. Even Gruget's 1559 edition saw fit to censor certain phrases and to replace three of the tales; nonetheless, it was the version reprinted most frequently until the end of the seventeenth century.

2. Giovanni Niccolò Doglioni, who authored a biography of Fonte and saw to the publication of her work, was married to Fonte's "sister" in the family that adopted her after her parents' death. When this adoptive sister married Doglioni, Fonte accompanied her into her new home and stayed until her own marriage. For Doglioni's account of Fonte's life, see *Il merito delle donne* (1988, 3–10).

3. See esp. the work of Joy Hambuechen Potter (1985), who includes some review of the arguments on both sides before presenting her own case.

4. See Wallace 1990, esp. 184–90.

5. See Jordan 1990, 77–78: the courtier's "status vis-à-vis his lord is similar to that of a wife in relation to her husband." See also Scarpati 1992, 526. Lauro Martines (1993) discusses more generally the connections between the "courtly" praise of women and of rulers, that is, of love relations and political relations.

6. The book and section numbers allow for reference to any edition, Italian or English.

7. Laura Terracina's canto 37, stanza 6 (1549), although unclear in its final line, states clearly enough: "Ma perche il tacer nostro assai piu spinge / quel fervido desio, le menti ingorde, / Ciascun, come li pare, hor scrive, hor pinge / Tal contra a noi che mille orecchi assorde. / E così il nostro honor, sonando finge / ogni scrittor, con risonanti corde / E si lietan di dar a lor più altura / . . ." [But because our silence prods yet further / that fervent wish, with greedy minds / each (man) as he likes now writes now paints (incites) / such things against us that he deafens a thousand ears, / And so every writer feigns playing / the tune of our honor in resounding chords. / And they delight in elevating their own / success . . . (trans. in Shemek 1998, 141–42)]. Fonte's Cornelia, responding to Verginia's question of whether the many treatises by men about the honor of women prove men's love and respect, says that perhaps some have written this way from love, "ma la più parte, credetemi, si ha messo a tale impresa più per suo utile ed onor proprio che per il nostro" (43) [but most of them, believe me, have undertaken such an enterprise more for their own utility and honor than for ours].

8. Constance Jordan's *Renaissance Feminism* (1990) addresses this concept of constructed versus essential gender identity in regard to a number of different treatises on women discussed in her chapters 2 and 3.

9. It has been suggested by Mario Baratto (1970, 47) that the female audience is a symbolic or coded way of indicating a broader—that is, vernacular—readership and that Boccaccio had to justify to the learned his interest in writing for such an audience. Virginia Cox (1992, 45) indicates similarly, in regard to Renaissance dialogues: "Female interlocutors . . . were much exploited in the vernacular dialogue as stand-ins for an unschooled audience."

10. Cited by Cox in the introduction to her translation of *Il merito* (1997, 3–4).

11. Cox in Fonte 1997, 3: "It is striking that in the sixteenth century Venice produced no aristocratic women poets to rank with the Neapolitan Vittoria Colonna, the Emilian Veronica Gambara, or the Tuscan Chiara Matraini." She notes that Stampa and Franco, one "a musical virtuoso" and the other a courtesan, were "released from the rigorous codes of decorum that governed the lives of their Venetian 'betters.'"

12. An exception enters these classical models through the presence of Diotima's teachings in the *Symposium*. However, her position is anomalous in that she is not directly a member of the symposium but instead has her teachings reported indirectly. Thus she is both included and excluded from the conversation. Moreover, her status as a female priest with special authority was incongruous within Renaissance Christian culture. On the other hand her topic, an ennobling and chaste love, seemed perfectly relevant to a woman speaker, and the few Renaissance dialogues that include women are often on that topic, as Virginia Cox (2000) has pointed out. Halperin (1990) has argued that Plato's use of Diotima functions rather to silence women than to include them. Nonetheless, her figure became in the Renaissance one of the classical models and excuses for allowing women's voices to enter even a more philosophical dialogue, and women themselves were happy to make use of it, as we have seen in the case of Tullia d'Aragona.

13. Bargagli 1982, 158; cited by Adriana Chemello in her introduction to Fonte 1988 (xxxi).

14. See Ehrmann 1968, esp. his citation from Caillois's *Les jeux et les hommes* (35).

15. Chemello focuses much of her introduction to *Il merito delle donne* on its ludic aspects, noting that a number of other treatises on women situate their conversations during carnival (Fonte 1997, xxv, lx n. 40) and interpreting the opening praises of Venetian liberty as similarly establishing a context for free play (xxix).

16. See also Jon Snyder's chapter on Speroni's "Apologia dei dialoghi" (1989, esp. 96–102).

17. Deleuze and Guattari 1987, e.g., 3–4, 9–10, 14–15, 203–5, 503–5, 508–10. These concepts are in use throughout their book.

18. See Fontanella 1981, 374, 377–78. But note also the warnings of Nicole Cazauran (1976, 20–21) on the uncertainties concerning the dates and process of writing.

19. Winn (1993b, 91–96) refers to the lack of character development or change in viewpoint of the discussants as an indication of the failure of dialectic.

20. This is an amusing inversion of the common habit of calling a woman "like a man" when she is learned or intelligent "beyond her sex." Maleness is being identified by Marguerite, as it was by Helisenne, with the appetites rather than with reason. Quotations in French are from the edition by M. François (1967); the English is taken from P. A. Chilton's translation (1984).

21. Literally, believed his advice "more than he wished."

22. Bideux (1992, 312) notes the recurrences in the mouths of various speakers.

23. As Tetel remarks (1973, 8–9), Marguerite speaks through all ten narrators' voices and not just through one or two or three. This view is reinforced by Mathieu-Castellani (1992, 202), who points out various ways in which Parlamente's position is undermined. Her argument is in turn supported further by Cazauran's discussion (1976, 227–49) of the concept of "perfect love," which is set forth by Parlamente but ultimately severely criticized and undermined by the rest of the work. Thus Parlamente cannot be taken as Marguerite's mouthpiece. Thysell (1998), however, argues against Tetel's relativistic reading and claims that Marguerite clearly conveys at least some of her own views through the narrating group's moments of agreement.

24. There is an excellent discussion of this issue throughout part 3 of Cazauran's *L'Heptaméron de Marguerite de Navarre* (1976). See also the discussion of the pervasive theme of masking and unmasking with its continual "mise en doute," in Mathieu-Castellani 1992 (esp. 231–34).

25. Lyons (1986, 159–60) notes the incongruity of this tale and its moral.

26. Cazauran (1976, 86) suggests that this may be a textual error and that his final comment should be attributed to Simontault; but her discomfort with the contradiction is her only basis for this suggestion. Ferguson (1994, 145–50) discusses the narrator's "volte-face" for tale 26, pointing out indications already within the tale that prepare for the narrator's later comment.

27. Ann Rosalind Jones (1990, 1) begins her book with the thesis "that female poets were able to write and to publish because they drew upon certain potentially productive contradictions in early modern culture." Mutatis mutandis, this is essentially my point here. See also Sinfield's notion of "faultlines" in any cultural system, which create the possibility of alternate interpretation or dissent (1992).

28. See also Lyons 1986, 152–56, about this story.

29. A similar reversal of the traditional hierarchy between husband and wife appears in tale 8, where the wife tells her errant husband: "Mais, s'il vous plaist cognoistre vostre faulce oppinion, et vous deliberer de vivre selon Dieu, gardant ses commandemens, j'oblieray toutes les faultes passées, comme je veulx que Dieu oblye l'ingratitude à ne l'aymer comme je doibz" (46) [But if you will acknowledge that you've been in the wrong, and make up your mind to live according to the ways of God and His commandments, then I'll overlook all your past misbehaviour, even as I hope God will forgive me *my* ingratitude to Him, and failure to love Him as I ought (111)]. Here the analogy relates wife to husband as God to man, an analogy clinched by the act of pardon. See also the reversals of traditional gender hierarchy in the writings of Helisenne.

30. See Mary McKinley (Lyons and McKinley 1993, 146–71) on women's resistance to the abuses of confession by wicked clergymen.

31. Literally, "found unbearable."

32. This is a repeated motif in the comments on tales, but one clear and early example is in tale 4, when the princess who has fought off a rapist is advised by her lady in waiting to thank God humbly, recognizing that "ce n'a pas esté par vostre vertu" (32) [it was not your virtue that saved you (95)]. Tale 30 makes an emphatic case for this point, which is seized on in the ensuing discussion.

33. This is the thesis for her entire *La conversation conteuse* (1992), but see esp. 231–34: "Le project global de *l'Heptaméron* est en effet de découvrir et de mettre à nu ce que femmes et hommes dissimulent" (233) [The global project of the *Heptameron* is indeed to discover and lay bare what women and men dissimulate].

34. Deleuze and Guattari 1987, 3. Interestingly Catherine of Siena, with whose work Marguerite may well have been familiar, has a similar notion of the self as a collection of distinct parts; thus her dialogue *Libro della divina dottrina* (cap. 51) interprets the scriptural verse "For where two or three are gathered together in my name, there I am in the midst of them" (Matt. 18:20) as referring to the presence of God in the soul that has "congregated" all its operations and powers.

35. See also Lyons's focus on the opposition between objective events in the stories and subjective judgments in the discussion (1986, 150–52).

36. Marcel Tetel (1973, 15) refers to "a narrative technique that . . . purposely confuses the concepts of fiction and reality." Tetel remarks further (196) that historicity itself becomes a fiction, "a mere veil of verisimilitude," in which the supposed renaming of characters in order to protect them is a device to produce a sense of realism. See also discussions of the truth claims in Mathieu-Castellani 1992 (esp. 7–21) and Cazauran 1976 (28–37). Philippe de Lajarte (1984, 71–72) points out that although the tales are presented as true exempla, the contradictory lessons from one tale to the next

end up deconstructing the whole notion of exemplarity. Edwin Duval (Lyons and McKinley 1993, 241–62) argues that we should not think of the "nouvelles" as stories at all but rather as "news" or "reports," as the word is generally used within the book.

37. Edwin Duval (Lyons and McKinley 1993, 251–52): "The whole point [of Marguerite's project], it would seem, is to probe the articulation between the Good News of redemption and daily news in a fallen world."

38. All citations in Italian are from Chemello's edition (1988); the English is from the translation by Virginia Cox (1997).

39. Cox (1995, 569–75) indicates another model that Fonte may have known: Cristoforo Zabata's *Ragionamento di sei nobili fanciulli genovesi* (1583). While the two works share the unusual feature of representing a conversation entirely among females, including a discussion of the pros and cons of marriage, Zabata's "lively initial discussion airing views felt to be extreme or 'paradoxical' is followed by an unconditional surrender to a single conventional viewpoint" (570). "The *Ragionamento*," according to Cox, "uses the fiction of a conversation between women to lend an air of impartiality and authority to its frequent misogynistic darts" (574).

40. Sara Grieco (1994, 308–9) observes the production of sixteenth- and seventeenth-century images of Saint Ann teaching the Virgin Mary how to read or sew, images that served as a model for the same kinds of charitable instruction being done by women both in convents and in lay institutions. Cox (Fonte 1997, 17) notes that "for a series of economic and social reasons, the marriage prospects of upper-class Venetian women were sharply diminishing, and unprecedented numbers were being pressured into taking the veil or kept on as unpaid servants in the family home." This too supported the search for new options for unmarried women, who were becoming a social problem. For more detailed discussion of the changing economic and social conditions affecting women in Venice and on the status and way of life of the *dimessa*, see Cox 1995, esp. 527–57. For more on images of Ann teaching Mary or Mary teaching the young Jesus how to read, see Plebani 1996, 33–34.

41. His sonnet at the beginning of her first published volume praises, along with her talent, the modesty with which she has concealed her identity behind a pseudonym (Fonte 1988, x). This kind of mixed signal is typical in the treatment of humanist women in Italy.

42. See note 2, this chapter.

43. He is praised as an excellent lawyer rather than as a husband: Corinna says that she has made use of his very good legal services and that his service to the state is also well respected.

44. Adriana's argument that for women living with male relatives marriage may be preferable to an even worse servitude in one's father's or brother's home provides a balancing view to Catherine des Roches's, for whom an unwed life meant life in a household of women. See also the view of Erasmus, in "The Girl with No Interest in Marriage," and of his devoted Paleario (1933, 72), that marriage brings a new and desired "liberty" to the woman.

45. Christine de Pizan and Marie de Romieu made long lists; Catherine des Roches includes a shorter list, all of Italian women; others, such as Laura Cereta, Veronica Gambara, Cornelia Cotta, and Lucia Bertani dell'Oro, at least name one or two other female writers in a mutually supportive manner.

46. For example, Gaspara Stampa, Veronica Franco, Irene Stilimbergo, Polissena Pecorino, and so on. Granted, these were of a previous generation, and at least two of

them were courtesans. Cox comments on Venice's relative sparsity of women writers from the honorable classes (see note 11, this chapter). Nonetheless, Fonte might well have known other women of her own time who wrote the occasional poem or elegant letter.

47. Corinna, in praising the beauty and virtue of one lady, even refers quite uncritically to her husband as the "dignissimo e felicissimo possessor d'una tanta gloria" (150) [most worthy and lucky possessor of such a glory (my trans.)]; the word "possessor" comes out as a natural expression of the relation of this man to his wife. Of course, the lists of notable men do not mention their wives.

48. "Forza" or "force" is even stronger than "obligation" in its suggestion of physical compulsion, such as the beatings by which men were commonly advised to assert their dominance over ornery wives.

49. Chemello (1983, 145–46) suggests that it is. Cox too, in the introduction to her translation of Fonte (1997, 5), supports this identification with the observation that Fonte's *Floridoro* (1581, 10.37–38) similarly contains a fountain associated with writers: on it are carved the images of Venetian poets including Fonte herself. Price (1989, 169) observes that in the description of the fountain in *Il merito*, the six marble statues of women produce "ad arte" or "artistically" "acque, chiare, fresche e dolci," a phrase whose Petrarchan evocation implies a female production of poetry.

50. See Chemello in Fonte 1988, xiv; Price 1989, 171; King 1991, 231–32.

51. See King 1976, 280–304. One can add the cases of Vittoria Colonna, who wrote most of her poetry after her husband's death, and Veronica Gambara, whose husband was absent much of the time and later dead, leaving her free for cultural pursuits. For some discussion of Fonte's difficulties in combining the desire to dedicate herself to a life of letters with the duties of a woman, wife, and mother, see Collina 1989, 142–64.

52. See also Collina 1989, 160–61, for discussion of this passage.

53. Chemello (1983, 114–26) discusses at length the theme of "merit" versus "envy" that runs through Fonte's book.

54. There too education in reading and writing is classified as a "virtù" that cannot possibly generate "vizio" the way some foolish people say.

55. See also the aim of Sigea's dialogue in conveying to the Portuguese princess a compendium of learning.

56. Patricia Labalme (1981, 90) suggests that "the main purpose of the work is not the condemnation of the male sex with old and new arguments. The dialogue is a vehicle for the display of Modesta's and Corinna's encyclopedic, if superficial, learning." I do not see these two purposes as mutually incompatible. The demonstration of women's abilities is part of the case for the injustice of men's attitudes and actions regarding women.

57. Paola Malpezzi Price (1989, 167) sees the combination of serious and playful aims as mutually supportive: "Fonte unmasks the injustice of such a tenet through a playful enumeration of men's vices and the uncovering of women's merits."

58. See also the discussions in chapters 3 and 4 concerning the presentation by both Helisenne de Crenne and Catherine des Roches of men disagreeing and arguing about the capabilities of women and what they should be allowed to do.

Chapter 7

1. Colet's letter, addressed to two female readers who have requested him to render Helisenne's text more easily readable, comes at the end of the 1560 edition. The

title page of the volume notes of this new edition: "Le tout reveu & corrigé de nouveau par elle." I take this to signify that Colet, whose letter expresses his hesitation to make changes that would render the author unhappy, had asked Helisenne to look over his editing and had received her consent. It may also signify, of course, that she was simply correcting errors in the previous editions. See also La Charité 1988, 84.

2. Morata oddly translated two of the *Decameron* tales into Latin, but this may have been an exercise for her teacher. Both in Italy and in France the novella was identified as a popular genre to be written most appropriately in the vernacular.

3. So too we find the copious lists of citations in a writer like Sigea frankly tedious to plow through. Yet for Sigea, these copious lists were the chief value of her work; it is these that she offers proudly in her dedication.

4. Denys Janot printed the first editions of *Les angoysses* (1538), *Les epistres* (1539), *Le songe* (1540), and her *Aeneid* translation (1541), as well as of her collected *Oeuvres* (1543). See Mustacchi and Archambault's introduction to Helisenne 1986 (3–5).

5. See chapter 2, note 59.

6. For a fairly thorough and objective discussion of Labé's contemporary moral reputation, see Cartier 1914–17.

7. Court society is a different matter, but the women who wrote dialogues in Italy were seldom at court, and the noblewomen immersed in court life, such as Vittoria Colonna or Veronica Gambara, did not write dialogues.

8. Christiane Lauvergnat-Gagnière (1990) discusses Labé's ready use of classical rhetoric in these orations and addresses the puzzling question of how she could have attained such knowledge.

9. See also the discussion of this topos in Vianello 1993 (14–18).

10. Kenneth Wilson (1985, 50–60) comments on the pervasive use of disputational and oratorical training in Renaissance education and the combination of the two in academic "oratorical disputations." David Marsh (1998, 166) notes the popularity of the oratorical contest as a form of dialogue.

11. Even though Valla's contemporaries, and critics since then as well, have suspected that Valla's own real views are represented by the Epicurean, the pattern still holds for his formal organization.

12. Similarly, Jean-Louis Fournel (1990, 121–68) describes the work of Sperone Speroni as seeking its own appropriate space, neither courtly nor academic, and ultimately creating "une grande 'conversation' italienne, aux espaces et aux formes multiples" (162) [one great Italian 'conversation' with multiple spaces and forms]. See also Mesnard 1967, 17: "l'humanisme correspond à un essai d'émancipation par la culture d'une nouvelle classe sociale qui, pour se faire reconnaître ses droits, s'attachèrent à définir ses idéaux propres à travers des relations purent formelles établies cette fois non plus de cité à cité ou d'église à église, mais d'individu à individu, quel que soit le rang ou la dignité social des intéressés, pourvu qu'ils aient le style e la mentalité requis."

Renaissance Dialogues

ISOTA NOGAROLA (1418–66)

De pari aut impari Evae atque Adae peccato (Isota Nogarola, Ludovico Foscarini; written 1451).

Dialogus quo utrum Adam vel Eva magis peccaverit, questio satis nota, sed non adeo explicata, continetur. Venice: Aldus, 1563.

Eugenius Abel, ed. In *Isotae Nogarolae Veronensis opera quae supersunt omnia*, vol. 2. Vienna: Gerold et Socios, 1886.

Margaret King and Albert Rabil, ed. and trans. "On the Equal or Unequal Sin of Adam and Eve." In *Her Immaculate Hand: Selected Works by and about the Women Humanists of Quattrocento Italy*. Binghamton: Medieval and Renaissance Texts and Studies, 1983.

CATHERINE D'AMBOISE (d. 1550)

La complaincte de la dame pasmée contre Fortune (written 1524–25). B.N. nouv. acq. fr. 19738.

MARGUERITE DE NAVARRE (1492–1549)

Dialogue en forme de vision nocturne (Charlotte, Marguerite; written 1524). First published with *Le miroir* and other works. Alençon: S. du Bois, 1533. Pierre Jourda, ed. In *Revue du Seizième Siècle* 13 (1926).

La navire, ou Consolation du roi François Ier à sa soeur Marguerite (François, Marguerite; written 1547; unpublished during the sixteenth century).

Robert Marichal, ed. Bibliothèque de l'Ecole des Hautes Etudes 306. Paris: Librairie Ancienne Honoré Champion, 1956.

Abel Lefranc, ed. In *Les dernières poésies*. Paris: Armand Colin and Cie, 1896.

L'Heptaméron (written 1540s).

Claude Gruget, ed. Paris: Jean Caveiller, 1559.

Michel François, ed. Paris: Garnier, 1967.

P. A. Chilton, trans. New York: Penguin Books, 1984.

HELISENNE DE CRENNE (1500/1515?–52?)

Les epistres familieres et invectives de ma dame Helisenne (invectives include dialogic exchange with husband).

Paris: Denys Janot, 1539.

Jean-Philippe Beaulieu with Hannah Fournier, eds. Montreal: Les Presses de l'Université de Montréal, 1995.

Jerry Nash, ed. Paris: Honoré Champion, 1996.

Marianna M. Mustacchi and Paul J. Archambault, trans. *A Renaissance Woman: Helisenne's Personal and Invective Letters*. Syracuse: Syracuse University Press, 1986.

Le songe de Madame Helisenne

Paris: Denys Janot, 1540.

In *Les oeuvres de ma dame Helisenne* [1560]. Geneva: Slatkine Reprints, 1977.

Jean-Philippe Beaulieu, ed. Paris: Indigo and Côté-femmes Éditions, 1995.

Lisa Neal, trans. In *Writings by Pre-Revolutionary French Women*, ed. Anne Larsen and Colette H. Winn. New York: Garland Publishing, 2000.

TULLIA D'ARAGONA (1510–56)

Dialogo dell'infinità di amore (Tullia, Benedetto Varchi, Lattanzio Benucci). Venice: Giolito, 1547.

Giuseppe Zonta, ed. In *Trattati d'amore del cinquecento*. Scrittori d'Italia 37. Bari: Gius. Laterza and Figli, 1912, 185–248.

Rinaldina Russell and Bruce Merry, trans. *Dialogue on the Infinity of Love*. Chicago: University of Chicago Press, 1997.

LOUISE LABÉ (1515/1524?–66)

Débat de Folie et d'Amour,

First published in *Oeuvres complètes*. Lyon: Jean de Tournes, 1555.

Enzo Giudici, ed. Geneva: Librairie Droz, 1981.

Edith Farrell, ed. and trans. In *Louise Labé's Complete Works*. Troy, N.Y.: Whitston Publishing Co., 1986.

Anne-Marie Bourbon, trans. *Debate of Folly and Love*. New York: Peter Lang, 2000.

OLYMPIA MORATA (1526–55)

"Lavinia Ruverensis Ursina & Olympia Morata colloquuntur" (written 1550) and "Theophila & Philotima colloquuntur" (written 1551).

First published in Celio Secondo Curione, ed. *Opera omnia*. Basel: Petrus Perna, 1562.

Lanfranco Caretti, ed. In *Opere*, vol. 2: *Orationes, dialogi et carmi*. R. Deputazione di Storia Patria Per L'Emilia e la Romagna, sezione di Ferrara. Ferrara: Premiata Tipografia Sociale, 1940.

Holt N. Parker, ed. and trans. In *The Complete Writings of an Italian Heretic*. Chicago: University of Chicago Press, 2003.

CATHERINE DES ROCHES (1542–87)

"Dialogue de Vieillesse et Jeunesse," "Dialogue de Vertu et Fortune," "Dialogue de la Main, du Pié et de la Bouche," "Dialogue de la Pauvreté et la Faim," "Dialogue d'Amour, de Beauté et de Physis," and "Dialogue de Sincero et de Charite."

First published in *Les oeuvres*. Paris: Abel l'Angelier, 1578.

Anne Larsen, ed. In *Les oeuvres*. Geneva: Droz, 1993.

"Dialogue de Placide et Sevère" and "Dialogue d'Iris et Pasithée."

First published in *Les secondes oeuvres*. Poitiers: Nicolas Courtoys, 1583.

Anne Larsen, ed. In *Les secondes oeuvres*. Geneva: Droz, 1998.

"Iris and Pasithee."

Anne Larsen, trans. In *Women writers of the Renaissance and Reformation*, ed. Katerina Wilson. Athens: University of Georgia Press, 1987.

CHIARA MATRAINI (1515–1604)

Dialoghi spirituali (probably written c. 1580).

First published in Venice: Fioravante Prati, 1602.

MODERATA FONTE (1555–92)

Il merito delle donne (written 1592).

First published in Venice: Domenico Imberti, 1600.

Adriana Chemello, ed. Venice: Editrice Eidos, 1988.

Virginia Cox, trans. *The Merit of Women*. Chicago: University of Chicago Press, 1997.

MARIE LE GENDRE, DAME DE RIVERY (fl. 1590s)

Dialogue des chastes amours d'Eros et de Kalisti.
Paris: Jean le Blanc, 1596. [B. N. Arsenal.]
L'exercice de l'âme vertueuse, augmenté d'un dialogue des chastes amours d'Eros et de Kalisti. Paris: Claude Micard et Gilles Robinot, 1597.
Colette H. Winn, ed. Paris: Honoré Champion, 2001.

LUISA SIGEA (1522–60)

Duarum virginum colloquium (written 1552; unpublished).
Odette Sauvage, ed. and trans. *Dialogue de deux jeunes filles sur la vie de la cour et la vie de retraite*. Paris: Presses Universitaires de France, 1970.

Bibliography

Adler, Sara. 1988. Veronica Franco's Petrarchan terze rime: Subverting the master's plan. *Italica* 65 (3): 213–33.

Altman, Janet. 1986. The letter book as a literary institution 1539–1789: Toward a cultural history of public correspondence in France. *Yale French Studies* 71:17–62.

Arbour, Romeo. 1975. *L'ére baroque en France: Répertoire chronologique des éditions de textes littéraires*. Premiére partie: 1585–1615. Geneva: Droz.

———. 1985. *L'ére baroque en France: Répertoire chronologique des éditions de textes littéraires*. Quatriéme partie: supplement 1585–1643. Geneva: Droz.

Atance, Felix R. 1974. Les religieux de *L'Heptaméron*: Marguerite de Navarre et les novateurs. *Archiv für Reformationsgeschichte/Archive for Reformation History* 65:185–209.

———. 1975. Marguerite de Navarre et la reforme dans *La comedie de Mont-de-Marsan*. *Bulletin de l'Assoc. des Professeurs des Universités Canadiennes* (February): 38–63.

Aubailly, Jean-Claude. 1976. *Le monologue, le dialogue et la sottie: Essai sur quelques genres dramatiques de la fin du moyen âge et du début du XVIe siècle*. Paris: Honoré Champion.

Augustijn, Cornelis. 1991. *Erasmus: His life, works, and influence*. Trans. J. C. Grayson. Toronto: University of Toronto Press.

Augustine. 1961. *Confessions*. Trans. William Watts. 2 vols. Loeb Classical Library. Cambridge: Harvard University Press.

———. 1990. *Soliloquiorum libri duo; De immortalitate animi; Soliloquies and immortality of the soul*. Facing trans. Gerard Watson. Warminster: Aris and Phillips.

Bainton, Roland. 1971. *Women of the Reformation in Germany and Italy*. Minneapolis: Augsburg Publishing House.

———. 1992. *Donne della Riforma in Germania, in Italia e in Francia*. Trans. Flavio Sarni. Torino: Claudiana.

Bakhtin, Mikhail. 1986. The problem of speech genres. In *Speech genres and other late essays*, trans. Vernon W. McGee, ed. Caryl Emerson and Michael Holquist, 60–102. Austin: University of Texas Press.

Baldacci, Luigi, ed. 1975. *Lirici del cinquecento*. Classici della Società Italiana 7. Milano: Longaresi.

Ballaster, Ross. 1996. The first female dramatists. In *Women and literature in Britain 1500–1700*, ed. Helen Wilcox, 267–90. Cambridge: Cambridge University Press.

Balsamo, Jean. 1999. Abel L'Angelier et ses dames: Les dames des Roches, Madeleine de l'Aubespine, Marie Le Gendre, Marie de Gournay. In Courcelle and Val Julián 1999, 117–36.

Baratto, Mario. 1970. *Realtà e stile nel* Decameron. Vicenza: N. Pozza.

Barberino, Francesco da. 1957. *Reggimento e costumi di donna*. Ed. Giuseppe Sansone. Torino: Loescher-Chiantore.

Bargagli, Girolamo. 1982. *Dialogo de' giuochi che nelle vegghie sanesi si usano di fare*. Ed. Patrizia D'Incalca Ermini. Introd. Riccardo Bruscagli. Monografie di storia e letteratura senese 9. Siena: Accademia Senese degli Intronati.

Barish, Jonas. 1994. The problem of closet drama in the Italian Renaissance. *Italica* 71 (1): 4–30.

Bassanese, Fiora. 1988. Private lives and public lies: Texts by courtesans of the Italian Renaissance. *Texas Studies in Literature and Language* 30(3): 295–319.

Baurmeister, Ursula, and Marie-Pierre Laffitte. 1992. *Des livres et des rois: La bibliothèque royale de Blois*. Paris: Bibliothèque Nationale.

Bausi, Francesco. 1994. Le rime di e per Tullia d'Aragona. In Ulysse 1994, 275–92.

Beaulieu, Jean-Philippe. 1994. La fonction du dialogue épistolaire dans les *Epistres invectives* de Helisenne de Crenne. In *Les femmes de lettres: Ecriture féminine ou spécificité générique?* ed. Benoit Melançon and Pierre Popovic, 7–19. Centre universitaire de lecture sociopoétique de l'epistolaire et des correspondances. Montreal: University de Montréal.

———. 1998. *L'avision Christine* ou la tentation autobiographique. In Desrosiers-Bonin 1998, 15–30.

Beaulieu, Jean-Philippe, and Diane Desrosiers-Bonin. 1999. Allégorie et épistolarité: Les jetées de l'érudition féminine chez Hélisenne de Crenne. *Revue d'Histoire Littéraire de la France* 99 (6): 1155–67.

Bembo, Pietro. 1966. *Prose e rime*. Ed. Carlo Dionisotti. Torino: UTET.

Bénouis, Mustapha Kemal. 1976. *Le dialogue philosophique dans la littérature française du seizième siècle*. Paris: Mouton.

Berlaire, Franz. 1978. *Les Colloques d'Érasme: Réforme des études, réforme des moeurs et réforme de l'Église au XVIe siècle*. Paris: Société d'Edition "Les Belles Lettres."

Bernardo, Aldo S. 1951. Dramatic dialogue and monologue in Petrarch's works. Part I. *Symposium* 5:302–16.

———. 1953. Dramatic dialogue and monologue in Petrarch's works. Part II. *Symposium* 7:92–119.

Berriot-Salvadore, Evelyne. 1990a. *Les femmes dans la société française de la Renaissance*. Histoire des idées et critique littéraire 285. Geneva: Droz.

———. 1990b. Les héritières de Louise Labé. In Demerson 1990, 93–106.

Bideux, Michel. 1992. *Marguerite de Navarre: L'Heptaméron de l'enquête au débat*. Mont-de-Marsan: Editions InterUniversitaires.

Billanovich, Giuseppe. 1996. *Petrarca e il primo umanesimo*. Studi sul Petrarca 25. Padova: Editrice Antenore.

Boccaccio, Giovanni. 1976. *Decameron*. Ed. Vittore Branca. Tutte le Opere 4. Milano: Mondadori.

Bömer, Aloys Wilhelm. 1897. *Die lateinischen Schülergespräche der Humanisten*. Berlin: J. Harrwitz.

Bonnet, Jules. 1856. *Vie d'Olympia Morata, épisode de la renaissance et de la réforme en Italie*. 3d ed., rev. et aug. Paris: Charles Meyrueis.

Borsellino, Nino. 1967. *Rozzi e intronati: Esperienze e forme di teatro dal Decameron al Candelaio*. 2d ed. Rome: Bulzoni.

Braybrook, Jean. 1999. Language in Louise Labé's *Débat de Folie et d'Amour*. In Ford and Jondorf 1999, 145–57.

Briçonnet, Guillaume, and Marguerite d'Angoulême. 1975. *Correspondance (1521–1524)*. Vol. 1: *Années 1521–1522*. Ed. Christine Martineau and Michel Veissière. Travaux d'Humanisme et Renaissance 141. Geneva: Droz.

———. 1979. *Correspondance (1521–1524)*. Vol. 2: *Années 1523–1524*. Ed. Christine Martineau and Michel Veissière. Travaux d'Humanisme et Renaissance 173. Geneva: Droz.

Bridenthal, Renata, and Claudia Koonz, eds. 1977. *Becoming visible: Women in European history*. Boston: Houghton Mifflin.

Bryant, Gwendolyn. 1984. The French heretic beguine: Margaret Porete. In *Medieval women writers*, ed. Katharina Wilson, 204–10. Athens: University of Georgia Press.

Bullock, Alan, and Gabriella Palange. 1980. Per una edizione critica delle opere di Chiara Matraini. In *Studi di Onore di Raffaele Spongano*, 235–62. Bologna: Massimiliano Boni Editore.

Bushnell, Rebecca. 1996. *A culture of teaching: Early modern humanism in theory and practice*. Ithaca: Cornell University Press.

Cammelli, Giuseppe. 1941. Olimpia Morata. Review of *Opere*, by Olympia Morata, ed. Lanfanco Caretti, with textual corrections. *La Rinascita* 4:453–58.

Campo, Roberto. 1998. Review of *Odes à Pasithée*, by Jean Tagaut. *Renaissance Quarterly* 51 (3): 989–90.

Carron, Jean-Claude. 1991. The persuasive seduction: Dialogue in sixteenth-century France. In Logan and Rudnytsky 1991, 90–108.

Cartier, Alfred. 1914–17. Louise Labé, le procès yvard à Genève, et le *Philosophe de court* par Philibert de Vienne. *Revue de Livres Anciens* 2:321–32.

Castiglione, Baldesar. 1959. *The book of the courtier*. Trans. Charles Singleton. New York: Anchor Books.

———. 1972. *Il libro del cortegiano*. Ed. Ettore Bonora. Milano: Mursia.

Caterina da Siena. 1912. *Libro della divina dottrina volgarmente detto Dialogo della divina provvidenza*. Ed. Matilde Fiorilli. Scrittori d'Italia 34. Bari: Gius. Laterza and Figli.

Cazauran, Nicole. 1976. *L'Heptaméron de Marguerite de Navarre*. Paris: Société d'Edition d'Enseignement Superieur.

Cereta, Laura. 1640. *Laurae Ceretae brixiensis feminae clarissimae epistolae . . .* Ed. Phillip Jacob Tomasini. Padua: Sebastiano Sardi.

———. 1997. *Collected letters of a Renaissance feminist*. Ed. and trans. Diana Robin. Chicago: University of Chicago Press.

Champdor, Albert. 1982. *Louise Labé, son oeuvre et son temps*. Trevoux: Editions de Trevoux.

Charpentier, Françoise. 1990. Le *Débat* de Louise et de l'Amour. In Demerson 1990, 147–59.

Chemello, Adriana. 1983. La donna, il modello, l'immaginario: Moderata Fonte e Lucrezia Marinelli. In Zancan 1983b, 95–170.

Cholakian, Patricia. 1992. Signs of the "feminine": The unshaping of narrative in Marguerite de Navarre's *Heptameron*, nouvelles 2, 4, and 10. In *Reconsidering the Renaissance*, ed. Mario Di Cesare, 229–44. Binghamton: Medieval and Renaissance Texts and Studies.

Cicero. *De oratore*. 1948. Trans. H. Rackham. 2 vols. Loeb Classical Library. Cambridge: Harvard University Press.

———. 1950. *Tusculan disputations*. Trans. J. E. King. Loeb Classical Library. Cambridge: Harvard University Press.

———. 1951. *De finibus*. Trans. H. Rackham. Loeb Classical Library. Cambridge: Harvard University Press.

Cioranesco, Alexandre. 1975. *Bibliographie de la littérature française du seizième siècle*. Geneva: Slatkine Reprints.

Clements, Robert J. 1941. Marguerite de Navarre and Dante. *Italica* 18(1): 37–50.

Collina, Beatrice. 1989. Moderata Fonte e *Il merito delle donne*. In West and Cervigni 1989, 142–64.

Colonna, Vittoria. 1892. *Carteggio*. Ed. Ermanno Ferrero and Giuseppe Müller. 2d ed. Torino: Ermanno Loescher.

Combes, André. 1963. *La théologie mystique de Gerson*. Rome: Editores Pontificii.

Connolly, James. 1928. *Jean Gerson: Reformer and mystic*. Louvain: Libraire universitaire.

Cottrell, Robert. 1986. *The grammar of silence: A reading of Marguerite de Navarre's poetry*. Washington, D.C.: Catholic University of America Press.

Courcelle, Dominique de, and Carmen Val Julián, eds. 1999. *Des femmes et des livres: France et Espagne XIVe–XVIIe siècle*. Études et rencontres de l'école des Chartres 4. Paris: École de Chartres.

Cox, Virginia. 1992. *The Renaissance dialogue: Literary dialogue in its social and political contexts, Castiglione to Galileo*. Cambridge Studies in Renaissance Literature and Culture. Cambridge: Cambridge University Press.

———. 1995. The single self: Feminist thought and the marriage market in early modern Venice. *Renaissance Quarterly* 48 (3): 513–81.

———. 2000. Seen but not heard: Women speakers in cinquecento literary dialogue. In Panizza 2000, 385–400.

Daenens, Francine. 1999. Donne valorose, eretiche, finte sante: Note sull'antologia giolitana del 1548. In *Per lettera: La scrittura epistolare femminile tra archivio e tipografia secoli XV–XVII*, ed. Gabriella Zarri, 181–207. Rome: Viella.

Dagens, Jean. 1963. Le miroir des simples ames et Marguerite de Navarre. In *La Mystique Rhénane, Colloque de Strasbourg, 16–19 mai 1961*, 281–89. Paris: Presses Universitaires de France.

D'Ancona, Alessandro. 1996. *Origini del teatro italiano*. 2 vols. Roma: Bardi Editore.

Davis, Natalie Zemon. 1975. *Society and culture in early modern France*. Stanford: Stanford University Press.

De Blasi, Jolanda, ed. 1930. *Antologia delle scrittrici italiane dalle origini al 1800*. Florence: Casa Editrice "Nemi."

Defaux, Gerard. 1999. Marguerite de Navarre et la guerre des sexes: *Heptaméron*, premiere Journée. *French Forum* 24 (2): 133–61.

Deleuze, Gilles, and Félix Guattari. 1987. *A thousand plateaus*. Trans. Brian Massumi. Minneapolis: University of Minnesota Press.

Demerson, Guy, ed. 1990. *Louise Labé: Les voix du lyrisme*. Paris: Éditions du CNRS.

De Montmorency, J. E. G. 1970. *Thomas à Kempis: His age and book*. Port Washington, N.Y.: Kennikat Press.

Derwa, Marcel. 1974. Un aspect du colloque scolaire humaniste: La dialogue à variations. *Revue de Littérature Comparée* 48 (2): 190–202.

Des Roches, Madeleine, and Catherine des Roches. [1579] 1993. *Les oeuvres*. Ed. Anne Larsen. Geneva: Droz.

———. [1583] 1998. *Les secondes oeuvres*. Ed. Anne Larsen. Geneva: Droz.

Desrosiers-Bonin, Diane, ed. 1998. *L'écriture des femmes à la Renaissance française*, special issue. *Littératures* 18.

Diller, George. 1936. *Les dames des Roches: Etude sur la vie littéraire á Poitiers dans la deuxième moitié du XVIe siècle*. Paris: Droz.

Dionisotti, Carlo. 1967. La letteratura italiana nell'età del Concilio di Trento. In *Geografia e storia della letteratura italiana*, 183–204. Torino: G. Einaudi.

Doglio, Maria Luisa. 2000. Letter writing, 1350–1650. In *A history of women's writing in Italy*, Letizia Panizza and Sharon Wood, ed. 13–24. Cambridge: Cambridge University Press.

Dolce, Lodovico. 1547. *Dialogo della institution delle donne*. Venice: Giolito.

Duchène, Roger. 1971. Réalité vécue et réussite littéraire: Le statut particulier de la lettre. *Revue d'Histoire Littéraire de la France* 71 (2): 177–94.

Duval, Edwin. 1993. "Et puis, quelles nouvelles?": The project of Marguerite's unfinished *Decameron*. In Lyons and McKinley, 241–62.

Ehrmann, Jacques. 1968. Homo ludens revisited. In *Game, play, literature*, ed. Jacques Ehrmann, 31–57. Boston: Beacon Press.

Erasmus Roterdamus, Desiderius. 1964. *Enchiridion militis christiani*. Ed. Annemarie Holborn and Hajo Holborn. Munich: C. H. Becksche Verlagsbuchhandlung.

———. 1965. *The colloquies of Erasmus*. Trans. Craig R. Thompson. Chicago: University of Chicago Press.

———. 1969–77. *Opera omnia Erasmi Roterdami*. Ordinis Primi. 7 vols. Amsterdam: North-Holland Publishing Company.

Fahy, Conor. 2000. *Women and Italian Cinquecento literary academies*. In Panizza 2000, 438–52.

Favez, Charles. 1937. *La consolation latine chrétienne*. Paris: Librairie Philosophique J. Vrin.

Febvre, Lucien. 1944. *Amour sacré, amour profane: Autour de l'Heptaméron*. Paris: Gallimard.

Fedele, Cassandra. 2000. *Letters and orations*. Ed. and trans. Diana Robin. Chicago: University of Chicago Press.

Feliciangeli, B. 1891. *Notizie e documenti sulla vita di Caterina Cybo-Varano duchessa di Camerino*. Camerino.

Ferguson, Gary. 1992. *Mirroring belief: Marguerite de Navarre's devotional poetry*. Edinburgh: Edinburgh University Press.

———. 1994. Gendered oppositions in Marguerite de Navarre's *Heptameron*: The rhetoric of seduction and resistance in narrative and society. In Larsen and Winn 1994, 143–59.

Finucci, Valeria. 1989. La donna di corte: Discorso istituzionale e realtà nel libro del cortegiano di B. Castiglione. In West and Cervigni 1989, 88–103.

———. 1992. *The lady vanishes: Subjectivity and representation in Castiglione and Ariosto*. Stanford: Stanford University Press.

Firenzuola, Agnolo. 1957. *Opere scelte*. Ed. Giuseppe Fatini. Torino: UTET.

Firpo, Massimo. 1987. Valdesianesimo ed evangelismo: Alle origini dell' *Ecclesia viterbiensis* (1541). In Prosperi and Biondi 1987, 53–71.

Floriani, Piero. 1981. *I gentiluomini letterati: Studi sul dibattito culturale nel primo cinquecento*. Le Forme del Significato 29. Napoli: Liguori.

Fontaine, Guylaine. 1998. Amour et imagination dans les fictions des femmes écrivains de la première moitié du seizième siècle. In Desrosiers-Bonin 1998, 133–50.

Fontaine, Marie Madeleine. 1993. L'ordinaire de la Folie. In *Libertés et savoirs du corps à la Renaissance*, 283–301. Caen: Paradigme.

Fontanella, Lucia. 1981. Un codice sconosciuto delle "Nouvelles" di Margherita di Navarra: Contributo allo studio della genesi della raccolta. In Sozzi 1981, 361–78.

Fonte, Moderata. 1988. *Il merito delle donne*. Ed. Adriana Chemello. Mirano, Venezia: Eidos.

———. 1997. *The merit of women*. Trans. Virginia Cox. Chicago: University of Chicago Press.

Ford, Philip, and Gillian Jondorf, eds. 1999. *Women's writing in the French Renaissance*. Proceedings of the Fifth Cambridge French Renaissance Colloquium, 7–9 July. Cambridge: Cambridge French Colloquia.

Forni, Carla. 1992. *Il "libro animato": Teoria e scrittura del dialogo nel cinquecento*. Torino: Tirrenia Stampatori.

Foucault, Michel. 1988. Technologies of the self. In *Technologies of the self*, ed. Luther Martin, Huck Gutman, and Patrick Hutton, 16–49. Amherst: University of Massachusetts Press.

Fournel, Jean-Louis. 1990. Le monde des dialogues de Sperone Speroni: Langue(s), commune(s), et communauté(s) de culture(s). In *Quêtes d'une identité collective chez les italiens de la Renaissance*, 121–68. Centre Universitaire de Recherche sur la Renaissance Italienne 18. Paris: Université de la Sorbonne Nouvelle.

Freccero, Carla. 1991. Rewriting the rhetoric of desire in the *Heptameron*. In Logan and Rudnytsky 1991, 298–312.

Gelernt, Jules. 1966. *World of many loves: The* Heptameron *of Marguerite de Navarre*. Chapel Hill: University of North Carolina Press.

Gerson, Jean. 1966. *Oeuvres complètes*. Ed. Mgr. Glorieux. Vol. 7: *L'oeuvre français*. Paris: Desclée and Cie.

Gersonii, Joannis. 1706. *Opera omnia*. 5 vols. Antwerp: N.p.

Gill, Katherine. 1994. Women and the production of religious literature in the vernacular, 1300–1500. In *Creative women in medieval and early modern Italy: A religious and artistic renaissance*, ed. E. Ann Matter and John Coakley, 64–104. Philadelphia: University of Pennsylvania Press.

Gilman, Donald. 1993. Theories of dialogue. In Winn 1993a, 7–76.

Girardi, Raffaele. 1989. *La società del dialogo: Retorica e ideologia nella letteratura conviviale del cinquecento*. Biblioteca di critica e letteratura 28. Bari: Adriatica Editore.

Giudici, Enzo. 1965. *Amore e Follia nell'opera della "Belle Cordière."* Napoli: Liguori Editore.

———. 1981. *Louise Labé. Essai*. Paris: Librairie A. G. Nizet.

Godard, Anne. 2001. *Le dialogue à la Renaissance*. Paris: Presses Universitaires de France.

Goldsmith, Elizabeth C., and Dena Goodman, eds. 1995. *Going public: Women and publishing in early modern France*. Ithaca: Cornell University Press.

Gothein, Percy. 1943. L'amicizia fra Lodovico Foscarini e l'umanista Isotta Nogarola. *La Rinascita* 6:394–413.

Grafton, Anthony, and Lisa Jardine. 1986. *From humanism to the humanities: Education and the liberal arts in fifteenth- and sixteenth-century Europe*. Cambridge: Harvard University Press.

Greene, Thomas M. 1979. *Il cortegiano* and the choice of a game. *Renaissance Quarterly* 32 (2): 173–86.

Grieco, Sara F. Mathews. 1994. Modelli di santità femminile nell'Italia del Rinascimento e della Controriforma. In Scaraffia and Zarri 1994, 303–25.

Guidi, José. 1980. *De l'amour courtois à l'amour sacre: La condition de la femme dans l'oeuvre de B. Castiglione*. Paris: Université de la Sorbonne Nouvelle.

Guillerm, Jean-Pierre, Laurence Hordoir, and Marie-France Piejus, eds. 1983. *Le miroir des femmes: Moralistes et polémistes au XVIe siècle*. Lille: Presses Universitaires de Lille.

Halperin, David. 1990. Why is Diotima a woman? Platonic *eros* and the figuration of gender. In *Before sexuality: The construction of erotic experience in the ancient Greek world*, ed. David Halperin, John Winkler, and Froma Zeitlin, 257–308. Princeton: Princeton University Press.

Hart, Jonathan, ed. 1996. *Imagining culture: Essays in early modern history and literature*. New York: Garland Publishing.

Helisenne de Crenne. [1560] 1977. *Les oeuvres*. Paris: Estienne Grouleau. Reprint, Geneva: Slatkine.

———. 1986. *A Renaissance woman: Helisenne's personal and invective letters*. Trans. Marianna M. Mustacchi and Paul J. Archambault. Syracuse: Syracuse University Press.

———. 1995a. *Les epistres familieres et invectives de ma dame Helisenne*. Ed. Jean-Philippe Beaulieu with Hannah Fournier. Montreal: Les Presses de l'Université de Montréal.

———. 1995b. *Le songe de madame Hélisenne de Crenne*. Ed. Jean-Philippe Beaulieu. Paris: Indigo and Côté-femmes Éditions.

———. 1996. *Les epistres familiers et invectives*. Ed. Jerry Nash. Paris: Honoré Champion, 1996.

———. 1997. *Les angoysses douloureuses qui procedent d'amours*. Ed. Christine de Buzon. Paris: Honoré Champion.

———. 2000. *Le songe de madame Hélisenne de Crenne* [Lady Hélisenne Dream] Trans. Lisa Neal. In *Writings by pre-revolutionary French women*, ed. Anne Larsen and Colette H. Winn, 63–105. New York: Garland Publishing.

Heller, Henry. 1971. Marguerite de Navarre and the reformers of Meaux. *Bibliothèque d'Humanisme et Renaissance* 33:271–310.

Heywood, Thomas. 1963. *Pleasant dialogues and drammas, selected out of Lucian, Erasmus, Textor, Ovid, &c*. London: 1637. Reprint, *Materials for the study of Old English drama*, series 1, vols. 1–3. Ed. W. Bang. Louwain: Uystpruyst, 1902; Vaduz: Kraus Reprint Ltd.

Hirzel, Rudolf. 1895. *Der Dialog. Ein literarhistorischer Versuch*. 2 vols. Leipzig: Verlag Von S. Hirzel.

Holm, Janis Butler. 1991. Struggling with the letter: Vives's preface to the *Instruction of a Christen woman*. In Logan and Rudnytsky 1991, 265–97.

Jacquot, Jean, ed. 1964. *Le lieu théâtral à la Renaissance*. Paris: Centre National de Recherche Scientifique.

Jones, Ann Rosalind. 1986. Surprising fame: Renaissance gender ideologies and women's lyric. In *The poetics of gender*, ed. Nancy Miller, 74–95. New York: Columbia University Press.

———. 1990. *The currency of eros: Women's love lyric in Europe, 1540–1620*. Bloomington: Indiana University Press.

———. 1993. The muses of indirection: Feminist ventriloquism in the dialogues of Catherine des Roches. In Winn 1993a, 190–222.

Jones-Davies, M. T., ed. 1984. *Le dialogue au temps de la Renaissance*. Université de Paris-Sorbonne, Institut de Recherches sur les Civilisations de l'Occident Moderne. Paris: Jean Touzot.

Jordan, Constance. 1990. *Renaissance feminism*. Ithaca: Cornell University Press.

———. 1993. Renaissance women and the question of class. In Turner 1993, 90–106.

Jourda, Pierre. 1930. *Marguerite d'Angoulême, Duchesse d'Alençon, Reine de Navarre (1492–1549): Étude biographique et littéraire*. Paris: Librairie Ancienne Honoré Champion.

———. N.d. *Une princesse de la Renaissance, Marguerite d'Angoulême Reine de Navarre (1492–1549)*. Paris: Desclée de Brouwer et cie.

Kahn, Victoria. 1985. *Rhetoric, prudence, and skepticism in the Renaissance*. Ithaca: Cornell University Press.

Keating, Clark. 1941. *Studies on the literary salon in France, 1550–1615*. Cambridge: Harvard University Press.

Kelly, Joan. 1984. *Women, history, theory*. Chicago: University of Chicago Press.

King, Margaret Leah. 1976. Thwarted ambitions: Six learned women of the Italian Renaissance. *Soundings* 59:280–304.

———. 1978. The religious retreat of Isotta Nogarola (1418–66): Sexism and its consequences in the fifteenth century. *Signs* 3 (4): 807–22.

———. 1980. Book-lined cells: Women and humanism in the early Italian Renaissance. In Labalme 1980, 66–90.

———. 1991. *Women of the Renaissance*. Chicago: University of Chicago Press.

———. 1994. Isotta Nogarola (1418–1466). In Russell 1994, 313–22.

King, Margaret L., and Albert Rabil, eds. 1983. *Her immaculate hand: Selected works by and about the women humanists of Quattrocento Italy*. Binghamton: Medieval and Renaissance Texts and Studies.

Kirkham, Victoria. 2001. *Fabulous vernacular: Boccaccio's Filocolo and the art of medieval fiction*. Ann Arbor: University of Michigan Press.

Kupisz, Kasimierz. 1981. Autour de la technique de *l'Heptaméron*. In Sozzi 1981, 379–95.

———. 1990. Le théâtre de Louise Labé. In Demerson 1990, 125–45.

Kushner, Eva. 1972. Reflexions sur le dialogue en France au XVIe siècle. *Revue des Sciences Humaines* 148:485–501.

———. 1977. Renaissance dialogue: Work of art or instrument of inquiry? *Zagadniena Rodzajow Literackich (Revue des Genres Littéraires)* 39: 23–35.

———. 1978. Le dialogue en France à la Renaissance: Quelques critères génologiques. *Revue canadienne de littérature comparée*, 5 (spring): 142–53.

————. 1982. Le dialogue (1580–1630): Fonctions et articulations. In Lafond and Stegmann 1982, 149–61.

————. 1983. Vers un poétique du dialogue de la Renaissance. In *Comparative litera- ture studies: Essays presented to György Mihály Vajda*, ed. István Fried, Zoltán Kanyó, and József Pal, 131–36. Szeged: Jozsef Attila Tudomanyegyetem.

————. 1984. Le dialogue en France de 1550 à 1560. In Jones-Davies 1984, 151–67.

————. 1993. Epilogue: The dialogue of dialogues. In Winn 1993a, 259–83.

————. 2000. Trois locutrices du XVIe siècle; Deux miroirs. *Dalhousie French Studies* 52 (fall): 14–21.

Labalme, Patricia. 1981. Venetian women on women: Three early modern feminists. *Archivio Veneto* ser. 5, no.152, anno 112, 81–109.

Labé, Louise. 1981. *Oeuvres complètes*. Ed. Enzo Giudici. Geneva: Droz.

————. 1986. *Louise Labé's complete works*. Ed. and trans. Edith Farrell. Troy, N.Y.: Whitston Publishing Co.

————. 2000. *Debate of Folly and Love*. Trans. Anne-Marie Bourbon. New York: Peter Lang.

La Charité, Claude. 1988. L'emergence de la lettre familière érasmienne: Le cas de Jean Bouchet et d'Helisenne de Crenne. In Desrosiers-Bonin 1998, 65–87.

Lafond, Jean, and André Stegmann, eds. 1981. *L'automne de la Renaissance 1580–1630*. Vingt-deuxième Colloque International d'Études Humanistes, Tours, July 2–13, 1979. Paris: Librairie Philosophique J. Vrin.

Lajarte, Philippe de. 1981. Le prologue de *l'Heptaméron* et le processus de production de l'oeuvre. In Sozzi 1981, 397–423.

————. 1984. Modes du discours et formes d'alterité dans les nouvelles de Marguerite de Navarre. *Littérature* 55 (October): 64–73.

Lanson, Gustave. 1938. *Histoire de la littérature française*. Paris: Hachette.

Larsen, Anne. 1983. Louise Labé's *Debat de Folie et d'Amour:* Feminism and the defense of learning. *Tulsa Studies in Women's Literature* 2 (1): 43–55.

————. 1987. Catherine des Roches (1542–1587): Humanism and the learned woman. *Journal of the Rocky Mountain Medieval and Renaissance Association* 8:97–117.

————. 1990a. Legitimizing the daughter's writing: Catherine des Roches's proverbial good wife. *Sixteenth Century Journal* 21 (4): 559–74.

————. 1990b. "Un honneste passetems": Strategies of legitimation in French Renais- sance women's prefaces. *L'Esprit Créateur* 30 (4): 11–22.

————. 1999. La réflexivité dans les dialogues de Catherine des Roches (1583). In *Dans les miroirs de l'écriture*, ed. Jean-Philippe Beaulieu and Dian Desrosiers-Bonin, 61–72. Montreal: Paragraphes (Université de Montréal).

Larsen, Anne, and Colette H. Winn, eds. 1994. *Renaissance women writers: French texts/American contexts*. Detroit: Wayne State University Press.

L'Aubespine, Madeleine de. 2001. *Cabinet des saines affections*, ed. Colette Winn. Paris: Honore Champion.

Lauvergnat-Gagnière, Christiane. 1990. La rhetorique dans le *Débat de Folie et d'Amour*. In Demerson 1990, 53–67.

Lazard, Madeleine. 1980. *Le théâtre en France au XVIe siècle*. Paris: Presses Universi- taires de France.

————. 1985. *Images littéraires de la femme à la Renaissance*. Paris: Presses Universitaires de France.

Lefranc, Abel. 1969. *Les idées religieuses de Marguerite de Navarre d'après son oeuvre poé-tique*. Paris, 1898. Reprint, Geneva: Slatkine Reprints.

Le Gendre, Marie, Dame de Rivery. 1596. *Dialogue des chastes amours d'Eros et de Kalisti*. Paris: Jean le Blanc.

———. 2001. *L'exercice de l'âme vertueuse*. Ed. Colette H. Winn. Paris: Honoré Cham-pion.

Le Guern, Michel. 1981. Sur le genre du dialogue. In Lafond and Stegmann 1981, 141–48.

Lenzi, Maria Ludovica, ed. 1982. *Donne e madonne: L'educazione femminile nel primo Rinascimento italiano*. Torino: Loescher.

Leone Ebreo. 1929. *Dialoghi d'amore*. Ed. Santini Caramella. Scrittori d'Italia 114. Bari: Laterza.

Logan, Marie-Rose, and Peter L. Rudnytsky, eds. 1991. *Contending kingdoms: Historical, psychological, and feminist approaches to the literature of sixteenth-century England and France*. Detroit: Wayne State University Press.

Longeon, Claude. 1973. *Documents sur la vie intellectuelle en Forez au XVIe siècle*. Forez: Centre d'Etudes Foreziennes.

Losse, Deborah. 1982. Distortion as a means of reassessment: Marguerite de Navarre's *Heptameron* and the "Querelle des femmes." *Journal of the Rocky Mountain Medieval and Renaissance Association* 3:75–84.

———. 1994. Women addressing women: The differentiated text. In Larsen and Winn 1994, 23–37.

Loviot, Louis. 1914–17a. *Cabinet des saines affections* (1595). *Revue de Livres Anciens* 2:274–82.

———. 1914–17b. Helisenne de Crenne. *Revue de Livres Anciens* 2:137–45.

Lyons, John. 1986. The *Heptameron* and the foundation of critical narrative. *Images of Power: Medieval History/Discourse/Literature: Yale French Studies* 70:150–63.

Lyons, John, and Mary B. McKinley, eds. 1993. *Critical tales: New studies of the* Hep-tameron *and early modern culture*. Philadelphia: University of Pennsylvania Press.

Maclachlan, Elena. 1992. The conversion of Chiara Matraini: The 1597 rewriting of the *Rime* of 1555. *NEMLA Italian Studies* 16:21–32.

Magliani, Eduardo. 1885. *Storia letteraria delle donne italiane: Le trovatrici-preludi-trecen-tiste-quattrocentiste-cinquecentiste*. Napoli: Cav. Antonio Morano, Editore.

Malenfant, Marie Claude. 1998. L'ambiguité finale du *Débat de Folie et d'Amour* de Louise Labé. In Desrosiers-Bonin 1998, 105–31.

Marcus, Leah. 1992. Renaissance/early modern studies. In *Redrawing the boundaries: Transformation of English and American literary studies*, ed. Giles Gunn and Stephen Greenblatt, 41–63. New York: MLA.

Marguerite de Navarre. 1896. *Les dernières poésies*. Ed. Abel Lefranc. Paris: Armand Colin and Cie.

———. 1926. Dialogue en forme de vision nocturne. Ed. Pierre Jourda. *Revue du seiz-ième siècle* 13: 1–49.

———. 1956. *La navire, ou Consolation du Roi François Ier a sa soeur Marguerite*. Ed. and introd. Robert Marichal. Paris: Librairie Ancienne Honoré Champion.

———. 1963. *Théâtre profane*. Ed. Verdun L. Saulnier. Geneva: Librairie Droz.

———. 1967. *L'Heptaméron*. Ed. Michel François. Paris: Editions Garnier Frères.

———. [1547] 1970. *Les Marguerites de la marguerite des princesses*. Ed. Felix Frank. Geneva: Slatkine Reprints.

————. 1978. *Les prisons*. Ed. Simone Glasson. Geneva: Droz.

————. 1984. *The Heptameron*. Trans. P. A. Chilton. New York: Penguin.

————. 1992. *Théâtre profane*. Trans. Régine Reynolds-Cornell. Carleton Renaissance Plays in Translation 25. Ottawa: Dovehouse Editions.

Marsh, David. 1980. *The Quattrocento dialogue: Classical tradition and humanist innovation*. Cambridge: Harvard University Press.

————. 1998. *Lucian and the Latins: Humor and humanism in the early Renaissance*. Ann Arbor: University of Michigan Press.

Martineau, Christine, and Christian Grouselle. 1970. La source première et directe du *Dialogue en forme de vision nocturne*: La lettre de Guillaume Briçonnet à Marguerite de Navarre, du 15 septembre 1524. *Bibliothèque d'Humanisme et Renaissance* 32:559–577.

Martineau-Génieys, Christine. 1977. *Le thème de la mort dans la poésie française de 1450 à 1550*. Paris: Honoré Champion.

Martines, Lauro. 1993. The politics of love poetry in Renaissance Italy. In *Historical criticism and the challenge of theory*, ed. Janet L. Smarr, 129–44. Urbana: University of Illinois Press.

Mason, Amelia Gere. 1891. *The women of the French salons*. New York: Century Co.

Massebieau, L. 1878. *Les colloques scolaires du seizième siècle et leurs auteurs (1480–1570)*. Paris: J. Bonhoure et Cie.

Masson, Georgia. 1975. *Courtesans of the Italian Renaissance*. London: Secker and Warburg.

Mathieu-Castellani, Giselle. 1992. *La conversation conteuse: Les nouvelles de Marguerite de Navarre*. Paris: Presses Universitaires de France.

Matraini, Chiara. 1597. *Lettere di madonna Chiara Matraini Gentildonna Lucchese con la prima e seconda parte delle sue Rime*. Venice: Nicolò Moretti.

————. 1602. *Dialoghi spirituali*. Venice: Fioravante Prati.

————. 1989. *Rime e lettere*. Ed. Giovanna Rabitti. Scelta di Curiosità Letterarie 279. Bologna: Commissione per i Testi di Lingua.

Matter, E. Ann, and John Coakley, eds. 1994. *Creative women in medieval and early modern Italy: A religious and artistic renaissance*. Philadelphia: University of Pennsylvania Press.

Matusevich, Yelena. 1998. The golden age of French mysticism: A different perspective: The study of the spiritual literature of the late Middle Ages, from Jean Gerson to Lefevre D'Étaples. Ph.D. diss., University of Illinois at Urbana-Champaign.

————. 2000. From monastic to individual spirituality: Another perspective on Jean Gerson's attitude towards women. *Magistra* 6(1): 61–88.

Mayer, C. A. 1973. Lucien et la Renaissance. *Revue de Littérature Comparée* 47 (1): 5–22.

McCutcheon, Elizabeth. 1992. "Tongues as ready as men's": Erasmus' representations of women and their discourse. *Erasmus of Rotterdam Society Yearbook* 12:64–86.

Mesnard, Pierre. 1967. Le commerce épistolaire comme expression sociale de l'individualisme humaniste. In *Individu e Société à la Renaissance, Colloque international tenu en avril 1965*, 17–31. Travaux de l'Institut pour l'Étude de la Renaissance et de l'Humanisme 3. Brussels: Presses Universitaires de Bruxelles.

Michel, Alain. 1984. L'influence du dialogue ciceronien sur la tradition philosophique et litteraire. In Jones-Davies 1984, 9–24.

Morata, Olympia. 1580. *Opera omnia cum eruditorum testimoniis*. Basel: Petrus Perna.

———. 1940. *Opere*. Vol. 1: *Epistolario (1540–1555)*. Ed. Lanfranco Caretti. R. Deputazione di Storia Patria Per L'Emilia e la Romagna, sezione di Ferrara. Atti e Memorie N.S. XI. Ferrara: Premiata Tipografia Sociale.

———. 1954. *Opere*. Vol. 2: *Orationes, Dialogi et Carmi*. Ed. Lanfranco Caretti. R. Deputazione di Storia Patria Per L'Emilia e la Romagna, sezione di Ferrara. Atti e Memorie N.S. XI. Ferrara: Premiata Tipografia Sociale.

———. 2003. *The complete writings of an Italian heretic*. Ed. and trans. Holt N. Parker. Chicago: University of Chicago Press.

Morigi, Giovanna Wyss. [1947]. *Contributo allo studio del dialogo all'epoca dell'Umanesimo e del Rinascimento*. Monza: Scuola tipgrafica Artigianelli.

Mouton, Léo. 1931. Le capitaine François Le Poulchre de la Motte-Messemé. *Revue d'Histoire Littéraire de la France* 38:262–82.

Nash, Jerry C. 1990. "Exerçant oeuvres viriles": Feminine anger and feminist (re)writing in Helisenne de Crenne. *L'Esprit Créateur* 30 (4): 38–48.

———. 1997. Renaissance misogyny, biblical feminism, and Hélisenne de Crenne's *Epistres familiers et invectives*. *Renaissance Quarterly* 50 (2): 379–410.

———. 2000. Constructing Hélisenne de Crenne: Reception and identity. In *Por le soie amisté: Essays in honor of Norris J. Lacy*, ed. Keith Busby and Catherine M. Jones, 371–83. Atlanta: Editions Rodopi B.V.

Nieto, Jose. 1970. *Juan de Valdés and the origins of the Spanish and Italian Reformation*. Travaux d'Humanisme et Renaissance 108. Geneva: Droz.

Nogarola, Isota. 1563. *Dialogus quo utrum Adam vel Eva magis peccaverit*. Venice: Aldus.

———. 1886. *Isotae Nogarolae Veronensis opera quae supersunt omnia*. Ed. Eugenius Abel. 2 vols. Vienna: Gerold et Socios.

Nolhac, Pierre de. 1921. Le premier salon littéraire à Paris. *La Revue Universelle* 5:337–52.

Ochino, Bernardino. 1540a. *Dialogi quattro*. Venice: Nicolo d'Aristotile detto il Zoppino.

———. 1540b. *Dialogi sette*. Venice: Nicolo d'Aristotile detto il Zoppino.

———. 1563. *Dialogi XXX*. Basil: Petrus Perna.

———. 1985. *I "dialogi sette" e altri scritti del tempo della fuga*. Introd. and ed. Ugo Rozzo. Torino: Claudiana.

O'Connor, Dorothy. 1926. *Louise Labé: Sa vie et son oeuvre*. Paris: Les Presses Françaises.

Omont, Henri. 1908. *Anciens inventaires et catalogues de la Bibliothèque Nationale*. Vol.1: *La librairie royale a Blois Fontainebleau et Paris au XVIe siècle*. Paris: Ernest Leroux.

Orth, Myra Dickman. 1997. Dedicating women: Manuscript culture in the French Renaissance, and the cases of Catherine d'Amboise and Anne de Graville. *Journal of the Early Book Society for the Study of Manuscripts and Printing History* 1 (1): 17–47.

Osorio, Jorge Alves. 1990. Enoncé et dialogue dans les *Colloques* d'Erasme. In *Actes du Colloque International Érasme (Tours 1986)*, ed. Jacques Chomart, André Godin, and Jean-Claude Margolin, 19–34. Travaux d'Humanisme et Renaissance 239. Geneva: Droz.

Ouy, Gilbert. 1967. Gerson, émule de Petrarque: Le "Pastorium carmen," poème de jeunesse de Gerson, et la renaissance de l'eglogue en France à la fin du XIVe siècle. *Romania* 88:175–231.

Paladino, Giuseppe, ed. 1927. *Opuscoli e letter di Riformatori Italiani del cinquecento*, vol. 2. Scrittori d'Italia 99. Bari: Laterza.

Paleario, Aonio. 1933. *Dell'economia o vero del governo della casa.* Ed. and introd. Salvatore Caponato. Biblioteca dell'"Archivium Romanicum" ser. 1, v. 172. Firenze: Leo S. Olschki.

Panizza, Letizia, ed. 2000. *Women in Italian Renaissance culture and society.* Oxford: European Humanities Research Centre.

Pauphilet, Albert, Louis Pichard, and Robert Barroux, eds. 1996. *Dictionnaire des lettres françaises: Le XVIIe siècle.* Paris: Fayard.

Pédron, François. 1984. *Louise Labé, la femme d'amour.* Paris, Fayard.

Pellegrini, Carlo. 1920. *La prima opera di Margherita di Navarra e la terza rima in Francia.* Catania: Francesco Battisto.

———. 1947. Riflessi di cultura italiana in Margherita di Navarra. In *Tradizione italiana e cultura europea,* 19–38. Messina: Casa Editrice G. D'Anna.

Perry, T. Anthony. 1980. *Erotic spirituality: The integrative tradition from Leone Ebreo to John Donne.* University: University of Alabama Press.

Petrarca, Francesco. 1950. *Invective contra medicum.* Ed. Pier Giorgio Ricci. Roma: Edizioni di Storia e Letteratura.

———. 1957. *Rime e trionfi.* Ed. Raffaello Ramat. Milano: Rizzoli.

———. 1967. *Four dialogues for scholars.* Ed. and with facing trans. by Conrad Rawski. Cleveland: Press of Western Reserve University.

———. 1968. *A dialogue between reason and adversity: A late Middle English version of Petrarch's De remediis.* Ed. with facing Latin text by F. N. M. Diekstra. Assen, Netherlands: Van Gorcum and Comp.

Plebani, Tiziana. 1996. Nascita e caratteristiche del pubblico di lettrici tra medioevo e prima età moderna. In *Donna, disciplina, creanza cristiana dal XV al XVII secolo: Studi e testi a stampa,* ed. Gabriella Zarri, 23–44. Rome: Edizioni di Storia e Letteratura.

Plutarch. 1985. *Oeuvres morales,* vol. 2. Ed. and trans. Jean Defradas, Jean Hani, and Robert Klaerr. Paris: Société d'Editions "Les Belles Lettres."

———. 1990. *Oeuvres morales,* vol. 5. Ed. and trans. Françoise Frazier and Christian Froidefond. Paris: Société d'Editions "Les Belles Lettres."

Potter, Joy Hambuechen. 1985. Woman in the *Decameron.* In *Studies in the Italian Renaissance,* ed. Gian Paolo Biasin, Albert N. Mancini, and Nicolas J. Perella, 87–103. Naples: Soc. Ed. Napoletana.

Price, Paola Malpezzi. 1989. A woman's discourse in the Italian Renaissance: Moderata Fonte's *Il merito delle donne.* In West and Cervigni 1989, 165–81.

———. 2003. *Venetia figurata* and women in sixteenth-century Venice: Moderata Fonte's writings. In *Italian women and the city,* ed. Janet Smarr and Daria Valentini, 18–34. Teaneck: Fairleigh Dickinson University Press.

Prine, Jeanne. 1987. Louise Labé: Poet of Lyon. In *Women writers of the Renaissance and Reformation,* ed. Katharina Wilson, 132–48. Athens: University of Georgia Press.

Prosperi, Adriano. 1994. Lettere spirituali. In Scaraffia and Zarri 1994, 227–51.

Prosperi, Adriano, and Albano Biondi, eds. 1987. *Libri, idee e sentimenti religiosi nel Cinquecento Italiano.* Istituto di Studi Rinascimentali Ferrara. Ferrara: Edizioni Panini.

Pugliese, Olga Zorzi. 1996. Sperone Speroni and the labyrinthine discourse of Renaissance dialogue. In Hart 1996, 57–72.

Quondam, Amadeo, ed. 1981. *Carte messaggiere: Retorica e modelli di comunicazione epistolare.* Rome: Bulzoni.

Rabil, Albert. 1981. *Laura Cereta, Quattrocento humanist*. Binghamton: Medieval and Renaissance Texts and Studies.

Rabitti, Giovanna. 1981. Linee per il ritratto di Chiara Matraini. *Studi e Problemi di Critica Testuale* 22:141–65.

———. 1994. Chiara Matraini (1515–1604). In Russell 1994, 243–52.

Rambaldi, Susanna Peyronel. 1992. Introduzione: Per una storia delle donne nella Riforma. In *Donne della Riforma in Germania, in Italia e in Francia*, ed. Roland Bainton, trans. Flavio Sarni, 9–52. Torino: Claudiana.

Ravisius Textor, Ioan. 1651. *Dialogi aliquot festivissimi, studiosae iuventuti cum primis utiles*, in *Dialogi et epigrammata nec non epistolae*. Rotterdam: Arnoldum Leers.

Relihan, Joel. 1993. *Ancient Menippean satire*. Baltimore: Johns Hopkins University Press.

Richards, Sylvie. 1996. Speaking politically correct in the feminine voice: Examples from the *Decameron* and the *Heptaméron*. In Hart 1996, 121–32.

Rigolot, François, ed. 1990. *Writing in the feminine in the Renaissance*, special issue. *L'Esprit Créateur* 30 (4).

———. 1997. *Louise Labé Lyonnaise ou la Renaissance au féminin*. Paris: Honoré Champion Éditeur.

Romieu, Marie de. 1972. *Les premières oeuvres poétiques*. Ed. André Winandy. Geneva: Librairie Droz.

Rosenthal, Margaret. 1989. Veronica Franco's *Terze rime:* The venetian courtesan's defense. *Renaissance Quarterly* 42 (2): 227–57.

———. 1993. Venetian women writers and their discontents. In Turner 1993, 107–32.

Rummel, Erika, ed. 1996. *Erasmus on women*. Toronto: University of Toronto Press.

Russell, Rinaldina, ed. 1994. *Italian women writers: A bio-bibliographical sourcebook*. Westport, Conn.: Greenwood Press.

Saccaro Battisti, Giuseppa. 1980. La donna, le donne nel *Cortegiano*. In *La corte e il "Cortegiano,"* ed. Carolo Ossola, 1: 219–49. Roma: Bulzoni.

Sald, Michael N. 1994. *La bibliothèque de François Ier au Château de Blois*. Les Cahiers de la Bibliothèque Municipale de Blois 12. Blois: Bibliothèque Municipale.

Sankovitch, Tilde A. 1988. *French women writers and the book: Myths of access and desire*. Syracuse: Syracuse University Press.

Scaraffia, Lucetta, and Gabriella Zarri, eds. 1994. *Donne e fede: Santità e vita religiosa in Italia*. Roma-Bari: Editori Laterza.

Scarpati, Claudio. 1992. Osservazioni sul terzo libro del *Cortegiano*. *Aevum* 66 (3): 519–37.

Schmitt, Jean-Claude. 1994. *Les revenants: Les vivants et les morts dans la société médiévale*. Mesnil-sur-l'Estrée: Gallimard.

Schutz, Alexander Herman. 1933. The group of the dames des Roches in sixteenth-century Poitiers. *PMLA* 48 (3): 648–54.

Scrivano, Riccardo, ed. 1966. *Cinquecento minore*. Classici Italiani 10. Bologna: Zanichelli.

———. 1985. Nelle pieghe del dialogare bembesco. In *Il dialogo: Scambi e passaggi della parola*, ed. Giulio Ferroni, 101–9. Palermo: Sellerio editore.

Sénemond, E. 1861. *La bibliothèque de Charles d'Orléans Comte d'Angoulême au Chateau de Cognac*. Paris: A. Claudin.

Shemek, Deanna. 1998. *Ladies errant: Wayward women and social order in early modern Italy*. Durham, N.C.: Duke University Press.

Sigée, Louise [Sigea, Luisa]. 1970. *Dialogue de deux jeunes filles sur la vie de cour et la vie de retraite (1552)*. [Duarum Virginum Colloquium.] Ed. and facing trans. Odette Sauvage. Paris: Presses Universitaires de France.

Sinfield, Alan. 1992. *Faultlines: Cultural materialism and the politics of dissident reading*. Oxford: Oxford University Press.

Singleton, Charles. 1977. *An essay on the* Vita nuova. Baltimore: Johns Hopkins University Press.

Smarr, Janet. 1995. The uses of conversation: Moderata Fonte and Edmund Tilney. *Comparative Literature Studies* 32 (1): 1–25.

———. 1998. A dialogue of dialogues: Tullia d'Aragona and Sperone Speroni. *MLN* 113:204–12.

———. 2004. Olympia Morata: From classicist to reformer. In *Phaethon's children: The Este court and its culture in early modern Ferrara*, ed. Deanna Shemek and Dennis Looney. Tempe, AZ: Medieval and Renaissance Texts and Studies.

Snyder, Jon. 1989. *Writing the scene of speaking: Theories of dialogue in the late Italian Renaissance*. Stanford: Stanford University Press.

Sommers, Paula. 1983. Feminine authority in the *Heptaméron*: A reading of Oysille. *Modern Language Studies* 13 (2): 52–59.

———. 1995. Marguerite de Navarre and the body-centered text: Re-reading *La Navire*. In *Les visages et les voix de Marguerite de Navarre: Actes du Colloque International sur Marguerite de Navarre (Duke University), 10–11 avril 1992*, ed. Marcel Tetel, 169–79. Paris: Klincksieck.

Sowards, J. K. 1982. Erasmus and the education of women. *Sixteenth-Century Journal* 13:77–89.

Sozzi, Lionello, ed. 1981. *La nouvelle française à la Renaissance*. Geneva: Editions Slatkine.

Speroni, Sperone. 1544. *Dialoghi di M. Sperone Speroni. Nuovamente ristampati & con molta diligenza rivedutai & corretti*. Venice: Aldus.

———. 1978. Apologia dei dialogi. In *Trattatisti del Cinquecento*, ed. M. Pozzi, 683–724. Milano-Napoli: Ricciardi.

———. 1989. *Opere*. Introd. Mario Pozzi. 5 vols. Rome: Vechiarelli.

Sproxton, Judith. 1999. The indemnity of Folly. In Ford and Jondorf 1999, 159–70.

Stock, Brian. 1996. The dialogues. In *Augustine the reader: Meditation, self-knowledge, and the ethics of interpretation*, 130–37. Cambridge: Harvard University Press, 1996.

Stortoni, Laura Anna, ed. 1997. *Women poets of the Italian Renaissance: Courtly ladies and courtesans*. Trans. Laura Anna Stortoni and Mary Prentice Lillie. New York: Italica Press.

Tateo, Francesco. 1967. *Tradizione e realtà nell'Umanesimo italiano*. Bari: Dedalo Libri.

Tedeschi, John. 1987. The cultural contributions of Italian Protestant reformers in the late Renaissance. In Prosperi and Biondi 1987, 81–108.

Telle, Emile. 1937. *L'oeuvre de Marguerite d'Angoulême reine de Navarre et la querelle des femmes*. Toulouse: Lion et Fils.

Terracina, Laura. 1549. *Discorso sopra il principio di tutti i canti d'Orlando Furioso*. Venice.

Tetel, Marcel. 1973. *Marguerite de Navarre's Heptameron: Themes, language, and structure*. Durham, N.C.: Duke University Press.

———. 1981. *L'Heptaméron*: Première nouvelle et fonction des devisants. In Sozzi 1981, 449–58.

————, ed. 1995. *Les visages et les voix de Marguerite de Navarre. Actes du Colloque International sur Marguerite de Navarre (Duke University), 10–11 avril 1992*. Paris: Klincksieck.

Thysell, Carol. 1998. Gendered virtue, vernacular theology, and the nature of authority in the *Heptameron*." In *Sixteenth-Century Journal* 29: 39–53.

Tomlinson, Sophie. 1992. "My brain the stage": Margaret Cavendish and the fantasy of female performance. In *Women, texts and histories 1575–1760*, ed. Clare Brant and Diane Purkiss, 134–63. London: Routledge.

Tullia d'Aragona. 1912. *Dialogo dell'infinità di amore*. In *Trattati d'amore del Cinquecento*, ed. Giuseppe Zonta, 185–248. Scrittori d'Italia 37. Bari: Gius, Laterza and Figli.

————. 1997. *Dialogue on the infinity of love*. Trans. Rinaldina Russell and Bruce Merry. Chicago: University of Chicago Press.

Turner, James Grantham, ed. 1993. *Sexuality and gender in early modern Europe: Institutions, texts, images*. Cambridge: Cambridge University Press.

Ulysse, Georges, ed. 1994. *Les femmes écrivains en Italie au moyen âge et à la Renaissance*. Aix-en Provence: Publications de l'Université de Provence.

Vaganay, Hugues. 1935. Quatre noms propres dans la littérature: Délie, Philothélie, Ophélie, Pasithée. *Revue de Littérature Comparée* 15:279–88.

Valdés, Giovanni di [Juan de]. 1938. *Alfabeto cristiano: Dialogo con Giulia Gonzaga*. Introd. and notes Benedetto Croce. Bari: Laterza and Figli.

Vecce, Carlo. 1994. Vittoria Colonna: Il codice epistolare della poesia femminile. In Ulysse 1994, 213–34.

Veracruysse, Jerome. 1967. *Helisenne de Crenne: Notes biographiques*. Studi Francesi 31:77–81.

Vianello, Valerio. 1993. *Il "giardino" delle parole: Itinerari di scrittura e modelli letterari nel dialogo cinquecentesco*. Materiali e Ricerche N.S. 21. Roma: Jouvence.

Virtanen, Reino. 1977. *Conversations on dialogue*. University of Nebraska Studies N.S. 54. Lincoln: University of Nebraska Press.

Vives, Juan Luis. [1547] 1996. *De institutione feminae Christianae*. Liber primus. Ed. C. Fantazzi and C. Matheeussen. Facing trans. C. Fantazzi. Leiden: Brill.

Voss, Bernd Reiner. 1970. *Der Dialog in der frühchristlichen Literatur*. Munchen: Fink.

Wallace, David. 1990. When she translated was. In *Literary practice and social change in Britain 1380–1530*, ed. Lee Patterson, 156–215. Berkeley: University of California Press.

Warner, Lyndan. 1999. Marie Le Gendre, the *Saines affections*, and moral thought in the late sixteenth century. In Ford and Jondorf 1999, 221–38.

Weil, Michèle. 1990. *Dialogie* de Louise Labé. In Demerson 1990, 161–86.

Wesling, Donald, and Tadeusz Slawek. 1995. *Literary voice: The calling of Jonah*. Albany: SUNY Press.

West, Rebecca, and Dino Cervigni, eds. 1989. *Women's voices in Italian literature*, special issue. *Annali d'Italianistica* 7.

Wiesner, Merry E. 1993. *Women and gender in early modern Europe*. Cambridge: Cambridge University Press.

Wilson, Katharina, ed. 1987. *Women writers of the Renaissance and Reformation*. Athens: University of Georgia Press.

Wilson, Kenneth. 1985. *Incomplete fictions: The formation of English Renaissance dialogue*. Washington, D.C.: Catholic University of America Press.

Winn, Colette H., ed. 1993a. *The dialogue in early modern France, 1547–1630: Art and argument*. Washington, D.C.: Catholic University of America Press.

———. 1993b. Toward a dialectic of reconciliation: The *Navire* and the *Heptameron* of Marguerite de Navarre. In Winn 1993a, 79–120.

———. 1999. Marie Le Gendre et l'échec du stoïcisme. In Ford and Jondorf 1999, 207–20.

Wood, Diane. 1991. The evolution of Helisenne de Crenne's persona. *Symposium* 45 (2): 140–51.

Wright, Julianne Jones, and François Rigolot. 1990. Les irruptions de la Folie: Fonction idéologique du porte-parole dan les *Oeuvres* de Louise Labé. *L'Esprit Créateur* 30 (4): 72–84.

Xenophon. 1938. *Oeconomicus*. Trans. E. C. Marchant. Loeb Classical Library. Cambridge: Harvard University Press.

Yates, Frances. 1988. *The French academies of the sixteenth century*. New York: Routledge.

Zancan, Marina. 1983a. La donna nel "Cortegiano" di B. Castiglione: Le funzioni del femminile nell'immagine di corte. In Zancan 1983b, 13–56.

———, ed. 1983b. *Nel cerchio della luna: Figure di donna in alcuni testi del XVI secolo*. Venice: Marsilio.

Zarri, Gabriella. 1987. Note su diffusione e circolazione di testi devoti (1520–1550). In Prosperi and Biondi 1987, 131–54.

———. 1994. Dalla profezia alla disciplina (1450–1650). In Scaraffia and Zarri 1994, 177–225.

Zimmerman, Margaret. 1999. Querelle des femmes, querelle du livre. In Courcelle and Val Julián 1999, 79–94.

Zumthor, Paul. 1978. *Le masque et la lumière: La poétique des grands rhétoriquers*. Paris: Seuil.

Index

241, 249, 275nn. 28, 32–33, 276n. 40;
dialogues in the *Secondes oeuvres*
(Placide and Sevère, Iris and
Pasithée), 99, 102, 117–29, 148, 187,
246, 267–68n. 29, 268nn. 31, 33
des Roches, Madeleine (Catherine's
mother), 103, 117, 119, 120, 128, 172,
275n. 28
Desrosiers-Bonin, Diane, 163, 271n. 19,
274n. 14
Diekstra, F. N. M., 20, 255n. 25
Diller, George, 268n. 28, 275n. 33
Diotima, 3, 16, 20, 85, 104, 109, 113,
115, 240, 257n. 18, 278n. 12
disputation, 11, 14, 26, 46–47, 87,
98–99, 132, 152, 156, 158, 160, 165,
167, 245–47, 273n. 10, 282n. 10
Dolce, Lodovico, 9, 16–17, 27, 87, 264n.
80
Domenichi, Lodovico, 88
Duval, Edwin, 213, 280nn. 36–37

education, 20, 22, 30, 83, 84, 126–27,
257n. 19; women's, 2, 4, 6, 9, 15–16,
23, 34–36, 40, 45, 74, 84, 86, 87, 90,
92, 93, 97, 98, 101–4, 106, 117,
119–25, 127, 128, 131, 136, 150, 163,
166, 182, 188–89, 192, 217, 220, 226,
230, 231–32, 233, 235, 236, 238, 240,
242, 245–47, 264n. 80, 268n. 31,
269nn. 8–9, 281n. 54, 282n. 8
Elizabeth I, Queen, 45
Erasmus, 3, 5, 8–9, 22, 26, 30, 76, 95,
102, 105, 125–27, 139, 141, 156–57,
158, 167, 187, 247, 253–54n. 9,
254nn. 10, 14–15, 256n. 39, 257–58n.
21, 262n. 68, 264n. 87, 265n. 90,
268n. 33, 280n. 44
Esther, Queen, 77, 79, 124
exchange of poems, 24–25, 122, 175,
179, 264–65n. 89

Fahy, Conor, 100
fame, 4, 59, 89, 90, 118, 178, 181, 224,
228. *See also* glory, desire for
father, 3, 7, 12, 14, 33, 35, 56, 72–73, 99,
103, 105, 107, 119–25, 128, 148, 157,
180, 187, 197, 204, 217–18, 220, 227,

236, 237, 244, 268n. 33, 269n. 8,
280n. 44
Fedele, Cassandra, 14, 17, 124, 130, 238,
268n. 35
Finucci, Valeria, 6, 9, 254n. 12
Firenzuola, Angelo, 14–16, 46, 231, 246,
257n. 18
Fontaine, Guylaine, 167, 168, 275n. 34
Fonte, Moderata (Modesta Pozzo), 3, 5,
99, 190–91, 192, 193, 195, 196,
215–30, 232–48, 269n. 4, 277n. 2,
278n. 15, 280n. 39, 281nn. 46, 49
Forni, Carla, 29, 131, 255nn. 31, 34
Foucault, Michel, 32
Fournel, Jean-Louis, 282n. 12
Franco, Veronica, 25, 106, 277n. 11,
280n. 46
friendship, 3, 4, 16, 21, 30, 39–40, 44,
56, 73–74, 76, 78, 80, 90, 102,
132–33, 136, 138, 142, 180, 181, 200,
202, 225, 235–36, 237, 242, 249,
253n. 5, 262–63n. 68

Gambara, Veronica, 14, 17, 95, 254n.
20, 268n. 34, 277n. 11, 280n. 45,
281n. 51, 282n. 7
game (playfulness), 5–6, 22, 24, 25, 26,
29, 69, 110, 113, 117, 123, 126–27,
136, 142, 156, 160, 191–92, 194–96,
210, 213–14, 215, 227–28, 229–30,
235, 245–46, 247, 253–54n. 9, 257n.
19, 281n. 57
garden, 3, 5, 10, 14, 83–86, 88–90, 92,
96, 99, 154–55, 190, 193, 195, 212,
216, 219, 222, 239, 245–47, 264n. 80
Gerson, Jean, 33, 34–38, 39, 44, 46, 51,
57, 58, 71, 74, 85, 91, 243, 256nn. 11,
13, 257nn. 15, 17–19, 258nn. 22,
26–27, 29, 36
Gill, Katherine, 45, 263n. 74
Gilman, Donald, 265n. 3, 273n. 10
Girardi, Raffaele, 29, 40, 255nn. 28, 31,
35, 256n. 8, 258n. 38, 273n. 6
Giudici, Enzo, 166–67, 168, 274n. 25
Glasson, Simone, 261n. 59
glory, desire for, 73, 89–90, 101, 110,
111, 125, 185, 192–93, 239, 255n. 32.
See also fame